Taking Sides: Clashing Views
in Social Psychology,
Fifth Edition

Wind Goodfriend

http://create.mheducation.com

ISBN-10: 1259359611   ISBN-13: 9781259359613

Contents

Preface

Human beings are inherently social creatures, and this book examines many important questions about the social nature of our existence from the unique perspective of social psychology. Ever since Kurt Lewin's famous equation that suggested any given person's behaviors are a function of both his or her individual personality and the social environment or situation, social psychology has acknowledged how complicated it can be to truly understand our social world. This complexity gives rise to many controversies, which is the purpose of this book.

Like all books in the Taking Sides series, all of the selections are organized around controversial questions, with each reading presenting one side of the argument. Due to its very nature, this book may set up readers to fall into the trap of false dichotomies. While each issue presents articles that support a "yes" and a "no" side of the argument, it is doubtful that many of the authors of these articles would exclusively believe in their side. Indeed, it is more likely that people who have spent many years studying each particular issue are the most willing individuals to admit that nothing is monolithic or as simple as it seems. For most issues, common ground may be found. An accessible example of this point may be seen in the classic "nature versus nurture" debate. While most academics and scholars may have a preference for one side over the other, those same people are likely to admit that for almost any particular issue, the answer to the "nature versus nurture" question is, inevitably, "both." Thus, after each controversy, a brief section follows that discusses common ground that might be found.

In some cases, the selected articles are reviews of literature; the advantage of these comprehensive reviews is that they can present more data, collected from many studies. However, other selections present one or two studies with original data found by the authors themselves. The benefit of reading these original reports is that you can see the first-hand description of the research rather than someone else's interpretation. This provides you the venue to interpret the results and conclusions for yourself, as well as the ability to think critically about the strengths and weaknesses of the experimental procedure.

Plan of the Book

The book is composed of controversial issues in the field of social psychology. Each issue begins with an *issue introduction*

that provides you with the background necessary to understand the context of the debate and its importance to social psychology. In addition to the two selections that address each perspective on the debate, *Critical Thinking and Reflection* questions, designed to spark thought-provoking discussions, are included in each issue. *Learning Outcomes* are also offered to help guide readers or classroom instructors in exact academic objectives found within each issue, or to provide a way to assess your learning. Brief biographies are also provided for contributors/authors of the articles selected. After a discussion and description titled *Is There Common Ground?*, additional resources—including both relevant readings and online resources—are listed, so that you can find out more if you are interested in exploring any given issue with more depth.

Acknowledgments

I would like to thank all of my colleagues and mentors in the world of social psychology who helped me see the value of critical thinking about controversial issues; this includes (but is not limited to) Chris Agnew, Amanda Diekman, and Ximena Arriaga, as well as all of my fellow graduate students from Purdue. I also want to thank my research partner and friend Pamela Cathey for her support over many years. Finally, I must thank two of my students, Stephanie Anders and Patrice Crall, for their help in gathering the materials used in this book.

Editor of This Volume

WIND GOODFRIEND is an associate professor of psychology and the co-director of both the gender and women's studies program and the trauma advocacy program at Buena Vista University in Storm Lake, Iowa. She earned her bachelor's degree at Buena Vista University, then earned her master's and PhD in social psychology from Purdue University. In addition to her work as a professor, she is also the vice president and principal investigator of the Institute for the Prevention of Relationship Violence, a national organization dedicated to education and prevention of child abuse, stalking, domestic violence, and elder abuse. She has co-authored a book titled *Voices of Hope: Breaking the Silence of Relationship Violence*, with Pamela Lassiter Cathey. They are currently writing a second book together: *Before the Boil: Warning Signs of a Potentially Violent Relationship*. Dr. Goodfriend has won the "Faculty of the Year" award at BVU three times in the past nine years, and in 2011 she also won the Wythe Award for Excellence in Teaching, the largest teaching award in the nation.

Academic Advisory Board Members

Members of the Academic Advisory Board are instrumental in the final selection of articles for each edition of TAKING SIDES. Their review of articles for content, level, and appropriateness provides critical direction to the editors and staff. We think that you will find their careful consideration well reflected in this volume.

Grace Auyang
University of Cincinnati

Richard Ayre
University of Maine, Presque Isle

Anita Barbee
University of Louisville

Shawn Bediako
University of Maryland, Baltimore County

Hector Betancourt
Loma Linda University

Robert Blodgett
Buena Vista University

Cheryl Boglarsky
University of Detroit Mercy

Kimberly Brackett
Auburn University, Montgomery

Amy Bradshaw
Embry-Riddle Aeronautical University

Ngoc Bui
University of La Verne

Bernardo J. Carducci
Indiana University Southeast

Paul Chrustowski
Wayne State University

Samuel L. Clay II
Brigham Young University, Idaho

Cheryl Dickter
College of William & Mary

Christopher Ferguson
Texas A&M International University

Herb French
Portland Community College

William Fry
Youngstown State University

Edwin E. Gantt
Brigham Young University

Marissa A. Harrison
Penn State Harrisburg

Helen Harton
University of Northern Iowa

Steven Hendrix
James Sprunt Community College

Christopher Henry
Guilford College

Kathryn Holcomb
Indiana University, Kokomo

MJ Hubertz
Florida Atlantic University

Steven Hurwitz
Tiffin University

Alisha Janowsky
University of Central Florida

Barry Johnson
Davidson County Community College

Brian Johnson
University of Tennessee, Martin

Nancy Karlin
University of Northern Colorado

James C. Kaufman
University of Connecticut

Barbra LaRue
Baker College, Cadillac

David LoConto
Jacksonville State University

Tani McBeth
Portland Community College

Tammy McClain
West Liberty University

Rusty McIntyre
Wayne State University

Eric Miller
Kent State University

David Myers
Hope College

Paul Nesselroade
Asbury College

Diana Odom Gunn
University of California

David Oxendine
University of North Carolina–Pembroke

Carol Oyster
University of Wisconsin, La Crosse

Sandra Sims Patterson
Spelman College

Stephen Peck
University of Michigan

Jack Powell
University of Hartford

Frank Prerost
Midwestern University

David Reuman
Trinity College

Vicki Ritts
St. Louis Community College, Meramec

D. Keith Roach
Mid-Continent University

Tonya Rondinone
St. Joseph College

Terry M. Salem
Lake Land College

Shannon Sexton
Rose-Hulman Institute of Technology

Lori Sheppard
Winston-Salem State University

Mark Sibicky
Marietta College

Robert Stennett
University of North Georgia, Gainesville

Betsy Stern
Milwaukee Area Technical College

Mark Stewart
American River College

John Terrell
Reedley College

Katherine Van Wormer
University of Northern Iowa

Theresa Vescio
Pennsylvania State University

T. Joel Wade
Bucknell University

David Wagner
University at Albany, SUNY

Robert Woody
University of Nebraska, Omaha

Elizabeth Yost
University of Alabama, Birmingham

Introduction

Social psychology is a relatively new but ambitious discipline. Social psychologists have not shied away from fundamental questions about human nature, including both the best and the worst in our species. Experiments have focused on positive social constructs, such as empathy, altruism, and heroism, as well as negative social constructs, including ostracism, prejudice, and aggression.

Unresolved Issues

But despite this vigorous commitment to addressing big questions about human nature, many important questions about social thought and behavior remain unresolved by social psychologists. This book and the selections that you will read are designed to stimulate critical thinking by encouraging you to carefully examine each debate from different perspectives. Sometimes, you may conclude that one perspective is right and another is wrong. At other times, you may feel that there is an element of truth to both viewpoints, or that compromise may be possible. Regardless of your feelings about the validity of each position, the process of examining both sides of the debate via critical thinking will leave you with a deeper and more thorough understanding of each issue. After having read both sides of each argument, you can weigh the merits of each position and make a decision for yourself as to which argument is more convincing.

But how do social psychologists attempt to answer these unresolved questions? At first glance, it may seem as if we can rely upon common sense and intuition to settle social psychological questions. After all, we are all social beings and we have our own beliefs about the world, which we have formed on the basis of own personal experiences. Perhaps these commonsense beliefs are sufficient to understand our social environment. Although intuition and commonsense are valuable for understanding our social world, scientific studies show that they are often mistaken. In fact, there is a great deal of social psychological research that documents the reasons why our beliefs and intuitions are imperfect. As a result, social psychologists use empirical data from carefully controlled studies, rather than intuition or common sense, to answer enduring questions about human nature.

The Importance of Scientific Evidence

Consider the case of Cognitive Dissonance Theory. This influential theory was first tested in an admittedly artificial laboratory experiment conducted by social psychologists Leon Festinger and J. Merrill Carlsmith (1959). In their classic experiment, participants were asked to perform a series of incredibly boring tasks, such as repeatedly rotating a spool of wood. After performing these mind-numbing tasks for half an hour, participants were asked to lie about how much they enjoyed the tasks, and tell another person that the tasks were enjoyable. The details of Festinger and Carlsmith's experiment are somewhat strange and bear no resemblance to any real-world situation. Most of us have never been asked to rotate a small spool of wood and then lie to someone else about how enjoyable it was. Yet, this is precisely what participants did in this study. And it turned out to be incredibly important, because over 50 years later social psychologists still study cognitive dissonance and its potential application to real-world situations. For example, Cognitive Dissonance Theory has been successfully used to improve racial attitudes (Leippe & Eisenstadt, 1994), encourage condom usage among sexually active young people (Stone, Aronson, Crain, Winslow, & Freid, 1994), and promote water conservation (Dickerson, Thibodeau, Aronson, & Miller, 1992).

This artificial laboratory experiment eventually resulted in numerous real-world applications. That is what makes Festinger and Carlsmith's study important. As social psychologist Douglas Mook (1983) pointed out, it is not the details of an experiment that must have some real-world counterpart or generalize to some real-world situation; it is the *theory* that generalizes to the real world. An artificial laboratory experiment can have very important, but indirect, real-world applications, because it can be used to test and refine an important theory, and the theory may have numerous real-world applications. This was certainly the case with Festinger and Carsmith's famous study, and it is also true of many other social psychology experiments.

The Reality of Social Psychology Experiments

Some people who read about the results of laboratory experiments in social psychology may believe that the results have little importance because participants do not become engaged by these experiments. Because the situations are artificial and not realistic, they do not involve participants in the same way that "real-life" situations engage us. As a result, one might be tempted to conclude that experiments are unimportant. Social psychologists have thought carefully about this concern and what it means for an experiment to be "realistic." According to Aronson, Ellsworth, Carlsmith, and Gonzales (1990), experiments can be realistic in different ways, and these authors draw a distinction between Mundane Realism and Experimental Realism.

Mundane Realism is the extent to which the details of an experiment resemble a particular real-world setting. As has already been discussed, most experiments take place in contexts that do not resemble any real-world setting, so most social psychology experiments do not have much Mundane Realism. On the other hand, Experimental Realism is the extent to which participants become psychologically involved in the experiment and take the experiment seriously. According to Aronson and his colleagues, as long as an experiment has Experimental Realism, it has the potential to yield important results.

To illustrate the importance of the distinction between Mundane Realism and Experimental Realism, consider how "real" reality television is. In the vast majority of reality television shows, the contestants find themselves in highly artificial situations, and because of the contrived nature of these shows, many critics contend that the shows are not real at all. Indeed, after some reality television shows are over, many contestants confess that some aspects of the show seemed quite strange. At the same time, many contestants also testify to a depth of emotion that they felt during the experience. For example, in the reality television program *Big Brother,* a group of 13 strangers are required to live in single house, with no outside contact for 3 months. This situation is completely artificial. There are few real-world situations that would require you to be cooped up with same people for months with no contact with the outside world. Nevertheless, this program has been an international hit, with dedicated fans in both the United States and Europe. What can account for its popularity? Aside from its voyeuristic appeal, it is an engaging show because the contestants become completely gripped by the situation. Despite the contrived nature of the situation, the way contestants behave and the emotions they feel are very real to themselves and to the audience.

So, is reality television real? In one sense of the word, reality television is not real at all, but in another sense it is very real. To use the jargon of social psychology, reality television is extremely high in Experimental Realism despite a complete lack of Mundane Realism. Because reality television bears little resemblance to the real world, it does not have Mundane Realism. So by that measure it is not real. However, because contestants often become totally immersed in the show and experience genuine emotions, reality television appears to be high in Experimental Realism. So in that sense of the word, reality television is quite real. And just as people become totally engrossed in these artificial situations that we see on television, participants can become completely immersed in psychology experiments despite their contrived nature. As a result, the way participants behave and the emotions they feel are real, in the sense that their reactions seem authentic to the participants themselves.

Applying Social Psychology

Evident in the discussion of Cognitive Dissonance Theory is the notion that the results of social psychological research should be applied to address serious social issues. The list of social problems that social psychologists have tackled is impressive and include (to name a few) prejudice, hypocrisy, destructive obedience, violence, intergroup conflict, depression, physical illnesses, prison strife, and brainwashing. The list could go on and on. Social psychologists have also been inspired to understand both the origins and nature of prejudice—including racism, sexism, homophobia, ageism, and more—and attempt to decrease these intergroup conflicts and hostilities.

Thus, social psychologists have not been satisfied to simply study these issues from afar and then hope that the results of the research are useful in some way. Social psychologists have actively sought to apply their research to real-world circumstances and have lobbied to make their voices heard. Some social psychologists have engaged in this kind of work on an individual basis and conducted their own research examining the usefulness of their ideas in the real world. Other social psychologists have also attempted to put their research to good use on a collective level, through their involvement in various organizations.

The most prominent of these organizations is the Society for the Psychological Study of Social Issues (SPSSI), which is devoted to ameliorating social problems through the application of psychological research. This group, which was originally founded in 1937, comprises thousands of social scientists, including many social psychologists. SPSSI actively lobbies to influence policy decisions, to ensure that policy is informed by the results of the relevant social psychological research. This means that social psychologists, and the organizations to which they belong, are sometimes involved in highly politicized debates. Although some have questioned the wisdom of entering the political fray, the vast majority of social psychologists enthusiastically agree that social psychological research should play a prominent role in policy decisions. These efforts have proven useful in a number of instances. For example, SPSSI holds congressional briefings on a fairly regular basis. At these briefings, members of the U.S. Congress listen to presentations given by prominent social scientists who describe the results of their research and its relevance to social policies, such as affirmative action and hate crime legislation. It is through efforts like this that social psychologists hope to apply the results of their research and promote positive social change.

If you are currently a student of social psychology, I encourage you to consider getting directly involved with either conducting basic research on theories and processes of social behavior or applying the findings of research to improve the social condition. Current "hot topics" within social psychology are addressed in part within this book, but there are certainly many other social issues that could benefit from more scientists applying findings to the outside world. Scientific breakthroughs in other fields have resulted in amazing advances that have benefited a wide variety of people, such as in the fields of physics, engineering, medicine, computer science, and more. Social psychology should be leading the way toward advances in our social world, helping the world community to improve conditions regarding an increase in empathy, altruism, heroism, and love, while simultaneously putting an end to needless aggression, prejudice, and hatred. Is there are more noble pursuit?

References

Aronson, E., Ellsworth, P., Carlsmith, J. M., & Gonzales, M. H. (1990). *Methods of Research in Social Psychology* (2nd ed.). New York: McGraw-Hill.

Dickerson, C. A., Thibodeau, R., Aronson, E., & Miller, D. (1992). Using cognitive dissonance to encourage water conservation. *Journal of Applied Social Psychology, 22,* 841–854.

Festinger, L., & Carlsmith, J. M. (1959). The cognitive consequences of forced compliance. *Journal of Abnormal and Social Psychology, 58,* 203–210.

Leippe, M. R., & Eisenstadt, D. (1994). Generalization of dissonance reduction: Decreasing prejudice through induced compliance. *Journal of Personality and Social Psychology, 67,* 395–413.

Mook, D. G. (1983). In defense of external invalidity. *American Psychologist, 38,* 379–387.

Stone, J., Aronson, E., Crain, A. L., Winslow, M. P., & Freid, C. (1994). Inducing hypocrisy as a means of encouraging young adults to use condoms. *Personality & Social Psychology Bulletin, 20,* 116–128.

Wind Goodfriend
Buena Vista University

Unit 1

UNIT

Social and Cultural Influence

*E*ver since classic studies by Lewin, Milgram, Asch, and Zimbardo were done on the power of social influence, social psychology has examined how behavior is predicted by both the individual and the situation. The first unit thus focuses on a wide variety of social influences that may affect any given person's social experience, as well as the reciprocal: how any given individual can have an impact on his or her larger social world. Several issues in this section are not only important to social psychologists, but also currently being debated in larger media outlets. Clearly, these issues matter on a variety of levels.

Selected, Edited, and with Issue Framing Material by:
Wind Goodfriend, *Buena Vista University*

ISSUE

Is There a "Prejudiced Personality" Type?

YES: Kevin O. Cokley et al. from "Predicting Student Attitudes About Racial Diversity and Gender Equity," *Journal of Diversity in Higher Education* (2010)

NO: B. Corenblum and Walter G. Stephan, from "White Fears and Native Apprehensions: An Integrated Threat Theory Approach to Intergroup Attitudes," *Canadian Journal of Behavioural Science* (2001)

Learning Outcomes
After reading this issue, you will be able to: • List and explain two "personality traits" or constructs that some social psychologists claim measure a "prejudiced personality."   • Discuss other possible predictors of prejudice that do not come from the individual personality level, but instead come from the level of intergroup relationships.   • Explain how variables on either side of the controversy are measured in research studies.

ISSUE SUMMARY

YES: This team of psychologists from Texas present data supporting the idea that three personality traits (social dominance orientation, authoritarianism, and openness to experience) predict college students' attitudes about racial and gender diversity.

NO: Using data from white and Native Canadians, researchers Corenblum and Stephan argue that prejudice stems from a combination of factors, including feelings of group threat, anxiety, history of intergroup conflict, and more.

Since its inception after World War II, one of social psychology's most central priorities is to understand and, hopefully, prevent stereotypes, prejudice, and discrimination. In order to accomplish this extremely challenging task, it is essential for psychologists and researchers in related fields to first understand the origins, or foundational framework, from which stereotypes and prejudice come.

Over the years, social psychology has proffered a wide variety of theories in attempting to thus explain the origins of prejudice. Some theories discuss how prejudice against other groups may help individuals maintain self-esteem. Some theories discuss how prejudice may arise from hostile intergroup relations or fighting over limited resources, such as land.

One popular theory, and the article on the "yes" side of this controversial issue, suggests that there is such a thing as a "prejudiced personality." Kevin Cokley and his team of researchers (who, at the time this article was published, were all working for universities in Texas) present data from a racially diverse sample of college students who provided data on two key measures: Social Dominance Orientation and Right-Wing Authoritarianism. For several years, these two constructs have been used in scores of research studies to predict participants' higher levels of prejudice *in general*. In other words, high scores on these two scales (Social Dominance Orientation and Right-Wing Authoritarianism) are positively correlated with being prejudiced against a wide variety of people who are different from oneself, including other races, the other gender, other political groups, and so on.

Examples of items on the scale for Social Dominance Orientation are:

- "Some groups of people are just more worthy than others."
- "If certain groups of people stayed in their place, we would have fewer problems."

Examples of items on the scale for Right-Wing Authoritarianism are:

- "The only way our country can get through the crisis ahead is to get back to our traditional values, put some tough leaders in power, and silence the troublemakers spreading bad ideas."
- "This country would work a lot better if certain groups of troublemakers would just shut up."

However, the "no" article presented here suggests that stereotypes and prejudice are more complicated than simply boiling down to certain individuals who have prejudiced personalities. By limiting prejudice to the individual level, this side argues that we are ignoring influences on the intergroup level. B. Corenblum and Walter Stephan

write, "Any particular form of stereotyping or prejudice, such as racism, is in all likelihood multiply determined by cognitive, motivational and social learning processes." Further, they state in this article that ". . . threat leads to prejudice. . . . [T]here are at least four such threats: realistic threats, symbolic threats, intergroup anxiety and negative stereotypes."

In their article, Corenblum and Stephan present data from both white and Native Canadians regarding stereotypes and prejudice toward each other, using this threat model and paradigm. They also explain further each of these four levels of "threat" and explain how they were measured in the study. Finally, they measure even more variables that they call "distal" variables, including negative intergroup contact and perceived intergroup conflict. In this way, they attempt to be more comprehensive than the authors on the "yes" side. However, it is important to note that these researchers do not include measures of prejudiced personality. If they had, it is possible that their results may have been different.

Whatever the source of stereotypes, prejudice, and discrimination, it is hard to deny that these pervasive social problems have led to murder, war, and genocide. While the answer to why humans seem to perpetually continue these problems may be complicated, that does not mean that pursuit of the answer is not worthwhile. Indeed, perhaps understanding prejudice is one of the most noble challenges within social psychology.

YES ↵

Kevin O. Cokley et al.

Predicting Student Attitudes About Racial Diversity and Gender Equity

The educational relevance of racial diversity has been a hotly contested debate in higher education (Bowen & Bok, 1998; Gurin, Lehman, & Lewis, 2004; Gurin, Nagda, & Lopez, 2004; Gurin, Dey, Gurin, & Hurtado, 2003). A growing body of research suggests that racial diversity positively impacts educational outcomes. Racial diversity has been found to promote critical and complex thinking, as well as intellectual engagement (Antonio et al., 2004; Gurin et al., 2003; Pascerella, Palmer, Moye, & Pierson, 2001). Racial diversity is particularly important to consider in college because college is a formative time for the development of identity and is a time when students experiment with new ideas and roles (Gurin, Dey, Hurtado, & Gurin, 2002). Racial diversity has also been found to promote racial understanding, perspective taking, and involvement in community service during and after college (Gurin et al., 2003). Diversity experiences provide increased cultural awareness, promote cognitive complexity and critical thinking, and enhance academic skills (e.g., Antonio et al., 2004; Chang, 1999; Gurin et al., 2002; Pascerella et al., 2001). Diversity experiences have also been found to positively impact student achievement (Chang, 1999). It is important for students to embrace racial diversity because of academic benefits that are associated with two educationally important outcomes: cognitive openness and attitudes favoring equal opportunity (Gottfredson et al., 2008).

These positive effects are consistent with student development theories such as Chickering's theory of identity development (Chickering & Reisser, 1993) and Perry's theory of intellectual and ethical development (Perry, 1981). For example, developing competence (the first of seven vectors in Chickering's theory) includes intellectual and interpersonal competence. Students in racially diverse institutions will likely encounter situations where they will need to be able to effectively communicate and work with diverse individuals, as well as use critical thinking skills to solve intergroup conflict. In courses that address difficult social issues involving race, racial diversity creates the conditions under which students are likely to express a diversity of perspectives (Gurin, Nagda, & Lopez, 2004). This diversity of perspectives can facilitate students to move from viewing the world in overly simplistic terms such as good-bad, right-wrong (Perry's dualism) to becoming more cognitively complex (Perry's relativism).

In spite of these known benefits some students harbor mixed feelings and are uncertain about the implications of pursuing diversity, especially racial diversity. For example, student organizations that promote the cultural heritage of specific ethnic groups are generally viewed more positively among African American and Hispanic American students than European American students, who tend to see them as promoting separatism (Negy & Hunt, 2008). Even among some ethnic minority students, there is uncertainty about whether ethnic student organizations are beneficial and necessary (Negy & Hunt, 2008).

Why do individuals harbor mixed feelings and/or negative attitudes about diversity in light of its demonstrated positive effects? What are the factors that contribute to the negative attitudes that some individuals have toward racial diversity? Answers to these questions can be used to better understand resistance to efforts to promote diversity on college campuses. Diversity can be defined as "individual differences (e.g., personality, learning styles, and life experiences) and group/social differences (e.g., race/ethnicity, class, gender, sexual orientation, country of origin, and ability as well as cultural, political, religious, or other affiliations) that can be engaged in the service of learning" (American Association of Colleges and Universities, n.d.). Attitudes toward racial diversity and gender equity in particular are believed to be linked because racism and sexism involve similar underlying beliefs (Sidanius, 1992). Therefore, these attitudes are the focus of this study.

From Cokley, Kevin O.; Tran, Kimberly; Hall-Clark, Brittany; Chapman, Collette; Bessa, Luana; Finley, Angela; Martinez, Michael, "Predicting Student Attitudes About Racial Diversity and Gender Equity," *Journal of Diversity in Higher Education,* vol. 3(3), September 2010, pp. 187–199.

Attitudes Toward Racial Diversity and Gender Equity

Attitudes toward issues related to racial diversity, such as affirmative action, have been consistently linked to race, ethnicity, and gender (Kluegel & Smith, 1983; Kravitz & Platania, 1993). Typically, European Americans have more negative attitudes toward affirmative action than racial minorities (Bobo, 1998; Kravitz & Platania, 1993), and males have more negative views toward affirmative action than females (Ozawa, Crosby, & Crosby, 1996). Given the connection between supporting affirmative action and promoting racial diversity, it logically follows that European Americans and males would also have more negative views toward racial diversity. However, attempts to link race, ethnicity, and gender to negative attitudes toward affirmative action, and by extension racial diversity, are overly simplistic. Race and gender have been referred to as *self-interest* variables, and are reasons that influence attitudes toward affirmative action (Golden, Hinkle, & Crosby, 2001). However, one study has found that the effects of race and gender on attitudes toward affirmative action are minimal when variables such as color-blind attitudes are included in the analysis (Awad, Cokley, & Ravitch, 2005). Similarly, we believe it is most helpful to go beyond race, ethnicity, and gender to identify psychological variables, such as social ideologies and personality traits, that are predictive of racial diversity attitudes.

Individuals who hold negative racial attitudes often also harbor negative sexist attitudes (Sidanius, 1993; Swim, Aiken, Hall, et al., 1995). While old-fashioned sexism is overt, modern sexism is covert and centered around a denial of continued discrimination, resistance to policies benefiting women, and antagonism toward the demands of women (Swim et al., 1995). Some students minimize the impact of gender discrimination, believing that they will enter a workplace that is gender-neutral (Sipe, Johnson, & Fisher, 2009). Thus, the endorsement of gender equity that is so prevalent in modern society does not seem to necessarily follow or lead to parallel changes in behaviors (Swim et al., 1995).

Social Dominance Orientation, Right-Wing Authoritarianism, and Openness to Experience

Important predictors of attitudes toward racial minorities and women's rights are social ideologies such as social dominance orientation (SDO) and right-wing authoritarianism (RWA). These two constructs have been found to

be consistently related to prejudicial attitudes (Duckitt & Sibley, 2007; Sibley & Duckitt, 2008; Sibley, Robertson, & Wilson, 2006). SDO is defined as a preference for hierarchy over equality between social groups (Pratto, Sidanius, Stallworth, & Malle, 1994). Social dominance theory is based on the tenet that social groups reduce group conflict by creating consensus on ideologies that some groups are superior to others, or hierarchy-legitimizing myths (Pratto et al., 1994). Pratto et al. (1994) argue that such beliefs form the basis of discrimination and oppression. By believing that some groups are inferior, social dominators legitimize societal practices that sustain or reinforce unequal treatment. Consistent with this thinking, people who are social dominators often disapprove of affirmative action (Haley & Sidanius, 2006). Therefore, people who are high in SDO are less inclined to endorse policies that attempt to address sociopolitical inequalities and discriminatory practices. In addition, those high in SDO are more likely to report prejudicial attitudes toward Blacks, Arabs, and women (Pratto et al., 1994).

Based upon the earlier work of Adorno, Frenkel-Brunswik, Levinson, and Sanford (1950) on the authoritarian personality, Altemeyer (1996) conceptualized RWA as consisting of three covarying factors: authoritarian submission, authoritarian aggression, and conventionality. Authoritarian submission refers to an uncritical and high level of deference to authority. Authoritarian aggression describes the ability to be aggressive toward out-groups, especially when sanctioned by societal authority. Finally, conventionality involves a pronounced respect and adherence to traditional values. While they both can be exclusionary, RWA is distinct from SDO because it is defensive and is based upon fear of threats to existing values and traditions by members of an outgroup (Van Hiel, Pandelaere, & Duriez, 2004), versus a perception of the world as a competitive arena where weaker members are subordinate (Duckitt, Wagner, du Plessis, & Birum, 2002). RWA has been demonstrated to be a strong predictor of prejudicial attitudes in a number of studies (Altemeyer, 1998; Van Hiel & Mervielde, 2005; Whitley, 1999). More specifically, investigations with college students have found that RWA facilitates negative attitudes toward African Americans by European Americans (Strube & Rahimi, 2006) and encourages the maintenance of traditional gender roles and sexism (Duncan, Peterson, & Winter, 1997). Thus, SDO and RWA are very relevant constructs for higher education administrators to understand when addressing tensions involving diversity.

A personality trait that may be predictive of attitudes toward racial diversity is openness to experience (OTE). OTE can be characterized as embodying a combination of "intellectual curiosity with broad interests, liberal views, adventurous tendencies, and a need for variety" (McCrae, 1994, p. 257). It suggests a preference for new and different experiences in many aspects of life (McCrae, 1994). European Americans low in OTE are more likely to engage in negative stereotyping of African Americans than those high in OTE (Flynn, 2005). In addition, European Americans who score relatively high on OTE exhibit less prejudice (Flynn, 2005). Given the many new experiences that college students encounter, OTE is also an important construct for higher education staff.

Purpose of Study

Most studies of prejudicial attitudes toward racial minorities and women include majority European American samples or relatively few ethnic minorities. Because prejudicial attitudes are not limited to European Americans, it is important to study these attitudes among ethnically diverse samples. Furthermore, it is important to assess prejudice more comprehensively than previous studies which usually focus only on race or ethnicity (e.g., usually African Americans) or gender separately. In the current study we examined ethnicity, gender, political views, SDO, RWA, and OTE as predictors of prejudicial attitudes. After controlling for the self-interest variables, we were interested in how much social ideology variables and a personality variable would account for prejudicial attitudes.

We were interested in three research questions. First, do factors of self-interest (i.e., ethnicity, gender, and political views), social ideologies (i.e., SDO, RWA), and personality traits (i.e., OTE) significantly predict cognitive attitudes toward racial diversity? Second, do factors of self-interest, social ideologies, and personality traits significantly predict comfort with interracial interaction? Third, do factors of self-interest, social ideologies, and personality traits significantly predict gender equity?

Method

Participants

Participants were recruited from a subject pool in the Educational Psychology department at the University of Texas at Austin, a large, urban public university located in the Southwest. The University of Texas at Austin has a Division of Diversity and Community Engagement (DDCE). The DDCE was created as a result of the recommendations of a Task Force on Racial Respect and Fairness and is responsible for integrating diversity into the core mission of the university. The University of Texas at Austin is

an ideal campus to do research on student attitudes about racial diversity and gender equity because it has been the focus of major legal battles involving the use of race in admissions. In addition, a Gender Equity Task Force recently recommended the creation of a plan to eliminate faculty gender inequity.

Four hundred thirty-three undergraduate students (235 women, 193 men, and five unknown; mean age = 20.39 years, $SD = 2.2$) participated in the present institutional review board-approved study in exchange for course credit. Surveys were completed online and participation was confidential. Participants were from a variety of racial and ethnic backgrounds. There were 167 European Americans, 83 African Americans, 81 Asian Americans, and 82 Hispanic Americans. Less than 1% of the remaining students were American Indian, Biracial, International, and from other backgrounds. Overall, the numbers of Asian American and Hispanic American students reflect the student population, while the numbers of African American students are higher and the numbers of European American students are lower.

Instruments

A demographic questionnaire was given to all participants. Information included ethnicity, gender, as well as political views. Ethnicity was initially coded 1 = "African American," 2 = "European American," 3 = "Asian American," 4 = "Hispanic American," 5 = "Biracial," 6 = "American Indian," and 7 = "International." Because of the small numbers of biracial, American Indian, and international students, they were excluded from data analyses. Ethnicity was then collapsed so that all racial minorities were coded as 1 and European Americans were coded as 2. Gender was coded 1 = "Male" and 2 = "Female." Although participants were asked to identify sex (i.e., male/female which involves biology), the discussion reflects the use of gender (i.e., men/women) as is consistent with contemporary psychology of women and gender scholarship (Unger, 1979). Political views were coded 1 "Far left," 2 "Liberal," 3 "Middle of the road," 4 "Conservative," and 5 "Far right."

Prejudicial attitudes were measured using the *Quick Discrimination Index (QDI)*. The QDI is a 30-item scale that measures cognitive attitudes regarding racial diversity, affective comfort with interracial interaction, and gender-based attitudes around issues of gender equity (Ponterotto, Burkard, & Reiger, 1995). Respondents are asked to determine their feelings about statements on a 4-point Likert scale. Responses range from 1 = *strongly disagree* to 4 = *strongly agree*. Cronbach's alphas for the three subscales have been reported as .85 for cognitive attitudes,

.83 for affective attitudes, and .65 for gender-based attitudes. Cronbach's alphas for the subscales in the current study were .85, .81, and .71, respectively. Criterion related validity has been established through finding expected differences by race, gender, and political affiliation. Convergent validity has been established through significant correlations with the New Racism Scale (Jacobson, 1985). The QDI has been used in a number of studies across ethnicities (Green, Kiernan-Stern, & Baskind, 2005; Liu, Pope-Davis, Nevitt, & Toporek, 1999; Neville, Lilly, Duran, Lee, & Browne, 2000; Ponterotto, Potere, & Johansen, 2002; Pope & Mueller, 2000) and has been found to be relatively free of social desirability contamination. Sample items include: "Overall, I think racial minorities in America complain too much about racial discrimination" (cognitive attitudes; reverse-scored), "I feel I could develop an intimate relationship with someone from a different race" (affective attitudes) and "I think feminist perspectives should be an integral part of the higher education curriculum" (gender-based attitudes; Ponterotto et al., 1995).

Social ideologies and personality traits were measured using three instruments. SDO was measured using the *Social Dominance Orientation Scale (SDOS)*. The SDOS is a 16-item scale that measures the degree to which individuals prefer social group inequality, a desire for ingroup dominance, and the belief in the inferiority of certain people (Strube & Rohimi, 2006). Respondents endorse items on a 7-point Likert scale ranging from 1 = *very negative* to 7 = *very positive*. Sample items include: "All groups should be given an equal chance in life," (reverse-scored) and "Some people are just inferior to others" (Duckitt, 2001). Cronbach's alphas ranging from .80 to .89 have been reported (Pratto et al., 1994) in previous studies. The Cronbach's alpha in the current study was .77. Known-groups validity has been demonstrated through findings that men are higher in SDO than women, and predictive validity has been found through SDO being linked to anti-Black racism and sexism (Pratto et al., 1994). Research also indicates that high scorers are more likely than low scorers to endorse a broad variety of hierarchy-legitimizing beliefs, exhibit prejudice, and hold positions and roles that maintain social inequality (Strube & Rohimi, 2006).

RWA was measured using the *Right-Wing Authoritarianism-Revised scale (RWA-R)*. The RWA-R is a 14-item measure that has been validated as an acceptable shorter version of the original RWA measure (Rattazzi, Bobbio, & Canova, 2007). The RWA-R measures two authoritarianism dimensions, broken into two subscales: (1) conservatism, and (2) authoritarian aggression and submission. Cronbach's alphas of .77 have been reported for the entire 14-item scale, with reliability coefficients of .72 and .75 being reported for the two subscales respectively (Rattazi et al., 2007). The

Cronbach's alpha for the current study was .85. Convergent validity has been found through high correlations with acceptance of government injustice (Altemeyer, 1981). Items are on a 7-point Likert scale and responses range from 1 = *totally disagree* to 7 = *totally agree*. Sample items include: "What our country really needs instead of more 'civil rights' is a good stiff dose of law and order" (authoritarian aggression and submission) and "Homosexuals and feminists should be praised for being brave enough to defy 'traditional family values' " (conservatism; reverse-scored).

OTE was measured using the *Openness to Experience* subscale taken from the *Big Five Inventory (BFI)* (John, Donahue, & Kentle, 1991). In the 10-item Openness to Experience (OE) subscale, persons are asked to agree or disagree with statements about characteristics that may or may not apply to themselves. The OE subscale is scored on a 5-point Likert scale ranging from 1 = *agree strongly* to 5 = *disagree strongly*. Cronbach's alphas ranging from .80 to .83 have been reported (Flynn, 2005). The Cronbach's alpha in the current study was .77. Construct validity has been found through positive correlations with higher SAT verbal scores (Noftle & Robins, 2007). Sample items include: "Has an active imagination," and "Likes to reflect, play with ideas." Scores from the OE subscale have been negatively correlated with self-report measures of racial attitudes (Flynn, 2005).

Procedure

Participants were recruited through the Educational Psychology department's subject pool and an introductory psychology class. All data were collected through an online survey system, Survey Monkey. Before participants began taking the survey they were prompted to enter their student ID and email address. Participants were then instructed to read the consent form, and their participation in the study indicated their informed consent. Participants completed a demographic form and measures of SDO, RWA, OTE, and prejudicial attitudes (Quick Discrimination Index; QDI). Respondents who completed the survey received course credit for their participation.

Descriptive statistics (i.e., means, standard deviations, correlations) were calculated for all study variables. Three hierarchical multiple regressions were conducted with each of the subscales of the QDI serving as a criterion variable. In Step 1, the self-interest variables were controlled for first (i.e., ethnicity, gender, and political view). OTE was entered in the second step because it was anticipated that OTE would account for additional variance beyond the self-interest variables. Finally, SDO and RWA were entered in the third step because it was hypothesized that these variables would account for the largest amount of variance.

Results

. . .

Predicting Cognitive Attitudes Toward Racial Diversity

In Step 1 of the first regression, the self-interest variables accounted for a significant amount of variance, $F(3, 425) = 52.31, p < .001$ (adjusted $R^2 = .27$). The self-interest variables differed and are presented in order of significance: (a) More conservative political views predicted more negative attitudes toward racial diversity ($\beta = -.34, p < .001$); (b) European American students had more negative attitudes toward racial diversity than racial minority students ($\beta = -.24, p < .001$), and (c) women had more positive attitudes toward racial diversity than men, ($\beta = .22, p < .001$). In Step 2, the addition of OTE ($\beta = .19$) resulted in a significant change in R^2 of .03 ($p < .001$), meaning that students more open to experience had more positive attitudes toward racial diversity. In Step 3, the addition of SDO and RWA accounted for a significant amount of variance, $F(6, 425) = 58.75, p < .001$ (adjusted $R^2 = .45$). Being higher in SDO was a significantly stronger and more negative predictor of attitudes toward racial diversity ($\beta = -.43, p < .001$) than RWA ($\beta = -.09, p < .05$). Thus, the final model accounted for 45% of the variance, with SDO being the strongest predictor of racial diversity attitudes followed by ethnicity, political views, gender, OTE, and RWA. Although political views were a stronger predictor than ethnicity in the first step, once all variables were in the model ethnicity became a stronger predictor.

Predicting Affective Comfort with Interracial Interaction

In Step 1 of the second regression, the self-interest variables accounted for a significant amount of variance, $F(3, 425) = 14.77, p < .001$ (adjusted $R^2 = .09$). The self-interest variables differed and are presented in order of significance: (a) More conservative political views predicted less comfort with interracial interaction ($\beta = -.27, p < .001$); (b) European American students had less comfort with interracial interaction than racial minority students ($\beta = -.10, p < .05$). In Step 2, the addition of OTE ($\beta = .23$) resulted in a significant change in R^2 of .05 ($p < .001$), meaning that students more open to experience had more comfort with interracial interaction. In Step 3, the addition of SDO and RWA to the model accounted for a significant amount of variance, $F(6, 425) = 33.32, p < .001$ (adjusted $R^2 = .31$). Being higher in SDO was a significantly stronger and more negative predictor of comfort with interracial interaction ($\beta = -37, p < .001$) than RWA ($\beta = -.26, p < .001$). Thus, the final model accounted for 31% of the variance, with SDO being the strongest predictor of comfort with interracial interaction followed by RWA, gender, ethnicity, and OTE. Political views were no longer a significant predictor once all variables were in the model, and gender became a significant predictor once all variables were in the model.

Predicting Cognitive Attitudes About Gender Equity

In Step 1 of the third regression, the self-interest variables accounted for a significant amount of variance, $F(3, 425) = 42.39, p < .001$ (adjusted $R^2 = .23$). The self-interest variables differed and are presented in order of significance: (a) More conservative political views predicted lower support for gender equity ($\beta = -.32, p < .001$); (b) women had stronger support for gender equity than males ($\beta = .29, p < .001$). In Step 2, the addition of OTE ($\beta = .07$) did not result in a significant change in R^2, meaning that being more open to experience did not relate to attitudes about gender equity. In Step 3, the addition of SDO and RWA to the model accounted for a significant amount of variance, $F(6, 425) = 35.54, p < .001$ (adjusted $R^2 = .33$). Being higher in RWA was a stronger and more negative predictor of attitudes about gender equity ($\beta = -.25, p < .001$) than SDO ($\beta = -.22, p < .001$). Thus, the final model accounted for 33% of the variance, with RWA being the strongest predictor of gender equity attitudes followed by gender, SDO, political views, and ethnicity. Ethnicity became a significant predictor once all variables were in the model. Table 1 includes a summary of the regression models.

Discussion

Every year many incidents of prejudice and discrimination occur on college campuses across the country. Students come to colleges with personalities and attitudes that either become more open and sympathetic to diversity issues or become more close-minded to diversity issues. To better understand why these incidents may occur, two overarching questions framed our study. First, why do individuals harbor mixed feelings and/or negative attitudes about diversity in light of its demonstrated positive effects? Second, what are the factors that contribute to the negative attitudes that some individuals have toward racial diversity? These overarching questions were operationalized by three research questions.

Table 1

Hierarchical Regression on Cognitive and Affective Racial Attitudes and Cognitive Gender Attitudes

Variable	Cognitive attitudes toward racial diversity				Affective comfort with interracial interaction				Cognitive attitudes about gender equity and women's roles			
	B	Standard error B	β	Adj. R^2	B	Standard error B	β	Adj. R^2	B	Standard error B	β	Adj. R^2
Step 1				.27				.09				.23
Race	-2.76	.49	-.24***		-1.02	.48	-.10*		-.66	.30	-.10*	
Gender	2.47	.46	.22***		-.28	.46	-.03		1.99	.29	.30***	
Political views	-2.30	.29	-.34***		-1.62	.29	-.27***		-1.33	.18	-.32***	
Step 2				.30				.14				.30
Openness to experience	1.88	.42	.19***		2.06	.42	.23***		.46	.27	.08	
Step 3				.45				.31				.33
Social dominance orientation	-2.70	.26	-.43***		-2.07	.26	-.37***		-.85	.18	-.22***	
Right-wing authoritarianism	-.52	.25	-.09*		-1.38	.25	-.26***		-.92	.17	-.25***	

*$p < .05$. ***$p < .001$.

Attitudes Toward Racial Diversity

Regarding the first research question, we were interested in whether factors of selfinterest were significantly related to cognitive attitudes toward racial diversity. Previous research has found that attitudes toward affirmative action differ by race and gender (Kravitz & Platania, 1993). Consistent with previous research, ethnicity, gender and political views significantly predicted attitudes toward racial diversity. Racial minorities held more positive attitudes toward racial diversity than European Americans, women held more positive attitudes than men, and individuals who self-identified as being more liberal held more positive attitudes than individuals who self-identified as being more conservative. These findings can be explained in part by the idea of self-interest (Golden, Hinkle, & Crosby, 2001). Individuals will tend to support ideas and policies that benefit their group interests. In environments where European American men are often in the majority and in positions of power, it is in the group interests of ethnic minorities and women to support the goal of diversity.

We were most interested in whether personality traits (i.e., OTE) and social ideology (i.e., SWO and RWA) would significantly predict attitudes toward racial diversity after controlling for self-interest variables. As hypothesized, SDO, RWA, and OTE all predicted attitudes toward racial diversity. Individuals higher in SDO and RWA held more negative attitudes toward racial diversity, while individuals higher in OTE held more positive attitudes. These findings are consistent with previous research showing that SDO and RWA are strong predictors of racial prejudice (Altemeyer, 1996; Pratto et al., 1994). Thus, programs designed to promote racial equality and change existing institutions would be viewed negatively by individuals high in SDO and RWA. The findings regarding OTE are also consistent with previous research which shows that individuals who are more openminded exhibit less prejudice (Flynn, 2005).

Comfort with Interracial Interaction

Regarding the second research question, ethnicity and political views significantly predicted comfort with interracial interaction. Racial minorities were more comfortable with interracial interaction than European Americans, and more liberal students were more comfortable with interracial interaction than more conservative students. While research has shown interracial interactions to be cognitively demanding for both European Americans (Richeson & Shelton, 2003) and racial minorities (Shelton, Richeson, & Salvatore, 2005), research has also shown that racial minorities value interracial interaction and want colleges to find ways to foster more of it (Schmidt, 2007).

As hypothesized, SDO, RWA and OTE were predictors of comfort with interracial interaction. Individuals higher in SDO and RWA had less comfort with interracial interaction while individuals higher in OTE had more comfort. These findings are consistent with previous research showing that (a) SDO is negatively related to support of interracial dating (Lalonde, Giguere, Fontaine, & Smith, 2007), and (b) individuals high in RWA exhibit more prejudice during negative interracial contact (Dhont & Van Hiel, 2009). The findings regarding OTE are consistent with previous research that shows individuals high in OTE have more tolerant interracial attitudes because they tend to be more curious and broad-minded (Flynn, 2005).

Attitudes About Gender Equity

Regarding the third research question, we examined whether self-interest variables, personality traits and social ideology were significantly related to attitudes about gender equity. Gender and political views both significantly predicted attitudes about gender equity. Not surprisingly, women held more positive attitudes about gender equity than men. Individuals who self-identified as being more conservative held more negative attitudes about gender equity than individuals who self-identified as being more liberal. As hypothesized, SDO and RWA were both negative predictors of attitudes about gender equity. These findings were also consistent with previous research that has found SDO and RWA to be significant predictors of hostile sexism and benevolent sexism, respectively (Christopher & Mull, 2006). Individuals higher in SDO prefer hierarchy in relations, and are likely to believe that men are more capable in leadership than women. Unlike the previous analyses, RWA was the strongest predictor of attitudes about gender equity. Research has found RWA to be a strong predictor of sexism (Altemeyer, 1998), and individuals higher in RWA are followers of social convention and tradition. Few attitudes better exemplify traditional beliefs than attitudes about the roles of women, and because individuals higher in RWA are more likely to be dogmatic (Altemeyer, 1998), they are likely to have very strong feelings about the roles of women (Whitley, 1999).

Implications for Practice

Results from this study can be used to refine programming and diversity education efforts on college campuses. More specifically, specialized training should be developed for staff and administrators involved in diversity education efforts. This training should involve presenting the latest research on factors such as SDO and RWA that impact attitudes about diversity, and helping the staff and administra-

tors design developmentally appropriate programming and diversity education efforts. There is evidence that diversity education reduces racial prejudice (Hogan & Mallott, 2005). However, diversity education and related programming should be theoretically grounded and supported by research. Therefore, it is important for individuals working in higher education to have knowledge of the factors that give rise to specific prejudicial attitudes related to racial diversity, interracial interaction, and gender equity. Programming and diversity education efforts should also recognize that there are different motives for prejudice which require tailored interventions to reduce different types of prejudice (Duckitt, 2006). A one-size-fits-all intervention that targets general prejudice is likely to be less successful than specific interventions that target racial prejudice versus gender prejudice. A common experience on college campuses involves incidents related to racial insensitivity (e.g., parties that involve students dressing or acting in a racially stereotypical manner). An administrator or staff person who has undergone specialized diversity education training will understand that different interventions are needed depending on the motives for prejudice. For example, a few years ago 1st year law students at the University of Texas at Austin participated in a ghetto-fabulous themed costume party and posted the pictures online. The Dean of the law school, along with the Vice-President for Diversity and Community Engagement, met with the students to chide them about their behavior and to inform them about how this incident could impact their future prospects for employment. There were no disciplinary actions, and the students indicated that they did not mean to offend anyone. If the students had been high in RWA they would have been most likely motivated by a perceived threat of racial minorities (in this case African Americans and Latino Americans). In this instance prejudice reduction strategies involving conflict resolution and threat reduction would have been appropriate (Duckitt, 2006). However, if the students had been high in SDO they would have most likely been motivated by perceiving racial minorities as socially subordinate, in which case prejudice reduction strategies should focus on creating equal status intergroup contacts, which is consistent with the contact hypothesis (Allport, 1954). Similarly, a residence hall director might deal with a roommate conflict situation where an individual does not want to room with someone from a different ethnic background. Individuals low in OTE may not want to room with someone from a different cultural background because of a fear of the unknown or lack of familiarity with another culture. In this instance the residence hall director should educate the individual about the personal benefits of a crosscultural roommate experience. It is important that higher education institutions create diversity program initiatives that involve support by the entire institution from the highest to lowest levels (de Pillis & de Pillis, 2008). Furthermore, diversity programs are likely to become more widely endorsed and sanctioned by university administrators and faculty if they are perceived to be based on theory and research rather than emotion and political correctness. Diversity initiatives must extend beyond just increasing the number of diverse students into the same environment. Instead, they must include curricular and extracurricular opportunities for crossgroup interactions (Gurin, Nagda, & Lopez, 2004).

Limitations

There are several limitations of this study. First, the research design is correlational, thus it cannot be concluded from this study that SWO and RWA cause negative attitudes toward racial diversity, comfort with interracial interaction, and gender equity. Nor can it be concluded that OTE causes positive attitudes toward the aforementioned. Future studies should employ an experimental design to allow stronger conclusions to be drawn about the presumed cause-effect relationship of social ideologies, personality traits and prejudice.

A second limitation is the failure to control for social desirability. Given the nature of the items on the Quick Discrimination Index, it is possible that students responded in a socially desirable way. Research shows that individuals tend to portray themselves as less prejudiced than they really are on self-report prejudice instruments (Holmes, 2009). Future research using the Quick Discrimination Index should include a measure of social desirability to provide further evidence of its validity.

A third limitation is the failure to use a more proximal measure of race or ethnicity such as racial or ethnic identity. All people have a racial and ethnic identity, and are subject to internalizing harmful messages about that identity. The use of racial or ethnic identity is an additional way of addressing the oversimplification of the self-interest variables of race and ethnicity (Cokley & Awad, 2007).

A fourth limitation is the lack of representation of Native American students as well as international and biracial students. Future studies would benefit from including these underrepresented groups.

Conclusion

This study has made a significant contribution to the higher education and social psychological literatures. The constructs of SDO and RWA are two of the most prominent theoretical approaches for studying prejudice in the

social psychology literature (Duckitt & Sibley, 2007), yet surprisingly virtually no research in higher education or college student development has included these constructs in studies related to diversity or prejudice reduction. The present study provides researchers the analytical framework to better understand student attitudes toward racial diversity and gender equity. Similarly, the construct of OTE has rarely been examined in the higher education or college student development literature, and should be incorporated in future research because the college experience is full of new experiences for students. Given the well-documented benefits of diversity, it is especially important for professors and university personnel to better understand the factors that influence negative student views, so that they may be better equipped to respond to resistance to diversity and racist classroom or campus incidents (Garcia & Van Soest, 2000). It is hoped that the results of this study will encourage future diversity education efforts to include interventions informed by social psychological research that can be directly translated to prejudice reduction efforts.

References

Adorno, T. W., Frenkel-Brunswik, E., Levinson, D. J., & Sanford, R. N. (1950). *The authoritarian personality.* Oxford, England: Harpers.

Allport, G. (1954). *The nature of prejudice.* Cambridge, MA: Perseus Books.

Altemeyer, B. (1981). *Right-wing authoritarianism.* Winnipeg: University of Manitoba Press.

Altemeyer, B. (1996). *The authoritarian specter.* Cambridge, MA: Harvard University Press.

Altemeyer, B. (1998). "'The other 'authoritarian personality.'" In M. Zanna (Ed.), *Advances in experimental social psychology* (Vol. 30, pp. 47–92). San Diego: Academic Press.

American Association of Colleges and Universities. (n.d.). Making excellence inclusive. Retrieved from http://www.aacu.org/inclusive_excellence/index.cfm

Antonio, A. L., Chang, M. J., Hakuta, K., Kenny, D. A., Levin, S., & Milem, J. F. (2004). Effects of racial diversity on complex thinking in college students. *Psychological Science, 15,* 507–510.

Awad, G. H., Cokley, K., & Ravitch, J. (2005). Attitudes toward affirmative action: A comparison of color-blind versus modern racist attitudes. *Journal of Applied Social Psychology, 35,* 1384–1399.

Bobo, L. (1998). Race, interests, and beliefs about affirmative action. *American Behavioral Scientist, 41,* 985–1003.

Bowen, W. G., & Bok, D. (1998). *The shape of the river: Long-term consequences of considering race in college and university admissions.* Princeton, NJ: Princeton University Press.

Chang, M. J. (1999). Does racial diversity matter?: The education impact of racially diverse undergraduate population. *Journal of College Student Development, 40,* 377–395.

Chickering, A. W., & Reisser, L. (1993). *Education and identity.* San Francisco: Jossey-Bass.

Christopher, A. N., & Mull, M. S. (2006). Conservative ideology and ambivalent sexism. *Psychology of Women Quarterly, 30,* 223–230.

Cokley, K., & Awad, G. (2007). Conceptual and methodological issues related to multicultural research. In P. Heppner, D. Kivlighan, & B. Wampold (Eds.), *Research design in counseling* (3rd ed., pp. 366–384). Belmont, CA: Brooks/Cole. Belmont.

de Pillis, E., & de Pillis, L. (2008). Are engineering schools masculine and authoritarian? The mission statements say yes. *Journal of Diversity in Higher Education, 1,* 33–44.

Dhont, K., & Van Hiel, A. (2009). We must not be enemies: Interracial contact and the reduction of prejudice among authoritarians. *Personality and Individual Differences, 46,* 172–177. doi:10.1016/j.paid.2008.09.022

Duckitt, J. (2001). A dual process cognitive-motivational theory of ideology and prejudice. In M. Zanna (Ed.), *Advances in experimental social psychology* (Vol. 33, pp. 41–113). San Diego: Academic Press.

Duckitt, J. (2006). Differential effects of right wing authoritarianism and social dominance orientation on outgroup attitudes and their mediation by threat from and competitiveness to outgroups. *Personality and Social Psychology Bulletin, 32,* 684–696. doi:10.1177/0146167205284282

Duckitt, J., & Sibley, C. G. (2007). Right wing authoritarianism, social dominance orientation and the dimensions of generalized prejudice. *European Journal of Personality, 21,* 113–130.

Duckitt, J., Wagner, C., du Plessis, & Birum, I. (2002). The psychological bases of ideology and prejudice:

Testing a dual process model. *Journal of Personality and Social Psychology, 83,* 75–93.

Duncan, L. E., Peterson, B. E., & Winter, D. G. (1997). Authoritarianism and gender roles: Toward a psychological analysis of hegemonic relationships. *Personality and Social Psychology Bulletin, 23,* 41–49.

Flynn, F. J. (2005). Having an open mind: The impact of openness to experience on interracial attitudes and impression formation. *Journal of Personality and Social Psychology, 88,* 816–826.

Garcia, B., & Van Soest, D. (2000). Facilitating learning on diversity: Challenges to the professor. *Journal of Ethnic & Cultural Diversity in Social Work: Innovation in Theory, Research & Practice, 9,* 21–39. doi:10.1300/J051v09n01_02

Golden, H., Hinkle, S., & Crosby, F. (2001). Reactions to affirmative action: Substance Semantics. *Journal of Applied Social Psychology, 31,* 73–88.

Gottfredson, N. C., Panter, A. T., Daye, C. E., Allen, W. A., Wightman, L. F., & Deo, M. E. (2008). Does diversity at undergraduate institutions influence student outcomes? *Journal of Diversity in Higher Education, 1,* 80–94.

Green, R. G., Kiernan-Stern, M., & Baskind, F. R. (2005). White social workers' attitudes about people of color. *Journal of Ethnic & Cultural Diversity in Social Work, 14,* 47–68.

Gurin, P., Lehman, J. S., & Lewis, E. (2004). *Defending diversity: Affirmative action at the University of Michigan.* Ann Arbor, MI: University of Michigan Press.

Gurin, P., Nagda, B. A., & Lopez, G. E. (2004). The benefits of diversity in education for democratic citizenship. *Journal of Social Issues, 60,* 17–34.

Gurin, P. Y., Dey, E. L., Gurin, G., & Hurtado, S. (2003). How does racial/ethnic diversity promote education? *The Western Journal of Black Studies, 27,* 20–29.

Gurin, P. Y., Dey, E. L., Hurtado, S., & Gurin, G. (2002). Diversity and higher education: Theory and impact on educational outcomes. *Harvard Educational Review, 72,* 330–367.

Haley, H., & Sidanius, J. (2006). The positive and negative framing of affirmative action: A group dominance perspective. *Personality and Social Psychology Bulletin, 32,* 656–668.

Hogan, D. E., & Mallott, M. (2005). Changing racial prejudice through diversity education. *Journal of College Student Development, 46,* 115–125.

Holmes, J. (2009). Transparency of self-report racial attitude scales. *Basic and Applied Social Psychology, 31,* 95–101. doi:10.1080/01973530902876884

Jacobson, C. R. (1985). Resistance to affirmative action: Self-interest or racism. *Journal of Conflict Resolution, 29,* 306–329.

John, O. P., Donahue, E. M., & Kentle, R. L. (1991). *The "Big Five" Inventory: Versions 4a and* 54 (Tech. Rep.). Berkeley: Institute of Personality and Social Research, University of California, Berkeley.

Kluegel, J. R., & Smith, E. R. (1983). Affirmative action attitudes: Effects of self-interest, racial affect, and stratification beliefs on Whites' views. *Social Forces, 61,* 797–824.

Kravitz, D. A., & Platania, J. (1993). Attitudes and beliefs about affirmative action: Effects of target and of respondent sex and ethnicity. *Journal of Applied Psychology, 78,* 928–938.

Lalonde, R., Giguère, B., Fontaine, M., & Smith, A. (2007). Social dominance orientation and ideological asymmetry in relation to interracial dating and transracial adoption in Canada. *Journal of Cross-Cultural Psychology, 38,* 559–572. doi:10.1177/ 0022022107305238

Liu, W. M., Pope-Davis, D. B., Nevitt, J., & Toporek, R. L. (1999). Understanding the function of acculturation and prejudicial attitudes among Asian Americans. *Cultural Diversity & Ethnic Minority Psychology, 5,* 317–328.

McCrae, R. R. (1994). Openness to experience: Expanding the boundaries of factor V. *European Journal of Personality, 8,* 251–272.

Negy, C., & Lunt, R. (2008). What college students really think about ethnic student organizations. *Journal of Diversity in Higher Education, 1,* 176–192. doi:10.1037/a0012751

Neville, H. A., Lilly, R. L., Duran, G., Lee, R. M., & Browne, L. (2000). Construction and initial validation of the Color-Blind Racial Attitudes Scales (CoBRAS). *Journal of Counseling Psychology, 47,* 59–70.

Noftle, E., & Robins, R. (2007). Personality predictors of academic outcomes: Big five correlates of GPA and SAT scores. *Journal of Personality and Social Psychology, 93,* 116–130. doi:10.1037/ 0022–3514.93.1.116

Ozawa, K., Crosby, M., & Crosby, F. (1996). Individualism and resistance to affirmative Action: A comparison of Japanese and American samples. *Journal of Applied Social Psychology, 26,* 1138–1152.

Pascerella, E. T., Palmer, B., Moye, M., & Pierson, C. T. (2001). Do diversity experiences influence the development of critical thinking? *Journal of College Student Development, 42,* 257–271.

Perry, W. G., Jr. (1981). Cognitive and ethical growth: The making of meaning. In A. W. Chickering (Ed.), *The modern American college: Responding to the new realities of diverse students and a changing society* (pp. 76–116). San Francisco: Jossey-Bass.

Ponterotto, J. G., Burkard, A., Rieger, B. P., Grieger, I., D'Onofrio, A., Dubuisson, A., . . . Sax, G. (1995). Development and initial validation of the Quick Discrimination Index (QDI). *Educational and Psychological Measurement, 55,* 1016–1031.

Ponterotto, J. G., Potere, J. C., & Johansen, S. A. (2002). The Quick Discrimination Index: Normative data and user guidelines for counseling researchers. *Journal of Multicultural Counseling and Development, 30,* 192–207.

Pope, R. L., & Mueller, J. A. (2000). Developmental and initial validation of the Multicultural Competence in Student Affairs–Preliminary 2 Scale. *Journal of College Student Development, 41,* 599–608.

Pratto, F., Sidanius, J., Stallworth, L. M., & Malle, B. F. (1994). Social dominance orientation: A personality variable predicting social and political attitudes. *Journal of Personality and Social Psychology, 67,* 741–763.

Rattazzi, A. M. M., Bobbio, A., & Canova, L. (2007). A short version of the Right-Wing Authoritarianism (RWA) Scale. *Personality and Individual Differences, 43,* 1223–1234.

Richeson, J., & Shelton, J. N. (2003). When prejudice does not pay: Effects of interracial contact on executive function. *Psychological Science, 14,* 287–290.

Schmidt, P. (2007). Minority students want colleges to foster interracial interaction, survey finds. Retrieved from http://chronicle.com/ news/article/ 3379/minority-students-want-colleges-to-fosterinterracial-interaction-survey

Shelton, J. N., Richeson, J., & Salvatore, J. (2005). Expecting to be the target of prejudice: Implications for interethnic interactions. *Personality and Social Psychology Bulletin, 31,* 1189–1202.

Sibley, C., & Duckitt, J. (2008). Personality and prejudice: A meta-analysis and theoretical review. *Personality and Social Psychology Review, 12,* 248–279. doi:10.1177/1088868308319226

Sibley, C. G., Robertson, A., & Wilson, M. S. (2006). Social dominance orientation and right-wing authoritarianism: Additive and interactive effects. *Political Psychology, 27,* 755–768.

Sidanius, J. (1993). The interface between racism and sexism. *Journal of Psychology: Interdisciplinary and Applied, 127,* 311–322.

Sipe, S., Johnson, C., & Fisher, D. (2009). University students' perceptions of gender discrimination in the workplace: Reality versus fiction. *Journal of Education for Business, 84,* 339–349. doi:10.3200/JOEB.84.6.339–349

Strube, M. J., & Rahimi, A. M. (2006). "Everybody knows it's true": Social dominance orientation and right-wing authoritarianism moderate false consensus for stereotypic beliefs. *Journal of Research in Personality, 40,* 1038–1053.

Swim, J., Aikin, K., Hall, W., & Hunter, B. (1995). Sexism and racism: Old-fashioned and modern prejudices. *Journal of Personality and Social Psychology, 68,* 199–214.

Unger, R. K. (1979). Toward a redefinition of sex and gender. *American Psychologist, 34,* 1085–1094.

Van Hiel, A., & Mervielde, I. (2005). Authoritarianism and social dominance orientation: Relationships with various forms of racism. *Journal of Applied Social Psychology, 35,* 2323–2344.

Van Hiel, A., Pandelaere, M., & Duriez, B. (2004). The impact of need for closure on conservative beliefs and racism: Differential mediation by authoritarian submission and authoritarian dominance. *Personality and Social Psychology Bulletin, 30,* 824–837. doi: 10.1177/0146167204264333

Whitley, B. E., Jr. (1999). Right-wing authoritarianism, social dominance orientation, and prejudice. *Journal of Personality and Social Psychology, 77,* 126–134.

Kevin O. Cokley teaches educational psychology at the University of Texas at Austin, where he focuses on African American psychology, which addresses the development of ethnic and racial identities and how those items impact academic successes. His research focuses on how African American students' academic achievements are influenced by environmental and psychological factors.

Kimberly Tran is an assistant professor of counseling psychology at Fayetteville State University in North Carolina. She has published much research on how mental health is impacted by multicultural issues among ethnic/racial minorities.

Brittany Hall-Clark is a licensed psychologist and post-doctoral fellow in the Department of Psychiatry and the Division of Behavioral Medicine at the University of Texas Health Science Center at San Antonio. Her research focuses on culturally sensitive treatment of anxiety and stress disorders.

Collette Chapman is a psychology professor at the College of Staten Island in New York. Her research focuses on ethnic and racial psychological functioning and identity development, social identity, and cultural consciousness.

Luana Bessa is a counselor and psychologist in Boston, Massachusetts, where she conducts psychological assessments, individual psychotherapy, and couples counseling.

Angela Finley is a former counseling psychology doctoral student at the University of Texas in Austin.

Michael Martinez is on the clinical psychology staff in counseling services at the University of Texas at San Antonio.

B. Corenblum and Walter G. Stephan

White Fears and Native Apprehensions: An Integrated Threat Theory Approach to Intergroup Attitudes

Research on intergroup relations has traditionally focused on emotions people experience when thinking about or interacting with out-group members. Adorno, Frenkel-Brunswick, Levinson, and Sanford (1950), for example, argued that repressed hostility and anger underlie the authoritarian personality. The scapegoat theory of prejudice (Dollard, Doob, Miller, Mower, & Sears, 1939) postulated that displaced hostility underlies intolerant attitudes and beliefs. Along similar lines, Allport (1954) suggested that attitudes toward out-group members often reflect hatred and aggression, emotions that nonprejudiced individuals are able to keep in check (Devine, 1989). Negative affect has also been shown to predict attitudes toward out-group members. Stephan and Stephan (1985) found that anxiety about interacting with out-group members predicted attitudes toward them, and Stangor, Sullivan, and Ford (1991, Experiment 1) and Dijker (1987) report that emotions were better predictors than stereotypes of attitudes toward ethnic, cultural, and religious groups. The basic assumption behind these and other studies is that affective and motivational variables play an important role in attitudes and behaviours toward own and other group members (see Ashmore & Del Boca, 1981; Harding, Proshansky, Kutner, & Chein, 1969 for reviews).

Recently, social psychologists have turned to cognitive determinants of prejudice and discrimination (Fiske & Taylor, 1991; Hamilton, 1981; Kunda, 1999), and have downplayed motivational and affective factors. Much of the research on cognitive factors has been on the manner in which stereotypes influence people's processing of information about own and other group members (see Hewstone, Brown, & Smith, 1992; Mullen, 1990 for reviews). The cognitive approach has been very successful in drawing attention to how category-based expectancies influence all phases of the information processing sequence. For both adults (Duncan, 1976; Hewstone &

Jaspars, 1982; Taylor & Jaggi, 1974) and children (Bigler, Jones, & Lobliner, 1997; Powlishta, 1995; Yee & Brown, 1992) own group members are evaluated more favourably, their successes are attributed to internal factors, and more is recalled about them (Bodenhausen, 1988; Corenblum, Annis, & Young, 1996). How people process information (i.e., the social categories used to encode and recall information) (Ostrom, Pryor, & Simpson, 1981) plays an important role in attitudes toward, evaluations, and memory of own and other group members.

Both motivational and information processing approaches to prejudice typically focus on a single factor that underlies intolerant attitudes and beliefs. While such an approach facilitates research, no single approach can provide a complete explanation of prejudice or its consequences (Duckitt, 1992). In their discussion of the cognitive approach, Hamilton and Trolier (1986) state the "strategy has been to push the cognitive analysis as far as it could go . . . exploring the extent to which it *alone* (italics original) could produce judgmental and behavioral outcomes . . ." (p. 153). They go on to say, however, that

> Any particular form of stereotyping or prejudice, such as racism, is in all likelihood multiply determined by cognitive, motivational and social learning processes, whose effects combine in a given social context to produce specific judgmental and behavioral manifestations. Therefore, any attempt to understand such phenomena as a product of one process alone is probably misguided. (p. 153)

While theorists agree that prejudice is multiply determined, few agree about what those determinants are or how they should be measured. Allport (1954), for example, differentiated between proximal (e.g, situational personality, and phenomonological) and distal (historical, economic, cultural) causal factors. Other researchers have

From Corenblum, B; Stephan, Walter G. "White Fears and Native Apprehensions: An Integrated Threat Theory Approach to Intergroup Attitudes," *Canadian Journal of Behavioural Science,* vol. 33(4), 2001, pp. 251–268.

proposed somewhat similar configurations (see Duckitt, 1992 for a review), but apart from Agnew, Thompson, and Gaines (2000), model development and assessment has been lacking.

In the present study, a multicomponent model of prejudice is presented and tested. The integrated threat model of prejudice (Stephan & Stephan, 2000) considers attitudes toward out-group members in relation to affective reactions, thoughts about, and interactions with out-group members, as reported in responses to questionnaires. While the model and tests of it are correlational, with the attendant limitations of such designs, results reported here support the plausibility of hypothesized antecedent factors being associated with negative out-group attitudes. Before presenting the model, two aspects of the present study should be noted. First, in this study we examine "old fashioned," "traditional" or overt racism in contrast to current work on symbolic or covert racism in which expressions of intolerance are often masked or ambiguous (Dovidio & Gaertner, 1998). Second, prejudice and its consequences are typically studied only within majority groups (Esses, Haddock, & Zanna, 1993); what is often omitted are minority group members' attitudes toward majority group members. Hardly any research on the attitudes of subordinate groups toward dominant groups has been done. It is just as important to study minority group attitudes because those attitudes influence the behaviour of majority group members. Word, Zanna, and Cooper (1974), for example, found that Whites, when treated as Blacks are typically treated, responded with hostility and withdrawal to an interviewer's questions, reactions which lead, in turn, to a downward spiral during the interaction (for a review of studies on expectancy confirmation, see Neuberg, 1994). The present study examines attitudes of Native and EuroCanadians toward one another using the integrated threat theory.[1]

The Integrated Threat Model of Prejudice

Proximal Factors

The integrated threat theory focuses on a domain of variables that are thought to influence prejudice in all groups. These variables are taken from previous research and theory concerning intergroup relations and embody the idea that threat leads to prejudice. The theory suggests that there are at least four such threats: realistic threats, symbolic threats, intergroup anxiety, and negative stereotypes. Realistic threats refer to threats to the economic and

political power of the in-group along with threats to the welfare of the in-group and its members. The concept has its origins in realistic group conflict theories (Bobo, 1988; Coser, 1956; LeVine & Campbell, 1972; Sherif, 1966). Although such fears have been used primarily to understand the attitudes of dominant groups toward subordinate groups, it is unclear whether such fears are necessarily associated with prejudice toward the dominant group. For such fears to be expressed, some challenge to the political or economic power of the minority group must be perceived. While this may be the case for African Americans or Hispanics, it may not be for Native Canadians who, as a group, have little real political influence and are often on the bottom of the socioeconomic scale.

The idea of symbolic threats plays a central role in theories of symbolic racism, modern racism, ambivalence-amplification, and social dominance among others (Esses et al., 1993; Katz, Wackenhut, & Glass, 1988; Kinder & Sears, 1981; McConahay, 1986; Sears, 1988; Sidanius, Devereux, & Pratto, 1992). Symbolic threat refers to perceived violation of in-group's symbolic beliefs, (i.e., prescriptive and proscriptive norms and values about society and how society should function). Esses et al. (1993), for example, found that perceived differences in symbolic beliefs predicted majority group member's attitudes toward gays and ethnic minorities better than did affect. The idea that symbolic threat underlies negative out-group attitudes can be traced (in part) to Rokeach, Smith, and Evans (1960) who argued that differences in beliefs, not race, underlie prejudice and discrimination. In the integrated threat theory, symbolic threats consist of perceived group differences in worldviews of in-group and out-group members. Relevant dimensions of difference include morals, values, standards, beliefs, and attitudes. Although much research on symbolic threats has been done on dominant groups (for exceptions see Glick & Fiske, 1996; Sidanius & Pratto, 1999; Swim, Aiken, Hail & Hunter, 1995; Tougas, Brown, Beaton, & Joly, 1995), there is every reason to think that minority groups too should view negatively those who they believe hold their cherished beliefs, values, and morals in disdain or disregard.

Intergroup anxiety refers to feelings of discomfort that people experience when anticipating or engaging in intergroup interactions. While intergroup anxiety can result from a number of sources (see Britt, Boneicki, Vescio, & Brown, 1996; Vorauer, Main, & O'Connell, 1998), the ones we are stressing here are feelings of social rejection from out-group members. These feelings arise when people are concerned about such negative outcomes as being embarrassed, rejected, or ridiculed by out-group members (Stephan & Stephan, 1985). The idea that intergroup interaction can generate anxiety appears in several theories (Dovidio & Gaertner, 1998; Gudykunst, 1995). Gudykunst (1995) regards it as one of the primary causes of ineffective communication between groups (i.e., the message sent is not the one received), Stephan and Stephan (1985) argue that intergroup anxiety leads to a reliance on cognitive heuristics and amplifies emotional reactions to out-group members. Here, too, the majority of previous research has been on dominant groups, but there has been some attention paid to subordinate groups (e.g., Stephan & Stephan, 1989). Anxiety concerning intergroup interaction should be just as prevalent, perhaps more so, among members of subordinate as among members of dominant groups. This is because, as Fiske (1993) argues, subordinate group members are often outcome dependent on dominant group members; as a result, their social position is often precarious. Saying or doing the "wrong" or inappropriate thing, or believing that powerful others hold you in low regard because of your group membership creates anxiety when interacting with high status others. Dominant groups are in a stronger position to cause negative outcomes for subordinate groups than vice versa.

Realistic and symbolic threats as well as intergroup anxiety reflect affective or emotional reactions to out-group members. Negative stereotypes, on the other hand, reflect a cognitive component of prejudicial attitudes and may, like the affective components, embody threats to the in-group. The belief that out-group members are hostile, manipulative, unintelligent, unclean, or irresponsible causes in-group members to be wary or guarded when interacting with them. Stephan, Renfro et al. (2001, Experiment 2) found negative stereotypic traits attributed to an out-group resulted in more unfavourable evaluations than descriptions consisting of positive or positive and negative attributes. The relationship between stereotypes and prejudice has been extensively studied in dominant groups. This research indicates that it is primarily negative stereotypes that are related to prejudice; the simple fact of stereotyping is not closely related to prejudice (Brigham, 1971; Stephan, Agevev, Coates-Shrider, & Abalkina, 1994; see Boneicki & Brown, 1998; Gardner, 1994 for alternate positions on this issue). Although it has been studied less, it appears that subordinate groups have negative stereotypes of dominant groups. For instance, Allen (1996) found that stereotypic traits attributed by Blacks and Whites to the other racial group were more negative and rated higher on anxiety than those attributed to own group members. Negative stereotypes should be linked to out-group attitudes in Euro and Native Canadian groups.

Previous research has generally supported hypothesized links between threats and prejudice. Realistic threats have been found to be predictors of prejudice in correlational, as well as experimental, studies (Duran, Renfro, Stephan, & Clason, 2001; Esses, Jackson, & Armstrong, 1998; Stephan, Diaz-Loving, & Duran, 2000; Stephan, Ybarra, & Bachman, 1999; Stephan, Ybarra, Martinez, Schwarld, & Turk-kapsa, 1998). Symbolic threats have also been found to predict prejudice in correlational and experimental studies (Duran et al., 2001; Stephan et al., 1998, 1999, 2000). Intergroup anxiety has been found to predict prejudice in a number of different studies (Britt, Boniecki, Vescio, Biernat, Brown, 1996; Duran et al., 2001; Islam & Hewstone, 1993; Stephan et al., 1998, 1999, 2000). Negative stereotypes too have been found to predict prejudice in correlational and laboratory studies (Duran et al., 2001; Stangor, Sechrist, & Jost, 2000; Stephan et al., 1998, 1999, 2000).

Distal Factors

There are many potential antecedents of prejudice. Allport (1954) listed four; Agnew et al. (2000), in a test of Allport's ideas, discuss two: family status and contextual factors. In the integrated threat theory, the four types of threats are believed to be associated with four antecedent or "causal" variables selected on the basis of past research and theory on intergroup relations. The four distal variables are: strength of in-group identification, negative out-group contact, history of intergroup conflict, and between-group status differences (Stephan & Stephan, 2000). People who strongly identify with their group have an emotional stake in its welfare and preservation and the well-being of its members. According to social identity theory (Tajfel & Turner, 1979), people identify with their group to enhance their social identity and maintain self-esteem. Social identity is enhanced by accentuating in a positive direction, differences between own and other group members (see also Brewer, 1991). For the strongly identified, the out-group is perceived as a threat to the self and the in-group because the out-group is seen as constraining, at a number of levels, growth and development of in-group identity (Duran et al., 2001; Stephan, Boniecki et al., 2001).

Negative out-group contact should increase feelings of threat (Stephan, Boniecki et al., 2001). The more extensive the negative contacts (e.g., disagreements, fights, losing team efforts, unpleasant intergroup interactions) the more the other group is likely to be perceived as a threat (Stephan, Boniecki et al., 2001; Stephan & Stephan, 2000; Stephan et al, 2000). Likewise, the more violent and protracted the history of intergroup conflict, the more threatened people are likely to feel by the other group (Stephan, Boniecki et al., 2001). When the two groups are perceived to differ in status, this, too, may lead to feelings of threat (Stephan, Boniecki et al., 2001). Dominant group members may worry that attempts by lower status groups to improve their social and economic position threatens the in-group's way of life, calls into question in-group values and beliefs, challenges prevailing stereotypes of out-group members, and increases intergroup anxiety. Vorauer, Main, and O'Connell (1998), for example, report that some Whites stereotype Natives as (among other attributes) rebellious, disrespectful, defiant, and bitter—attributes that suggest perceptions of Native people as attempting to alter the status quo. Among subordinate groups, the relationship between perceived status differences and threats is more tenuous, and may reflect perceived extremity and "cause" of status differences as well as perceived permeability of status boundaries. Among subordinate groups with a growing middle class and attendant social and political influence, status differences could be associated with negative intergroup attitudes directly as well as indirectly through proximal, threat variables. Where those groups are economically, socially or politically oppressed, and there is little evidence of change, perceived status differences should be unrelated to perceived threats or negative intergroup attitudes (Runciman, 1966).

One assumption underlying the integrated threat model is that similar factors are associated with intolerant attitudes in dominant and subordinate groups. This assumption will be tested here. The model also assumes, as do other theories of prejudice, that intolerance is intolerance; that is, the same factors underlie negative out-group attitudes regardless of the group's status. Allport (1954) states that prejudicial thoughts reflect the presence of simple categories and the use of the principle of least effort. Hamilton and Trolier (1986) argue that ". . . as cognitive categories, all stereotypes are assumed to have the same basic structural properties and to influence information processing in the same ways" (p. 152). While support for a generalized model of prejudice is limited, Agnew et al. (2000) found that the same proximal and distal factors were associated with dominant groups' attitudes toward gays, African Americans, and the elderly. In only a few studies of which we are aware are attitudes of subordinate groups assessed, and no study assesses reciprocal attitudes within a single theoretical framework. The current study examines the attitudes of White and Native Canadians toward one another using the integrated threat theory. . . .

Method

Participants

One hundred and ten Whites (80 females) and 127 Native (93 females) volunteered to participate in a survey of racial attitudes. Most (97%) of the White sample indicated their age as being between 16 and 25. The age distribution of the Native sample was more diverse: 6% indicated an age between 16–20, 19% indicated an age between 21–25, 28% said their age was between 26–30, and 22% indicated an age range of 31–35.

White and Native samples were drawn from a variety of classes in Arts, Science, and Education, as well as Education classes designed for Native people living in rural areas or northern Canada. A number of plains and boreal forest First Nation groups were represented in the Native sample. Overall, 40% indicated Ojibwa affiliation, 43% chose Cree as their First Nation affiliation, and the rest were divided among Sioux, Salteaux, and Metis (people of Native and White heritage). First Nation peoples were grouped together for analysis since previous studies (e.g., Corenblum et al., 1996) have found no significant differences between people from First Nation groups on a number of dependent measures.

Measures

Attitudes toward out-groups. The measure of intergroup attitudes used here has been used in a number of previous studies (Stephan et al., 1998, 1999). It was designed to reflect negative affect associated with out-groups (Stephan & Stephan, 1993). Participants were asked to indicate the degree to which they felt 12 different evaluative or emotional reactions to Whites (Native people) on a 10-point scale running from 0, *No (e.g., hatred) at all*, to 9, *Extreme (e.g., hatred)*. The evaluative and emotional terms included: hostility, admiration, disliking, acceptance, superiority, affection, disdain, approval, hatred, sympathy, rejection, and warmth. For this measure and all other measures, the same items (with appropriate wording changes) were used for White and Native samples; on this measure and all other measures, positively worded words or statements were reverse scored so that all scales reflect greater negativity toward out-group members.

Proximal Variables

Realistic threats. The measure that was created to assess realistic threats consisted of 12 statements reflecting perceived economic or political threat from the out-group. Participants responded to such items as, "Natives/Whites hold too many positions of power and responsibility in this country," "Natives/Whites receive too much of the money spent on health and child care," on 10-point scales anchored by *Strongly disagree* to *Strongly agree.*

Symbolic threats. To capture threat posed by perceived differences in values and beliefs between Whites and Natives, a measure consisting of 12 statements was created. Participants rated their agreement on a 10-point, *Strongly disagree* to *Strongly agree* scale with statements such as, "Natives and Whites have many incompatible values," "Whites want their rights to be put ahead of the rights of Native people."

Intergroup anxiety. The measure of intergroup anxiety was modified from the intergroup anxiety scale developed by Stephan and Stephan (1985). The measure consisted of 12 items that asked participants how they would feel when interacting with members of the other group. The anxiety-eliciting terms were: apprehensive, friendly, uncertain, comfortable, worried, trusting, threatened, confident, awkward, safe, anxious, and at ease. For each term participants rated how they would feel on a 10-point scale labeled, *Not at all* to *Extremely.*

Negative Stereotype Index: To assess stereotypes, a measure developed by Stephan et al. (1994) was employed (see also Eagly & Mladinic, 1989; Esses et al., 1993). Participants were asked to indicate the percentage of members of the other racial group who possessed each of the 12 traits that previous research has shown to be associated with these groups (Gibbins & Ponting, 1977; Hanson & Rouse, 1987; Kirby & Gardner, 1973; Mackie, 1974). The response format consisted of a 10-point scale representing 10% increments running from 0% to 100%. The stereotypic attributes included: calm, uneducated, clean, boastful, lazy, loud, passive, sophisticated, reliable, spiritual, considerate, and aggressive. In addition to providing percentage estimates for each trait, participants rated the favourableness of each trait. These evaluations employed a 10-point format running from −5, (*Very unfavourable*) to +5 (*Very favourable*). The percentage estimate of each trait was multiplied by its evaluation and the resulting products were averaged to create a stereotype/evaluation index reflecting the negativity of out-group stereotypes.

Distal Variables

Negative intergroup contact. To measure negative intergroup contact, a measure modeled on the one developed by Stephan et al. (2001) was employed. Participants were

asked to indicate the frequency with which they had experienced a wide range of negative events at the hands of members of the other group. Examples of the 14 negative experiences included: being insulted, being discriminated against, being harassed, being verbally abused, being threatened, and being physically harmed. The 10-point response options ran from *Never* to *Very frequently.*

Identification with the in-group. The four-item scale developed by Luhtanen and Crocker (1992) was used to assess in-group identification. An example of an item from this scale is, "My racial/ethnic group is an important part of my self-image." Participants rated each statement along a 10-point Likert scale format that ran from *Strongly agree* to *Strongly disagree*

Perceived intergroup conflict. This measure employed four items set up in a 10-point Likert scale ranging from *Strongly disagree* to *Strongly agree.* A sample item is, "Relations between Whites and Natives have always been characterized by conflict."

Perceived status differences. Perceptions of status differences between Whites and Natives were assessed with three items using a 10-point Likert scale that ranged from *Strongly disagree* to *Strongly agree.* A sample item is, "There is a great difference between the status of Natives and Whites in this society."

In addition to collecting proximal, distal, and attitude measures, participants also completed a number of biographical questions, and, in an attempt to assess whether knowledge about Native people would be related to predictor and criterion variables, participants indicated the number of Native Studies courses taken at university or elsewhere.[2] The presentation of the questions was randomly determined, and all participants answered the same questions in the same fixed order.

Results

Between-Group Differences

. . . On the proximal variables, Native Canadians reported more realistic and symbolic threats and more intergroup anxiety about interacting with majority group members, but less negative stereotyping of majority group members than EuroCanadians reported in stereotyping Native Canadians. While between-group differences were highly significant, effect sizes (*d*; Cohen, 1988) indicate that these differences were quite meaningful. On all measures, effect sizes ranged from very large to moderately large. Native Canadians report very serious concerns about issues raised in the realistic and symbolic threat scales, whereas Whites report relatively little concern about these issues. Analysis of variance on the distal variables indicated that Native Canadians were more extreme in their ratings of negative intergroup contacts, intergroup conflicts, and perceived status differences; they also reported that ethnic identity was more important to their self-concept than did EuroCanadians. Effect sizes corresponding to these differences indicate that some were noticeably greater (intergroup contact, ethnic identity) than others (intergroup conflict, perceived status differences). As predicted, ethnic identity was a more important concern for Native than White respondents. . . .

Relating Distal and Proximal Factors

. . . It was predicted here that for people in both groups, perceived intergroup conflict and negative intergroup contact should predict all four proximal variables, and these, in turn, should predict negative out-group attitudes. These predictions were partially supported. Among Native Canadians, negative intergroup contact predicted negative intergroup attitudes directly, but more importantly for our purposes, negative contact predicted realistic threats and intergroup anxiety, but only the latter predicted negative out-group attitudes. Contrary to expectations, negative out-group conflict predicted only symbolic threat, and it, in turn, predicted (marginally) negative attitudes toward Whites. Relations between out-group conflict and negative intergroup contact, proximal variables, and negative out-group attitudes received stronger support among EuroCanadians. Negative intergroup contact significantly predicted all four proximal variables, and out-group conflict was significantly associated with symbolic threats and negative out-group stereotypes; all four threats, in turn, predicted negative attitudes toward Native people.

It was hypothesized that among Native respondents, ethnic identity should be associated with symbolic and realistic threats, and these, in turn, should be associated with negative attitudes towards majority group members. This hypothesis was partially supported. Increases in ethnic identity were significantly associated with greater perceived symbolic threat, but contrary to expectations, also increased intergroup anxiety; each of these, in turn, was associated with negative attitudes toward Whites. The more Native people identified with their own group, the more threat they perceived to their values and beliefs, and more anxiety they reported in

their dealings with Whites. These threats and anxieties were associated with more negative attitudes toward majority group members.

Among EuroCanadians, ethnic identity was not a significant predictor directly or indirectly of attitudes towards Native Canadians, nor were perceived status differences a significant predictor directly or indirectly of out-group attitudes for either group. While there was variability in EuroCanadians responses to identity questions, this variability was not significantly related to other variables. EuroCanadians are, in a number of ways, very much the dominant group, which as McGuire, McGuire, Child, & Fujioka (1978) point out, reduces the salience of ethnicity when making inferences about and evaluations of own and other group members. The between-group status hierarchy has been stable for many years, and while there has been a steady increase in a Native middle class, it will be some time before the existing status relations are altered to the point where significant numbers of majority group members feel threatened by any perceived changes in the social status of Native people.

Discussion

The basic assumption of the integrated threat theory of prejudice is that perceived threats from out-group members mediate relations between distal "causal" variables and negative attitudes toward out-group members. Results from this study support that idea: Theoretically important, distal variables were associated with perceived threats from out-group members; these threats, in turn, were associated with negative attitudes toward other group members, and did so while accounting for a substantial proportion of variance in both groups' out-group attitudes. It was predicted here that among Native Canadians, increases in ethnic identity would be associated with perceived out-group threat. This hypothesis, too, was supported. It was also predicted that for respondents in both groups, negative intergroup contact and out-group conflict would be related to negative out-group attitudes. This hypothesis too was supported. Overall, results reported here support the conclusion that perceived threats and attitudes toward out-groups are clearly intertwined; it is also clear, however, that relations between specific threats and prejudice received stronger support among majority than minority group members. A number of ideas and issues surrounding the observed relations between perceived threat and attitudes toward other group members deserve comment. . . .

Relations Between Distal Factors, Perceived Threats, and Attitudes Toward Other Group Members

According to integrated threat theory, feelings of threat from a number of sources predict negative out-group attitudes and indirectly mediate relations between distal factors and prejudicial attitudes. For Whites and Native Canadians these general predictions were supported. Among Whites, all four proximal threats predicted negative attitudes toward Natives and mediated relations of two of four distal variables. For Native Canadians, two threats (and a third nearly so) predicted negative attitudes towards Whites, and mediated the effects of two distal variables. In addition, one distal variable, negative intergroup contact, was directly related to out-group attitudes among Native respondents. For people in dominant and subordinate groups, perceived threats about the out-group and attitudes toward them were significantly related. . . .

Generalization of Results of the Present Study to Other Groups

In this study we examined factors associated with out-group attitudes of White and Native Canadians. An important question concerns the degree to which results reported here can be generalized to other groups. In a recent study, Stephan, Boniecki et al. (2001) used the same set of antecedent and proximal variables to examine out-group attitudes of White and African Americans. Stephan, Boneicki et al. (2001) found that the same threats that predicted negative attitudes towards Natives also predicted negative attitudes toward African Americans; in addition, the percentage of variance accounted for in those threats was the same in American and Canadian majority group members. Moreover, in both samples of majority group members, negative intergroup contact was associated with all four threats, and out-group conflict was associated with symbolic threats. The major difference between the Canadian and American samples were relations between in-group identity, threats, and out-group attitudes. In the Canadian sample, there were no significant relations between these factors, but in the American sample, identity predicted several threats which, in turn, predicted negative attitudes toward Blacks. Among American Whites, racial self-identification was an important predictor of negative out-group attitudes. . . .

Implications of the Present Results for Improving Intergroup Relations

The findings reported here have implications not only for theories of threat in intergroup relations, but for the application of these theories to improving relationships between Whites and Natives in particular and ethnic groups generally. The close relationship found between feelings of threat and prejudice suggests that programs designed to improve intergroup relations would do well to focus on problems posed by perceived threat. Realistic threats may be exaggerated or overblown, in which case correct and balanced information can be used to reduce them. Intergroup relations programs oriented toward providing information about various groups in which majority and minority group members participate equally, may be suitable for allaying some of these fears. Symbolic threats acknowledge the existence of group differences in values, beliefs, norms, and behaviours, but ignore or downplay the existence of shared values, common destinies, goals or desired end-states. Emphasizing what is shared or common among people, and creating superordinate goals that unite diverse groups, can work to offset not only perceptions of group differences but their inevitability and unchangeable nature as well (Gaertner, Dovidio, Nier, Ward, & Banker, 1999). Cooperative learning groups, in which participants work toward a common purpose, may well reduce perceptions of group differences (Aronson & Patnoe, 1997; Slavin, 1992). Intergroup relations training could be an effective antidote to intergroup anxiety. Intercultural relations programs with their emphasis on learning how to interact with members of other cultural groups have a long history providing these kinds of skills (Black & Mendenhall, 1990; Bochner, 1986). Negative stereotypes are often intractable, but research beginning with Allport (1954) suggests that such stereotypes can be modified, provided that stereotype-change programs conform to a rather long list of conditions (see Rothbart & John, 1985; Weber & Crocker, 1983), and people's willingness to deploy strategies to counteract their own stereotypes when they are activated (Devine, 1989). Intergroup relations programs such as intergroup dialogues (Gurin, Peng, Lopez, Nagda, 1999; Nagda, Zuniga, & Sevig, 1995) that provide opportunities to interact with numerous out-group members under conditions like those specified in the contact hypothesis hold the promise of fulfilling these and other stringent conditions (Amir, 1976).

Conclusion

In closing, we would like to emphasize two important findings from the present study. First, at a broad, theoretical level it was demonstrated here that the same principles used to understand prejudice toward minority groups can be applied to understanding prejudice toward majority groups. In both groups, threats and their antecedents were associated with negative out-group attitudes. The point here, however, is a more general and more important one—different groups of people may dislike each other for similar reasons. As Allport (1954) argued nearly 50 years ago, the underlying nature of prejudice is fundamentally the same for all groups. Second, this is the first study that we are aware of that directly examines White and Native peoples' attitudes toward the other group. What may be difficult for majority group members to understand or Native people to appreciate, is that—as witnessed by several Supreme Court decisions—perceived relationships between Whites and Natives are changing. There will be changes in how Whites and Natives think about each other, and how resources (broadly defined) will be allocated now and in the future. For Native people, attitudes toward Whites were associated with negative contacts with them, and by a strong sense of group identity. Among Whites, negative intergroup contacts were associated with threats concerning Natives and negative attitudes towards them. It is important for both groups to realize that fears and apprehensions stem, in part, from perceiving intergroup relations as a zero-sum game. While a useful metaphor in some contexts, thinking about relationships this way strains intergroup relationships and makes discussions and negotiations about a renewed social contract more difficult.

Notes

1. In this paper we use the terms *EuroCanadian* and *White* interchangeably to denote majority group members in society. We recognize and appreciate that not all Whites are EuroCanadians nor are all EuroCanadians necessarily White. Taken together, however, Whites/EuroCanadians are in the numerical majority. While there is some discussion as to what to call First Nation people, we shall use the terms *Native people, Native Canadians,* or *Natives* interchangeably in this paper to denote people of aboriginal ancestry.
2. Analysis of the number of Native Studies courses taken indicated that 83% of Native participants took such courses compared to 33% of White respondents. Specifically, 15% of Whites had taken one course, whereas 57% of Natives had done so, and 18% of White participants had taken three courses compared to 26% of Native participants.

References

Adorno, T.W., Frenkel-Burnswik, E., Levinson, D.J., & Sanford, R.N.(1950). *The authoritarian personality.* New York: Harper & Brothers.

Agnew, C.R., Thompson, V.D., & Gaines, S.O. (2000). Incorporating proximal and distal influences on prejudice: Testing a general model across out-groups. *Personality and Social Psychology Bulletin, 26,* 403–418.

Allen, B.P. (1996). African Americans' and European Americans' mutual attributions: Adjective generation technique stereotyping. *Journal of Applied Social Psychology, 26,* 884–912.

Allport, G.W. (1954). *The nature of prejudice.* Reading, MA: Addison-Wesley.

Amir, Y. (1976). The role of intergroup contact in change of prejudice and ethnic relations. In P.A. Katz (Ed.), *Toward the elimination of racism* (pp. 245–308). New York: Pergamon.

Aronson, E., & Patnoe, S. (1997). *The jigsaw classroom.* New York: Longman.

Ashmore, R.D., & Del Boca, F.K. (1981). Conceptual approaches to stereotypes and stereotyping. In D.L. Hamilton (Ed.), *Cognitive processes in stereotyping and intergroup behavior* (pp. 1–35). Hillsdale, NJ: Erlbaum.

Bigler, R.S., Jones, L.C., & Lobliner, D.B. (1997). Social categorization and the formation of intergroup attitudes in children. *Child Development, 68,* 530–543.

Black, J.S., & Mendenhall, M. (1990). Cross-cultural training effectiveness: A review and theoretical framework for future research. *Academy of Management Review, 15,* 113–136.

Bobo, L. (1988). Group conflict, prejudice, and the paradox of contemporary racial attitudes. In P. A. Katz & D.A. Taylor (Eds.), *Eliminating racism: Profiles in controversy* (pp. 85–116). New York: Plenum.

Bochner, S. (1986). Training intercultural skills. In C.R. Hollins & P. Trower (Eds.), *Handbook of social skills training: Applications across the life span* (Vol. 1). Oxford: Pergamon.

Bodenhausen, G.V. (1988). Stereotypic biases in social decision making and memory: Testing process models for stereotype use. *Journal of Personality and Social Psychology, 55,* 726–737.

Boniecki, K.A., & Brown, L.M. (1998, May). *The influence of prejudice on stereotype formation: The justification hypothesis revisited.* Paper presented at the American Psychological Association meeting, Washington, DC.

Brewer, M.B. (1991). The social self: On being the same and different at the same time. *Personality and Social Psychology Bulletin, 17,* 475–482.

Brigham, J.C. (1971). Ethnic stereotypes. *Psychological Bulletin, 76,* 15–38.

Britt, T.W., Boniecki, K.A., Vescio, T.K., Biernat, M.R., & Brown, L.M. (1996). Intergroup anxiety: A person X situation approach. *Personality and Social Psychology Bulletin, 22,* 1177–1188.

Cohen, J. (1988). *Statistical power analysis of the behavioral sciences* (2nd ed.). Hillsdale, NJ: Erlbaum.

Corenblum, B., Arulis, R., & Young, S. (1996). Effects of own group success and failure of judgements of task performance by children of different ethnicities. *European Journal of Social Psychology, 26,* 777–798.

Coser, L. (1956). *The functions of social conflict.* New York: Free Press.

Devine, P.G. (1989). Stereotypes and prejudice: Their automatic and controlled components. *Journal of Personality and Social Psychology, 56,* 5–18.

Dijker, A.J. (1987). Emotional reactions to ethnic minorities. *European Journal of Social Psychology, 17,* 305–325.

Dollard, J., Doob, L., Miller, N.E., Mowrer, O., & Sears, R. (1939). *Frustration and aggression.* New Haven, CT: Yale University Press.

Dovidio, J.F., & Gaertner, S.L. (1986). *Prejudice, discrimination, and racism.* Orlando FL: Academic Press.

Dovidio, J.F., & Gaertner, S.L. (1998). On the nature of contemporary prejudice. In J.L. Eberhardt & S.T. Fiske (Eds.), *Confronting racism: The problem and the response* (pp. 3–32). Thousand Oaks, CA: Sage.

Duckitt, J. (1992). Psychology and prejudice: A historical analysis and integrative framework. *American Psychologist, 47,* 1182–1193.

Duncan, S. (1976). Differential social perception and attribution of intergroup violence: Testing the lower limits of stereotyping of blacks. *Journal of Personality and Social Psychology, 34,* 590–598.

Duran, A., Renfro, L., Stephan, W.G., & Clason, N. (2001). *The role of threats in attitudes toward affirmative action and its beneficiaries.* Unpublished manuscript. New Mexico State University Las Cruces, NM.

Eagly, A.H., & Mladinic, A. (1989). Gender stereotypes and attitudes toward women and men. *Personality and Social Psychology Bulletin, 15,* 543–558.

Esses, V.M., Haddock, G., & Zanna, M.P. (1993). Values, stereotypes, and emotions as determinants of intergroup attitudes. In D.M. Mackie & D.L. Hamilton (Eds.), *Affect, cognition and stereotyping: Inter-active processes in-group perception* (pp. 137–166). Orlando, FL: Academic Press.

Esses, V.M., Jackson, L.M., & Armstrong, T.L. (1998). Intergroup competition and attitudes toward immigrants and immigration: An experimental model of intergroup conflict. *Journal of Social Issues, 54,* 699–724.

Fiske, S.T. (1993). Controlling other people: The impact of power on stereotypes. *American Psychologist, 6,* 621–628.

Fiske, S.T., & Taylor, S. E. (1991). *Social cognition* (2nd ed.) New York: McGraw-Hill.

Gaertner, S.L., Dovidio, J.F., Nier, J.A., Ward, C.M., & Banker, B.S. (1999). Across cultural divides: The value of superordinate identity. In D.A. Prentice & D.T. Miller (Eds.), *Cultural divides: Understanding and overcoming group conflict* (pp. 173–212). New York: Russell Sage Foundation.

Gardner, R.C. (1994). Stereotypes as consensual beliefs. In M.P. Zanna & J. M. Olson (Ed.), *The psychology of prejudice: The Ontario symposium* (Vol. 7, pp. 1–32). Hillsdale, NJ: Erlbaum.

Gibbons, R., & Ponting, J.R. (1977). Contemporary perceptions of Canada's Native peoples. *Prairie Forum, 2,* 57–81.

Glick, P., & Fiske, S.T. (1996). The ambivalent sexism inventory: Differentiating hostile and benevolent sexism. *Journal of Personality and Social Psychology, 70,* 491–512.

Gudykunst, W.B. (1995). Anxiety/uncertainty management (AUM) theory: Development and current status. In R.L. Wiseman (Ed.), *Intercultural communication theory.* Thousand Oaks, CA: Sage.

Gurin, P., Peng, T., Lopez, G., & Nagda, B. (1999). Context, identity, and intergroup relations. In D.A. Prentice & D.T. Miller (Eds.), *Cultural divides: Understanding and overcoming group conflict* (pp. 133–172). New York: Russell Sage Foundation.

Hamilton, D.L., & Trolier, T.K. (1986). Stereotypes and stereotyping: An overview of the cognitive approach. In J.F. Davidio & S.L Gaertner (Eds.), *Prejudice, discrimination and racism* (pp. 127–158). Orlando, FL: Acadmic Press.

Hamilton, D.L. (1981). *Cognitive processes in stereotyping and intergroup behavior.* Hillsdale, NJ: Erlbaum.

Hanson, J.R., & Rouse, L.P. (1987). Dimensions of Native American stereotyping. *American Indian Culture and Research Journal, 11,* 33–58.

Harding, J., Proshansky, H., Kutner, B., & Chein, I. (1969). Prejudice and ethnic relations. In G. Lindzey & E. Aronson (Eds.), *Handbook of social psychology: Vol. 5.* (2nd ed., pp. 1021–1061). Reading, MA: Addison-Wesley.

Hewstone, M. (1990). The ultimate attribution error'? A review of the literature on integroup causal attribution. *European Journal of Social Psychology, 20,* 311–335.

Hewstone, M., & Jaspars, J.M. (1982). Intergroup relations and attribution process. In H. Tajfel (Ed.), *The social dimension: European developments in social psychology* (pp. 379–404). Cambridge, UK: University of Cambridge Press.

Islam, R.M., & Hewstone, M. (1993). Dimensions of contact as predictors of intergroup anxiety, perceived outgroup variability, and out-group attitude: An integrative model. *Personality and Social Psychology Bulletin, 19,* 700–710.

Katz, I., Wackenhut, J., & Glass, D.C. (1988). An ambivalence-amplification theory of behavior toward the stigmatized. In S. Worchel & W.G. Austin (Eds.), *Psychology of intergroup relations* (2nd ed.). Chicago IL: Nelson-Hall.

Kinder, D.R., & Sears, D.O. (1981). Prejudice and politics: Symbolic racism versus racial threats to the good life. *Journal of Personality and Social Psychology, 40,* 414–431.

Kirby, D.M., & Gardner, R.C. (1973). Ethnic stereotypes: Determinants in children and their parents. *Canadian Journal of Psychology, 27,* 127–143.

Kunda, Z. (1990). The case for motivated reasoning. *Psychological Bulletin, 108,* 480–498.

LeVine, R.A., & Campbell, D.T. (1972). *Ethnocentrism: Theories of conflict, ethnic attitudes, and group behavior.* New York: Wiley.

Luhtanen, R., & Crocker, J. (1992). A collective self-esteem scale: Self-evaluation of one's own identity. *Personality and Social Psychology Bulletin, 18,* 302–318.

Mackie, M. (1974). Ethnic stereotypes and prejudice— Alberta Indians, Hutterites, and Ukrainians. *Canadian Ethnic Studies, 6,* 40–51.

McConahay, J.G. (1986). Modern racism, ambivalence, and the modern racism scale. In J.F. Dovidio & S.L. Gaertner (Eds.), *Prejudice, discrimination, and racism* (pp. 91–125). Orlando, FL: Academic Press.

McGuire, W.J., McGuire, C.V., Child, P., & Fujioka, T. (1978). Salience of ethnicity in the spontaneous self-concept as a function of one's ethnic distinctiveness in the social environment. *Journal of Personality and Social Psychology, 36,* 511–520.

Mullen, B., Brown, R., & Smith, C. (1992). Ingroup bias as a function of salience, relevance, and status: An integration. *European Journal of Social Psychology, 22,* 103–122.

Nagda, B., Zuniga, X., & Sevig, T. (1995). Bridging differences through peer facilitated intergroup dialogues. In S. Hatcher (Ed.), *Peer programs on a college campus: Theory, training, and the voices of peers* (pp. 378–414). San Diego, CA: New Resources.

Neuberg, S. (1994). S.L. Expectancy-confirmation processes in stereotype-tinged social encounters: The moderating goal of social goals. In M.P. Zanna & J.M. Olson (Eds.), *The psychology of prejudice: The Ontario symposium* (Vol. 7, pp. 103–130). Hillsdale, NJ: Erlbaum.

Ostrom, T.M., Pryor, J.B., & Simpson, D.D. (1981). The organization of social information. In E.T. Higgins, C.P. Herman, & M.P. Zanna (Eds.), *Social cognition: The Ontario symposium* (Vol. 1, pp. 3–38), Hillsdale, NJ: Erlbaum

Powlishta, K. (1995). Intergroup processes in childhood: Social categorization and sex role development. *Developmental Psychology, 31,* 781–788.

Rokeach, M., Smith, P.W., & Evans, R.I. (1960). Two kinds of prejudice or one. In M. Rokeach (Ed.), *The open and closed mind* (pp. 132–170). New York: Basic Books.

Rothbart, M., & John, O.P. (1985). Social categorization and behavioral episodes: A cognitive analysis and the effects of intergroup contact. *Journal of Social Issues, 41,* 81–104.

Runciman, W.G. (1966). *Relative deprivation and social justice.* London: Routledge & Kegan Paul.

Sears, D.O. (1988). Symbolic racism. In P.A. Katz & D.A. Taylor (Eds.), *Eliminating racism* (pp. 53–84). New York: Plenum.

Sherif, M. (1966). *Group conflict and cooperation.* London: Routledge & Kegan Paul.

Sidanius, J., Devereux, E., & Pratto, F. (1992). A comparison of symbolic racism theory and social dominance theory as explanations for racial policy attitudes. *Journal of Social Psychology, 132,* 377–395.

Sidanius, J., & Pratto, F. (1999). *Social dominance: An intergroup theory of social hierarchy and oppression.* Cambridge: Cambridge University Press.

Slavin, R.E. (1992). Cooperative learning: Applying contact theory in the schools. In J. Lynch, C. Modgil, & S. Modgil (Eds.), *Cultural diversity in the schools* (Vol. II, pp. 333–348). London: Falmer Press.

Stangor, C., Sechrist, G., & Jost, J. (2001). Changing racial beliefs by providing concensus information. *Personality and Social Psychology Bulletin, 27, 4,* 486–496.

Stangor, C., Sullivan, L.A., & Ford, T.E. (1991). Affective and cognitive determinants of prejudice. *Social Cognition, 9,* 359–380.

Stephan, W.G., Ageyev, V.S., Coates-Shrider, L., Stephan, C.W., Abalakina, M. (1994). On the relationship between stereotypes and prejudice: An international study. *Personality and Social Psychology Bulletin, 20,* 277–284.

Stephan, W.G., Boneicki, K.A., Ybarra, O., Bettencourt, A., Ervin, K.S., Jackson, L.A., McNatt, P.S., & Renfro, C.L. (2001). *Racial attitudes of Blacks and Whites: An integrated threat theory analysis.* Unpublished manuscript. New Mexico State University, Las Cruces, NM.

Stephan, W.G., Diaz-Loving, R., & Duran, A. (2000). Integrated threat theory and intercultural attitudes: Mexico and the United States. *Journal of Cross-Cultural Psychology, 31,* 240–249.

Stephan, W.G., Renfro, C.L., Esses, V.M., Stephan, C.W., Martin, T. (2001). *The effect of threat on attitudes toward immigrants.* Unpublished manuscript. New Mexico State University Las Cruces, NM.

Stephan, W.G., & Stephan, C.W. (1985). Intergroup anxiety. *Journal of Social Issues, 41,* 157–175.

Stephan, W.G., & Stephan, C.W. (1989) Antecedents of intergroup anxiety in Asian-American and Hispanic-Americans. *International Journal of Intercultural Communications, 13,* 203–219.

Stephan, W.G., & Stephan, C.W. (1993). Cognition and affect in stereotyping: Parallel interactive networks. In D.M. Mackie & D.L. Hamilton (Eds.), *Affect, cognition, and stereotyping: Interactive processes in-group perception,* (pp. 111–136). Orlando FL: Academic Press.

Stephan, W.G., & Stephan, C.W. (2000). An integrated threat theory of prejudice. In S. Oskamp (Ed.), *Reducing prejuice and discrimination* (pp. 23–46). Hillsdale, NJ: Erlbaum.

Stephan, W.G., Ybarra, O., & Bachman, G. (1999). Prejudice toward immigrants: An integrated threat theory. *Journal of Applied Social Psychology, 29,* 2221–2237.

Stephan, W.G., Ybarra, O., Martinez, C., Schwarld, J., & Tur-kapsa, M. (1998). Prejudice toward immigrants in Spain and Israel: An integrated threat theory analysis. *Journal of Cross-Cultural Psychology, 29,* 559–576.

Swim, J.K., Aiken, K.J., Hall, W.S., & Hunter, B.A. (1995). Sexism and racism: Old-fashioned and modern prejudices. *Journal of Personality and Social Psychology, 68,* 199–214.

Tajfel, H., & Turner, J.C. (1979). An integrative theory of intergroup conflict. In S. Worchel & W. G. Austin (Eds.), *Psychology of intergroup relations.* Monterey, CA: Brooks-Cole.

Taylor, D.M., & Jaggi, V. (1974). Ethnocentrism and causal attribution within a south Asian context. *Journal of Social Psychology, 5,* 162–174.

Tougas, F., Brown, R., Beaton, A.M., & Joly, S. (1995). Neosexism: Plus ca change, plus c'est pareil. *Personality and Social Psychology Bulletin, 21,* 842–849.

Vorauer, J.D., Main, K.J., & O'Connell, G.B. (1998). How do individuals expect to be viewed by members of lower status groups? Content and implications of meta-stereotypes. *Journal of Personality and Social Psychology, 75,* 917–937.

Weber, R., & Crocker, J. (1983). Cognitive processing in the revision of stereotypic beliefs. *Journal of Personality and Social Psychology, 45,* 961–977.

Word, C.O., Zanna, M.P., & Cooper, J. (1974). The nonverbal mediation of self-fulfilling prophecies in interracial interactions. *Journal of Experimental Social Psychology, 10,* 109–120.

Yee, M.D., & Brown, R. (1992). Self-evaluations and intergroup attitudes in children aged three to nine. *Child Development, 63,* 619–629.

B. CORENBLUM is a psychology professor at Brandon University in Brandon, Manitoba, Canada.

WALTER G. STEPHAN is a social psychology professor at New Mexico State University. His research focuses on emotional expression, prejudice and stereotyping, intercultural relations, and attribution processes.

EXPLORING THE ISSUE

Is There a "Prejudiced Personality" Type?

Critical Thinking and Reflection

1. Do you know of anyone you believe has a "prejudiced personality," such that this person seems to be prejudiced against a wide variety of groups? What do you think causes high levels of prejudice in this type of person?
2. Do you believe that personality can explain people's prejudice fully, or are additional variables needed, such as historic conflict between one group versus another? Are the variables identified in the "no" article convincing additions to explain prejudice?
3. Is it possible for someone with a high level of prejudice—from any cause—to change his or her mind? If so, what does it take to accomplish this task? Is it possible for an entire group of people to change their mind about another group?
4. If it's true that people could simply have a "prejudiced personality," does this mean it's inevitable that they will show hatred toward people unlike themselves? Is prejudice between people simply an inevitable part of being human—a basic instinct that's impossible to avoid?

Is There Common Ground?

The authors on both sides of this debate would probably agree on a few basic ideas. First, they might agree that stereotypes and prejudice are negative social phenomena that hurt both groups involved. Second, they might agree that fighting prejudice is worthwhile. It's clear that they already agree that understanding the nature and origins of prejudice is an interesting psychological topic and worthy of discussion.

Psychologists who devote their research careers to studying "prejudiced personality traits" such as Social Dominance Orientation and Right-Wing Authoritarianism likely believe in the power of these constructs to predict prejudice across a wide variety of other groups, but they might also agree that personality is not the entire answer to the question, "What makes someone prejudiced?"

On the other hand, psychologists who try to be comprehensive and list a variety of sources of prejudice would very likely at least include prejudiced personality as an important predictor of prejudice, and agree that this variable cannot be ignored. Most social psychologists seem to

agree that prejudice is very complicated, and that battling it is just as challenging. However, most social psychologists agree that the battle may be well worth it.

Additional Resources

Altemeyer, B., & Hunsberger, B. (1992). Authoritarianism, religious fundamentalism, quest, and prejudice. *International Journal for the Psychology of Religion, 2,* 113–133.

Luchins, A. S. (1950). Personality and prejudice: A critique. *Journal of Social Psychology, 32,* 79–94.

MacFarland, S. (2010). Authoritarianism, social dominance, and other roots of generalized prejudice. *Political Psychology, 31,* 453–477.

Rutland, A., Killen, M., & Abrams, D. (2010). A new social-cognitive developmental perspective on prejudice: The interplay between morality and group identity. *Perspectives on Psychological Science, 5,* 279–291. doi: 10.1177/1745691610369468

Internet References . . .

Minority Studies

http://dmc122011.delmar.edu/socsci/rlong/race/
far-02.htm

Prejudice and Discrimination

http://psychology.jrank.org/pages/502/Prejudice-
Discrimination.html

Understanding Prejudice

http://www.understandingprejudice.org/

Selected, Edited, and with Issue Framing Material by:
Wind Goodfriend, *Buena Vista University*

ISSUE

Is Terror Management Real?

YES: Jeff Greenberg, from "Terror Management Theory: From Genesis to Revelations," *American Psychological Association* (2012)

NO: Daniel M. T. Fessler and C. David Navarrete, from "The Effect of Age on Death Disgust: Challenges to Terror Management Perspectives," *Evolutionary Psychology* (2005)

Learning Outcomes

After reading this issue, you will be able to:

- Define the following terms: (1) worldview, (2) mortality salience, and (3) death disgust sensitivity.
- List and explain some of the basic tenets or beliefs within Terror Management Theory.
- Generate at least one new hypothesis that would support Terror Management Theory, if the data could be found.

ISSUE SUMMARY

YES: Jeff Greenberg, one of the original creators of Terror Management Theory (TMT), reviews its main hypotheses and several findings from a variety of studies that support the main principles of the theory, including that thoughts of our own deaths lead to a variety of psychological reactions.

NO: Daniel Fessler and C. Navarrete, both professors of anthropology, present research and arguments against Terror Management Theory. Instead, they find that as age increases, sensitivity to death decreases, and that TMT predictions may be bound to certain cultures.

There's an old saying that only two things are guaranteed: death and taxes. The former is the central concept in one of the most controversial recent ideas within social psychology: Terror Management Theory. With both zealous fans and zealous detractors, Terror Management Theory has divided the field more than almost any other issue in the last 20 years.

First proposed in 1984 by Tom Pyszczynski, Sheldon Solomon, and Jeff Greenberg, Terror Management Theory has several basic tenets or premises:

1. All living things want to continue living, and humans are uniquely capable of realizing that we are, unfortunately, mortal beings.
2. The realization that we are going to die is terrifying.
3. We attempt to distract ourselves—or "manage" this fear—by instead thinking about culture, religion, or leaving a legacy; these things bring us comfort and validate our existence.
4. When we are reminded of death, this is called "mortality salience."
5. Under mortality salience (reminders of death), we cling to comforting and validating concepts more strongly; this is called validation of "worldviews."

The original creators, as well as fans of Terror Management Theory, have presented scores of studies that they claim support these principles. In their book *In the Wake of 9/11: The Psychology of Terror*, Pyszczynski, Solomon, and Greenberg attempt to explain the rapid changes seen in the United States due to increased fears of terrorism. For example, they note that the number of couples who got engaged to be married shot up after the terrorist attacks on the Twin Towers and American Pentagon building. Perhaps, they posit, clinging to a close relationship or getting married brought people comfort, and the idea of having children might have helped people feel that they were leaving a lasting legacy. Other people have presented ideas that managing terror is related to patterns of stereotypes and prejudice, juror decisions during criminal trials, or political judgments such as how people decide to vote in important elections.

Thus, in the relatively recent article for the "yes" side of this debate, Jeff Greenberg presents three specific hypotheses regarding how mortality salience might be related to self-esteem striving, anxiety and defensiveness, and threats to terror management resources. He also reviews recent research findings from a variety of studies about how terror management is related to brain and neurological processes, religion, fame seeking, fantasy, aging, and more.

However, there are many social psychologists who doubt the basic ideas within Terror Management Theory, or at least doubt the theory's utility. In the "no" article for this controversy, Daniel Fessler and C. David Navarrete focus their critique on the connection between mortality and aging. It is in alignment with Terror Management Theory that as people age, mortality should become increasingly salient and terrifying. If this is true, then older individuals should increasingly cling to their worldviews, in attempts to bring themselves the resultant validation and comfort. In addition, seeing how we (humans) are different from other animals should make us feel special and should assuage fears about our mortality.

Going against these hypotheses that they argue should happen if Terror Management Theory is correct, they present data that age is negatively—not positively—correlated with "death disgust sensitivity," and they find this pattern in two different cultures (North America and Costa Rica). In other words, they found that as their participants got older, those individuals actually seemed to be increasingly comfortable with their own animal natures and their mortality. In addition, when they gave their participants the typical "mortality salience prime" experimental manipulation in which people write essays describing their own deaths before completing the rest of the study materials, this increased focus on death seemed to have no effects. This is compared to a control group, who wrote the same essays, but not until after they had completed the rest of the study materials. Thus, they conclude that their data refute two central ideas within Terror Management Theory.

Perhaps it is because this theory is so new that many social psychologists are still undecided about whether it will be enduring; some scientists may be holding their opinions until more data have been gathered. However, other, even newer theories have been presented without the visceral reaction that Terror Management Theory seems to cause when people hear about it at conferences or read about it in books and articles. Perhaps it is jarring simply because reading about mortality salience has the ironic effect of, indeed, making mortality salient. If we acknowledge that we are afraid of death, do the distractions suggested by the theory become automatically ineffective?

YES ↵

Jeff Greenberg

Terror Management Theory: From Genesis to Revelations

Humans live by existential illusions. These fictions about existence help us cope with the big five existential concerns: death, identity, meaning, social isolation, and freedom (Pyszczynski, Greenberg, Koole, & Solomon, 2010). They allow us to feel as though we are significant and enduring beings in a meaningful world, even though science tells us we are just material organisms with a brief life span in an indifferent universe and members of a species that will likely eventually become extinct. Death is inevitable. Our identities and meanings are cultural constructions that don't amount to a hill of beans in the context of billions of years of time and the vast enormity of space. Our most cherished relationships are inherently limited; we can never know the inner life of another person or reliably expect someone else to put our interests above their own. We strive for freedom while we are all imprisoned by our cultural upbringing and largely dependent on following others' rules for survival. If we have too much freedom, it causes us anxiety and stress, and we often don't know what to do with it.

. . . In the present chapter, I focus on my least favorite existential problem, which also happens to be the one that generated the first large-scale program of XXP research: Death. Terror management theory (TMT) has directly focused on how people cope with this problem and has generated a wide range of novel hypotheses that have been supported by over 400 studies conducted in over 15 countries. . . . Here, I concisely summarize the basic findings and some recent developments, and consider the broad contributions of TMT so far.

Origin and Roots of Terror Management Theory

As social psychology graduate students at the University of Kansas from 1978–1981, Sheldon Solomon, Tom Pyszczynski, and I found ourselves amused but dissatisfied with the prevailing view of humans as dispassionate, albeit imperfect, information processors. It simply did not ring true with respect to our families and peer groups or from our knowledge of history or the understanding of humans gleaned from our favorite novelists, poets, philosophers, and filmmakers.

We began discussing two well-established propensities that seemed to us central aspects of human social behavior: the inability of people from different cultures to peacefully coexist and the proneness for people to go to great lengths to protect their self-esteem. It occurred to us that we needed to understand why people were so defensive of their cultural beliefs, ingroups, and positive self-image. But surveying the existing literature in social psychology, we saw no clues as to what people are trying to accomplish in their daily lives or how the basic motivations underlying their actions lead to the intergroup biases and egotism so well-documented in social psychology experiments. Thus, we became determined to seek answers outside our own discipline.

After a few years of searching, we stumbled on an interdisciplinary Pulitzer Prize–winning book by cultural anthropologist Ernest Becker. That book, *The Denial of Death* (Becker, 1973), in conjunction with Becker's earlier *The Birth and Death of Meaning* (Becker, 1962/1971) and later *Escape from Evil* (Becker, 1975), provided the answers we were looking for and became the primary basis of TMT. These books also revealed the rich tradition of existential psychoanalytic thought that Becker built on, a tradition that can be traced to figures such as Sigmund Freud, Otto Rank, Gregory Zilboorg, Harry Stack Sullivan, and Robert Jay Lifton. Our elaboration of TMT owes much to these figures, along with Becker, our training in social psychology, and to sociologists George Herbert Mead and Erving Goffman.

Terror Management Theory: The Basic Theory and Hypotheses and Key Elaborations

All humans are biologically predisposed to want to continue living, and at the same time we are smart enough to realize that we are going to die and that it could happen at virtually any time for a wide variety of reasons. Given this existential predicament, how do we humans function without being perpetually anxious? According to TMT, we do so by viewing ourselves as enduring beings living in a permanent, meaningful world full of symbols instead of as mere material animals in an indifferent universe fated only to cease existing on death.

From birth on, we are socialized into a worldview that tells us we are significant beings in a meaningful world. We have souls and possible afterlives, and we are part of lasting entities such as nations and family lines. We have identities that will live on past our physical deaths in the seemingly permanent marks we have made on the world: children, memorials, artistic creations, accomplishments in business and science, and so forth. Thus, we function with our deepest anxiety under wraps as long as we believe we are enduring, significant contributors to a meaningful, permanent world. When we are not simply seeking survival or pleasurable experiences, we spend much of our time buttressing our claims of legacy within the symbolic reality we psychologically inhabit. When this view of ourselves and the world is threatened, we experience anxiety and defend against such threats by reasserting our own value and that of our groups, and strengthening our faith in the meaningful world in which we believe.

Many TMT studies converge on three primary points that support the theory. The first is known as the *mortality salience* (MS) hypothesis. If worldviews and self-worth protect people from anxiety regarding mortality, then reminders of your mortal nature should instigate efforts to bolster the value of yourself and your groups (self-esteem striving), and faith in an orderly, stable view of the world and one's self (for reviews, see Greenberg Landau, & Arndt, in press, and Greenberg Solomon, and Arndt, 2008). For example, regarding self-esteem striving, MS leads people who base their self-worth on driving ability to drive more boldly. One common consequence of the need to bolster faith in one's worldview is to derogate and lash out at people and ideas that call the validity of your beliefs into question (worldview defense). Thus, people who identify with a certain nation become more negative in their reactions to someone who criticizes that nation.

A fundamental terror management function of worldviews is to provide an orderly, structured, and sensible view of reality and oneself that allows for the possibility of being a significant contributor to a meaningful existence. Thus, MS should motivate people to want their cognitions to fit together, for people and events to be consistent, for the world to be just, for art to be meaningful,

and for the self to seem to be an enduring entity, linked from past to present to future. A wide range of fairly recent studies have supported these notions, especially for people relatively high in need for structure in their lives (see Greenberg et al., in press).

The methods used to induce MS, or what is more precisely heightened death-thought accessibility, warrant brief consideration. The first and most commonly used MS induction involves asking participants to respond to two prompts. First, they are asked to describe the emotions that thinking about their own death arouses in them. Second, they are asked what they think will happen to them as they are dying and once they are dead. Interestingly, so far, content analyses have not found any evidence that what the individual specifically writes in response to these death-focused prompts affects his or her reactions to the induction. The control condition for this induction has consisted of either writing about a neutral topic or, more commonly, an unpleasant, potentially anxiety-provoking topic not directly connected to death. Controls have included thinking of dental pain, intense pain, unpredictable bouts of severe pain, an upcoming exam, failure, public speaking, general anxieties, worries after college, feelings of uncertainty, temporal discontinuity, meaninglessness, unexpected events, expectancy violations, social exclusion, and being paralyzed. In the majority of studies, MS has shown different effects than the salience of these other potentially aversive topics.

In addition, many other methods of increasing the accessibility of death-related thoughts have been employed (e.g., accident footage; proximity to a funeral home; word puzzles with death words imbedded; writing one sentence about death, health or risk warnings; images or reminders of terrorism or destruction), and these other methods have yielded converging support for TMT hypotheses. For example, studies have found that subliminal priming with the word *dead* intensified American subjects' negative reactions to an anti-American author relative to subliminally priming with the word *pain* or *fail* (Pyszczynski, Greenberg, & Solomon, 1999).

The second hypothesis supported by substantial evidence is that stably high or temporarily raised self-esteem and bolstered faith in one's worldview allow people to function with minimal anxiety and defensiveness. The first set of studies demonstrated this by showing that if self-esteem was boosted by false feedback, people were able to endure normally anxiety-provoking images of death and threats of electric shock with no self-reported or physiological signs of increased anxiety (see Greenberg et al., in press). Additional evidence has shown that affirming important values eliminates worldview defense after MS and that, following MS, the opportunity to display pro-American bias reduced the accessibility of death-related thoughts back to baseline levels. . . .

The third central hypothesis is that threats to terror management resources will increase the accessibility of death-related thought. Studies have shown that threats to one's self-worth, threats to the belief that we humans are more than just animals, threats to cherished beliefs (e.g., the righteousness of one's nation), and threats to cherished close relationships all bring thoughts of death closer to mind. In one interesting example, Landau et al. (2004) found that learning that the victim of a brutal knife attack was a really good person led to higher death-thought accessibility if the victim was portrayed in a positive rather than a negative way. Landau et al. argued that this was because something bad happening to a good person threatens belief in a just world. There are now over 90 TMT studies that have measured the accessibility of death-related thought, a literature recently reviewed by Hayes, Schimel, Arndt, and Faucher (2010). . . .

Some Recent Directions in Terror Management Theory Research

. . .

Brain Processes Associated with Terror Management

A social neuroscience approach to terror management is still in its early stages. Ideally, I would suggest that terror management involves high-level thoughts produced by the prefrontal cortex that generate a path toward amygdala activation, which sparks other high-level thoughts buttressing faith in one's worldview and a sense of personal significance, which then deactivates the potentiation of processes in the amygdala that generate fear, dread, or terror. Some initial evidence consistent with this sequence of processes was provided by the only functional magnetic resonance imaging TMT study to date. Quirin et al. (in press) showed that answering questions about death was associated with increased activation of the right amygdala, left rostral anterior cingulate cortex, and right caudate nucleus. The first two structures seem to play a role in anxiety responses, whereas the caudate nucleus has been suggested to be an indicator of stereotypic thinking as well as love-oriented emotions. . . .

A recent study of Americans by Kosloff, Greenberg, Allen, and Martens (2011) using EEG showed that MS shifted people toward greater activation of the right

prefrontal cortex. In addition, this study showed that for people prone to eyeblink startle responses, extent of right hemispheric shift was associated with larger eyeblink responses to anti-American images but not other negative images. This study suggests that MS activates the hemisphere of the brain associated with anxiety and withdrawal motivation, a finding opposite research suggesting a left-hemisphere shift in response to concerns with uncertainty (McGregor, Nash, Mann, & Phills, 2010). This may make sense in that uncertainty may motivate approach-oriented proactive responses, whereas MS activates defensive ones. . . .

Managing Terror Through Assimilation to One's Worldview

TMT theorists proposed that people historically have used four strategies to defuse the threat posed by those who espouse alternative worldviews: derogation, assimilation, accommodation, and annihilation. Many studies have supported the first and last of these defenses by showing that MS increases negativity toward people who implicitly or explicitly challenge the validity of one's own culture's worldview (see Solomon et al., in press).

Research has also shown that MS can contribute to aggression and even a desire to annihilate such different others. McGregor et al. (1998) showed that MS increased allocation of painfully hot salsa to critics of the participants' political views. Pyszczynski, Abdollahi, et al. (2006) showed that MS intensified support among Iranians for lethal violence directed at Americans, and similarly intensified support among conservative Americans for lethal violence directed against potentially threatening groups. Hayes, Schimel, and Williams (2008) showed that, after MS, reading about Muslims being killed reduced death-thought accessibility in Canadians.

The two other proposed defenses against worldview threat have not garnered much attention. Accommodation involves incorporating aspects of alternative worldviews into one's own in a manner that does not threaten core values of one's worldview. Research has yet to examine this defense. However, Kosloff, Cesario, and Martens (2011) studied MS-induced assimilation. Assimilation involves attempting to convert people with alternative worldviews to abandon their views and adopt one's own. Missionary activity and efforts to spread ideologies such as secular democratic capitalism and communism are real-life examples.

In their first study, Kosloff, Cesario, and Martens (2011) had Christians and non-Christians think about mortality or a control topic and then had them read about either a successful or an unsuccessful conversion of a Hindu person to Christianity. MS generally increased death-thought accessibility in the non-Christians. It also increased death-thought accessibility in Christians who read about the failed conversion. However, the death-thought accessibility of Christians who read about the successful conversion was as low as that of participants in the non-MS control condition.

In a second study, after an MS manipulation, Christians engaged in an advice-giving task after they read two passages supposedly written by another student, one of which revealed the target's attitudes toward religion. One condition conveyed that the target was a staunch atheist, whereas the other portrayed the target as an atheist open to alternatives. The Christian participants then wrote advice to that person, believing that the advice would be returned to the target and the effect of it on the target would be tracked over the next semester. After giving advice, participants privately rated their attitudes about the target. Content analysis of the advice given found that MS increased advising the target to consider giving belief in God a try but only if the target seemed open to persuasion. The liking measure showed that MS led to more liking of the potentially receptive target and less liking of the nonreceptive target.

... This line of work reveals one motivation for persuading others and has the potential to broaden our understanding of important forms of terror management.

Terror Management and the Allure of Stardom

The notion that one could attain symbolic immortality—having one's identity live forever—dates back at least to the ancient Greeks. Thus, one way to cope with concerns about mortality seems to be to seek fame and reinforce the possibility of symbolic immortality through fame. In the age of YouTube, mass media celebrity-watching such as on TMZ, reality television, and a de-emphasis in many cultures on traditional religious modes of immortality striving, it seems likely this form of terror management is becoming more and more popular. Thousands of young women move to Los Angeles every year seeking acting fame. Many other folks around the world try for fame through singing or through enduring horrendous challenges for shows such as *American Idol* and *Survivor*. Other people, perhaps less convinced of their own capacity to become famous, seek to connect themselves to the famous.

The most unfortunate version of this fame seeking may manifest itself through committing heinous acts. Individuals repeatedly feeling humiliated and

insignificant have killed to become immortal. John David Chapman admitted that this was one of his motives for assassinating John Lennon. Seung-Hui Cho, the Virginia Tech killer, provided perhaps the most compelling example of this horrid form of fame seeking. After killing two people on the campus, he left the campus to mail a video to NBC in which he proclaimed he was like Jesus and would be immortalized for standing up for the meek by committing the largest-scale school shooting in history. He then returned to the campus to complete his mission.

Consistent with a terror management analysis of fame seeking in its many forms, Greenberg, Kosloff, Solomon, Cohen, and Landau (2010) found that MS, relative to the salience of intense pain, temporal discontinuity, general uncertainty, and meaninglessness, led to a postdelay increased self-reported desire for fame, interest in having a star named for oneself, and liking for an abstract painting if it was attributed to a celebrity. Additional research will explore phenomena such as the potential terror management value of negative fame (notoriety), responses to celebrities who have fallen from grace, and reactions to those who advocate alternative worldviews. We also hope to explore Internet behavior directed toward gossiping about and connecting to celebrities.

Terror Management and Supernatural Fantasy

In addition to gravitating toward real-life superstars, people also seem to be drawn to deities and fictional superheroes, a phenomenon dating back as long as recorded history and, in the case of superheroes, at least to Hercules. The impulse to become famous and to admire those with special powers may be the same: to try to feel larger than life, so special as to be exempt from the normal limitations of mortal life. You can do this either by connecting with those who seem larger than life or fantasizing being so yourself. Celebrity is one way to feel this, and we have seen how MS draws people to that. Wealth is another way, and research shows that MS does increase the desire for wealth and status (Solomon et al., in press).

Defying the laws of nature may be another way. Many of the most popular movies and best-selling books of all time involve characters with special powers: the "Force" utilized by Luke Skywalker; the amazing powers of Superman and Spiderman, the X-Men, Harry Potter and the vampires and werewolves of Twilight; or the technology-aided superfeats of Iron Man. It is interesting that most admired superheroes have the power of flight in one form or other. In addition, fantasies of human flight are extremely common across cultures and are often linked to attainment of immortality. This led Cohen et al. (2010) to posit that fantasies of flight may serve a special terror management function by giving people a sense that they can transcend the human physical limitation due to gravity, and if that, why not mortality as well, like an immortal state of a disembodied soul ascending to heaven? In their first study, MS led participants to express greater desire to fly. A second study replicated this effect and showed that it did not extend to other supernatural feats such as walking through walls or reading minds. This suggests that flight fantasies may have a unique role in ameliorating concerns with mortality.

Consistent with this possibility, two subsequent studies showed that after MS, participants who engaged in flight fantasy did not subsequently show the typical increased worldview defense found in a nonflying fantasy condition (Cohen et al., 2010). A final study showed that flight fantasy, but not other pleasurable or empowering fantasies, decreased death-thought accessibility after MS, and this effect was mediated by a feeling of freedom from bodily limits. These findings help explain the popularity of flight fantasies and raise the possibility that other forms of fantasy may also mitigate the need for terror management defenses. . . .

Terror Management in Older People

Traumas bring people close to death, but so does the natural process of aging. Maxfield et al. (2007) recently spearheaded research examining how elderly people respond to MS. Older people are probabilistically closer to death and more likely to have experienced life-threatening illness and the death of members of their social network. This suggests a number of plausible questions regarding how they might react differently to MS than young and middle-aged adults. Is mortality so salient to them that our inductions would have no effect? Is it such an imminent issue for them that they would respond even more strongly? Is there a process by which as people get older they more effectively come to terms with their mortality and hence react less defensively?

We do not have definitive answers to these questions yet, but using American samples, we have found some interesting ways in which elderly people respond differently to MS than younger samples. First, they seem to respond more strongly to incidental exposure to death-related words than to the classic MS induction, suggesting that perhaps they are so used to blatant reminders of death that they are more likely to be affected by more subtle reminders. In three studies, we found that in a control condition elderly samples were harsher toward moral transgressors than were young adults and just as harsh as young adults toward a critic of the United States (Maxfield et al., 2007). However, in these three studies we found that MS had opposite effects for elderly and young adult samples. As usual, MS led the young adults to be more negative toward moral transgressors and critics of their culture. However, MS actually led older adults to become more lenient toward moral transgressors and more tolerant of a critic of the United States.

Our samples in these studies tended to be healthy, high-functioning older adults, people who had endured a lot but were still doing well. Therefore, we thought that this startling contrast may have occurred because, when confronted with mortality, well-functioning elderly people draw on a broader perspective on life and a more benevolent perspective on imperfections and differences among us humans. Thus, we hypothesized that the MS-leniency effect would be found in elderly people who exhibit effective executive functioning, whereas the usual MS-punitive effect would occur in older adults relatively poor in executive functioning.

Thus, in a follow-up study we first tested a broadly recruited elderly sample and a college student sample on executive functioning using a combination of three well-established cognitive tasks. Participants were then led to think of their own mortality and asked how much a set of hypothetical moral transgressors should be punished. MS led the young adults to be more punitive regardless of their level of executive functioning. However, as predicted, the MS responses of the older adults depended on their executive functioning. Those functioning well became more lenient after MS. However, those older people low in executive functioning became more punitive after MS, mirroring the general effect for the young adults. These findings suggest the hopeful notion that as people get older, they get more benevolent in response to reminders of their mortality, as long as they are functioning at a high cognitive level. Of course, more research is needed to fully understand why and how this happens.

More Constructive Forms of Terror Management?

The research on older adults' responses to MS raises the possibility that the potential terror of death can be managed in more benign ways than most terror management research implies. A number of other recent lines of research explore ways besides graceful aging that might lead to such constructive approaches. First, evidence suggests that people low in personal need for structure and in authoritarianism may embrace worldviews that encourage more open, tolerant ways of coping with mortality (e.g., Vess, Routledge, Landau, & Arndt, 2009). Evidence also suggests that creative thinking and deeper, more elaborate contemplation of death may encourage more constructive and open-minded reactions to reminders of death (see, e.g., Cozzolino, 2006; Greenberg et al., in press; Janoff-Bulman & Yopyk, 2004). At present, my colleagues and I are exploring how different ways of consciously construing one's own death may affect the extent to which death-related thoughts contribute to defensive versus growth-oriented responses. For example, could viewing death as an integral part of life lead to more openness and tolerance than viewing death as the opposite of life?

Terror Management and Other Psychological Motives

. . . TMT was originally developed to explain basic psychological propensities for self-esteem and negative reactions to different others. It also helps explain a variety of other human propensities ranging from aggression, conformity, and obedience, to political leanings and religiosity, to prosocial behavior and romantic love. However, we have always acknowledged that terror management is not the only psychological motive and that it is rarely, if ever, the only concern affecting a particular thought or action. It is not that any particular human behavior can be fully explained as terror management, but that terror management plays a role in many, if not most, aspects of human behavior. Similarly, not all psychological threats can be reduced to the problem of death. Although issues of uncertain beliefs and meaning, identity and social relationships, often arouse terror management concerns, they can be troubling for other reasons as well. People like some certainties and meanings and dislike others, depending on their implications. Just as such concerns cannot be reduced solely to serving terror management, the concern with mortality cannot be reduced to some broader, vague concern such as uncertainty and meaning. Death is a unique threat because so many of our biological systems are oriented toward averting it, and yet it is the only inevitable future event; further, death is the ultimate threat to all human desires as the potential end of control, social connections, meaning, competence, growth, cognition, and so forth. The need for denial of death cannot be denied. . . .

References

Becker, E. (1971). *The birth and death of meaning: An interdisciplinary perspective on the problem of man* (2nd ed.). New York, NY: Free Press. (Original work published 1962)

Becker, E. (1973). *The denial of death.* New York, NY: Free Press.

Becker, E. (1975). *Escape from evil.* New York, NY: Free Press.

Cohen, F., Sullivan, D., Solomon, S., Greenberg, J., & Ogilvie, D. (2010). Finding everland: Flight fantasies and the desire to transcend mortality. *Journal of Experimental Social Psychology, 47,* 88–102. doi:10.1016/j.jesp.2010.08.013

Cozzolino, P. J. (2006). Death, contemplation, growth, and defense: Converging evidence of a dual-existential system? *Psychological Inquiry, 17,* 278–287. doi:10.1080/10478400701366944

Greenberg, J., Kosloff, S., Solomon, S., Cohen, F., & Landau, M. J. (2010). Toward understanding the fame game: The effect of mortality salience on the appeal of fame. *Self and Identity, 9,* 1–18. doi:10.1080/15298860802391546

Greenberg, J., Landau, M. J., & Arndt, J. (in press). Mortal cognition: Viewing self and the world from the precipice. In D. Carlston (Ed.), *Handbook of social cognition.* Oxford, England: Oxford University Press.

Greenberg, J., Solomon, S., & Arndt, J. (2008). A uniquely human motivation: Terror management. In J. Shah & W. Gardner (Eds.), *Handbook of motivation science* (pp. 114–134). New York, NY: Guilford Press.

Hart, J., Shaver, P. R., & Goldenberg, J. L. (2005). Attachment, self-esteem, worldviews, and terror management: Evidence for a tripartite security system. *Journal of Personality and Social Psychology, 88,* 999–1013. doi:10.1037/0022-3514.88.6.999

Hayes, J., Schimel, J., Arndt, J., & Faucher, E. H. (2010). A theoretical and empirical review of the death-thought accessibility concept in terror management research. *Psychological Bulletin, 136,* 699–739. doi:10.1037/a0020524

Hayes, J., Schimel, J., & Williams, T. J. (2008). Fighting death with death: The buffering effects of learning that worldview violators have died. *Psychological Science, 19,* 501–507. doi:10.1111/j.1467-9280.2008.02115.x

Janoff-Bulman, R., & Yopyk, D. J. (2004). Random outcomes and valued commitments: Existential dilemmas and the paradox of meaning. In J. Greenberg, S. L. Koole, & T. Pyszczynski (Eds.), *Handbook of experimental existential psychology* (pp. 122–140). New York, NY: Guilford Press.

Kosloff, S., Cesario, J., & Martens, A. (2011). *Resistance is futile: Mortality salience increases efforts to assimilate others to one's own worldview.* Unpublished manuscript.

Kosloff, S., Greenberg, J., Allen, J. J. B., & Martens, A. (2011). *Mortality salience heightens neural and autonomic indices of withdrawal from symbolic threat.* Unpublished manuscript.

Landau, M. J., Johns, M., Greenberg, J., Pyszczynski, T., Solomon, S., & Martens, A. (2004). A function of form: Terror management and structuring of the social world. *Journal of Personality and Social Psychology, 87,* 190–210. doi:10.1037/0022-3514.87.2.190

Maxfield, M., Pyszczynski, T., Kluck, B., Cox, C., Greenberg, J., Solomon, S., & Weise, D. (2007). Age-related differences in responses to thoughts of one's own death: Mortality salience and judgments of moral transgressors. *Psychology and Aging, 22,* 341–353. doi:10.1037/0882-7974.22.2.341

McGregor, H. A., Lieberman, J. D., Solomon, S., Greenberg, J., Arndt, J., Simon, L., & Pyszczynski, T. (1998). Terror management and aggression: Evidence that mortality salience motivates aggression against worldview threatening others. *Journal of Personality and Social Psychology, 74,* 590–605. doi:10.1037/0022-3514.74.3.590

McGregor, I., Nash, K. A., Mann, N., & Phills, C. (2010). Anxious uncertainty and reactive approach motivation (RAM). *Journal of Personality and Social Psychology, 99,* 133–147. doi:10.1037/a0019701

Pyszczynski, T., Abdollahi, A., Solomon, S., Greenberg, J., Cohen, F., & Weise, D. (2006). Mortality salience, martyrdom, and military might: The Great Satan versus the Axis of Evil. *Personality and Social Psychology Bulletin, 32,* 525–537. doi:10.1177/0146167205282157

Pyszczynski, T., Greenberg, J., Koole, S., & Solomon, S. (2010). Experimental existential psychology: Coping with the facts of life. In S. Fiske, D. Gilbert, & G. Lindzey (Eds.), *Handbook of social psychology* (Vol. 2, pp. 724–760). London, England: Wiley.

Pyszczynski, T., Greenberg, J., & Solomon, S. (1999). A dual-process model of defense against conscious and unconscious death-related thoughts: An extension of terror management theory. *Psychological Review, 106,* 835–845. doi:10.1037/0033-295X.106.4.835

Pyszczynski, T., Greenberg, J., Solomon, S., & Maxfield, M. (2006). On the unique psychological import of the human awareness of mortality: Themes and variations. *Psychological Inquiry, 17,* 328–356. doi:10.1080/10478400701369542

Quirin, M., Loktyushin, A., Arndt, J., Kustermann, E., Lo, Y., Kuhl, J., & Eggert, L. D. (in press). Existential neuroscience: A functional magnetic resonance imaging investigation of neural responses to reminders of one's mortality. *Social Cognitive and Affective Neuroscience.*

Solomon, S., Greenberg, J., & Pyszczynski, T. (in press). *The worm at the core: On the role of death in life.* New York, NY: Random House.

Strachan, E., Schimel, J., Arndt, J., Williams, T., Solomon, S., Pyszczynski, T., & Greenberg, J. (2007). Terror mismanagement: Evidence that mortality salience exacerbates phobic and compulsive behaviors. *Personality and Social Psychology Bulletin, 33,* 1137–1151. doi:10.1177/0146167207303018

Vess, M., Routledge, C., Landau, M. J., & Arndt, J. (2009). The dynamics of death and meaning: The effects of death-relevant cognitions and personal need for structure on perceptions of meaning in life. *Journal of Personality and Social Psychology, 97,* 728–744. doi:10.1037/a0016417

JEFF GREENBERG is a professor and head of the social psychology department at the University of Arizona, where he focuses his teachings on advanced social psychology and social psychology and cinema. He conducts research on stereotypes and prejudice, intergroup relations, the self and identity, and law and public policy.

Daniel M. T. Fessler and C. David Navarrete

The Effect of Age on Death Disgust: Challenges to Terror Management Perspectives

The Terror Management Account of Disgust

Disgust, first systematically studied by Darwin (1872), is widely considered a universal emotion (Ekman, Friesen, and Ellsworth, 1982; Oatley and Johnson-Laird, 1987; Scherer and Wallbott, 1994). Though long neglected, within the last two decades disgust has become the focus of rigorous investigation. Paul Rozin and Jonathan Haidt, the principal pioneers in this enterprise, have, together with their associates, generated a large body of empirical findings, shedding new light on disgust. Because their work constitutes a thematically coherent corpus, we refer to this team collectively as the Rozin School. The Rozin School proposes that a disgust-like emotion evolved to protect the body from the oral incorporation of pathogen- and toxin-bearing substances (Haidt, McCauley, and Rozin, 1994; Haidt, Rozin, McCauley, and Imada, 1997; Rozin and Fallon, 1987; Rozin, Haidt, and McCauley, 1993, 1999). However, being intimately linked to defending the body/self from contamination, disgust, the Rozin School argues, is readily extended to other domains.

A principal conceptual hazard that symbolically-mediated disgust ostensibly guards against is the recognition that humans are animals. Inspired by the work of anthropologist Ernest Becker (1973), and relying on the same premises as the theoretical framework now known as Terror Management Theory (TMT) (see Greenberg, Solomon, and Pyszczynski, 1997 for review), the Rozin School claims that knowledge of our own mortality induces existential anxiety, a condition that TMT proponents describe as a fitness-reducing paralytic state—consumed by an awareness of the inevitability of death, individuals are, it is postulated, unable to engage in the tasks that contribute to survival and reproductive success (Greenberg, Solomon, and Pyszczynski, 1997; Solomon, Greenberg, Schimel, Arndt, and Pyszczynski, 2004). Because humans are aware that animals are mortal, being reminded of our animality provokes this paralyzing anxiety. Disgust is thus purportedly adaptively employed as a defense against existential terror, an explanation invoked to account for the linkage between disgust and such stimuli as contact with animals, body products, violations of the body envelope, and the dead (Goldenberg, Pyszczynski, Greenberg, Solomon, Kluck, and Cornwell, 2001; Haidt, McCauley, and Rozin, 1994; Haidt, Rozin, McCauley, and Imada, 1997; Rozin, Haidt, McCauley, Dunlop, and Ashmore, 1999; Rozin, Haidt, McCauley, and Imada, 1997; Rozin, Haidt, and McCauley, 1993, 1999, 2000).

Consistent with the above reasoning, the Rozin School and allied Terror Management investigators hold that the application of disgust to the domain of sexual behavior is motivated by a panhuman need to distance oneself from the animality of mating (Haidt, McCauley, and Rozin, 1994; Haidt, Rozin, McCauley, and Imada, 1997; Rozin, Haidt, McCauley, Dunlop, and Ashmore, 1999; Rozin, Haidt, and McCauley, 1993, 1999, 2000; see also Goldenberg, Cox, Pyszczynski, Greenberg, and Solomon, 2002; Goldenberg, Pyszczynski, Greenberg, Solomon, Kluck, and Cornwell, 2001; Goldenberg, Pyszczynski, McCoy, Greenberg, and Solomon, 1999). Recently, we demonstrated that disgust sensitivity in the sexual domain, and only in the sexual domain, increases as a function of the likelihood of conception across the menstrual cycle (Fessler and Navarrete, 2003a). It is difficult to see how such patterned domain-specific changes in disgust sensitivity can be explained by the notion that sexual disgust derives from an intense need to avoid recognition of one's own mortality. In contrast, these changes are exactly what should be expected if women's sexual disgust is an evolved adaptation that reduces the probability of biologically suboptimal sexual unions (e.g., incest, bestiality, etc.) during the fertile phase. This led us to question the Rozin School's oft-repeated claim that, rather than directly reflecting the workings of

From Fessler, Daniel M. T.; Navarrete, C. David, "The Effect of Age on Death Disgust: Challenges to Terror Management Perspectives," *Evolutionary Psychology*, vol. 3, pp. 279–296 (ISSN 1474-7049).

an evolved mechanism, many aspects of disgust experience instead constitute an attempt to avoid existential terror. We therefore sought to examine the domain in which the postulated phenomenon ought to loom most large, namely disgust reactions to stimuli that are overtly associated with death.

If, as TMT proponents argue (Goldenberg, Pyszczynski, Greenberg, Solomon, Kluck, and Cornwell, 2001; Haidt, McCauley, and Rozin, 1994; Haidt, Rozin, McCauley, and Imada, 1997; Rozin, Haidt, McCauley, Dunlop, and Ashmore, 1999; Rozin, Haidt, McCauley, and Imada, 1997; Rozin, Haidt, and McCauley, 1993, 1999, 2000), disgust responses to reminders of death constitute an attempt to avoid the anxiety attending the recognition that we are mortal, and if, as part of that recognition, each of us knows that the passage of time inexorably brings us closer to the day that we will die, then disgust sensitivity in the death domain should increase with age, since the motivation to deny our impending death should be enhanced as the fateful day draws closer.

Although Quigley, Sherman, and Sherman (1997) noted that disgust sensitivity declines with age, their study focused only on young adults, and they report only overall disgust sensitivity, rather than disgust sensitivity by domain; similar considerations apply to Rozin, Haidt, and McCauley's observation that 'There are hints . . . that disgust sensitivity declines after the teen years,' (2000, p. 648). In the course of our investigation of changes in disgust sensitivity over the menstrual cycle, using the same instrument employed by both Quigley, Sherman, and Sherman and the Rozin School, we also found a decline in overall disgust sensitivity with age (Fessler and Navarrete, 2003a); however, our study involved only reproductive-age women. In a very large sample spanning a wide age range, Curtis, Aunger, and Rabie (2004) showed declines in disgust sensitivity with age; however, their study employed stimuli not directly related to death. As the literature thus does not illuminate the relationship between age and disgust sensitivity in the death domain, we sought to address this issue via three avenues. First, we reanalyzed data previously collected in two Internet-based surveys that employed the Disgust Scale (Haidt, McCauley, and Rozin, 1994), the instrument created by the Rozin School, the principal advocates of the Terror Management account of death disgust. Second, we conducted a new Internet-based survey using the Disgust Scale. Lastly, because attitudes toward death vary across cultures, in order to ensure that any patterns found were not the unique product of U.S. culture, we orally administered a translated version of the Disgust Scale in rural Costa Rica, a cultural environment in which individuals have greater familiarity with death, and in which death fears are more boldly confronted, than is generally true in the U.S.

Study 1—Reanalysis of Prior Internet-Based Administrations of the Disgust Scale

Method

In order to shed light on the relationship between age and death disgust, we revisited data collected previously in the course of two Internet studies conducted for other purposes. The first study, described to participants as 'Surveys on Diet, Disgust, and Motion Sickness,' consisted of a dietary inventory on the first web page, followed by the Disgust Scale on a second page, followed in turn by a questionnaire on susceptibility to motion sickness (see Fessler, Arguello, Mekdara, and Macias, 2003 for details). In the second study, titled 'Body Awareness and the Self,' the initial web page asked participants to rate how disgusting they found the prospect of transplantation of each of twenty different body tissues; the Disgust Scale was then presented on a separate page (see Fessler and Haley, in press, Study 3, for details). In both studies, participants were recruited through postings to clearinghouse web sites (e.g., Psychological Research on the Net, SocialPsychology. org) and listservs (e.g., Psych-L, Anthro-L). Participation was anonymous, and no compensation was offered.

Results and Discussion

We pooled data from the two studies, limiting the analysis to adults who completed every item on each questionnaire and eliminating multiple entries from the same IP address. This produced a combined sample of 921 individuals (635 women and 286 men, aged $18 - 79$; M = 29.5, S.D. = 11.3). To assess death disgust sensitivity, we examined responses to death-related questions on the Disgust Scale, including both true/false questions (e.g., "It would bother me to sleep in a nice hotel room if I knew that a man had died of a heart attack in that room the night before," etc.) and scalar 'how disgusting' questions (e.g., "You accidentally touch the ashes of a person who has been cremated," etc.) (see Haidt, McCauley, and Rozin, 1994). In a multiple regression analysis in which the independent variables were age, sex, and a dummy variable controlling for mean differences between the two samples, we found a significant main effect for age in which increasing age predicted lower disgust sensitivity to death stimuli. . . .

Although men were less disgust sensitive towards death stimuli than were women, the slopes predicting disgust sensitivity as a function of age did not differ between the sexes.

Study 2—Internet-Based Administration of the Disgust Scale Alone

Method

Because the materials analyzed in Study 1 were not originally collected for the purpose of examining age effects on death disgust sensitivity, in both of the surveys, the Disgust Scale was preceded by a questionnaire addressing a different topic; likewise, in both cases, demographic information was collected at the beginning of the survey. These procedures raise the possibility that the pattern evident in the results reflects age-dependent priming effects produced by stimuli not directly pertaining to death disgust. To address this limitation, we conducted an additional Internet survey in which the Disgust Scale was presented in isolation. A link labeled 'An Investigation of the Effects of Context on Emotional Reactions,' posted on clearinghouse web sites, led to the Disgust Scale, followed by a separate page containing questions regarding age, sex, and the setting in which participation took place (the latter information was collected for reasons not relevant to the present discussion).

Results

Employing the same criteria for inclusion as those used in Study 1 produced a sample of 692 individuals (506 women and 186 men, aged 18 − 81; M = 26.8, S.D. = 11.7). In a multiple regression analysis in which the independent variables were age, sex and their interactions, we found significant main effects for age and sex. Confirming previous results, death disgust sensitivity declined significantly with age, and men were less disgust sensitive than women. A second step in which interaction terms were added once again revealed that, although men had a lower mean level of death disgust sensitivity than did women, the slopes predicting disgust sensitivity as a function of age did not differ between the sexes.

Study 3—In-Person Oral Administration of the Disgust Scale in Rural Costa Rica

Participants for Studies 1 and 2 were recruited using web sites and listservs that are directed primarily at an English-speaking North American audience. It is therefore likely that many participants in Studies 1 and 2 either primarily identified with U.S. culture, or else were intimately familiar with it. Adherence to a cultural worldview plays a central role in TMT (Greenberg, Solomon, and Pyszczynski, 1997). Because attitudes toward death vary substantially across cultures (Counts and Counts, 1991), we therefore felt it important to demonstrate that the effects of age on death disgust sensitivity documented in Studies 1 and 2 are not unique to those who are well-versed in North American culture.

Rural Costa Rica differs along many important dimensions from the dominant culture of the U.S. (Hofstede, 1991), and numerous traditions, practices and beliefs remain relatively unadulterated by North American influences (Biesanz, Biesanz, and Biesanz, 1999). As in other agricultural areas in the Developing World, people in rural Costa Rica are frequently exposed to the death of animals, as animals are killed for food, pests and predators are exterminated, and farm animals die of injuries or age. In addition to the general exposure to the cycle of life and death typical of rural dwellers, Latin Americans are noteworthy for the degree to which they appear to have normalized death. Many Hispanic authors have noted that mortality concerns are expressed openly in Latin American cultures, rather than repressed as they often are in the U.S. (e.g. Delibes, 1966; Fierro, 1980). Likewise, death themes have been staples of Hispanic written and oral traditions for centuries, and may have pre-Columbian roots in both the Spanish and the Mayan and Aztec traditions (Siefken, 1993). Consistent with these generalizations, practices in rural Costa Rica reflect an easy familiarity with death. Dying relatives usually pass away in the home, not in hospitals, and surviving family members are present at the moment of death. In the immediate aftermath, family members often remain in close proximity to the deceased, sometimes embracing and kissing the corpse. More generally, people frequently visit relatives' graves and memorials, and picnics at a loved one's tomb are common, particularly during religious holidays; food is sometimes left at the grave for the deceased to consume. Correspondingly, with regard to overarching attitudes toward death and dying, rural Costa Ricans are more open about their anxieties, more familiar with the death process, and much more fatalistic in their attitude toward death than is typical in the U.S. (Biesanz, Biesanz, and Biesanz, 1999; Navarrete, 2004). Hence, because of the many relevant contrasts with contemporary U.S. culture, rural Costa Rica constitutes a promising setting in which to evaluate the degree of universality of patterns of emotional reactions to reminders of death.

In addition to examining the effects of age on death disgust in rural Costa Rica, we also used this opportunity to test a related prediction promulgated by proponents of a Terror Management approach to disgust. Goldenberg, Pyszczynski,

Greenberg, and Solomon (2000) and Goldenberg, Pyszczynski, Greenberg, Solomon, Kluck, and Cornwell (2001) argue that, because disgust defends against fitness-reducing existential anxiety, reminders of death should intensify the disgust reaction to stimuli, such as the body and its by-products, which remind people that they are animals, and hence are mortal. Goldenberg, Pyszczynski, Greenberg, Solomon, Kluck, and Cornwell (2001, Study 1) tested this hypothesis in a North American university sample by administering the Disgust Scale following contemplation of one's own death; results revealed that, relative to a control condition, mortality salience increased scores on the body products and animal disgust sensitivity subscales. The authors interpret this finding as supporting the Rozin School's notion that disgust responses serve as a symbolic, distal defense against death by differentiating humans from animals.

In previous research, we found that, contrary to the core predictions of TMT, reminders of death failed to increase worldview defense among Costa Rican participants (Navarrete, 2004; Navarrete, Kurzban, Fessler, and Kirkpatrick, 2004). We hypothesized that these null effects were due to cultural differences, as overt death fears may not be particularly salient to individuals in societies such as Costa Rica in which beliefs, practices, and fatalistic attitudes make exposure to death themes less problematic than is true for people living in societies that emphasize secular life and control over one's own destiny. Rural Costa Rica was thus a useful location for a test of the TMT claim that, due to evolved panhuman features of mind, mortality salience should enhance disgust sensitivity toward the corporeal aspects of human animality.

Method

Study participants were 82 Costa Rican citizens (29 men and 53 women) living in the community of Cariari, in the Limón Province of the Republic of Costa Rica—a region with a primarily agricultural economy in which bananas are the principal export. Participants were recruited door-to-door in their homes to participate in a survey on personality and social attitudes, and ranged in age from 16 to 73 (Mean Age: 28, S.D. = 11.1). Education ranged from 0 to 15 years (Mean 7.9, S.D. = 2.5) with the modal education level at the completion of primary school (6 years).

Because rural Costa Ricans have little or no familiarity with written surveys, we employed an in-person structured interview format. With the aid of literate local assistants, the second author translated the Disgust Scale into colloquial Costa Rican Spanish. The resulting translation was then inspected by two faculty members at the D'Amore Language School in Quepos, Costa Rica, who edited the translation for clarity. Finally, the edited version was presented to local assistants, who substituted familiar colloquial terms for any formal phrases. The survey was then administered by a male research assistant who was naïve to the hypotheses being tested.

Participants were given a mortality salience prime, the Positive And Negative Affect Schedule (PANAS) (Watson, Clark, and Tellegen, 1988), the Disgust Scale, and an assay of several demographic items. The mortality salience prime, similar to that used in typical TMT research, asked participants to describe the feelings that the thought of their own death aroused in them, and to describe what happens when one physically dies. Participants in the treatment condition were given the mortality salience prime before the administration of the Disgust Scale, while participants in the control condition were given the prime after the Disgust Scale. Following Terror Management protocols (Greenberg, Pyszczynski, Solomon, Simon, and Breus, 1994), the PANAS was administered as a delay and distraction before administration of the Disgust Scale.

Results and Discussion

In evaluating the effects of age and sex on death disgust sensitivity, we conducted a regression analysis similar to those described above. A dummy variable coded for whether participants were exposed to the mortality salience prime before or after administration of the Disgust Scale.

Analysis revealed a main effect for age, a marginally significant effect for sex, and no effect for mortality salience on death disgust sensitivity (see Table 1). Interaction terms were not significant and were removed from the model. As in our Internet studies, death disgust decreased as a function of age, and men showed less death disgust than did women. Mortality salience failed to produce a significant change in disgust sensitivity toward death stimuli.

In assessing the TMT prediction that reminders of death should intensify the disgust reaction to animality and by-products of the body, we conducted a multivariate

Table 1

Rural Costa Rica: Summary of Multiple Regression Analysis for Variables Predicting Death Disgust. Values reflect standardized beta-weights.

Variable	β	S.E.	t	Sig.
DEATH DISGUST				
Age	−.29	.04	−8.15	$p < .0001$
Gender (Male)	−.32	.08	−3.95	$p < .0001$

Table 2

Rural Costa Rica: Summary of Multivariate Regression Analysis for Variables Predicting Animal and Body-Function Disgust. Values reflect standardized beta-weights.

Variable	β	S.E.	t	Sig.
ANIMAL DISGUST				
Age	−.08	.10	−0.79	N.S.
Gender (Male)	−.49	.21	−2.29	$p = .03$
Death Reminder	−.08	.21	0.41	N.S.
BODY-FUNCTION DISGUST				
Age	−.04	.09	−0.47	N.S.
Gender (Male)	−.90	.20	−4.59	$p < .0001$
Death Reminder	−.01	.19	−0.04	N.S.

regression in which the animal and body products subscales of the Disgust Scale were the two dependent variables; mortality salience, sex, and age were the predictors. The analysis revealed no effect for mortality salience on either subscale, no age effects, and a main effect for sex, with men being less disgust sensitive toward animal and body-function disgust stimuli than women (see Table 2). Contrary to the predictions, and previous findings, of TMT researchers working in the U.S., in Costa Rica reminders of death failed to intensify the disgust reaction to those domains which blur the human–animal boundary. . . .

General Discussion

A straightforward reading of Terror Management Theory suggests that defenses against existential anxiety should progressively increase as the inevitability of senescence, and hence death, becomes increasingly evident. The Rozin School and allied TMT researchers assert that disgust reactions to death are part of such defenses, generating the prediction that death disgust should increase with age. Here, using the measure of disgust sensitivity devised by the Rozin School, we have shown that, contrary to this prediction, disgust sensitivity in the death domain declines with age. Recently, some proponents of TMT have argued that what they term 'successful aging' involves abandoning those defenses against death anxiety thought to be characteristic of younger adults, replacing them instead with coping mechanisms centering on what is described

as 'self-transcendence' (McCoy, Pyszczynski, Solomon, and Greenberg, 2000). This revised formulation of TMT fares no better in our tests. If disgust reactions to death and reminders of death are a defense against existential anxiety characteristic of one stage of life, and if defenses of this type are later replaced by self-transcendence, then the relationship between age and death disgust should shift sometime in old age. Younger individuals should exhibit a positive correlation between death disgust and age since, being still reliant on defense mechanisms involving denial and avoidance, with each passing year they should work harder to distance themselves from their approaching deaths. In contrast, older individuals should exhibit a negative correlation between death disgust and age since, the greater their age, the longer the opportunity they have had to work toward self-transcendence, and hence the less they should need to deny their mortality through disgust reactions to death. In each of our studies we found a significant main effect for age, indicating that the relationship between death disgust and age does not exhibit the inverted U-shaped function predicted by this version of TMT.

In addition to demonstrating that TMT is unable to predict the relationship between age and death disgust, our Costa Rican study reveals that, contrary to the predictions of Terror Management theorists, in at least one population, mortality salience induction does not enhance disgust responses to reminders of animality.

Although Terror Management Theory explicitly purports to provide an evolutionary account of human responses to death (Solomon, Greenberg, Schimel, Arndt, and Pyszczynski, 2004), viewed from the perspective of contemporary evolutionary psychology, TMT is premised on a number of questionable assumptions, including the view that anxiety is fitness-reducing, and the claim that all animals possess a domain-general survival instinct (for critiques see Boyer 2001, pp. 204–226; Buss, 1997; Leary, 2004; Leary and Schreindorfer, 1997; Matz, Evans, Geisler, and Hinsz, 1997; Navarrete and Fessler, 2005; Navarrete, Kurzban, Fessler, and Kirkpatrick, 2004). Elsewhere (Navarrete, Kurzban, Fessler, and Kirkpatrick, 2004) we have provided evidence that the experimental prime, mortality salience induction, employed in much TMT research lacks the uniqueness ascribed to it by TMT advocates. Together with the results presented above, these observations lead us to conclude that Terror Management Theory does not provide a solid foundation on which to construct theories of disgust.

Although Paul Rozin was one of the earliest proponents of a neo-Darwinian approach to behavior (cf. 1976), while noting the evolutionary origins of disgust as a motivator of behavioral prophylaxis, the Rozin School has nevertheless emphasized features of disgust, such as elicitation by culturally-defined morally objectionable behaviors, that deviate from this function (Haidt, Rozin, McCauley, and Imada, 1997; Rozin, Lowery, Imada, and Haidt, 1999). In contrast, following suggestions by Nesse and Williams (1995) and Pinker (1997), Curtis and Biran (2001) have sought to swing the pendulum back toward a more comprehensive evolutionary account of disgust, documenting that, across disparate cultures, this emotion is elicited by stimuli, such as feces, vomit, and spoiled food, that constitute avenues for pathogen transmission (see also Cosmides and Tooby, 2000; Wronska, 1990; compare with Kurzban and Leary, 2001). Consistent with this view, Curtis, Aunger, and Rabie (2004) recently showed that disgust elicitation is influenced by cues (wound type, color of liquids, etc.) that are discretely associated with sources of disease. In previous work, members of our research group have argued that a) the salience of animals and animal parts as disgust elicitors reflects the hazards of pathogen transmission that such objects posed in ancestral environments (Fessler and Navarrete, 2003b); and b) the relative salience of various parts of the human body in disgust events is a function of both their vulnerability to biological contamination and their role in producing contaminants (Fessler and Haley, in press). Recently, we demonstrated that food disgust sensitivity is elevated during the first trimester of pregnancy, a period when, due in part to reproductive immunosuppression, the costs of food-borne illness are greatly elevated (Fessler, Eng, and Navarrete, 2005). While we acknowledge that disgust experiences are importantly shaped by cultural beliefs, we believe that this growing corpus of evidence indicates that many features of disgust are best explained in terms of the functional importance that avoiding sources of biologically relevant contamination held for our ancestors. Given that a) for most of human history, death was often caused by disease, and b) pathogens proliferate on corpses and carcasses, it follows that disgust reactions to death are parsimoniously explained as one facet of an emotion that evolved to decrease exposure to fitness-reducing contamination (Boyer, 2001, pp. 212–215).

Declines in disgust sensitivity with age may reflect habituation as a result of repeated exposure to death-related stimuli over time. Habituation can be viewed as part of the adaptive modulation of responses to indices of potentially harmful circumstances: because caution and avoidance are costly due to the time, energy, and missed opportunities that they entail, it is adaptive to reduce such responses when experience reveals that, in the given environment, the stimuli at issue do not index significant hazards. Note that the habituation explanation is incompatible with the Rozin School's claim that death disgust defends against existential terror—defense mechanisms can be likened to mental calluses and, like their physical equivalents, they ought to become increasingly robust, rather than increasingly weak, with successive exposure to abrasive features of the environment. Our account of death disgust thus combines an acknowledgement of the evolutionary importance of disease avoidance with a recognition of the possible adaptive influence of habituation on response intensity. This perspective is both more parsimonious and better able to explain the influence of age on death disgust than the rather baroque psychodynamic processes postulated by Terror Management Theory. . . .

References

Becker, E. (1973). *The Denial of Death*. New York: The Free Press.

Biesanz, M. H., Biesanz, R. and Biesanz, K. Z. (1999). *The Ticos: Culture and social change in Costa Rica*. London: Lynne Rienner.

Boyer, P. (2001). *Religion Explained: The evolutionary origins of religious thought*. New York: Basic Books.

Buss, D. M. (1997). Human social motivation in evolutionary perspective: Grounding Terror Management Theory. *Psychological Inquiry, 8(1)*, 22–26.

Cosmides, L. and Tooby, J. (2000). Evolutionary psychology and the emotions. In Lewis, M., and Haviland-Jones, J. M. (Eds.), *Handbook of Emotions* (2nd ed., pp. 91–115). New York: Guilford Press.

Counts, D. R. and Counts, D. A. (Eds.) (1991). *Coping with the Final Tragedy: Cultural variation in dying and grieving*. Amityville, N.Y.: Baywood Publishing Company.

Curtis, V., Aunger, R. and Rabie, T. (2004). Evidence that disgust evolved to protect from risk of disease. *Proceedings of the Royal Society Biological Sciences Series B, 271(Suppl 4)*, S131–133.

Curtis, V. and Biran, A. (2001). Dirt, disgust, and disease: Is hygiene in our genes? *Perspectives in Biology and Medicine, 44(1)*, 17–31.

Darwin, C. (1872). *The Expression of the Emotions in Man and Animals*. London: J. Murray.

Delibes, M. (1966). *USA y yo*. Barcelona: Ediciones Destino.

Ekman, P., Friesen, W. V. and Ellsworth, P. (1982). Comparisons of facial behavior across cultures. In Ekman, P. (Ed.), *Emotion in the Human Face* (2nd ed., pp. 128–143). Cambridge, England: Cambridge University Press.

Fessler, D. M. T., Arguello, A. P., Mekdara, J. M. and Macias, R. (2003). Disgust sensitivity and meat consumption: A test of an emotivist account of moral vegetarianism. *Appetite, 41(1)*, 31–41.

Fessler, D. M. T., Eng, S. J. and Navarrete, C. D. (2005). Disgust sensitivity is elevated in the first trimester of pregnancy: Evidence supporting the compensatory prophylaxis hypothesis. *Evolution and Human Behavior* 26(4):344–351.

Fessler, D. M. T. and Haley, K. J. (in press). Guarding the perimeter: The outside-inside dichotomy in disgust and bodily experience. *Cognition and Emotion*.

Fessler, D. M. T. and Navarrete, C. D. (2003a). Domain-specific variation in disgust sensitivity across the menstrual cycle. *Evolution and Human Behavior, 24(6)*, 406–417.

Fessler, D. M. T. and Navarrete, C. D. (2003b). Meat is good to taboo: Dietary proscriptions as a product of the interaction of psychological mechanisms and social processes. *Journal of Cognition and Culture, 3(1)*, 1–40.

Fierro, A. (1980). A note on death and dying. *Hispanic Journal of Behavioral Sciences, 2(4)*, 401–406.

Goldenberg, J. L., Cox, C. R., Pyszczynski, T., Greenberg, J. and Solomon, S. (2002). Understanding human ambivalence about sex: The effects of stripping sex of meaning. *Journal of Sex Research, 39(4)*, 310–320.

Goldenberg, J. L., Pyszczynski, T., Greenberg, J. and Solomon, S. (2000). Fleeing the body: A terror management perspective on the problem of human corporeality. *Personality and Social Psychology Review, 4(3)*, 200–218.

Goldenberg, J. L., Pyszczynski, T., Greenberg, J., Solomon, S., Kluck, B. and Cornwell, R. (2001). I am not an animal: Mortality salience, disgust, and the denial of human creatureliness. *Journal of Experimental Psychology: General, 130(3)*, 427–435.

Goldenberg, J. L., Pyszczynski, T., McCoy, S. K., Greenberg, J. and Solomon, S. (1999). Death, sex, love, and neuroticism: Why is sex such a problem? *Journal of Personality and Social Psychology, 77(6)*, 1173–1187.

Greenberg, J., Pyszczynski, T., Solomon, S., Simon, L. and Breus, M. (1994). Role of consciousness and accessibility of death-related thoughts in mortality salience effects. *Journal of Personality and Social Psychology, 67(4)*, 627–637.

Greenberg, J., Solomon, S. and Pyszczynski, T. (1997). Terror management theory of self-esteem and cultural worldviews: Empirical assessments and conceptual refinements. *Advances in Experimental Social Psychology, 29*, 61–139.

Haidt, J., McCauley, C. and Rozin, P. (1994). Individual differences in sensitivity to disgust: A scale sampling seven domains of disgust elicitors. *Personality and Individual Differences, 16(5)*, 701–713.

Haidt, J., Rozin, P., McCauley, C. and Imada, S. (1997). Body, psyche, and culture: The relationship between disgust and morality. *Psychology and Developing Societies, 9(1)*, 107–131.

Hofstede, G. H. (1991). *Cultures and organizations: Software of the mind.* London; New York: McGraw-Hill.

Kurzban, R. and Leary, M. R. (2001). Evolutionary origins of stigmatization: The functions of social exclusion. *Psychological Bulletin, 127(2)*, 187–208.

Leary, M. R. (2004). The function of self-esteem in terror management theory and sociometer theory: Comment on Pyszczynski et al. (2004). *Psychological Bulletin, 130(3)*, 478–482.

Leary, M. R. and Schreindorfer, L. S. (1997). Unresolved issues with Terror Management Theory. *Psychological Inquiry, 8(1)*, 26–29.

Matz, D. C., Evans, B. A., Geisler, C. J. and Hinsz, V. B. (1997). Life, death, and terror management theory. *Representative Research in Social Psychology, 21*, 48–59.

McCoy, S. K., Pyszczynski, T., Solomon, S. and Greenberg, J. (2000). Transcending the self: A terror management perspective on successful aging. In Tomer, A. (Ed.), *Death Attitudes and the Older Adult: Theories, concepts, and applications* (pp. 37–63). New York: Brunner-Routledge.

Navarrete, C. D. (2004). *Challenge, Threat and Pronormative Bias: Coalitional psychology in two societies.* Unpublished Ph.D. thesis, University of California, Los Angeles, Los Angeles.

Navarrete, C. D. and Fessler, D. M. T. (2005). Pro-normative bias and adaptive challenges: A relational approach to coalitional psychology and a critique of Terror Management Theory. *Evolutionary Psychology, 3*, 297–325.

Navarrete, C. D., Kurzban, R., Fessler, D. M. T. and Kirkpatrick, L. A. (2004). Anxiety and intergroup bias: Terror management or coalitional psychology? *Group Processes and Intergroup Relations, 7(4)*:370–397.

Nesse, R. M. and Williams, G. C. (1995). *Why We Get Sick: The new science of Darwinian medicine.* New York: Times Books.

Oatley, K. and Johnson-Laird, P. N. (1987). Towards a cognitive theory of emotions. *Cognition and Emotion, 1(1),* 29–50.

Pinker, S. (1997). *How the Mind Works.* New York: Norton.

Quigley, J. F., Sherman, M. F. and Sherman, N. C. (1997). Personality disorder symptoms, gender, and age as predictors of adolescent disgust sensitivity. *Personality and Individual Differences, 22(5),* 661–667.

Rozin, P. (1976). The selection of food by rats, humans and other animals. In Hinde, R. A., Beer, C., and Shaw, E. (Eds.), *Advances in the Study of Animal Behavior* (Vol. 6, pp. 21–76). New York: Academic Press.

Rozin, P., and Fallon, A. E. (1987). A perspective on disgust. *Psychological Review, 94(1),* 23–41.

Rozin, P., Haidt, J., McCauley, C., Dunlop, L. and Ashmore, M. (1999). Individual differences in disgust sensitivity: Comparisons and evaluations of paper-and-pencil versus behavioral measures. *Journal of Research in Personality, 33(3),* 330–351.

Rozin, P., Haidt, J., McCauley, C. and Imada, S. (1997). Disgust: Preadaptation and the cultural evolution of a food-based emotion. In MacBeth, H. (Ed.), *Food Preferences and Taste* (pp. 65–82). Providence, RI: Berghahn Books.

Rozin, P., Haidt, J. and McCauley, C. R. (1993). Disgust. In Lewis, M., and Haviland, J. M. (Eds.), *Handbook of Emotions* (pp. 575–594). New York: The Guilford Press.

Rozin, P., Haidt, J. and McCauley, C. R. (1999). Disgust: the body and soul emotion. In Dalgleish, T., and Power, M. J. (Eds.), *Handbook of Cognition and Emotion* (pp. 429–445). Chichester, UK: John Wiley and Sons Ltd.

Rozin, P., Haidt, J., and McCauley, C. R. (2000). Disgust. In Lewis, M., and Haviland, J. (Eds.), *Handbook of Emotions* (2nd ed., pp. 637–653). New York: Guilford Press.

Rozin, P., Lowery, L., Imada, S. and Haidt, J. (1999). The CAD triad hypothesis: A mapping between three moral emotions (contempt, anger, disgust) and three moral codes (community, autonomy, divinity). *Journal of Personality and Social Psychology, 76(4),* 574–586.

Scherer, K. R. and Wallbott, H. G. (1994). Evidence for universality and cultural variation of differential emotion response patterning. *Journal of Personality and Social Psychology, 66(2),* 310–328.

Siefken, S. (1993). The Hispanic perspective on death and dying: A combination of respect, empathy, and spirituality. *Pride Institute Journal of Long Term Home Health Care, 12(2),* 26–28.

Solomon, S., Greenberg, J., Schimel, J., Arndt, J. and Pyszczynski, T. (2004). Human awareness of mortality and the evolution of culture. In Schaller, M., and Crandall, C. S. (Eds.), *The Psychological Foundations of Culture* (pp. 15–40). Mahwah, NJ: Lawrence Erlbaum Associates.

Watson, D., Clark, L. A. and Tellegen, A. (1988). Development and validation of brief measures of positive and negative affect: The PANAS scales. *Journal of Personality and Social Psychology, 54(6),* 1063–1070.

Wronska, J. (1990). Disgust in relation to emotionality, extraversion, psychoticism and imagery abilities. In Drenth, P. J. D., Sergeant, J. A. and Takens, R. J. (Eds.), *European Perspectives in Psychology* (Vol. 1, pp. 125–138). Chichester: Wiley.

DANIEL M. T. FESSLER is a professor of anthropology at the University of California in Los Angeles Center for Behavior, Evolution, and Culture, where he conducts research in biological anthropology, evolutionary psychology, and evolutionary medicine.

C. DAVID NAVARRETE is an assistant professor of psychology at Michigan State University, a research fellow in the MSU Consortium for Multicultural Psychology Research, and a member of the Core Faculty for the MSU Ecology, Evolutionary Biology, and Behavior Program. His research topics include social psychology, moral judgment, evolutionary psychology, and intergroup bias.

EXPLORING THE ISSUE

Is Terror Management Real?

Critical Thinking and Reflection

1. In the second article (the one that went against Terror Management Theory), they argue that by testing two different cultures, their conclusions were stronger than if they had only tested one culture. But are two cultures enough? How many cultures need to be included in order to say that a finding is true across cultures?
2. One of the learning outcomes for this issue was to create your own hypotheses to test an idea within Terror Management Theory. What was your hypothesis, and how could you set up a study that would test this hypothesis?
3. Is it possible that some people dismiss Terror Management Theory simply because it focuses on death, and people don't like to think about their own deaths?
4. Do you, personally, believe that people use culture, religion, or relationships to distract themselves from thinking about death? Do you think you do this yourself?

Is There Common Ground?

The creators of Terror Management Theory would probably be happy to admit that their hypotheses may not apply to every person in every culture; most social psychologists admit that individual differences have an influence on our decisions, life choices, relationships, etc. In addition, people who do not like this theory would probably find it hard not to admit that thoughts of our deaths can make us uncomfortable.

It is reasonable to believe that we all take a moment to reflect on our values and how we want to live our lives, when we are forced to confront mortality after the death of a loved one or even after coming close to death ourselves. It is thus likely that most psychologists would agree with some of the larger ideas within Terror Management Theory, and that disagreements lie in our understanding of the specific details or the degree to which fears of death affect our everyday decisions and lifestyles.

Additional Resources

Kirkpatrick, L. A. (2006). Reports of my death anxiety have been greatly exaggerated: A critique of terror management theory from an evolutionary perspective. *Psychological Inquiry, 17,* 288–298.

Navarrete, D. C., & Fessler, D. M. T. (2005). Normative bias and adaptive challenges: A relational approach to coalitional psychology and a critique of terror management theory. *Evolutionary Psychology, 3,* 297–325.

Pyszczynski, T., Solomon, S., & Greenberg, J. (2003). Terror management theory: An evolutionary existential account of human behavior. In T. Pyszczynski, S. Solomon, & J. Greenberg (Eds.), *In the wake of 9/11: The psychology of terror* (pp. 11–35). Washington, D.C.: American Psychological Association.

Solomon, S., Greenberg, J., Pyszczynski, T. (1991). A terror management theory of social behavior: The psychological functions of self-esteem and cultural worldviews. *Advances in Experimental and Social Psychology, 24,* 93–159.

Internet References . . .

Encyclopedia of Death and Dying

http://www.deathreference.com/

How Stuff Works: Terror Management Theory

http://science.howstuffworks.com/environmental/
green-science/doomsday-scenarios-climate-
change2.htm

Scientific American: Fear, Death, and Politics

http://www.scientificamerican.com/article/fear-
death-and-politics/

Viewzone: What's Behind Beauty?

http://viewzone.com/TMT.html

Selected, Edited, and with Issue Framing Material by:
Wind Goodfriend, *Buena Vista University*

ISSUE

Is Viewing Television Violence Harmful for Children?

YES: Mark Sappenfield, from "Mounting Evidence Links TV Viewing to Violence," *The Christian Science Monitor* (2002)

NO: John Grohol, from "TV, Violence, & Children: More Weak Pediatrics Studies," psychcentral.com (2013)

Learning Outcomes

After reading this issue, you will be able to:

- Identify some of the effects that television viewing is believed to have on children.
- Discuss the reasons why some researchers believe that violence on television is causing an increase in aggressive behaviors in children.
- Discuss the reasons why some researchers believe that television watching has not been studied in the correct way to support the negative effects that are reported.

ISSUE SUMMARY

YES: Mark Sappenfield, writer for *The Christian Science Monitor,* describes a new scientific report that links television viewing with violent behavior, even in adults.

NO: John Grohol, an author, researcher, and expert in mental health online, asserts that the studies that condemn television watching in children fail to consider a myriad of factors involved with children that might also be the cause of negative outcomes.

Almost everyone has access to television (TV). There is hardly any other factor so pervasive in our society as television viewing. What is the relationship of TV viewing to violent acts? Those who believe that TV viewing is the root of all evil support unplugging the "boob tube" and going back to the good old days of reading, listening to the radio, and swapping stories while sitting by the fireplace. At the other end of the continuum, those who argue that TV is merely the next evolution of communication technology would promote going with the flow, grinning and bearing TV for it is surely here to stay, and stop worrying about TV.

There are numerous studies on children who watch violent TV shows, as well as on the amount of TV children watch. Some research suggests that children who spend excessive amounts of time watching TV tend to do poorly in school. Other studies show that children who spend moderate amounts of time in front of the set perform better scholastically than those who watch no TV at all. Children are more likely to be overweight when they watch TV versus playing actively. If children are watching TV to excess, they are not communicating with adults in the family and are not learning family values.

The debate over TV violence rages on. Ask any group of people you meet today about violence in contemporary society. The responses will be remarkably similar. "Violence is in epidemic proportions. There is a lot more violence out on the streets now than when I was a kid. It's just not safe to be out anymore. We live in such violent times." The anecdotes and nostalgia about more peaceful times seem to be endless. The unison in which society decries the rise in violence begins to disintegrate, however, when one attempts to discern causes for the increases in crimes like murder, rape, robbery, and assault.

One segment of society that is regularly targeted as a contributing cause to the rise in violence is the media, particularly TV programming. A common argument is that TV is much too violent, especially in children's programming. It has been suggested, for example, that a child will witness in excess of 100,000 acts of simulated violence depicted on TV before graduating from elementary school! Lower socioeconomic status children may view even more hours of violent TV. Many researchers suggest that this TV violence is at least in part responsible for the climbing rates of violent crime, since children tend to imitate what they observe in life.

On the other side, critics argue that it is not what is on TV that bears responsibility for the surge in violence. Programming is merely reflective of the level of violence in contemporary society. The argument is that while TV watching may be associated with violence, it does not mean that it causes violence. As an example, the critics suggest that we have known for some time that aggressive children tend to watch more aggressive TV programming. However, does the aggression predispose an interest in aggressive programming, or does the programming cause the aggression? This is a question that sparks hotly contested debates.

Those who believe TV viewing is at least partly responsible for aggressive behavior in children want the U.S. Congress to more closely regulate the ratings, viewing times, and amount of violence that can be shown on American TV. Those on the other side of the issue point to the infringement on First Amendment rights of freedom of expression if such intense regulation is imposed on the media.

Other factors that contribute to the issue of TV viewing and violence are the types of programs and commercials that children watch. School-aged children are the most targeted when it comes to advertising. There are more commercial breaks per hour for children's programming than for other types of programs. Additionally, with the widespread access to cable TV, children can watch violent adult programming, many times in unsupervised homes.

Several organizations have emerged to address the issue of TV violence and its effects on society. The Center for Media Literacy provides practical information to children and adults by translating media literacy research and theory into easy-to-read resources. They also provide training and educational tools for teachers, youth leaders, parents, and caregivers of children. The National Institute on Media and the Family sponsors "Media Wise," which educates and informs the public, as well as encourages practices and policies that promote positive change in the production and use of mass media. According to their mission statement, they do not advocate censorship of any kind. They are committed to partnering with parents and other caregivers, organizations, and corporations in using the power of the free market to create healthier media choices for families, so that there are healthier, less violent communities. What should be done to effectively address this problem? Is it realistic to revert back to the days prior to the TV era? Or should we just relax and stop worrying about TV? After all, children are resilient; they can eventually understand TV's impact on their lives just as we adults have. Anyone reading this book grew up with the "magic" box and probably turned out OK.

The two articles that follow are typical of the debate centered around violence and TV as it affects children. In the YES article, Mark Sappenfield describes a study that links violent behavior and television viewing, even among adults. He details the evidence, which he refers to as "overwhelming" that explains how the two are linked. In the NO article, John Grohol identifies aspects of children's lives, such as social support, that are not included in the studies that condemn television watching for children. He argues that there are multiple factors involved in a child's outcome and blaming television solely is simply not justified.

YES

Mark Sappenfield

Mounting Evidence Links TV Viewing to Violence

A new scientific report released today says television can affect violent behavior even among adults.

For much of the past half century, the link between watching violence on television and violent behavior in everyday life has seemed an open question embraced by one study, rejected by another, and largely left unanswered by years of congressional inquiries.

That, however, is rapidly changing. To a growing number of scientists and psychiatrists, the correlation between the two is no longer a point of debate, it is an established fact.

A study released today in the journal *Science* adds to a large body of work that suggests some sort of connection. Already, six major pediatric, psychiatric, and medical associations have said that the evidence of a link is overwhelming, citing more than 1,000 studies in the past 30 years.

As a result, the debate is increasingly splintering into a fight that echoes the recent antitobacco or global-warming campaigns, as a preponderance of scientists square off against a besieged industry and a smattering of contrarian colleagues.

Many Americans are not yet convinced. On average, children still watch three hours of television a day, and calls to regulate the industry have resulted only in minor tweaks like the current ratings system. But with the scientific community presenting a more unified front and casting the issue as one of public health, not taste[,] the pressure for more change is gaining momentum.

"Clearly, with more exposure [to media violence, children] do become desensitized, they do copy what they see, and their values are shaped by it," says Susan Villani, a Baltimore, Md., psychiatrist who has reviewed the past 10 years of study on the subject.

Not even the most ardent critic of TV violence argues that images of gunplay and kung fu are the sole causes of youth violence. Yet they can be significant. One study last year found a 25 percent decrease in violence in a San Jose, Calif., grade school where kids received classroom lessons in media awareness and were asked to watch only seven hours of TV a week for several months. Another in North Carolina showed that teenage boys who regularly watched professional wrestling were 18 percent more likely to get into a physical confrontation with a date.

TV's Effect on Adult Behavior

Today's study, experts say, is particularly interesting for several reasons. It is the first survey of its scope to provide evidence that violent behavior is associated with television viewing beyond childhood well into adolescence and adulthood. In addition, it claims a connection even when other factors such as childhood neglect and low family income are taken into account.

"What this study serves to do is remove some of these variables," says Michael Brody of the American Academy of Child and Adolescent Psychiatry.

Adolescents who watched more than one hour a day of television regardless of content were roughly four times more likely to commit aggressive acts toward other people later in their lives than those who watched less than one hour. Of those who watched more than three hours, 28.8 percent were later involved in assaults, robberies, fights, and other aggressive behavior.

The study, led by Jeffrey Johnson of Columbia University in New York, followed 707 participants in upstate New York for 17 years, recording their TV viewing habits and tracking their behavior through periodic interviews and public documents.

What it did not do, say critics, is prove that the television viewing necessarily caused the violence. The comment goes to the heart of the debate over the issue: Does TV play a part in making violent people, or are violent people naturally inclined to watch violence on TV?

"I don't think there is any link at all," says Jonathan Freedman, a professor at the University of Toronto who disputes the statistic that thousands of studies have shown a link between television violence and violent behavior.

Doubts Within TV Industry

Members of the broadcasting industry share Mr. Freedman's skepticism of such media studies. "They spark a lot of interest, but nothing definite comes out that can establish a direct link," says Dennis Wharton of the National Association of Broadcasters in Washington.

The industry also touts their cleaner fare: A recent study by the Center for Media and Public Affairs in Washington found a 29 percent drop in TV violence last season compared with 1998–99.

Aspects of the criticism find broader support. It's true that some kids might be able to watch TV all day and not commit a single violent act. But some psychiatrists say that merely begs for more research about who might be influenced by TV and how.

But most also insist that the vast majority of studies support a link. Granted, no study can definitively say that TV caused a violent act; it can only infer. But the results of one of the most researched areas in social science are pretty consistent, says professor Craig Anderson of Iowa State University in Ames. "It doesn't matter how you study it, the results are the same," says Mr. Anderson.

Plus, for many, it's simply a matter of common sense. "If television doesn't influence kids, then why are so many people spending so many billions of dollars to advertise," says Dr. Brody. "It's not the sole cause, but even if it represents 10 percent of the reason [for violence], somebody should look at this."

MARK SAPPENFIELD is a staff writer for *The Christian Science Monitor*. Mark joined the *Monitor* in 1996 and has since written from Boston, the San Francisco Bay Area, the Pentagon, and India. In addition to reporting from Pakistan and Afghanistan during his time in South Asia, Mark has also written on issues of sports and science. He has covered five Olympic Games and attended various events at NASA's Jet Propulsion Laboratory, including the landing of the Mars rover Opportunity.

John Grohol

TV, Violence, & Children: More Weak Pediatrics Studies

Did you know that simply watching TV causes harm to children? Well, that's what the American Academy of Pediatrics would have you believe. And yet, here we are in the sixth decade since TV became popular, and we have not yet seen the end of the world based upon multiple generations that grew up with television as a mainstay

The latest issue of *Pediatrics* has two studies—and a bonus editorial!—that suggests television viewing by children is associated with greater criminality and antisocial personality, and that a child's behavior can be modified by simply changing what they're watching.

Pediatrics is the mouthpiece for the American Academy of Pediatrics. And while it's ostensibly an objective, scientific journal, it continually publishes weak research—especially on the effects of TV and children.

Let's check out the latest. . . .

The first study (Robertson, et al., 2013) followed 1,037 New Zealand children over the course of their early lives, from ages 5 to 26. Parents were asked how much time their children spent watching TV, until age 13, when the children themselves were asked directly. Then they looked at some other factors—like criminal convictions, antisocial personality disorder, IQ, and the socio-economic status of the families. Parental control was also measured twice—at ages 7 and 9—by asking the mom about what kinds of rules and procedures were used to run family life.

From this data, the researchers found that those with more criminal convictions or with antisocial personality traits watched significantly more TV as children.

But here's all the things the researchers **did not** measure:

- Social peer network and social support
- Relationships and quality of relationships with friends
- Existence of other mental disorders (because the researchers only focused on antisocial personality disorder)
- Parental marital status

- Parental relationship quality
- Parental role modeling behavior
- History of criminal convictions within the immediate family
- Limited understanding of family dynamics from just two data points, and just from the perspective of the mother
- Religion and moral upbringing
- Amount of time spent in creative play
- Amount of time attending or participating in sports
- And so on . . .

As you can see, the list of alternative explanations for this correlational relationship is *voluminous*. Without controlling for as many variables as possible in a child's environment, **there is no reasonable way you can isolate a single variable.** And without measuring the kinds of things in the list above (among others) you'd have no way to determine if one of those might provide a more reasonable—or at least alternative—explanation.

While two variables can often be associated with one another, an association rarely tells you much. Especially in this case, where the researchers never bothered to ask or measure what type of TV programs the children actually watched. For all we know, they could've all been heavy viewers of *The Waltons*. It seems incomprehensible that in a study that purports to study the importance of TV watching's effects on children such an oversight could've been made.

Only buried at the end of the study do you find this acknowledgment:

As with any observational research, we cannot prove that television viewing causes antisocial behavior, but the study has a number of features that enable us to make causal inferences. . . .

[It] is also possible that other unmeasured factors associated with the milieu in which television viewing occurs may explain the observed relationship.

Yes, of course it may. Which means you can't say anything about causation. So why do they then contradict themselves in the abstract of the study?

The findings are consistent with a causal association and support the American Academy of Pediatrics recommendation that children should watch no more than 1 to 2 hours of television each day.

And people wonder why social scientists often get a bad name in science?

That's Okay, You Can Watch This on TV Instead

But hey, maybe it *does* matter what your child actually watches on TV. Let's look at study 2 (Christakis, et al., 2013):

We devised a media diet intervention wherein parents were assisted in substituting high quality prosocial and educational programming for aggression-laden programming without trying to reduce total screen time. We conducted a randomized controlled trial of 565 parents of preschool-aged children ages 3 to 5 years recruited from community pediatric practices. Outcomes were derived from the Social Competence and Behavior Evaluation at 6 and 12 months.

The researchers found about a 2 point difference in the Social Competence and Behavior Evaluation (SCBE) scale between the two groups. This was a statistically significant difference (in their regression analysis according to the researchers).

However, it was a meaningless difference in the real world. The SCBE is a scale scored from 1 to 6 on 30 questions, resulting in a possible overall score of 180.

After 6 months, the control group scored a 106.38 versus a 108.36 of the intervention group. That's an average change of just two of the 30 questions changing just one point in the positive direction. (A similar point difference was seen at the 1 year followup mark.)

Their original hypothesis was to find a significant change in all the subscales and the overall score of the SCBE—that's four scales:

We hypothesized that the intervention would increase the overall score and each of the 3 subscale scores.

After one year, all they found was a statistically significant change in one subscale score and the overall score. So were the researchers cautiously optimistic in their findings' discussion, considering the tiny increases they found in the intervention group?

We demonstrated that an intervention to modify the viewing habits of preschool-aged children can **significantly enhance** their overall social and emotional competence and that low-income boys may derive the greatest benefit.

Not, "we found support for . . ." or "on one single measure of social and emotional competence. . . ."

The apparent lack of objectivity displayed here is, in my opinion, simply astounding.

Should your child spend 5 hours a day in front of the TV? In general, probably not. Nor should they spend 5 hours a day playing sports, a video game, or eating bananas. This is called "common sense," and no amount of psychological research—good or bad—can infuse it into parents who don't care how they raise their children. Why researchers insist on pursuing this questionable line of inquiry is beyond me.

References

Christaskis, D.A., et al. (2013). Modifying Media Content for Preschool Children: A Randomized Controlled Trial. *Pediatrics.* doi: 10.1542/peds.2012-1493

Robertson, L.A., McAnally, H.M. & Hancox, R.J. (2013). Childhood and Adolescent Television Viewing and Antisocial Behavior in Early Adulthood. *Pediatrics.* doi: 10.1542/peds.2012-158

JOHN GROHOL is the founder and CEO of Psych Central. He is an author, researcher, and expert in mental health online, and has been writing about online behavior, mental health, and psychology issues—as well as the intersection of technology and human behavior—since 1992. Dr. Grohol sits on the editorial board of the journal *Cyberpsychology, Behavior and Social Networking* and is a founding board member and treasurer of the Society for Participatory Medicine.

EXPLORING THE ISSUE

Is Viewing Television Violence Harmful for Children?

Critical Thinking and Reflection

1. Sappenfield asserts throughout his selection that violent television programming increases aggressive behavior. Do you agree with this assertion? Why or why not?
2. Because television is in virtually every household in America, is it reasonable to think that television programs could ever be regulated? Explain your answer.
3. Grohol argues that there are multiple alternative explanations for children's outcomes besides just television viewing. Which of these alternatives do you think contributes the MOST to children's development and why?

Is There Common Ground?

There are numerous studies on children who watch violent television (TV) shows, as well as on the amount of TV children watch. Some research suggests that children who spend excessive amounts of time watching TV tend to do poorly in school. Other studies show that children who spend moderate amounts of time in front of the set perform better scholastically than those who watch no TV at all. Children are more likely to be overweight when they watch TV versus playing actively. If children are watching TV to excess, they are not communicating with adults in the family and are not learning family values. Logically, there must be middle-ground solutions to the issue of children, TV viewing, and violence.

Ideally, society could move past this dichotomy of thinking of TV as simply good or bad. TV viewing could be thought of as an active endeavor rather than a passive one. Parents could become more involved with their children as they watch TV by controlling the amount and type of TV shows their children are watching. Through modeling, parents could teach children to be skeptical about TV advertisements, point out the differences between fantasy and reality, and argue that the moral values being portrayed on the tube are different from values that are important to the parents.

Additional Resources

American Academy of Pediatrics. Smart Guide to Kids Television. Retrieved on April 11, 2011, from www.fcctf.org/pdf%20files/Parenting%20info%20pdfs/Smart%20Guide%20to%20Kids%20TV.pdf

This website provides guidance for parents on how to handle their child(ren)'s television viewing.

KidsHealth. How TV Affects Your Child. Retrieved on April 11, 2011, from http://kidshealth.org/parent/positive/family/tv_affects_child.html

This website discusses the impact that television viewing can have on children.

PBS Parents. Children and Media. Retrieved on April 11, 2011, from www.pbs.org/parents/childrenandmedia/article-faq.html

This website addresses the most common questions that parents of children under 3 have about television viewing.

The University of Maine, Cooperative Extension Publications. Children, Television, and Screen Time. Retrieved on April 11, 2011, from http://umaine.edu/publications/4100e/

This website discusses the impact that television viewing can have on children, in addition to suggestions for what parents can do and alternatives to television viewing.

Internet References . . .

Action for Healthy Kids

> http://www.actionforhealthykids.org

Family: Single Parenting

> www.ivillage.com/parenting
> /search?q=single+parenting

National Institute on Out-of-School Time

> www.niost.org

Selected, Edited, and with Issue Framing Material by:
Wind Goodfriend, *Buena Vista University*

ISSUE

Is High Self-Esteem Really Beneficial?

YES: Sarah E. Lowery et al. from "Body Image, Self-Esteem, and Health-Related Behaviors Among Male and Female First Year College Students," *Journal of College Student Development* (2005)

NO: Jennifer Crocker and Lora E. Park, from "The Costly Pursuit of Self-Esteem," *Psychological Bulletin* (2004)

Learning Outcomes

After reading this issue, you will be able to:

- Define self-esteem and explain at least one way to measure it in a research study.
- List at least two concepts that are associated with low self-esteem and explain why some psychologists believe low self-esteem can be harmful.
- List at least two concepts that are associated with high self-esteem and explain why some psychologists believe that high self-esteem can be harmful.

ISSUE SUMMARY

YES: This team of health and counseling psychologists argues that positive self-esteem in college students predicts better body image, fitness, and other health-related behaviors.

NO: Researchers Crocker and Park believe that while high self-esteem leads to short-term gratification, it also leads to long-term negative effects, including poor self-regulation and poor mental and physical health.

Social psychology's range of topics is quite broad, including both explicitly concrete ideas such as discriminatory behaviors and extremely abstract concepts such as managing existential terror related to mortality. One of the field's more abstract concepts is covered in this controversy, which focuses on "the self."

Perhaps the most popular perspective from which to view and study the self is to focus on self-esteem. Thousands of articles, book chapters, and entire books have been published on the topic of self-esteem, and empirical measures of self-esteem count as some of the most popular scales in psychological research. A quick search of the term "self-esteem" on Amazon.com website reveals over 100,000 books are available on the subject.

For the past few decades, improving the next generation's self-esteem has been a focus of government programs, counseling, parenting programs, school interventions, and more. We have seen trends change in how children are treated in everyday settings such as gymnastics schools or martial arts studios, when every child who participates receives a certificate, ribbon, or even a trophy, just for participation. The goal of this shift seems to be a noble one: to ensure that every child—and, later, adult—feels confident and proud.

However, our culture has also experienced a split in people's views regarding how far parents, teachers, and counselors should go with these messages. This discrepancy of opinion can be found very quickly in any brief investigation into literature on self-esteem. For example, the popular website Psychology Today offers definitions of basic psychological concepts, and this is what they say about self-esteem:

> Possessing little self-regard can lead people to become depressed, to fall short of their potential, or to tolerate abusive situations and relationships. Too much self-love, on the other hand, results in an off-putting sense of entitlement and an inability to learn from failures. (It can also be a sign of clinical narcissism.) Perhaps no other self-help topic has spawned so much advice and so many (often conflicting) theories. Here are our best insights on how to strike a balance between accurate self-knowledge and respect for who you are.

Thus, even a website that's supposed to simply define the concept of self-esteem immediately focuses on the clashing views presented (at least in part) in the next two articles. In the "yes" article, written by a team of counseling and health psychologists, Sarah Lowery and her colleagues present original data focused on self-esteem in college students. They are specifically interested in how self-esteem is predictive of body image and health-related behaviors and experiences, such as stress, anxiety, eating choices, exercise, and the use of drugs/alcohol. They use a sample of over 400 first-year college students at a large university. Their findings indicate that for men, lower self-esteem is related to higher "body shame," which they define as "the degree to which the person has internalized cultural standards of body image that are virtually impossible for many and the shame that is experienced when these standards are not met."

For women, Lowery and her colleagues also find that lower self-esteem is also related to higher body shame, and that lower self-esteem is also correlated with more body surveillance (thinking about how other people view your body), discrepancy between one's current self and one's ideal self, and physical dissatisfaction. In general, higher self-esteem was related to better health behaviors for both men and women. Positive self-esteem thus seems very useful toward making people happier and healthier.

However, there is a powerful group of psychologists, educators, etc. who are concerned about the constant validation some people receive. The worry is that if one always wins a trophy, do things like pride, discipline, responsibility, and healthy competition get lost along the way? Is high self-esteem the same as arrogance or narcissism? While hundreds of studies provide evidence that positive views of the self are desirable, there are also hundreds of studies that warn against inflated self-esteem.

On the "no" side of this issue, professors Jennifer Crocker and Lora Park clearly argue that the relentless pursuit of high self-esteem may actually be more harmful than helpful. Near the beginning of their article, they write:

> Researchers have argued that the objective benefits of high self-esteem are small and limited. For example, a recent and extensive review concluded that high self-esteem produces pleasant feelings and enhanced initiative but does not cause high academic achievement, good job performance, or leadership, nor does low self-esteem cause violence, smoking, drinking, taking drugs, or becoming sexually active at an early age.

Thus, they directly disagree with the "yes" article's claims that high self-esteem is positively correlated to health behaviors (or, at least, some health behaviors). Of course, if high self-esteem simply produced *no* effects, it would not be harmful; it would simply be neutral. In order to claim that high self-esteem is *harmful,* they must produce more evidence. This article thus presents a thorough and detailed review of empirical research done by other scientists about how high self-esteem is tied to a wide variety of negative outcomes, including costs to autonomy, academic learning, and relationships. Importantly, they also include two sections about mental and physical health (again, going directly against the "yes" article).

It may be difficult to believe that lower self-esteem would really benefit the next generation of children. On the other hand, if the issue is framed in another way, it is easier to believe that a generation of entitled narcissists would be both unpleasant and even potentially dangerous. Is it possible that both sides of this argument are correct?

YES ↵

Sarah E. Lowery et al.

Body Image, Self-Esteem, and Health-Related Behaviors Among Male and Female First Year College Students

For women, being beautiful is important for social success. This may be especially true on college campuses where people are rapidly assessed for physical attractiveness (Pipher, 1994). Although the idealized standard for feminine beauty demands that women be thin (Cash & Green, 1986; Garner, Garfinkel, Schwartz, & Thompson, 1980), men typically have been exempt from this standard (Adame & Frank, 1990). However, cultural pressure for men to conform to a thin and muscular ideal has intensified since the 1970s (Lien, Pope, & Gray, 2001), and men are increasingly dissatisfied with their bodies (Cash, Winstead, & Janda, 1986) and want to lose weight or increase muscle tone (McCabe & Ricciardelli, 2004).

In 1950, Schilder described body image as "the picture of our own body which we form in our mind . . . [it is] the way in which the body appears to ourselves" (p. 11). More recently, the term body image has been used to reflect one's ability to regard parts of one's body as belonging to the self or to define the boundaries of one's own body (Thompson, 1990) and one's subjective, mental representation of his or her physical appearance. Body image is constructed from self-observation, the reactions of others, and a complicated interaction of attitudes, emotions, memories, fantasies, and experience, both conscious and unconscious. Grogan (1999) described body image as "a person's perceptions, thoughts and feelings about his or her body" and as "subjective and open to change through social influence" (pp. 1–2)

While there are various conceptualizations of body image, few would deny its importance and its link to well being. Research data indicate that body image dissatisfaction, often called body image disturbance (Thompson, 1990), has become more prevalent since the 1980s and has been associated with incidences of depression (Denniston, Roth, & Gilroy, 1992), heightened anxiety, and lowered

self-esteem (Thompson & Altabe, 1991), as well as the development of maladaptive eating behaviors and dieting (Cooley & Toray, 2001).

Dissatisfaction with one's body has become "a normative discontent" (Thompson, 1990) in today's culture and is closely related to a drive for thinness (Cooley & Toray, 2001). The inability to shed unwanted pounds can have a drastic effect on overall mood and self-confidence. Body image dissatisfaction, weight concerns, eating problems, and physical attractiveness have become especially significant issues on college campuses (Harris, 1995; Mintz & Betz, 1988), with up to 90% of college students reporting that they worry about body image (Delene & Brogowicz, 1990).

Historically, there have been sex differences in body image. In two large national surveys, women have reported greater body dissatisfaction than have men (Cash & Henry, 1995; Garner, 1997). Across all ages, women have reported being more concerned with body weight and appearance (Pliner, Chaiken & Flett, 1990). Moreover, women report experiencing more negative feelings when they are attentive to their bodies than do men (Franzoi, Kessenich, & Sugrue, 1989), they have a greater discrepancy between their ideal and actual body figures (Rozin & Fallon, 1998), and they tend to perceive themselves as larger or heavier than they actually are (Cash & Green, 1986). Adame and Frank (1990) found that among normal weight women (women who are neither medically underweight nor overweight), 61% perceived themselves to be overweight. In contrast, men, regardless of their actual weight, usually report more positive body images than do women (Demarest & Langer, 1996). Women tend to "feel" overweight much more than do men (Tiggemann, 1992), and men appear to be less obsessed with weight and becoming fat; therefore, pathogenic values related to eating and body size is lower among men (Akande, 1993).

From Lowery, Sarah E.; Robinson Kurplus, Sharon E.; Befort, C.; Blanks, Elva H.; Sollenberger, Sonja; Nicpon, Megan F.; Huser, L., "Body Image, Self-Esteem, and Health-Related Behaviors Among Male and Female First Year College Students," *Journal of College Student Development*, vol. 46, no. 6, pp. 612–623, November/December 2005. Published by The Johns Hopkins University Press.

It is evident that potential sex differences need to be considered when doing research on body image.

Another variable that needs to be considered is self-esteem, defined as liking and respecting oneself (Crandall, 1973). According to Rosenberg, Schooler, Schoenberg, and Rosenberg (1995), domain-specific self-esteem, or elements of self-esteem related to different self-perceptions, explains behavior. Franzoi and Shields (1984) suggested that physical self-worth is a component of self-esteem that relates to constructs such as perceived sport competence, physical condition, attractiveness, and weight concern. As an aspect of physical self-worth, body image dissatisfaction is related to global self-esteem. Indeed, the association between body image dissatisfaction and self-esteem has been well established (Harris, 1995; Stowers & Durm, 1996).

Given that women are biologically predisposed to have a higher percentage of body fat and that the standard of thinness is more extreme for women than for men (Rodin, Silberstein, & Striegel-Moore, 1984), it is reasonable to expect a stronger relationship between body image dissatisfaction and self-esteem for women. In fact, Kostanski and Gullone (1998) found that being female and having low self-esteem was most predictive of body image dissatisfaction for participants with healthy body weight. For college women, the pressure to achieve high standards of thinness and attractiveness in a competitive college environment is related to lower self-esteem (Harris, 1995; Mintz & Betz, 1988). These findings suggest that researchers need to examine the interactions of sex, body image, and self-esteem. It is also important to explore behaviors that may be linked to body image and self-esteem, such as exercise and other health behaviors.

In 2001, Parsons and Betz called for research on the interaction of physical exercise and body image. The literature on body image and exercise reveals some unexpected associations. For example, although women who exercise are generally leaner, they exhibit similar or even greater degrees of body dissatisfaction than women who do not exercise (Davis & Cowles, 1991). In addition, the degree to which women regularly exercise appears to influence their preoccupation with losing weight and dissatisfaction with their physiques (Kennedy & Reis, 1995).

McDonald and Thompson (1992) examined reasons for exercising and found that women exercised for more weight-related reasons than did men. In both males and females, exercising for weight, tone, and physical attractiveness was positively associated with body image dissatisfaction, while exercising for health, enjoyment, and fitness was negatively related to body image dissatisfaction. Studying men and women who identified them-

selves as regular exercisers, Davis and Cowles (1991) found that men and women were equally dissatisfied with their weights; however, women wanted to lose weight while men were divided between those with a desire to lose weight and those who wanted to gain weight. Women were more dissatisfied with their bodies and were more likely to exercise to try to lose weight as compared to men. Thus, the motives for exercising may moderate how body image is affected by exercise participation.

Purpose of This Study

This study examined the relationships among self-esteem, body image, exercise, and other health-related behaviors in first-year male and female college students. This study contributes to the literature by (a) examining whether sex differences in body image are still pronounced given more recent evidence that men may be experiencing increasing body dissatisfaction, (b) examining college students' health-related behaviors in relationship to body image and self-esteem, and (c) examining whether regular exercise is associated with more positive body image and higher self-esteem for men and women. Four hypotheses were posed:

H1. Male students will have a more positive body image than will female students.

H2. Self-esteem will be negatively related to body image dissatisfaction for both women and men.

H3. Men who regularly exercise will have higher self-esteem and a more positive body image than will women who regularly exercise; however, there will be no differences between women who regularly exercise and those who do not.

H4. Students with more positive health-related behaviors and attitudes will have higher self-esteem and a more positive body image.

Method

Participants

Participants were 433 first year college students enrolled in a three-credit semester-long course designed to help ease their transition to a large, southwestern, Research I university. Among the 267 female and 156 male participants, 327 were Euro-American, 40 Latino, 18 African American, 16 Asian American, 8 International Students, 4 Native American, and 4 classified as "Other." This sample represents approximately 10 percent of the incoming freshman class and also reflects the racial/ethnic diversity at this university. Age ranged from 17 to 32 with a mean age of 18.42 years ($SD = 1.32$).

Procedures

Course instructors were contacted to request their permission to administer the survey during their class time. Approximately mid-semester, graduate students or counseling psychology faculty distributed survey packets in 23 classes. Students were informed that their participation was voluntary and that their grades would not be affected if they elected not to participate. Of the students who were present on the day the survey was administered, approximately 90 percent completed the survey packet. The survey took approximately 30 to 40 minutes to complete. The few students who were unable to complete the surveys during the allotted class time were allowed to return it to their instructors during the following class period.

Instrumentation

In addition to the demographic sheet, the measures used to assess the study constructs were: the Objectified Body Consciousness Scale (McKinley & Hyde, 1996); the Weight and Appearance Visual Analogue Scales (Heinberg & Thompson, 1995); the Contour Drawing Rating Scale (Thompson & Gray, 1995); the Rosenberg Self Esteem Scale (Rosenberg, 1965); and measures of health-related behaviors.

The Objectified Body Consciousness Scale (OBC). The OBC is a measure of aspects of body image related to viewing one's own body as an object "to be looked at" (McKinley & Hyde, 1996). Using factor analysis, the authors formed three 8-item scales: body surveillance, body control, and body shame. Each item is rated on a seven-point Likert-type scale ranging from *strongly disagree* to *strongly agree.* Body surveillance refers to constant self-surveillance, seeing one's body as others see it. For women, it is linked theoretically to the sociocultural construction of the female body as an object of male desire. An example of an item from the body surveillance scale is: "I often worry about how I look to other people." Body control refers to the assumption that people are responsible for how their bodies look and that they can control their weight and appearance with enough effort. A sample item for body control subscale is: "I can weigh what I'm supposed to when I try hard enough." The third scale, body shame, reflects the degree to which the person has internalized cultural standards of body image that are virtually impossible for many and the shame that is experienced when these standards are not met. A sample item from the body shame scale is: "When I'm not the size I think I should be

I feel ashamed." Higher total scores on each factor reflect a greater prevalence of body surveillance, body control, or body shame.

McKinley and Hyde (1996) reported Cronbach's alpha internal consistencies ranging from .76 to .89 for body surveillance, .68 to .76 for body control, and .70 to .84 for body shame and 2-week test-retest reliabilities of .79 for body surveillance, .73 for body control, and .79 for body shame. Significant negative correlations were found between the Body Esteem Scales (Franzoi & Shields, 1984) and both body surveillance ($r = -.39$) and body shame ($r = -.51$). When correlated with the Self-Consciousness Scales, body surveillance correlated strongly with public self-consciousness ($r = .73$). For this study, the Cronbach's alphas were .77 for body surveillance, .82 for body shame, and .66 for body control.

Weight and Appearance Visual Analogue Scales. These scales consist of two visual analogues, each 100 millimeters long and anchored by *no dissatisfaction* and *extreme dissatisfaction* (Heinberg & Thompson, 1995). The two analogues measure weight/size dissatisfaction and overall appearance dissatisfaction. Participants put an X on each line that corresponds to their level of dissatisfaction. Scores are measured with a metric ruler, and higher scores represent greater dissatisfaction. Heinberg and Thompson examined the construct validity of the Weight and Appearance Visual Analogue Scales by correlating them with the Eating Disorders Inventory-Body Dissatisfaction subscale (EDI-BD; Garner, 1997). Both the Visual Analogue Scales correlated significantly with the EDI-BD. Because the two Visual Analogue Scales shared 65% of common variance, Heinberg and Thompson suggested combining the two scales into a single measure of body dissatisfaction. In this study, the two Visual Analogue Scales, which correlated at .76 ($p = .001$), were averaged to comprise a measure of physical dissatisfaction that could range from zero to 100.

Contour Drawing Rating Scale. This scale (Thompson & Gray, 1995) consists of nine male and nine female contour drawings of graduated sizes. Men responded to the male figures, and women responded to the female figures. Participants checked the figure that reflected their current figure and circled the figure that reflected their ideal figure. The discrepancy between the current and ideal selections represents a measure of self-ideal discrepancy in body image. Thompson and Gray reported a one-week test-retest reliability of .78 with college-aged women. Validity was established by having college students order the drawings from thinnest to heaviest and indicate the drawings they believed to be anorexic or obese. Ninety-five percent of the students gave the correct ordering.

Rosenberg Self-Esteem Scale. This 10-item scale was utilized to measure overall self-esteem (Rosenberg, 1965). Items are rated from *strongly disagree* (1) *to strongly agree* (4). A sample item is: "I take a positive attitude toward myself." Five items that are negatively worded were recoded so that higher scores reflected more positive self-esteem. Total scores can range from 10 to 40. Rosenberg (1979) reported test-retest reliabilities ranging from .80 to .85. Convergent validity has been established with high correlation with the Coopersmith Self Esteem Inventory and with peer ratings of self-esteem (Demo, 1985). For this study's sample, the Cronbach's alpha was .79.

Health-Related Behaviors. The 15 items used to assess health-related behaviors were adopted from a wellness survey that was used by the university Student Health Center. These items asked about stress, tension and anxiety, eating behaviors, use of drugs/alcohol, and exercise behaviors. Having a four-point response format, a typical item was "I know of several ways to relax my body without using drugs or alcohol" (responses range from *completely disagree* to *completely agree*). Items were scored so that more healthy responses were awarded higher numbers. Responses across the 15 items were summed so that total possible scores could range from 15 to 60. The Cronbach's alpha for item responses for this study sample was .80.

Results

Prior to analyzing the hypotheses, the correlations among the five body image variables (body surveillance, body shame, body control, physical dissatisfaction, and self-ideal discrepancy) were examined. Of the 10 correlations, 8 were significant at a probability level of .01. Therefore, multivariate procedures were utilized to examine the hypotheses predicting group differences.

The first hypothesis predicted that male college students would have a more positive body image than would female college students. To test for differences between men and women on body image, a multivariate analysis of variance (MANOVA) was conducted with the five body image scales. The Hotelling's Trace was significant, $F(5, 244) = 8.16, p < .001$. Follow-up analyses of variance (ANOVAs) revealed that there were sex differences in four out of the five measures of body image, including body surveillance, body shame, self-ideal discrepancy, and physical dissatisfaction (see Table 1 for descriptive statistics). Compared to men, women reported more body surveillance, greater body shame, greater discrepancy between their ideal and real body figures, and more dissatisfaction with their weight and physical appearance.

Table 1

Means and Standard Deviations for Body Image Across Men and Women

Body Image	Men		Women	
	M	SD	M	SD
Body Surveillance	33.83	8.23	37.80	8.61
Body Control	36.94	7.92	36.35	6.55
Body Shame	22.78	8.57	27.07	9.89
Physical Dissatisfaction	67.34	46.72	89.60	47.81
Self-Ideal Discrepancy	−0.11	1.32	1.02	1.31

The second hypothesis predicted that self-esteem would be negatively related to body image dissatisfaction for both women and men. The family-wise error rate was set at .05 for each set of correlations to help control for Type I error. For men, lower self-esteem was significantly related to higher body shame ($r = -.21, p < .01$). For women, lower self-esteem was related to more body image dissatisfaction on four out of five measures: body surveillance ($r = -.30, p < .001$), body shame ($r = -.40, p < .001$), self-ideal discrepancy ($r = -.24, p < .001$), and physical dissatisfaction ($r = -.36, p < .001$).

The third hypothesis predicted that men who regularly exercised would have higher self-esteem and a more positive body image than would women who regularly exercised, but that there would be no differences between women who exercised and women who did not. First, participants were categorized by consistency of exercising. Those who reported that they exercised not at all or very little were grouped together to form the non-exercise group (men, $n = 56$; women, $n = 111$). Those who reported that they consistently or very consistently exercised were grouped together to form the regularly exercise group (men, $n = 53$; women, $n = 84$). The MANOVA comparing men and women who regularly exercised on body image and self-esteem revealed significant differences, $F(6, 84) = 5.85, p < .001$. Follow-up ANOVAs indicated that men and women in the regularly exercise group were different in body surveillance, $F(1, 89) = 4.02, p < .05$, and in the self-ideal discrepancy, $F(1, 89) = 31.39, p < .001$. For both of these body image measures, women reported more negative body image. When women who regularly exercised and women who did not exercise were compared, no differences between these two groups of women were found for the five body image measures and self-esteem, $F(6, 116) = 1.53, p = .17$. Although not hypothesized, there were no differences between men who exercised consistently and those who did not on body image ($p < .41$). Descriptive statistics are presented in Table 2.

Table 2

Descriptive Statistics for Body Image Across Sex and Exercise Condition

Body Image		Men		Women	
		Non-Exercise	Exercise	Non-Exercise	Exercise
Surveillance	M	34.06	32.35	38.97	36.42
	SD	7.80	9.80	8.18	9.09
Control	M	37.17	36.43	35.74	36.78
	SD	7.64	8.89	6.45	6.96
Shame	M	22.20	23.59	26.78	26.09
	SD	10.06	7.48	9.64	10.04
SID	M	0.06	−0.35	1.00	1.14
	SD	1.59	1.13	1.59	1.29
Physical Dissatisfaction	M	69.00	64.94	94.27	78.21
	SD	47.78	46.43	45.87	46.69

The final hypothesis predicted that students with more positive health-related behaviors would have higher self-esteem and a more positive body image. Since sex differences were found between men and women in body image, men and women were analyzed separately in correlational analyses (see Table 3). When the inter-relationships among body image, self-esteem, and health-related behaviors for men were examined, health-related behaviors were positively correlated with self-esteem ($r = .26$, $p < .01$) and with body control ($r = .17$, $p < .05$) and were negatively related to body surveillance ($r = −.42$, $p < .001$), body shame ($r = −.46$, $p < .001$), and physical dissatisfaction ($r = −.34$, $p < .001$). For women, health-related behaviors were positively correlated with self-esteem ($r = .46$, $p < .001$) and to body control ($r = .17$, $p < .01$) and negatively related to body surveillance ($r = −.48$, $p < .001$), body shame ($r = −.64$, $p < .001$), self-ideal discrepancy ($r = −.34$, $p < .001$), and to physical dissatisfaction ($r = −.54$, $p < .001$).

Table 3

Correlations Among Health-Related Behaviors, Self-Esteem, and Body Image for Men and Women

	Health-Related Behaviors	
	Men	Women
Self-Esteem	0.26**	0.46***
Body Surveillance	−0.42***	−0.48***
Body Control	0.17*	0.17**
Body Shame	−0.46***	−0.64***
Self-Ideal Discrepancy	−0.31	−0.34***
Physical Dissatisfaction	−0.34***	−0.54***

*$p < 0.05$. **$p < 0.01$. ***$p < 0.001$.

Discussion

As Thompson (1990) noted, body image dissatisfaction is a normative discontent within Western society, particularly among college women, And, as recently as 2001, researchers called for investigations of the interaction of physical exercise and body image. In response to these concerns, this study explored the relationships among body image, self-esteem, and the health-related behaviors of first year college students.

As predicted and consistent with several studies (Cash & Henry, 1995; Demarest & Allen, 2000; Garner, 1997; Wade & Cooper, 1998), men exhibited more positive body images than did women. Sex differences in acceptable body size may be influenced by societal definitions of appropriate and attractive shapes for men and for women (Wright & Whitehead, 1987). There has been criticism of Western society for its emphasis on a slender female physique and negative stereotyping of obese figures (Lake, Staiger, & Glowinski, 2000). Tiggemann and Rothblum (1998) have suggested that the prominence given to weight and physique has resulted in mass dissatisfaction with body shape in the female population. Constant exposure to unrealistic "ideal" images through television, music videos, movies, and magazines seems to add to women's struggle to be perfect and their dissatisfaction with current bodies. As society moves toward the inclusion and objectification of men in the realm of media, there may also be a movement toward more dissatisfaction and body image disturbance in men (Cash, Winstead, & Janda, 1986). Indeed, the negative relationship between self-esteem and body shame for men in this study and reported by Thompson and Altabe (1991) provides support for this change.

The body image measures significantly correlated with self-esteem for women. For women, lower self-esteem scores were mirrored by reports of watching their bodies as an onlooker (body surveillance), having greater discrepancy between their current and ideal body figures, having greater overall physical dissatisfaction, and feeling bad because of their bodies (body shame). These results support Stowers and Durm's (1996) findings that physical self-worth is significantly related to overall self-esteem. Interestingly, the body control variable was not related to self-esteem. These young women viewed body control as positive and believed that if they controlled their weight and appearance, this was a good thing. They did not, however, link body control with their feelings of self-worth.

In contrast, only one aspect of the body image was significantly correlated with self-esteem for men. Feeling body shame, reflected in questions such as, "I would be ashamed for people to know what I really weigh," was significantly related to self-esteem. The more their body shame, the lower their self-esteem. Four components of body image were not related to self-esteem. It appears that for the men in this study, self-esteem is not as intertwined with their body image as it is for women. These men were generally satisfied with their physical appearance, having very little discrepancy between their real and ideal bodies. This finding is similar to that of Demarest and Allen's (2000) who reported that men are generally satisfied with their own shapes. Unlike the women, the men in this study were not particularly concerned about how others viewed their bodies. One aspect of body image became important only when fitness behaviors were examined.

When only the men and women who reported that they exercised regularly were compared, women still exhibited a more negative body image, particularly body surveillance and self-ideal discrepancy. In addition, women who regularly exercised did not have a more positive body image than women who did not regularly exercise. It is possible that women who exercise regularly may be working out primarily to feel more physically attractive and to increase their perceptions of others viewing their bodies more positively, however, exercising does not appear to make them feel any better about their bodies. While men probably work out for similar reasons stemming from the desire to be physically attractive, they are not faced with the extensive physical ideals of thinness that women must endure. For women, working out may be one piece of a long list of restrictions that may include dieting, avoiding certain foods, and avoiding certain types of clothing. With all the restrictions, being physically active may seem like just one more punishment for not being thin enough. This conclusion is supported by McDonald and Thompson (1992) who

reported that women exercised for more weight-related reasons than did men. Similarly, Parsons and Betz (2001) examined the relationship of participation in sports and physical activity with body objectification (as measured by the OBC) for women and found that the variable most consistently related to sports and physical activity was body shame, the degree of potential shame if one does not fulfill cultural expectations for the female body.

In contrast, it may be that men who exercise are trying to gain weight and be more muscular. With the emphasis on becoming larger, working out may be less of a punishment and more of confidence building experience. Unlike the women who are trying to make themselves smaller and less noticeable (in order to be noticed), men are working to become larger, more prominent, and to remain healthy. Conversely, women, instead of congratulating themselves for working to stay physically healthy, often think that they should still be thinner and that if they exercised just a few hours more per week they could attain the physical ideal they so desire and be noticed more positively by others.

All women, whether or not they regularly exercise, still struggled with body image concerns. In addition, regular exercise did not correlate with higher self-esteem in this sample of women. However, self-esteem was positively related to health-related behaviors in general. The more positive their health-related behaviors, the higher their self-esteem and their body control. This relationship was also found for men. When these students were taking care of themselves, both physically and psychologically, they felt better about themselves as people and believed they were exerting appropriate control over their bodies.

It was surprising that for both men and women, stronger beliefs in personal control over one's appearance were related to higher self-esteem and positive health behaviors. The body control scale was designed to reflect an internalized cultural ideal by measuring the extent to which a person believes that she or he can look thin and attractive with enough effort. In this study, however, participants' responses to statements such as "A large part of being in shape is having that kind of body in the first place," and "I can weigh what I'm supposed to when I try hard enough" indicated a positive view of control, as it was associated with a higher self-esteem and more positive physical behaviors for both men and women. Perhaps the extreme focus on the positive aspects of being in control in this society influenced their responses. They may have overlooked the physical and social implications of the phrase "supposed to" and thought that it would be best to fit themselves into a mold. Students may also have viewed some of the statements suggesting that they may not have power to change their bodies, due to reasons such as heredity, as negative due to the lack of control implied. Further understanding of how control beliefs influence body image is vital to understanding factors that influence body image dissatisfaction and more severe problems such as eating disturbance.

In contrast, better health-related behaviors were negatively related to body surveillance, body shame, and physical dissatisfaction for both men and women. In addition, health-related behaviors were also negatively related to self-ideal discrepancy for women. It should be noted that there was very little variance in the self-ideal discrepancy scores for men, indicating that they saw little difference between their real and ideal bodies.

Despite changes in the way men are presented in the media, this research indicates that there continue to be significant differences in how men and women perceive their bodies. Men consistently exhibit more positive body image, even when exercise is taken into account, than do women. Despite exercise patterns, body image dissatisfaction is rampant among young women. Even women who exercise report body image dissatisfaction similar to those who do not exercise. Finally, a hopeful aspect of the study is that students with more positive health-related behaviors had higher self-esteem.

There were some limitations to this study that need to be noted. The most prominent is the limited ethnic diversity. The sample consisted of predominately Euro-American women and men with an average age of 18 who presumably just graduated from high school. Thus, these findings are only generalizable to a similar sample of first year college students. Future studies that include more ethnic/racial minority men and women and upper level students are needed. Also, the study was conducted at a large southwestern university where the temperate climate may have influenced students' responses about body image. The year-round warm temperature impacts amount and choice of clothing, which may have served as an added pressure for women to be thin. Finally, this was a cross-sectional survey design, and causality between health-related behaviors, body image, and self-esteem cannot be determined.

Body image dissatisfaction is undoubtedly a central issue for young women and may be becoming one for young men. College personnel working with this population need to consider that, despite the fact that body image dissatisfaction will not likely be the reason a student seeks out counseling, it may be impacting their presenting problem and overall self-concept or self-esteem

(Befort et al., 2001). Future work is needed in the creation of helpful student interventions for body image disturbance. Programs that focus on positive health behaviors may help influence higher self-esteem and subsequently a more positive body image. Such programs may include positive media messages about healthy body acceptance, education to increase students' awareness of the negative and often subtle influence of the thin ideal (e.g., a campus based program such as Body Pride Week), and peer support programs that encourage students to focus foremost on making healthy choices.

References

Adame, D., & Frank, R. E. (1990). The relationship of self-perceived weight to actual weight, body image, and health behaviors of college freshmen. *Wellness Perspectives, 7*, 31–41.

Akande, A. (1993). Sex difference in preferences for ideal female body shape. *Health Care for Women International, 14*, 249–259.

Befort, C., Robinson Kurpius, S. E., Hull-Blanks, E., Foley Nicpon, M., Huser, L. L., & Sollenberger, S. (2001). Body image, self-esteem, and weight-related criticism from romantic partners, *Journal of College Student Development, 42*, 407–419.

Cash, T. F., & Green, G. K. (1986). Body weight and body image among college women: Perception, cognition, and affect. *Journal of Personality Assessment, 50*, 290–301.

Cash, F., & Henry, E. (1995). Women's body images: The results of a national survey in the USA. *Sex Roles, 33*, 19–28.

Cash, T. F., Winstead, B. A., & Janda, L. H. (1986). Body Image Survey Report: The great American shape-up. *Psychology Today, 20*, 30–37.

Cooley, E., & Toray, T. (2001). Body image and personality predictors of eating disorder symptoms during the college years. *International Journal of Eating Disorders, 30*, 28–36.

Crandall, J. E. (1973). Sex differences in extreme response style: Differences in frequency of use of extreme positive and negative ratings. *Journal of Social Psychology, 89*, 281–293.

Davis, C., & Cowles, M. (1991) Body image and exercise: A study of relationships and comparisons between physically active men and women. *Sex Roles, 25*, 33–44.

Delene, L., & Brogowicz, A. (1990). Student health care needs, attitudes, and behavior: Marketing implication for college health centers. *Journal of American College Health, 38,* 157–164.

Demarest, J., & Allen, R. (2000). Body image: Gender, ethnic, and age differences. *Journal of Social Psychology, 140,* 465–473.

Demarest, J., & Langer, E. (1996). Perception of body shape by underweight, average and overweight men and women. *Perceptual and Motor Skills, 83,* 569–570.

Demo, D. H. (1985). The measurement of self-esteem: Refining our methods. *Journal of Personality and Social Psychology, 48,* 1490–1502.

Denniston, C., Roth, D., & Gilroy, F. (1992). Dysphoria and body image among college women. *International Journal of Eating Disorders, 12,* 449–452.

Franzoi, S. L., Kessenich, J. L., & Sugrue, P. A. (1989). Gender differences in the experience of body awareness: An experimental sampling study. *Sex Roles, 21,* 499–515.

Franzoi, S. L., & Shields, S. (1984). Body Esteem Scale: Multidimensional structure and sex differences in college population. *Journal of Personality Assessment, 48,* 173–178.

Garner, D. M. (1997). The 1997 body image survey results. *Psychology Today, 30,* 30–44.

Garner, D. M., Garfinkel, P. E., Schwartz, D., & Thompson, M. (1980). Cultural expectations of thinness in women. *Psychological Reports, 47,* 483–491.

Grogan, S. (1999). *Body image: Understanding body dissatisfaction in men, women and children.* Routledge: London.

Harris, S. (1995). Body image attitudes and the psychosocial development of college women. *Journal of Psychology, 129,* 315–330.

Heinberg, L. J., & Thompson, J. K. (1995). Body image and televised images of thinness and attractiveness. *Journal of Social and Clinical Psychology, 14,* 325–338.

Kennedy, C., & Reis, J. (1995). A comparison of body image perceptions of exercising and non-exercising college students. *Wellness Perspectives, 11,* 3–16.

Kostanski, M., & Gullone, E. (1998). Adolescent body image dissatisfaction: Relationship with self esteem, anxiety, and depression controlling for body mass. *Journal of Child Psychology and Psychiatry, 39,* 255–262.

Lake, A. J., Staiger, P. K., & Glowinski, H. (2000). Effect of western culture on women's attitudes to eating and perceptions of body shape. *International Journal of Eating Disorders, 27,* 83–89.

Lien, A., Pope, H. G., & Gray, J. J. (2001). Cultural expectations of muscularity in men: The evolution of playgirl centerfolds. *International Journal of Eating Disorders, 29,* 90–93.

McCabe, M. P., & Ricciardelli, L. A. (2004). Body image dissatisfaction among males across the lifespan: A review of past literature. *Journal of Psychosomatic Research, 56,* 675–685.

McDonald, K., & Thompson, J. K. (1992). Eating disturbance, body image dissatisfaction, and reasons for exercising: Gender differences and correlational findings, *International Journal of Eating Disorders, 11,* 289–292.

McKinley, N. M., & Hyde, J. S. (1996). The objectified body consciousness scale: Development and validation. *Psychology of Women Quarterly, 20,* 181–215.

Mintz, L., & Betz, N. (1988). Prevalence and correlates of eating disordered behaviors among undergraduate women. *Journal of Counseling Psychology, 35,* 463–471.

Parsons, E. M., & Betz, N. E. (2001). The relationship of participation in sports and physical activity to body objectification, instrumentality, locus of control among young women. *Psychology of Women Quarterly, 25,* 209–222

Pipher, M. (1994). *Reviving Ophelia: Saving the selves of adolescent girls.* New York: Grosset/Putnam Books.

Pliner, P., Chaiken, S., & Flett, G. L. (1990). Gender differences in concern with body weight and physical appearance over the life span. *Personality and Social Psychology Bulletin, 16,* 263–273.

Rosenberg, M. (1965). *Society and the adolescent self-image.* Princeton, NJ: Princeton University Press.

Rosenberg, M. (1979). *Conceiving the self.* Malabar, FL: Krieger.

Rosenberg, M., Schooler, C., Schoenberg, C., & Rosenberg, F. (1995). Global self-esteem and specific self esteem: Different concepts, different outcomes. *American Sociological Review, 60,* 141–156.

Rodin, J., Silberstein, L., & Streigel-Moore, R. (1984). Women and weight: A normative discontent. *Nebraska Symposium on Motivation, 32,* 267–307.

Rozin, P., & Fallon, A. (1998). Body image, attitudes to weight, and misperceptions of figure preferences of the opposite sex: A comparison of men and women in two generations. *Journal of Abnormal Psychology, 97,* 342–345.

Schilder, P. F. (1950). *The image and appearance of the human body.* London: Kegan Paul, Trench and Trubner.

Stowers, W., & Durm, D. A. (1996). Does self-concept depend on body-image? A gender analysis. *Psychological Reports, 78,* 643–646.

Thompson, J. K. (1990). *Body image disturbance: Assessment and treatment.* Elmsford, NY: Pergamon.

Thompson, J. K., & Altabe, M. D. (1991). Psychometric qualities of the Figure Rating Scale. *International Journal of Eating Disorders, 10,* 615–619.

Thompson, J. K., & Gray, J. J. (1995). Development and validation of a new body image assessment scale. *Journal of Personality Assessment, 64,* 258–269.

Tiggemann, M. (1992). Body-size dissatisfaction. *Journal of Personality and Individual Differences, 13,* 39–43.

Tiggeman, M., & Rothblum, E. D. (1998). Gender differences in social consequences of perceived overweight in the United States and Australia. *Sex Roles, 18,* 75–86.

Wade, T. J., & Cooper, M. (1998). Sex differences in the links between attractiveness, self esteem, and the body. *Personality and Individual Differences, 27,* 1047–1056.

Wright, E. J., & Whitehead, T. L. (1987). Perceptions of body size and obesity: A selected review of the literature. *Journal of Community Health, 12,* 117–129.

SARAH E. LOWERY was a health psychologist in the Indianapolis, Indiana, area at the time the article in this volume was published.

SHARON E. ROBINSON KURPIUS is the Director of Clinical Training for the Counseling Psychology program and the CACREP Liaison for the Master of Counseling in clinical mental health counseling program at Arizona State University. She has published over 150 book chapters, journal articles, and books.

CHRISTIE BEFORT is an associate professor at the University of Kansas Medical Center, where she instructs on preventive medicine and public health. She is also a co-director of the Breast Cancer Survivorship Center, where she does research on cancer survivorship and behavioral weight control interventions.

ELVA HULL BLANKS was a postdoctoral intern at the Arizona State University Counseling and Consultation School. She is now a psychologist in Mesa, Arizona.

SONJA SOLLENBERGER is a counselor at the downtown Arizona campus for Arizona State University, where she counsels college students on the stressors relevant to the college atmosphere. She received her doctoral degree in psychology from Arizona State University.

MEGAN FOLEY NICPON is an associate professor at the University of Iowa where she teaches in the Counseling Psychology program, works within the Department of Psychological and Quantitative Foundations and the Center for Disability Research and Education, and is the director for research and clinic at the Belin-Blank Center for Gifted Education and Talent at the University of Iowa.

LAURA HUSER is a licensed psychologist at the Anxiety Treatment Center in Phoenix, Arizona. She received her doctoral degree in psychology in 2002 at Arizona State University.

Jennifer Crocker and Lora E. Park

The Costly Pursuit of Self-Esteem

The pursuit of self-esteem has become a central preoccupation in American culture (Baumeister, Campbell, Krueger, & Vohs, 2003; Heine, Lehman, Markus, & Kitayama, 1999; Pyszczynski, Greenberg, & Solomon, 1997; Sheldon, Elliot, Kim, & Kasser, 2001). Hundreds of books offer strategies to increase self-esteem, childrearing manuals instruct parents on how to raise children with high self-esteem (Benson, Galbraith, & Espeland, 1998; Glennon, 1999; P. J. Miller, 2001), and schools across the United States have implemented programs aimed at boosting students' self-esteem in the hopes of reducing problems such as high dropout rates, teenage pregnancy, and drug and alcohol abuse (Dawes, 1994; McElherner & Lisovskis, 1998; Mecca, Smelser, & Vasconcellos, 1989; Seligman, 1998). The preoccupation with self-esteem can also be seen in the volume of scholarly research and writing on the topic. More than 15,000 journal articles on self-esteem have been published over the past 30 years, and interest in this topic has not waned (Baumeister, 1998; Baumeister et al., 2003).

Empirical research has documented the many ways people seek to maintain, enhance, and protect their self-esteem (Baumeister, 1998). The desire to believe that one is worthy or valuable drives behavior and shapes how people think about themselves, other people, and events in their lives (e.g., Crocker, 2002a; Greenberg, Pyszczynski, Solomon, Pinel, Simon, & Jordan, 1993; Kunda & Sanitioso, 1989; Leary & Baumeister, 2000; Ross, 2002). For example, the best predictor of satisfaction with positive events is their impact on self-esteem (Sheldon et al., 2001). The pursuit of self-esteem is so pervasive that many psychologists have assumed it is a universal and fundamental human need (Allport, 1955; Baumeister, Heatherton, & Tice, 1993; Maslow, 1968; Rogers, 1961; Rosenberg, 1979; Solomon, Greenberg, & Pyszczynski, 1991; Taylor & Brown, 1988); some have even argued that humans evolved as a species to pursue self-esteem (Leary & Baumeister, 2000; Leary & Downs, 1995).

With a few notable exceptions, the vast majority of the published articles on self-esteem has focused exclusively on level of trait self-esteem—whether people typically or characteristically have high or low self-regard.

Hundreds of studies have demonstrated that high self-esteem is strongly related to the beliefs people hold about themselves. High self-esteem people believe they are intelligent, attractive, and popular, for example (Baumeister et al., 2003); although high self-esteem people acknowledge that they had flaws or made mistakes in the distant past, they see their present or recently past selves in a particularly positive light, believing they have changed for the better even when concurrent evaluations suggest they have not (Ross, 2002; Wilson & Ross, 2001). High self-esteem people believe they are superior to others in many domains (Brown, 1986; Campbell, 1986), and they expect their futures to be rosy relative to other people's (Taylor & Brown, 1988). Consequently, high self-esteem people have more self-confidence than low self-esteem people, especially following an initial failure (McFarlin & Blascovich, 1981).

In light of these positive beliefs about the self, high self-esteem is assumed to have beneficial effects, and low self-esteem detrimental effects. Recently, however, researchers have argued that the objective benefits of high self-esteem are small and limited. For example, a recent and extensive review concluded that high self-esteem produces pleasant feelings and enhanced initiative but does not cause high academic achievement, good job performance, or leadership; nor does low self-esteem cause violence, smoking, drinking, taking drugs, or becoming sexually active at an early age (Baumeister et al., 2003).

We suggest that the importance of self-esteem lies not only in whether trait self-esteem is high or low but also in the pursuit of self-esteem—what people do to achieve boosts to self-esteem and avoid drops in self-esteem in their daily lives. Because increases in self-esteem feel good, and decreases in self-esteem feel bad, state self-esteem has important motivational consequences. Thus, in the domains in which self-worth is invested, people adopt the goal of validating their abilities or qualities, and hence their self-worth. When people have the goal of validating their worth, they may feel particularly challenged to succeed, yet react to threats or potential threats in ways that are destructive or self-destructive. They interpret events

From Jennifer Crocker and Lora E. Park, "The Costly Pursuit of Self-Esteem," *Psychological Bulletin*, 2004, vol. 130, no. 3, pp. 392–414.

and feedback in terms of what they mean about the self; they view learning as a means to performance outcomes, instead of viewing success and failure as a means to learning; they challenge negative information about the self; they are preoccupied with themselves at the expense of others; and when success is uncertain, they feel anxious and do things that decrease the probability of success but create excuses for failure, such as self-handicapping or procrastination.

The pursuit of self-esteem, when it is successful, has emotional and motivational benefits, but it also has both short- and long-term costs, diverting people from fulfilling their fundamental human needs for competence, relatedness, and autonomy, and leading to poor self-regulation and poor mental and physical health (Baumeister & Leary, 1995; Crocker, 2002a; Deci & Ryan, 2000). We argue that in the pursuit of self-esteem, people often create the opposite of what they need to thrive and that this pursuit has high costs to others as well. People pursue self-esteem through different avenues, and some of these have higher costs than others, but we argue that even "healthier" ways of pursuing self-esteem have costs, and it is possible to achieve their benefits through other sources of motivation. . . .

The Costs of Seeking Self-Esteem

Regardless of how people pursue self-esteem, there are costs associated with this pursuit. In our view, the pursuit of self-esteem impedes the satisfaction of the needs for competence, relatedness, and autonomy, as well as the ability to self-regulate behavior. These costs may not be apparent in the short term because they may be outweighed by immediate emotional benefits when the pursuit of self-esteem is successful. In the long run, however, the benefits dissipate while the costs accumulate. In some cases, the costs of pursuing self-esteem are not borne by the self but by others, even strangers. Thus, a full appreciation of the costs of this pursuit requires a global and long-term perspective to consider costs both to the self and to others.

What Do People Need to Thrive?

Evaluating the costs of the pursuit of self-esteem requires a conception of what people need psychologically to thrive. Our analysis of what humans need draws heavily on self-determination theory, which states that competence, relatedness, and autonomy are essential for continued personal growth, integrity, and well-being (Deci & Ryan, 1995, 2000). Daily activities that facilitate the fulfillment

of these basic psychological needs lead to increased well-being, whereas activities that detract from meeting these needs lead to decreased well-being (Reis, Sheldon, Gable, Roscoe, & Ryan, 2000; Sheldon & Elliot, 1999; Sheldon et al., 2001). We add self-regulation of behavior and mental and physical health to the list of what humans need to thrive. In self-determination theory, needs are distinct from goals; needs are like nutriments required for health—one fails to thrive without them, regardless of whether one has the goal to satisfy the needs. Goals, on the other hand, consciously or unconsciously regulate behavior; specific activities are enacted for the purpose of moving one toward the goal (Deci & Ryan, 2000). Consistent with self-determination theory, we assume that relatedness, competence, autonomy, and self-regulation are always needs (but are not always adopted as goals). We assume that self-esteem or self-worth is often a goal but not necessarily a need.

Costs to Autonomy

Autonomy refers to the sense of being the causal origin of one's behavior (deCharms, 1968), with the internalized self experienced as the source of motivation. Autonomous behavior is self-determined, volitional, and accompanied by the feeling of choice (Deci & Ryan, 2000). When autonomy is low, people experience pressure from internal or external demands, expectations, and standards—they feel that they are at the mercy of these pressures.

Autonomy is the most controversial of the fundamental needs posited by self-determination theory, perhaps because the construct is sometimes confused with independence, individualism, or emotional detachment (Deci & Ryan, 2000). In fact, autonomy is positively related to satisfying, authentic relationships with others (Hodgins, Koestner, & Duncan, 1996) and to well-being (Ryan & Lynch, 1989), even in collectivistic cultures (Deci & Ryan, 2000). Autonomy in goal pursuits is related to increased behavioral persistence, more effective performance, and better mental and physical health (see Deci & Ryan, 2000, for a review).

The pursuit of self-esteem sacrifices autonomy. As Deci, Eghrari, Patrick, and Leone (1994) suggested,

> The type of ego involvement in which one's "worth" is on the line—in which one's self-esteem is contingent upon an outcome—is an example of internally controlling regulation that results from introjection. One is behaving because one feels one has to and not because one wants to, and this regulation is accompanied by the experience of pressure and tension. (p. 121)

When people have the higher order goal of protecting, maintaining, and enhancing self-esteem, they are susceptible to stress, pressure, and anxiety because failure leads to a loss in self-esteem (Deci & Ryan, 1995; Ryan, 1982). For example, students whose self-esteem is contingent on academic performance experience pressure to succeed and lose intrinsic motivation (Deci, Nezlek, & Sheinman, 1981; Deci & Ryan, 2000; Ryan & Deci, 2000). College students who base their self-esteem on academic performance report experiencing more time pressure, academic struggles, conflicts with professors and teaching assistants, and pressure to make academic decisions than do less contingent students (Crocker & Luhtanen, 2003). These effects are independent of level of self-esteem, grade point average, and personality variables such as neuroticism and conscientiousness.

In sum, these findings suggest that when people seek to protect, maintain, and enhance their self-esteem, they lose the ability to act autonomously. Converging evidence is provided by studies of people with unstable self-esteem. College students with unstable self-esteem showed less self-determination (i.e., autonomy) in the motivations underlying their personal strivings and greater feelings of tension associated with those strivings than college students with stable self-esteem (Kernis, Paradise, Whitaker, Wheatman, & Goldman, 2000). Children with unstable self-esteem also showed less curiosity and interest in their school work and less preference for challenge than did children with stable self-esteem (Waschull & Kernis, 1996).

Narcissistic men appear to represent an exception to this general rule; in contrast to nonnarcissists and narcissistic women, they show increased intrinsic motivation when their competence is assessed relative to others, instead of relative to themselves (Morf, Weir, & Davidov 2000). Morf et al. (2000) suggested that the congruence between narcissists' chronic preoccupation with satisfying ego concerns and the situational goal of outperforming others leads to increased intrinsic interest in the task. The suggestion that congruence between chronic and situational self-validation goals increases, rather than decreases, intrinsic motivation is potentially important because it implies that for some people, the pursuit of self-esteem may actually increase the satisfaction of the need for autonomy rather than decrease it (Harackiewicz & Sansone, 1991). However, because the goal to outperform others is distinct from the goal of self-validation and has distinct consequences (Grant & Dweck, 2003), more research is needed. It seems plausible that people with chronic self-validation goals find opportunities to validate their abilities and qualities inherently interesting and enjoyable, unless the task is too challenging, in which case

failure could invalidate their worth, and intrinsic motivation may decrease. In addition, the distinction between approach and avoidance self-esteem goals may be important; narcissists typically have the approach goal of demonstrating their superiority and uniqueness (Rhodewalt & Sorrow, 2003); perhaps it is only avoidance self-esteem goals that undermine intrinsic motivation.

Costs to Learning and Competence

Competence and mastery, or learning, have been recognized as a fundamental human need in several theoretical traditions (Bowlby, 1969; Deci & Ryan, 2000; White, 1959). In these theoretical frameworks, competence refers not to the content of one's knowledge or to the level of one's skills but rather to the ability and willingness to learn and grow from experience which is essential for humans to thrive (see Pyszczynski, Greenberg, & Goldenberg, 2003, for a discussion).

The pursuit of self-esteem interferes with learning and mastery (Covington, 1984; Deci & Ryan, 2000; Dweck, 2000). When people have self-validation goals, mistakes, failures, criticism, and negative feedback are self-threats rather than opportunities to learn and improve. In domains in which self-worth is invested, the goal of obtaining outcomes that validate self-worth is paramount; learning becomes a means to desired performance outcomes that validate the self, instead of performance outcomes being opportunities for learning. For example, Crocker (2003) recently administered a measure of contingencies of self-worth (Crocker, Luhtanen, Cooper, & Bouvrette, 2003) and achievement goals (Grant & Dweck, 2003) to a sample of 75 college students enrolled in Introduction to Psychology. As previously noted, the more students based their self-esteem on academics, the stronger their goal to validate their intelligence through their schoolwork. In addition, basing self-esteem on academics was strongly correlated with the performance goal of obtaining a high grade but was nonsignificantly related to the goal of learning. Entering all the achievement goals as predictors of the academic contingency in a regression, the goals of validating ability, getting a high grade, and outperforming others were each uniquely and positively related to the academic contingency; learning goals were negatively related to basing self-esteem on academics ($\beta = -.19$, $p < .06$). Apart from its usefulness for obtaining grades, outperforming others, and validating ability, students who based their self-worth on academics seem uninterested in learning for its own sake. When asked to choose between learning goals and getting high grades, more academically contingent students reliably chose grades over learning

($r = .34$, $p < .01$). True mastery, we argue, reverses this relation between learning and performance goals; performance, including mistakes and failures, is a means for learning, not for self-esteem (Dweck, 2000).

When people are driven by self-esteem goals, they are eager to take credit for their success (for reviews, see Blaine & Crocker, 1993; Bradley, 1978; Greenberg & Pyszczynski, 1985; D. T. Miller & Ross, 1975). Because self-esteem is the end goal, when people succeed in a domain of contingency, they may consider it the end of the story, without really trying to understand what led to the success (Carver, 2003). In the experience of pride that accompanies success, people may envision even greater achievements (Fredrickson & Branigan, 2001). The tendency to take credit for success that accompanies self-esteem goals can interfere with learning from experience. When people boost their self-esteem by taking full credit for success, they do not explore many other factors that may have contributed to the success, including the efforts of other people, changed circumstances, and so on. Consequently, they do not learn all they can about how to recreate success in the future.

Because negative self-relevant information in domains of contingent self-worth implies that one is lacking the quality on which self-esteem is staked, people resist and challenge such information (Baumeister, 1998). People minimize the amount of time they spend thinking about negative information about the self, unless the presence of an audience makes this difficult (Baumeister & Cairns, 1992). People selectively forget failures and negative information about the self, while remembering their successes and positive information (Crary, 1966; Mischel, Ebbesen, & Zeiss, 1976). After failure in domains linked to self-esteem, people make excuses (for reviews, see Blaine & Crocker, 1993; Bradley, 1978; Greenberg & Pyszczynski, 1985; D. T. Miller & Ross, 1975). For example, they derogate a test as invalid or inaccurate when they fail but not when they succeed (Frey, 1978; Greenberg, Pyszczynski, & Solomon, 1982; Shrauger, 1975) and evaluate evidence about the validity of the test in self-serving ways (Pyszczynski, Greenberg, & Holt, 1985). People with high and unstable self-esteem are particularly likely to make excuses following failure (Kernis & Waschull, 1995); a self-affirmation manipulation reduces this self-serving attributional bias, supporting the view that taking credit for success and avoiding blame for failure follows from the pursuit of self-esteem (Sherman & Kim, 2002).

If failure or negative feedback cannot be explained away, people search for other ways to restore their self-esteem through compensatory self-enhancement (e.g., Baumeister & Jones, 1978; Gollwitzer & Wicklund, 1985;

Greenberg & Pyszczynski, 1985), downward comparison (Beauregard & Dunning, 1998; Crocker, Thompson, McGraw, & Ingerman, 1987; Pyszczynski, Greenberg, & Laprelle, 1985; Wills, 1981; Wood, Giordano-Beech, & Ducharme, 1999), remembering negative information about others (Crocker, 1993), or distancing themselves from others who outperform them (Tesser, 1988, 2000). They may derogate out-groups, portraying others as being worse off than themselves to restore self-esteem following a self-threat (Aberson, Healy, & Romero, 2000; Crocker & Luhtanen, 1990; Crocker et al., 1987; Fein & Spencer, 1997; Spencer, Fein, Wolfe, Fong, & Dunn, 1998; Wills, 1981).

When self-worth is at stake, people pursue many strategies to avoid failure—even if they undermine learning—including arguing and cheating (Covington, 1984, 2000; Dweck, 2000). For example, students with contingent self-worth in the academic domain have reported that they would be willing to cheat if they were unable to succeed at a task (Covington, 1984).

All of these reactions to self-threat are focused on maintaining, protecting, or restoring self-esteem following receipt of negative self-relevant information rather than on learning from the experience. The tendency to discount, excuse, minimize, or forget failures and negative feedback limit how much can be learned from experiences of failure. The effort to dismiss or discredit negative information is incompatible with focusing on what could be important to learn from the failures or criticisms people experience. When people discount, dismiss, or excuse their mistakes and failures, they are unable to appraise their flaws and shortcomings realistically to identify what they need to learn. Even if the test is unfair, the evaluator is biased, or there is a good excuse for failure, there is often some important information or lesson to be learned from these negative experiences. Yet, when people have the goal of validating their worth, they do not seem open to these lessons.

When failure or criticism in domains in which self-worth is invested cannot be discounted, it may be overgeneralized as an indictment of the entire self, lowering global self-esteem (Carver & Ganellen, 1983; Carver, la Voie, Kuhl, & Ganellen, 1988; Crocker, Karpinski, et al., 2003; Crocker et al., 2002). Although overgeneralizing failure exaggerates rather than dismisses failure and criticism, it nonetheless interferes with realistically identifying one's strengths and weaknesses or learning from one's mistakes and failures. People who view their past failures as specific show more constructive self-criticism than people who view their past failures as broader or more global. For example, specific failure on a shape perception test led to less negative emotional reactions and less self-improvement processes than global failure on an intelligence test in a recent study by Kurman (2003). Concluding that one is a terrible person or that everything is one's own fault typically leads to intensely negative self-focused attention and emotions instead of a cooler, less emotional appraisal of what went wrong and what to do differently next time. Realistic appraisal and acknowledgement of one's responsibility for mistakes may actually be more painful for self-esteem than the sweeping overgeneralization that one is a terrible person, which is neither entirely true nor focused on the real issue of what specific aspects of the self need improvement.

The stress and anxiety associated with the pursuit of self-esteem can also undermine learning and performance. Stress affects the ability to learn and recall information through the effects of cortisol on the brain (de Quervain, Roozendaal, & McGaugh, 1998; de Quervain, Roozendaal, Nitsch, McGaugh, & Hock, 2000; Vedhara, Hyde, Gilchrist, Tytherleigh, & Plummer, 2000). Stress also impedes decision making in students undergoing medical training (Cumming & Harris, 2001). Although arousal improves performance on well-learned tasks, it undermines performance when the task is complex, difficult, or at the limits of one's ability, as in high-stakes testing situations (Covington, 1984; Steele, 1997; Stone, 2002).

Costs to Relationships

Psychologists generally agree that humans are social creatures and have a fundamental need for relatedness (Baumeister & Leary, 1995; Bowlby, 1969; Deci & Ryan, 2000). True relatedness is more than simply believing that one is liked by others, is cared about, or has others on whom one can rely when needed. Relatedness involves close, mutually caring and supportive relationships with others and having and providing a safe haven in times of distress—it involves giving as well as receiving (Baumeister & Leary, 1995; Collins & Feeney, 2000; Deci & Ryan, 2000). Close, mutually caring relationships provide a sense of felt security (Collins & Feeney, 2000), which contributes to more effective coping (Cohen, Sherrod, & Clark, 1986), better mental and physical health, and overall longevity (Ryff, 1995).

When self-esteem is the goal, relatedness is hindered because people become focused on themselves at the expense of others' needs and feelings (Park & Crocker, 2003). People pursuing self-esteem want to be superior to others (Brown, 1986; Taylor & Brown, 1988). Consequently, life becomes a zero-sum game, and other people become competitors and enemies rather than supports and

resources. Responding to self-esteem threats with avoidance, distancing, and withdrawal or with blame, excuses, anger, antagonism, and aggression (Baumeister, 1998; Baumeister, Bushman, & Campbell, 2000; Baumeister, Smart, & Boden, 1996; Crocker & Park, 2003; Heatherton & Vohs, 2000; Kernis & Waschull, 1995; Tice, 1993) is incompatible with caring for or being cared for by others. Whether the response is distancing, avoidance, and withdrawal or blaming, anger, and aggression, connections with others are sacrificed. These defensive reactions may result in isolation and disconnection from others and hinder the formation of meaningful authentic supportive relationships (Pyszczynski et al., 2003).

A recent study shows how the pursuit of self-esteem can cause people to be less attuned to the needs and feelings of others (Park & Crocker, 2003). In this study, 2 unacquainted same-sex students participated in each experimental session. One of the participants (the partner) wrote an essay about a personal problem while the other participant (the target) completed either a Graduate Record Exam (GRE) analogies test and received failure feedback or completed a non-GRE word associations task and received no feedback. In the second part of the experiment, the essay partner discussed his or her personal problem with the target. At the conclusion of the conversation, partners rated the target on various interpersonal qualities, such as how compassionate, helpful, preoccupied, or bored the target was, and indicated how much they liked the target, wanted to interact with him or her again, and wanted to disclose another personal problem to him or her in the future.

The results showed that for targets in the failure feedback condition, the combination of having high self-esteem and being highly contingent on academic competence was related to being perceived by their partners as being less caring, supportive, concerned, and invested and as being more interrupting, preoccupied, and bored with the perceiver's personal problem. Furthermore, high self-esteem, highly contingent targets who failed were rated as less likable, less desirable for future interactions, and less appealing as people with whom to discuss one's problems in the future. In the no threat condition, highly contingent, high self-esteem targets were not rated negatively or disliked by their partners (Park & Crocker, 2003). Taken together, these findings suggest that people whose self-worth is at stake, especially if they have high self-esteem, may have difficulty disengaging from the pursuit of self-esteem following threat, and thus are not really "present" to support others. In the long run, this reaction to self-threat detracts from forming and maintaining close, mutually caring and supportive relationships with others (Deci & Ryan, 1995).

Level of trait self-esteem moderates how people pursue self-esteem and, consequently, the costs of this pursuit for relationships. People with high self-esteem sacrifice mutually caring relationships with others for the sake of maintaining, enhancing, and protecting self-esteem through achievement (e.g., Baumeister et al., 1996; Heatherton & Vohs, 2000; Vohs & Heatherton, 2001). But what about people who pursue self-esteem through the principles of "be loved," "be included," or "be accepted"— the pattern more characteristic of people with low self-esteem (e.g., Joiner, Katz, & Lew, 1999; Joiner, Metalsky, Katz, & Beach, 1999; Vohs & Heatherton, 2001)? People who base their self-esteem on others' regard and approval tend to have poor relationships and behave in ways that make those relationships worse over time.

People whose self-worth is tied to others' regard and approval respond to self-threats by seeking reassurance from others (Murray, Holmes, Griffin, Bellavia, & Rose 2001). Joiner and his colleagues have explored the antecedents and consequences of reassurance seeking (Joiner, Alfano, & Metalsky, 1992; Joiner, Katz, & Lew, 1999; Joiner, Metalsky, Gencoz, & Gencoz, 2001; Joiner, Metalsky, et al., 1999). Joiner, Katz, and Lew (1999) argued that

> excessive reassurance seeking is a maladaptive interpersonal coping strategy specifically aimed at negotiating doubts about one's lovability and worthiness (i.e., self-esteem) and doubts about future prospects and safety (i.e., anxiety). According to this view, people seek reassurance to assuage the experience of lowered self-esteem and heightened anxiety. (p. 631)

In a study of college undergraduates, Joiner, Katz, and Lew (1999) found that negative life events increased anxiety and decreased self-esteem, which, in turn, increased reassurance seeking.

The desire for others' approval and reassurance creates sensitivity to real or imagined signs of rejection. People high in rejection sensitivity base their self-worth on others' acceptance and anxiously expect, readily perceive, and overreact to rejection (Downey & Feldman, 1996; Downey, Feldman, & Ayduk, 2000; Downey, Freitas, Michaelis, & Khouri, 1998). These behaviors harm, rather than enhance, relationships. Highly rejection sensitive people assume that their significant others' negative behavior reflects hostile intentions, report feeling more insecure and dissatisfied with their relationships, and are more likely to exaggerate their partners' dissatisfaction and desire to leave the relationship than low rejection sensitive people (Downey & Feldman, 1996). Men who are high in rejection sensitivity

tend to react with jealousy, hostility, and attempts to control their partner, whereas women high in rejection sensitivity tend to withdraw support and become despondent (Downey & Feldman, 1996). Over time, this style of interaction may hinder relationship partners from supporting each other and ultimately lead to the dissolution of the relationship (Downey et al., 1998). Ironically, people who seek the approval of others (and simultaneously fear rejection from them) create exactly what they do not want—in a self-fulfilling prophecy, their fears of rejection and attempts to seek reassurance result in rejection (Downey et al., 1998; Joiner, 1994; Joiner et al., 1992; Joiner, Metalsky, et al., 1999; Murray, Holmes, & Griffin, 2000).

Attachment theory also suggests that approval seekers do not achieve the relationship security they seek. According to attachment theory, people with a preoccupied attachment style have a positive mental model of others and a negative mental model of the self (Bartholomew, 1990; Bartholomew & Horowitz, 1991). Their self-esteem is highly dependent on others' approval, and they crave constant reassurance from their partners (Bartholomew, 1990). People with this attachment style tend to be obsessive and preoccupied with their relationships, fearing that their partners will not want to be as intimate or as close as they desire them to be (Collins & Read, 1990; Feeney & Noller, 1990; Simpson, Rholes, & Nelligan, 1992). Recent research has also shown that whereas people with secure attachment styles engage in more effective forms of support seeking and caregiving, people with insecure attachment styles are less effective support seekers and caregivers (Collins & Feeney, 2000). Taken together, the findings on attachments styles suggest that people who are highly contingent on the approval of others may have a diminished capacity for creating and maintaining mutually supportive caring relationships.

In sum, people with low self-esteem, high reassurance seeking, rejection sensitivity, and certain insecure attachment styles pursue self-esteem by trying to earn the acceptance and approval of others. However, they rarely get what they want and instead behave in ways that increase the chances they will be rejected by others. Moreover, when people pursue self-esteem, they sometimes behave and think in ways that are incompatible with forming mutually caring supportive relationships. They do not provide a secure base for others and do not elicit caring and supportive relationships from others, consequently undermining their connections with others.

The pursuit of self-esteem not only undermines satisfaction of the need for relatedness for the self, it also has implications for the experience of others (Crocker, Lee, & Park, 2004). Researchers have rarely considered how one person's pursuit of self-esteem affects other people. We suggest that preoccupation with the implications of events and behavior for the self causes people to lose sight of the implications of events and their own actions for others. They have fewer cognitive resources to take the perspective of the other and therefore fail to consider what others need or what is good for others. Consequently, others have reason to mistrust their motives and do not feel safe. The goal of validating self-worth often creates competition or the desire to be superior to others. This, in turn, triggers competition in others, who do not want to be inferior, and can create the desire for revenge or retaliation. These ripple effects rebound to the self, creating a lack of safety for the self, and in the end, create the opposite of what most people really want and need.

Costs to Self-Regulation

Self-regulation involves restraining impulses to engage in behaviors that have known costs to the self (e.g., smoking, binge eating, or breaking laws), as well as the ability to pursue goals that have future benefits (Metcalfe & Mischel, 1999). Self-regulation and self-control have demonstrated long-term benefits (Mischel & Shoda, 1995; Shoda, Mischel, & Peake, 1990). As Baumeister (1998) noted, "A high capacity for self-regulation appears to be an unmitigated good in that it improves one's chances of success in nearly every endeavor to which it is relevant" (p. 717).

The pursuit of self-esteem may involve behavioral self-regulation, emotional self-regulation, or both. That is, people sometimes regulate their behavior to achieve a success that will enhance their self-esteem; at other times, they may abandon efforts at behavioral self-regulation and pursue strategies that protect their feelings of self-worth, such as blaming others (Tice & Bratslavsky, 2000; Tice, Bratslavsky, & Baumeister, 2001).

When self-regulation occurs with the higher order goal of self-esteem, people have difficulty self-regulating their behavior. Metcalfe and Mischel (1999) argued that there are two systems for self-control and self-regulation: a cool, cognitive system, which "allows a person to keep goals in mind while pursuing them and monitoring progress along the route" (p. 5), and a hot, emotional system that is fast, simple, reflexive, accentuated by stress, and under stimulus control. Because self-esteem has powerful consequences for emotion, the pursuit of self-esteem is largely under the control of the hot system. When self-esteem is threatened, people often indulge in immediate impulses to make themselves feel better, giving short-term affect regulation priority over other self-regulatory goals (Tesser, 1988; Tice & Bratslavsky, 2000; Tice et al., 2001).

Procrastination and self-handicapping, for example, protect self-esteem by creating excuses for failure but decrease the chances of success (Tice, 1991).

When people have self-esteem goals, they are motivated to see themselves in a positive light, deflecting responsibility for failure and taking credit for success. As a result, self-regulation suffers because they have difficulty realistically appraising their current state and comparing it with their ideal state; they may become either overly positive or overly negative about the discrepancy, or they may avoid considering it altogether by focusing on other people's shortcomings. People also have difficulty assessing their rate of progress toward a goal (Wilson & Ross, 2000, 2001). Effective self-regulation also requires disengaging from goals when progress is too slow (Carver & Scheier, 1998), but people often have difficulty disengaging from goals that are connected to their self-worth (Baumeister et al., 1993; Pyszczynski & Greenberg, 1987).

In addition to these examples of self-regulatory failure, the pursuit of self-esteem may also deplete self-regulatory resources in domains that are linked to self-esteem, so that one is unable to exercise self-control in other domains. For example, Vohs and Heatherton (2000) showed that chronic dieters who exerted self-control by not eating a good-tasting snack food were subsequently less able to exert self-control on a task that required inhibiting emotional expression; nondieters did not show this depletion of self-regulatory ability. We suspect that these effects extend broadly to the pursuit of self-esteem; when people successfully self-regulate in domains on which self-worth is staked, this is likely to consume self-regulatory resources for various reasons, including the effort required to overcome hot system responses. Consequently, the pursuit of self-esteem may be associated with poor self-regulation in other domains.

Use of time is an important aspect of self-regulation. One of the most pernicious costs of the pursuit of self-esteem is that people use this limited resource to demonstrate their worth or value. For example, students who base their self-esteem on academic performance spend more time studying but do not get better grades; students who base their self-esteem on their appearance spend more time shopping for clothes and partying (Crocker, Luhtanen, et al., 2003). Perfectionists have high standards and find failure to meet them unacceptable (Blatt, 1995); consequently, they misuse their time and sometimes sacrifice long-term goals.

The pursuit of self-esteem also makes it difficult to plan one's use of time. People consistently underestimate how long it will take them to complete a project, in part because they protect their self-esteem by attributing failure to external causes (Buehler, Griffin, & Ross, 1994). When avoiding responsibility for past failures, it is difficult to estimate accurately the likelihood that one will experience similar personal difficulties in the future.

Less obvious, but perhaps more important, is the amount of time people spend diverted from pursuing their immediate goals because of self-esteem concerns. Time spent worrying or procrastinating rather than doing, self-handicapping rather than preparing, or seeking perfection rather than moving forward imperfectly, is time that cannot be recovered for activities that are more likely to achieve other goals and satisfy fundamental human needs. Particularly pernicious is the tendency to focus on the shortcomings of others as a way to avoid looking at one's own weaknesses and faults. When this behavior triggers defensive responses in others, it may create conflicts that consume time. Of the many costs of such diversions, perhaps the least appreciated is the cost of time.

Costs to Physical Health

Although research has not directly examined the links, the pursuit of self-esteem likely has long-term costs to physical health. Self-esteem goals may lead to physical health problems through anxiety and stress (Suinn, 2001). People with self-esteem goals tend to be highly anxious (Dykman, 1998), and anxiety has negative effects on health (Suinn, 2001). Stress and anxiety are associated with activation of the pituitary–adrenal–cortical system, which releases corticosteroids from the adrenal cortex (Hellhammer & Wade, 1993; Stroebe, 2000). Corticosteroids increase levels of triglycerides and cholesterol in the blood; thus, chronic and frequent stress is often associated with heart disease. Corticosteroids also reduce immune system functioning (Kiecolt-Glaser, Cacioppo, Malarkey, & Glaser, 1992; Kiecolt-Glaser & Glaser, 1994), resulting in greater susceptibility to illnesses such as upper respiratory infections (Kiecolt-Glaser, Dura, Speicher, Trask, & Glaser, 1991). It is not surprising, then, that students who procrastinate early in an academic semester are ill more frequently and report more stress and illness late in the term (Tice & Baumeister, 1997).

Stress is associated with activation of the sympathetic-adrenal medullary system, which stimulates cardiovascular activity with consequences for cardiac health (Stroebe, 2000; Suinn, 2001). Hostility is also associated with the pursuit of self-esteem, especially through external avenues such as appearance, perhaps because people with external contingencies of self-worth feel angry when their worth is not validated by others (Crocker, 2002b). People who have high but fragile (i.e., unstable or contingent) self-esteem tend to be hostile, especially

when they experience threats to self-worth (Baumeister et al., 1996; Kernis, 2003). Hostility is a risk factor for coronary heart disease (T. Q. Miller, Smith, Turner, Guijarro, & Hallet, 1996; Suinn, 2001) and also diminishes immune system functioning (Kiecolt-Glaser et al., 1993).

Self-esteem goals also lead to physical health problems through unhealthy coping behavior. College students whose self-esteem is based on their appearance are particularly likely to spend time partying and use more alcohol and drugs (Crocker, 2002b). To cope with the negative affect associated with the pursuit of self-esteem, people may drink alcohol or have unprotected sex, with potentially serious health consequences (Cooper, Agocha, & Sheldon, 2000; Cooper, Frone, Russell, & Mudar, 1995, 1998; Hull, 1981; Hull, Levenson, Young, & Sher, 1983; Hull & Young, 1983; Stroebe, 2000; Suinn, 2001). When people pursue self-esteem, they tend to be highly self-focused or self-aware because their superordinate goals concern the self. When negative events occur in domains on which self-worth is staked, this self-awareness intensifies their painful emotional consequences. Consequently, the pursuit of self-esteem, especially when failure is experienced, should frequently lead to attempts to escape the self (Baumeister, 1991). People may escape the self by consuming alcohol (Hull, 1981), binge eating (Heatherton & Baumeister, 1991), masochism (Baumeister, 1991), and even suicide (Baumeister, 1990).

The pursuit of self-esteem can also lead to poor physical health outcomes through health risk behaviors (Leary & Jones, 1993; Leary, Tchividjian, & Kraxberger, 1994). People concerned about how they are perceived and evaluated by others tend to consume more alcohol (Faber, Khavari, & Douglass, 1980), smoke (Camp, Klesges, & Relyea, 1993), sunbathe (Leary & Jones, 1993), diet excessively (Gritz & Crane, 1991), undergo cosmetic surgery (Schouten, 1991), use steroids (Schrof, 1992), drive recklessly (Jonah, 1990), and engage in unsafe sex (Abraham, Sheeran, Spears, & Abrams, 1992; Schlenker & Leary, 1982) to obtain the approval of peers. Although these behaviors may boost self-esteem or reduce anxiety in the short term, they have health consequences that accumulate over time. In many cases, the cumulative damage to physical health is irreparable and poses a burden not only to individuals but also to others and to society.

Costs to Mental Health

The pursuit of self-esteem has implications for mental health, especially depression, narcissism, and anxiety.

Depression. Clinical psychologists have long debated the relation between self-esteem and depression. Although low self-esteem is correlated with the presence of depressive symptoms, evidence that low self-esteem is a risk factor for depression, rather than a symptom of it, is inconclusive (Roberts & Gamble, 2001; Tennen & Herzberger, 1987). Other theorists have argued that depression-prone people have self-esteem that is vulnerable, or contingent, in particular domains (Beck, Epstein, Harrison, & Emery, 1983; Bibring, 1953; Blatt, Quinlan, Chevron, McDonald, & Zuroff, 1982; Blatt & Shichman, 1983; Higgins, 1987). In our view, the pursuit of self-esteem is a risk factor for the development of depression.

People who tend to approach situations and events with self-esteem goals are high in symptoms of depression (Dykman, 1998). The tendency to overgeneralize negative events to the worth of the entire self, characteristic of people with self-esteem goals, is related to depression and prospectively predicts the development of depressive symptoms (Carver, 1998; Carver & Ganellen, 1983; Carver et al., 1988). Instability of self-esteem caused by success and failure in domains of contingency can contribute to depressive symptoms (Butler, Hokanson, & Flynn, 1994; Kernis et al., 1998; Kuiper & Olinger, 1986; Kuiper, Olinger, & MacDonald, 1988; Roberts & Gotlib, 1997; Roberts, Kassel, & Gotlib, 1995, 1996; Roberts & Monroe, 1992). For example, temporal variability in self-esteem, together with life stress, prospectively predicted the onset of depressive symptoms in a sample of college students (Roberts & Kassel, 1997). A daily report study of college students showed that the more students based their self-esteem on academic performance, the more their self-esteem tended to drop on days they received a worse-than-expected grade on an exam or paper. This instability of self-esteem, in turn, predicted increases in depressive symptoms over the 3 weeks of the study, especially among students who were initially high in depressive symptoms (Crocker, Karpinski, et al., 2003).

Narcissism.   Clinical and experimental descriptions of narcissism are remarkably similar to our description of the pursuit of self-esteem (see, e.g., Rhodewalt & Sorrow, 2003). Clinical accounts of narcissism describe a pathological self-focus and unstable self-esteem resulting from fragile or damaged self-views (see Kohut, 1971). Like most people pursuing self-esteem, narcissists put the goal of self-worth above other goals and are caught up in the question of whether they are worthless or wonderful. What distinguishes narcissists from others with contingencies, however, are their extremely positive self-concepts, extreme fears of being worthless (Morf & Rhodewalt, 2001; Rhodewalt & Morf, 1995), and their constant need for external validation in the form of attention and admiration from others to sustain their exaggeratedly positive self-views (Morf, 1994;

Morf & Rhodewalt, 1993, 2001; Rhodewalt & Morf, 1995). Narcissists' self-esteem fluctuates in response to their social interactions (Rhodewalt, Madrian, & Cheney, 1998). It has even been suggested that narcissists are addicted to self-esteem (Baumeister & Vohs, 2001).

Although narcissism and depression differ in many respects, both of these disorders are characterized by strong concerns about self-worth. This similarity raises an alarming possibility: that the pursuit of self-esteem, so strongly emphasized in American culture, encourages the development of both narcissistic and depressive tendencies. Indeed, as the self-esteem movement has taken hold in the United States, levels of depression, narcissism, and anxiety have been rising (Smith & Elliott, 2001; Twenge, 2000). For example, the average American child in the 1980s reported more anxiety than child psychiatric patients in the 1950s (Twenge, 2000), teenagers today are 10 times more likely to be depressed than teenagers a generation ago, and suicide rates among this age group have tripled (Smith & Elliott, 2001). . . .

Conclusion

. . .

Some readers may believe we have ignored many benefits of pursuing self-esteem, and we acknowledge that these benefits exist; in addition to the immediate emotional benefits of validating one's worth and value by succeeding in domains of self-worth contingency, research suggests that under some circumstances, some people are driven to accomplish great things in the pursuit of the recognition, acknowledgement, or fame that shores up their self-esteem. Although chasing after self-esteem can motivate excellent performance, performance itself is not a fundamental human need, and it can be achieved through other less destructive sources of motivation. Recognition and acknowledgement are not the same as love and acceptance, and they do not create the safety and security people desire. People cannot protect themselves from dangers they experienced in childhood by proving that they are smart, strong, beautiful, rich, or admired or that they satisfy some other contingency of self-worth. In the words of Claire Nuer (1997), a Holocaust survivor and leadership development trainer, "The only way to create love, safety, and acceptance is by giving them."

References

Aberson, C. L., Healy, M., & Romero, V. (2000). Ingroup bias and self-esteem: A meta-analysis. *Personality and Social Psychology Review, 4,* 157–173.

Abraham, C., Sheeran, P., Spears, R., & Abrams, D. (1992). Health beliefs and promotion of HIV-preventive intentions among teenagers: A Scottish perspective. *Health Psychology, 11,* 363–370.

Allport, G. W. (1955). *Becoming.* New Haven, CT: Yale University Press.

Averill, J. R. (1982). *Anger and aggression: An essay on emotion.* New York: Springer-Verlag.

Bartholomew, K. (1990). Avoidance of intimacy: An attachment perspective. *Journal of Social and Personal Relationships, 7,* 147–178.

Bartholomew, K., & Horowitz, L. M. (1991). Attachment styles among young adults: A test of a four-category model. *Journal of Personality and Social Psychology, 61,* 226–244.

Baumeister, R. F. (1990). Suicide as escape from self. *Psychological Review, 97,* 90–113.

Baumeister, R. F. (1991). *Escaping the self: Alcoholism, spirituality, masochism, and other flights from the burden of selfhood.* New York: Basic Books.

Baumeister, R. F. (1998). The self. In D. T. Gilbert, S. T. Fiske, & G. Lindzey (Eds.), *The handbook of social psychology* (4th ed., Vol. 2, pp. 680–740). New York: McGraw-Hill.

Baumeister, R. F., Bushman, B. J., & Campbell, W. K. (2000). Self-esteem, narcissism, and aggression: Does violence result from low self-esteem or from threatened egotism? *Current Directions in Psychological Science, 9,* 141–156.

Baumeister, R. F., & Cairns, K. J. (1992). Repression and self-presentation: When audiences interfere with self-deceptive strategies. *Journal of Personality and Social Psychology, 62,* 851–862.

Baumeister, R. F., Campbell, J. D., Krueger, J. I., & Vohs, K. D. (2003). Does high self-esteem cause better performance, interpersonal success, happiness, or healthier lifestyles? *Psychological Science in the Public Interest, 4,* 1–44.

Baumeister, R. F., Heatherton, T. F., & Tice, D. M. (1993). When ego threats lead to self-regulation failure: Negative consequences of high self-esteem. *Journal of Personality and Social Psychology, 64,* 141–156.

Baumeister, R. F., & Jones, E. E. (1978). When self-presentation is constrained by the target's knowledge: Consistency and compensation. *Journal of Personality and Social Psychology, 36,* 608–618.

Baumeister, R. F., & Leary, M. R. (1995). The need to belong: Desire for interpersonal attachments as a fundamental human motivation. *Psychological Bulletin, 111,* 497–529.

Baumeister, R. F., Smart, L., & Boden, J. M. (1996). Relation of threatened egotism to violence and aggression: The dark side of high self-esteem. *Psychological Review, 103,* 5–33.

Baumeister, R. F., & Vohs, K. D. (2001). Narcissism as addiction to esteem. *Psychological Inquiry, 12,* 206–210.

Beauregard, K. S., & Dunning, D. (1998). Turning up the contrast: Self-enhancement motives prompt egocentric contrast effects in social judgments. *Journal of Personality and Social Psychology, 74,* 606–621.

Beck, A. T., Epstein, N., Harrison, R. P., & Emery, G. (1983). *Development of the Sociotropy–Autonomy Scale: A measure of personality factors in psychopathology.* Unpublished manuscript, University of Pennsylvania.

Benson, P. L., Galbraith, J., & Espeland, P. (1998). *What kids need to succeed: Proven, practical ways to raise good kids.* Minneapolis, MN: Free Spirit Press.

Bibring, E. (1953). The mechanism of depression. In P. Greenacre (Ed.), *Affective disorders* (pp. 13–48). New York: International Universities Press.

Blaine, B., & Crocker, J. (1993). Self-esteem and self-serving biases in reactions to positive and negative events: An integrative review. In R. F. Baumeister (Ed.), *Self-esteem: The puzzle of low self-regard* (pp. 55–85). Hillsdale, NJ: Erlbaum.

Blatt, S. J. (1995). The destructiveness of perfectionism: Implications for the treatment of depression. *American Psychologist, 50,* 1003–1020.

Blatt, S. J., Quinlan, D., Chevron, E., McDonald, C., & Zuroff, D. (1982). Dependency and self-criticism: Psychological dimensions for depression. *Journal of Consulting and Clinical Psychology, 50,* 113–124.

Blatt, S. J., & Shichman, S. (1983). Two primary configurations in psychopathology. *Psychoanalysis and Contemporary Thought, 6,* 187–254.

Bowlby, J. (1969). *Attachment and loss: Vol. 1. Attachment.* New York: Basic Books.

Bradley, G. W. (1978). Self-serving biases in the attribution process: A reexamination of the fact or fiction question. *Journal of Personality and Social Psychology, 36,* 56–71.

Brown, J. D. (1986). Evaluations of self and others: Self-enhancement biases in social judgments. *Social Cognition, 4,* 353–376.

Buehler, R., Griffin, D., & Ross, M. (1994). Exploring the "planning fallacy": Why people underestimate their task completion times. *Journal of Personality and Social Psychology, 67,* 366–381.

Butler, A. C., Hokanson, J. E., & Flynn, H. A. (1994). A comparison of self-esteem liability and low trait self-esteem as vulnerability factors in depression. *Journal of Personality and Social Psychology, 66,* 166–177.

Camp, D. E., Klesges, R. C., & Relyea, G. (1993). The relationship between body weight concerns and adolescent smoking. *Health Psychology, 12,* 24–32.

Campbell, J. D. (1986). Similarity and uniqueness: The effects of attribute type, relevance, and individual differences in self-esteem and depression. *Journal of Personality and Social Psychology, 50,* 281–294.

Carver, C. S. (1998). Generalization, adverse events, and development of depressive symptoms. *Journal of Personality, 66,* 607–619.

Carver, C. S. (2003). Pleasure as a sign you can attend to something else: Placing positive feelings within a general model of affect. *Cognition & Emotion, 17,* 241–261.

Carver, C. S., & Ganellen, R. J. (1983). Depression and components of self-punitiveness: High standards, self-criticism, and overgeneralization. *Journal of Abnormal Psychology, 92,* 330–337.

Carver, C. S., la Voie, L., Kuhl, J., & Ganellen, R. J. (1988). Cognitive concomitants of depression: A further examination of the roles of generalization, high standards, and self-criticism. *Journal of Social and Clinical Psychology, 7,* 350–365.

Carver, C. S., & Scheier, M. F. (1998). *On the self-regulation of behavior.* New York: Cambridge University Press.

Cohen, S., Sherrod, D. R., & Clark, M. S. (1986). Social skills and the stress-protective role of social support. *Journal of Personality and Social Psychology, 50,* 963–973.

Collins, N. L., & Feeney, B. (2000). A safe haven: An attachment theory perspective on support seeking and care giving in close relationships. *Journal of Personality and Social Psychology, 78,* 1053–1073.

Collins, N. L., & Read, S. J. (1990). Adult attachment, working models, and relationship quality in dating couples. *Journal of Personality and Social Psychology, 58,* 644–663.

Cooper, M. L., Agocha, V. B., & Sheldon, M. S. (2000). A motivational perspective on risky behaviors: The role of personality and affect regulatory processes. *Journal of Personality, 68,* 1059–1088.

Cooper, M. L., Frone, M. R., Russell, M., & Mudar, P. (1995). Drinking to regulate positive and negative emotions: A motivational model of alcohol use. *Journal of Personality and Social Psychology, 69,* 990–1005.

Cooper, M. L., Shapiro, C. M., & Powers, A. M. (1998). Motivations for sex and risky sexual behavior among adolescents and young adults: A functional perspective. *Journal of Personality and Social Psychology, 75,* 1528–1558.

Covington, M. V. (1984). The self-worth theory of achievement motivation: Findings and implications. *Elementary School Journal, 85,* 5–20.

Covington, M. V. (2000). Goal theory, motivation, and school achievement: An integrative review. *Annual Review of Psychology, 51,* 171–200.

Crary, W. G. (1966). Reactions to incongruent self-experiences. *Journal of Consulting Psychology, 30,* 246–252.

Crocker, J. (1993). Memory for information about others: Effects of self-esteem and performance feedback. *Journal of Research in Personality, 27,* 35–48.

Crocker, J. (2002a). Contingencies of self-worth: Implications for self-regulation and psychological vulnerability. *Self and Identity, 1,* 143–149.

Crocker, J. (2002b). The costs of seeking self-esteem. *Journal of Social Issues, 58,* 597–615.

Crocker, J. (2003). [Contingencies of self-worth and self-validation goals in achievement domains]. Unpublished raw data.

Crocker, J., Karpinski, A., Quinn, D. M., & Chase, S. K. (2003). When grades determine self-worth: Consequences of contingent self-worth for male and female engineering and psychology majors. *Journal of Personality and Social Psychology, 85,* 507–516.

Crocker, J., Lee, S. J., & Park, L. E. (2004). The pursuit of self-esteem: Implications for good and evil. In A. G. Miller (Ed.), *The social psychology of good and evil: Understanding our capacity for kindness and cruelty* (pp. 271–302). New York: Guilford Press.

Crocker, J., & Luhtanen, R. K. (1990). Collective self-esteem and ingroup bias. *Journal of Personality and Social Psychology, 58*, 60–67.

Crocker, J., & Luhtanen, R. K. (2003). Level of self-esteem and contingencies of self-worth: Unique effects on academic, social, and financial problems in college freshmen. *Personality and Social Psychology Bulletin, 29*, 701–712.

Crocker, J., Luhtanen, R. K., Cooper, M. L., & Bouvrette, S. A. (2003). Contingencies of self-worth in college students: Theory and measurement. *Journal of Personality and Social Psychology, 85*, 894–908.

Crocker, J., & Park, L. E. (2003). Seeking self-esteem: Maintenance, enhancement, and protection of self-worth. In M. R. Leary & J. P. Tangney (Eds.), *Handbook of self and identity* (pp. 291–313). New York: Guilford Press.

Crocker, J., Sommers, S. R., & Luhtanen, R. K. (2002). Hopes dashed and dreams fulfilled: Contingencies of self-worth and admissions to graduate school. *Personality and Social Psychology Bulletin, 28*, 1275–1286.

Crocker, J., Thompson, L., McGraw, K., & Ingerman, C. (1987). Downward comparison, prejudice, and evaluation of others: Effects of self-esteem and threat. *Journal of Personality and Social Psychology, 52*, 907–916.

Cumming, S. R., & Harris, L. M. (2001). The impact of anxiety on the accuracy of diagnostic decision-making. *Stress and Health: Journal of the International Society for the Investigation of Stress, 17*, 281–286.

Dawes, R. M. (1994). *House of cards: Psychology and psychotherapy built on myth.* New York: Free Press.

deCharms, R. (1968). *Personal causation.* New York: Academic Press.

Deci, E. L., Eghrari, H., Patrick, B. C., & Leone, D. R. (1994). Facilitating internalization: The self-determination theory perspective. *Journal of Personality, 62*, 119–141.

Deci, E. L., Nezlek, J., & Sheinman, L. (1981). Characteristics of the rewarder and intrinsic motivation of the rewardee. *Journal of Personality and Social Psychology, 40*, 1–10.

Deci, E. L., & Ryan, R. M. (1995). Human autonomy: The basis for true self-esteem. In M. H. Kernis (Ed.), *Efficacy, agency, and self-esteem* (pp. 31–49). New York: Plenum Press.

Deci, E. L., & Ryan, R. M. (2000). The "what" and "why" of goal pursuits: Human needs and the self-determination of behavior. *Psychological Inquiry, 11*, 227–268.

de Quervain, D. J. F., Roozendaal, B., & McGaugh, J. L. (1998, August 20). Stress and glucocorticoids impair retrieval of long-term spatial memory. *Nature, 394*, 787–790.

de Quervain, D. J. F., Roozendaal, B., Nitsch, R. M., McGaugh, J. L., & Hock, C. (2000). Acute cortisone administration impairs retrieval of long-term declarative memory in humans. *Nature Neuroscience, 3*, 313–314.

Downey, G., & Feldman, S. (1996). Implications of rejection sensitivity for intimate relationships. *Journal of Personality and Social Psychology, 70*, 1327–1343.

Downey, G., Feldman, S., & Ayduk, O. (2000). Rejection sensitivity and male violence in romantic relationships. *Personal Relationships, 7*, 45–61.

Downey, G., Freitas, A. L., Michaelis, B., & Khouri, H. (1998). The self-fulfilling prophecy in close relationships: Rejection sensitivity and rejection by romantic partners. *Journal of Personality and Social Psychology, 75*, 545–560.

Dweck, C. S. (2000). *Self-theories: Their role in motivation, personality, and development.* Philadelphia: Psychology Press.

Dykman, B. M. (1998). Integrating cognitive and motivational factors in depression: Initial tests of a goal-orientation approach. *Journal of Personality and Social Psychology, 74*, 139–158.

Faber, P. D., Khavari, K. A., & Douglass, F. M. I. (1980). A factor analytic study of reasons for drinking: Empirical validation of positive and negative reinforcement dimensions. *Journal of Consulting and Clinical Psychology, 48*, 780–781.

Feeney, J. A., & Noller, P. (1990). Attachment style as a predictor of adult romantic relationships. *Journal of Personality and Social Psychology, 58*, 281–291.

Fein, S., & Spencer, S. J. (1997). Prejudice as self-image maintenance: Affirming the self through derogating others. *Journal of Personality and Social Psychology, 73*, 31–44.

Fiske, A. P., Kitayama, S., Markus, H. R., & Nisbett, R. E. (1998). The cultural matrix of social psychology. In D. Gilbert, S. T. Fiske, & G. Lindzey (Eds.), *The handbook of social psychology* (4th ed., Vol. 2, pp. 915–981). New York: McGraw-Hill.

Fredrickson, B. L., & Branigan, C. (2001). Positive emotions. In T. J. Mayne & G. A. Bonanno (Eds.), *Emotions: Current issues and future directions* (pp. 123–151). New York: Guilford Press.

Frey, D. (1978). Reactions to success and failure in public and private conditions. *Journal of Experimental Social Psychology, 14,* 172–179.

Glennon, W. (1999). *200 ways to raise a girl's self-esteem.* York Beach, ME: Conari Press.

Gollwitzer, P. M., & Wicklund, R. (1985). Self-symbolizing and the neglect of others' perspectives. *Journal of Personality and Social Psychology, 43,* 702–715.

Grant, H., & Dweck, C. S. (2003). Clarifying achievement goals and their impact. *Journal of Personality and Social Psychology, 85,* 541–553.

Greenberg, J., & Pyszczynski, T. (1985). Compensatory self-inflation: A response to the threat to self-regard of public failure. *Journal of Personality and Social Psychology, 49,* 273–280.

Greenberg, J., Pyszczynski, T., & Solomon, S. (1982). The self-serving attributional bias: Beyond self-presentation. *Journal of Experimental Social Psychology, 18,* 56–67.

Greenberg, J., Pyszczynski, T., Solomon, S., Pinel, E., Simon, L., & Jordan, K. (1993). Effects of self-esteem on vulnerability-denying defensive distortions: Further evidence of an anxiety-buffering function of self-esteem. *Journal of Experimental Social Psychology, 29,* 229–251.

Gritz, E. R., & Crane, L. A. (1991). Use of diet pills and amphetamines to lose weight among smoking and nonsmoking high school seniors. *Health Psychology, 10,* 330–335.

Harackiewicz, J. M., & Sansone, C. (1991). Goals and intrinsic motivation: You *can* get there from here. *Advances in Motivation and Achievement, 7,* 21–49.

Heatherton, T. F., & Baumeister, R. F. (1991). Binge eating as escape from self-awareness. *Psychological Bulletin, 110,* 86–108.

Heatherton, T. F., & Vohs, K. D. (2000). Interpersonal evaluations following threat to self. *Journal of Personality and Social Psychology, 78,* 725–736.

Heine, S. J., & Lehman, D. R. (1997). The cultural construction of self-enhancement: An examination of group-serving biases. *Journal of Personality and Social Psychology, 72,* 1268–1283.

Heine, S. J., Lehman, D. R., Markus, H. R., & Kitayama, S. (1999). Is there a universal need for positive self-regard? *Psychological Review, 106, 766–795.*

Hellhammer, D. H., & Wade, S. (1993). Endocrine correlates of stress vulnerability. *Psychotherapy and Psychosomatics, 60,* 8–17.

Higgins, E. T. (1987). Self-discrepancy: A theory relating self to affect. *Psychological Review, 94,* 319–340.

Hodgins, H. S., Koestner, R., & Duncan, N. (1996). On the compatibility of autonomy and relatedness. *Personality and Social Psychology Bulletin, 22,* 227–237.

Hull, J. G. (1981). A self-awareness model of the causes and effects of alcohol consumption. *Journal of Abnormal Psychology, 90,* 586–600.

Hull, J. G., Levenson, R. W., Young, R. D., & Sher, K. J. (1983). Self-awareness reducing effects of alcohol consumption. *Journal of Personality and Social Psychology, 44,* 461–473.

Hull, J. G., & Young, R. D. (1983). Self-consciousness, self-esteem, and success–failure as determinants of alcohol consumption in male social drinkers. *Journal of Personality and Social Psychology, 44,* 1097–1109.

Joiner, T. E. (1994). Contagious depression: Existence, specificity to depressed symptoms, and the role of reassurance seeking. *Journal of Personality and Social Psychology, 67,* 287–296.

Joiner, T. E., Alfano, M. S., & Metalsky, G. I. (1992). When depression breeds contempt: Reassurance seeking, self-esteem, and rejection of depressed college students by their roommates. *Journal of Abnormal Psychology, 101,* 165–173.

Joiner, T. E., Katz, J., & Lew, A. (1999). Harbingers of depressotypic reassurance seeking: Negative life events, increased anxiety, and decreased self-esteem. *Personality and Social Psychology Bulletin, 25,* 630–637.

Joiner, T. E., Metalsky, G. I., Gencoz, F., & Gencoz, T. (2001). The relative specificity of excessive reassurance-seeking to depressive symptoms and diagnoses among clinical samples of adults and youth. *Journal of Psychopathology and Behavioral Assessment, 23,* 35–41.

Joiner, T. E., Metalsky, G. I., Katz, J., & Beach, S. R. H. (1999). Depression and excessive reassurance-seeking. *Psychological Inquiry, 10,* 269–278.

Jonah, B. A. (1990). Age differences in risky driving. *Health Education Research, 5,* 139–149.

Kernis, M. H. (2003). Toward a conceptualization of optimal self-esteem. *Psychological Inquiry, 14,* 1–26.

Kernis, M. H., Paradise, A. W., Whitaker, D. J., Wheatman, S. R., & Goldman, B. N. (2000). Master of one's psychological domain? Not likely if one's self-esteem is unstable. *Personality and Social Psychology Bulletin, 26,* 1297–1305.

Kernis, M. H., & Waschull, S. B. (1995). The interactive roles of stability and level of self-esteem: Research and theory. In M. P. Zanna (Ed.), *Advances in experimental social psychology* (Vol. 27, pp. 93–141). San Diego, CA: Academic Press.

Kernis, M. H., Whisenhunt, C. R., Waschull, S. B., Greenier, K. D., Berry, A. J., Herlocker, C. E., & Anderson, C. A. (1998). Multiple facets of self-esteem and their relations to depressive symptoms. *Personality and Social Psychology Bulletin, 24,* 657–668.

Kiecolt-Glaser, J., Cacioppo, J., Malarkey, W., & Glaser, R. (1992). Acute psychological stressors and short-term immune changes: What, why, for whom and to what extent? *Psychosomatic Medicine, 53,* 345–362.

Kiecolt-Glaser, J., Dura, J., Speicher, C., Trask, O., & Glaser, R. (1991). Spousal caregivers of dementia victims: Longitudinal changes in immunity and health. *Psychosomatic Medicine, 53,* 345–362.

Kiecolt-Glaser, J., & Glaser, R. (1994). The effects of an acute psychological stressor on cardiovascular, endocrine, and cellular immune response: A prospective study of individuals high and low in heart rate reactivity. *Psychophysiology, 31,* 264–271.

Kiecolt-Glaser, J., Malarkey, W., Chee, M., Newton, T., Cacioppo, J., Mao, H., & Glaser, R. (1993). Negative behavior during marital conflict is associated with immunological down-regulation. *Psychosomatic Medicine, 55,* 395–409.

Kohut, H. (1971). Peace prize 1969: Laudation. *Journal of the American Psychoanalytic Association, 19,* 806–818.

Kuiper, N. A., & Olinger, L. J. (1986). Dysfunctional attitudes and a self-worth contingency model of depression. In P. C. Kendall (Ed.), *Advances in cognitive-behavioral research and therapy* (pp. 115–142). Orlando, FL: Academic Press.

Kuiper, N. A., Olinger, L. J., & MacDonald, M. R. (1988). Vulnerability and episodic cognitions in a self-worth contingency model of depression. In L. B. Alloy (Ed.), *Cognitive processes in depression* (pp. 289–309). New York: Guilford Press.

Kunda, Z., & Sanitioso, R. (1989). Motivated changes in the self-concept. *Journal of Experimental Social Psychology, 25,* 272–285.

Kurman, J. (2003). The role of perceived specificity level of failure in self-enhancement and in constructive self-criticism. *Personality and Social Psychology Bulletin, 29,* 285–294.

Leary, M. R., & Baumeister, R. F. (2000). The nature and function of self-esteem: Sociometer theory. In M. P. Zanna (Ed.), *Advances in experimental social psychology* (Vol. 32, pp. 1–62). San Diego, CA: Academic Press.

Leary, M. R., & Downs, D. L. (1995). Interpersonal functions of the self-esteem motive: The self-esteem system as sociometer. In M. H. Kernis (Ed.), *Efficacy, agency, and self-esteem* (pp. 123–144). New York: Plenum.

Leary, M. R., & Jones, J. L. (1993). The social psychology of tanning and sunscreen use: Self-presentational motives as a predictor of health risk. *Journal of Applied Social Psychology, 23,* 1390–1406.

Leary, M. R., Tchividjian, L. R., & Kraxberger, B. E. (1994). Self-presentation can be hazardous to your health: Impression management and health risk. *Health Psychology, 13,* 461–470.

Markus, H. R., & Kitayama, S. (1991). Culture and the self: Implications for cognition, emotion, and motivation. *Psychological Review, 98,* 224–253.

Maslow, A. H. (1968). *Motivation and personality.* New York: Harper & Row.

McElherner, L. N., & Lisovskis, M. (1998). *Jumpstarters: Quick classroom activities that develop self-esteem, creativity, and cooperation.* Minneapolis, MN: Free Spirit Press.

McFarlin, D. B., & Blascovich, J. (1981). Effects of self-esteem and performance feedback on future affective preferences and cognitive expectations. *Journal of Personality and Social Psychology, 40,* 521–531.

Mecca, A. M., Smelser, N. J., & Vasconcellos, J. (1989). *The social importance of self-esteem.* Berkeley: University of California Press.

Metcalfe, J., & Mischel, W. (1999). A hot/cool system analysis of delay of gratification: Dynamics of willpower. *Psychological Review, 106,* 1–17.

Miller, D. T., & Ross, M. (1975). Self-serving biases in attribution of causality: Fact or fiction? *Psychological Bulletin, 82,* 213–225.

Miller, P. J. (2001, April). *Self-esteem as folk theory: A comparison of ethnographic interviews.* Paper presented at the annual meeting of the Society for Research in Child Development, Minneapolis, MN.

Miller, T. Q., Smith, T. W., Turner, C. W., Guijarro, M. L., & Hallet, A. J. (1996). A meta-analytic review of research on hostility and physical health. *Psychological Bulletin, 119,* 322–348.

Mischel, W., Ebbesen, E. B., & Zeiss, A. R. (1976). Determinants of selective memory about the self. *Journal of Consulting and Clinical Psychology, 44,* 92–103.

Mischel, W., & Shoda, Y. (1995). A cognitive-affective system theory of personality: Reconceptualizing situations, dispositions, dynamics, and invariance in personality structure. *Psychological Review, 102,* 246–268.

Morf, C. C. (1994). Interpersonal consequences of narcissists' continual effort to maintain and bolster self-esteem. *Dissertation Abstracts International, 55,* 2430B.

Morf, C. C., & Rhodewalt, F. (1993). Narcissism and self-evaluation maintenance: Explorations in object relations. *Personality and Social Psychology Bulletin, 19,* 668–676.

Morf, C. C., & Rhodewalt, F. (2001). Unraveling the paradoxes of narcissism: A dynamic self-regulatory processing model. *Psychological Inquiry, 12,* 177–196.

Morf, C. C., Weir, C., & Davidov, M. (2000). Narcissism and intrinsic motivation: The role of goal congruence. *Journal of Experimental Social Psychology, 36,* 424–438.

Murray, S. L., Holmes, J. G., & Griffin, D. W. (2000). Self-esteem and the quest for felt security: How perceived regard regulates attachment processes. *Journal of Personality and Social Psychology, 78,* 478–498.

Murray, S. L., Holmes, J. G., Griffin, D. W., Bellavia, G., & Rose, P. (2001). The mismeasure of love: How self-doubt contaminates relationship beliefs. *Personality and Social Psychology Bulletin, 27,* 423–436.

Nuer, C. (Chair). (1997, August). *Personal mastery in action.* Learning as Leadership Seminar, Sausolito, CA.

Park, L. E., & Crocker, J. (2003). *The interpersonal costs of seeking self-esteem.* Unpublished manuscript.

Pyszczynski, T., & Greenberg, J. (1987). Self-regulatory perseveration and the depressive self-focusing style: A self-awareness theory of reactive depression. *Psychological Bulletin, 102,* 122–138.

Pyszczynski, T., Greenberg, J., & Goldenberg, J. L. (2003). Freedom versus fear: On the defense, growth, and expansion of the self. In M. R. Leary & J. P. Tangney (Eds.), *Handbook of self and identity* (pp. 314–343). New York: Guilford Press.

Pyszczynski, T., Greenberg, J., & Holt, K. (1985). Maintaining consistency between self-serving beliefs and available data: A bias in information evaluation following success and failure. *Personality and Social Psychology Bulletin, 11,* 179–190.

Pyszczynski, T., Greenberg, J., & Laprelle, J. (1985). Social comparison after success and failure: Biased search for information consistent with a self-serving conclusion. *Journal of Experimental Social Psychology, 21,* 195–211.

Pyszczynski, T., Greenberg, J., & Solomon, S. (1997). Why do we need what we need? A terror management perspective on the roots of human social motivation. *Psychological Inquiry, 8,* 1–20.

Reis, H. T., Sheldon, K. M., Gable, S. L., Roscoe, J., & Ryan, R. M. (2000). Daily well-being: The role of autonomy, competence, and relatedness. *Personality and Social Psychology Bulletin, 26,* 419–435.

Rhodewalt, F., Madrian, J. C., & Cheney, S. (1998). Narcissism, self-knowledge organization, and emotional reactivity: The effect of daily experiences on self-esteem and affect. *Personality and Social Psychology Bulletin, 24,* 75–87.

Rhodewalt, F., & Morf, C. C. (1995). Self and interpersonal correlates of the Narcissistic Personality Inventory: A review and new findings. *Journal of Research in Personality, 29,* 1–23.

Rhodewalt, F., & Sorrow, D. L. (2003). Interpersonal self-regulation: Lessons from the study of narcissism. In M. R. Leary & J. P. Tangney (Eds.), *Handbook of self and identity* (pp. 519–535). New York: Guilford Press.

Roberts, J. E., & Gamble, S. A. (2001). Current mood-state and past depression as predictors of self-esteem and dysfunctional attitudes among adolescents. *Personality and Individual Differences, 30,* 1023–1037.

Roberts, J. E., & Gotlib, I. H. (1997). Temporal variability in global self-esteem and specific self-evaluation as prospective predictors of emotional distress: Specificity in predictors and outcome. *Journal of Abnormal Psychology, 106,* 521–529.

Roberts, J. E., & Kassel, J. D. (1997). Labile self-esteem, life stress, and depressive symptoms: Prospective data testing a model of vulnerability. *Cognitive Therapy and Research, 21,* 569–589.

Roberts, J. E., Kassel, J. D., & Gotlib, I. H. (1995). Level and stability of self-esteem as predictors of depressive symptoms. *Personality and Individual Differences, 19,* 217–224.

Roberts, J. E., Kassel, J. D., & Gotlib, I. H. (1996). Adult attachment security and symptoms of depression: The mediating role of dysfunctional attitudes and low self-esteem. *Journal of Personality and Social Psychology, 70,* 310–320.

Roberts, J. E., & Monroe, S. M. (1992). Vulnerable self-esteem and depressive symptoms: Prospective findings comparing three alternative conceptualizations. *Journal of Personality and Social Psychology, 62,* 804–812.

Rogers, C. R. (1961). On becoming a person. Boston: Houghton Mifflin. Rosenberg, M. (1979). *Conceiving the self.* New York: Basic Books.

Ross, M. (2002). It feels like yesterday: The social psychology of subjective time judgments. Paper presented at the annual meeting of the Society for Personality and Social Psychology, Savannah, GA.

Ryan, R. M. (1982). Control and information in the interpersonal sphere: An extension of cognitive evaluation theory. *Journal of Personality and Social Psychology, 43,* 450–461.

Ryan, R. M., & Deci, E. L. (2000). Self-determination theory and the facilitation of intrinsic motivation, social development, and well-being. American *Psychologist, 55,* 68–78.

Ryan, R. M., & Lynch, J. (1989). Emotional autonomy versus detachment: Revisiting the vicissitudes of adolescence and young adulthood. *Child Development, 60,* 340–356.

Ryff, C. D. (1995). Psychological well-being in adult life. *Psychological Science, 4,* 99–104.

Schlenker, B. R., & Leary, M. R. (1982). Social anxiety and self-presentation: A conceptualization and model. *Psychological Bulletin, 92,* 641–669.

Schouten, J. W. (1991). Selves in transition: Symbolic consumption in personal rites of passage and identity reconstruction. *Journal of Consumer Research, 17,* 412–425.

Schrof, J. M. (1992, June 1). Pumped up. *U.S. News and World Report,* 55–63.

Seligman, M. E. P. (1998). The American way of blame. *Monitor on Psychology, 29,* 4.

Sheldon, K. M., & Elliot, A. J. (1999). Goal striving, need satisfaction, and longitudinal well-being: The self-concordance model. *Journal of Personality and Social Psychology, 76,* 482–497.

Sheldon, K. M., Elliot, A. J., Kim, Y., & Kasser, T. (2001). What is satisfying about satisfying events? Testing 10 candidate psychological needs. *Journal of Personality and Social Psychology, 80,* 325–339.

Sherman, D. K., & Kim, H. S. (2002). *Increasing attributions of personal responsibility in sports competitions via self-affirmation.* Unpublished manuscript, University of California, Los Angeles.

Shoda, Y., Mischel, W., & Peake, P. K. (1990). Predicting adolescent cognitive and self-regulatory competencies from preschool delay of gratification: Identifying diagnostic conditions. *Developmental Psychology, 26,* 978–986.

Shrauger, J. S. (1975). Responses to evaluation as a function of initial self-perceptions. *Psychological Bulletin, 82,* 581–596.

Simpson, J. A., Rholes, W. S., & Nelligan, J. S. (1992). Support seeking and support giving within couples in an anxiety-provoking situation: The role of attachment styles. *Journal of Personality and Social Psychology, 62,* 434–446.

Smith, L. L., & Elliott, C. H. (2001). *Hollow kids: Recapturing the soul of a generation lost to the self-esteem myth.* New York: Random House.

Solomon, S., Greenberg, J., & Pyszczynski, T. (1991). A terrormanagement theory of social behavior: The psychological functions of self-esteem and cultural worldviews. In M. P. Zanna (Ed.), *Advances in experimental social psychology* (Vol. 24, pp. 91–159). San Diego, CA: Academic Press.

Spencer, S. J., Fein, S., Wolfe, C. T., Fong, C., & Dunn, M. A. (1998). Automatic activation of stereotypes: The role of self-image threat. *Personality and Social Psychology Bulletin, 24,* 1139–1152.

Steele, C. M. (1997). A threat in the air: How stereotypes shape intellectual identity and performance. *American Psychologist, 52,* 613–629.

Stone, J. (2002). Battling doubt by avoiding practice: The effects of stereotype threat on self-handicapping in White athletes. *Personality and Social Psychology Bulletin, 28,* 1667–1678.

Stroebe, W. (2000). Health psychology (2nd ed.). Buckingham, England: Open University Press.

Suinn, R. M. (2001). The terrible twos—Anger and anxiety. *American Psychologist, 56,* 27–36.

Taylor, S. E., & Brown, J. D. (1988). Illusion and well-being: A social–psychological perspective on mental health. *Psychological Bulletin, 103,* 193–210.

Tennen, H., & Herzberger, S. (1987). Depression, self-esteem, and the absence of self-protective attributional biases. *Journal of Personality and Social Psychology, 52,* 72–80.

Tesser, A. (1988). Toward a self-evaluation maintenance model of social behavior. In L. Berkowitz (Ed.), *Advances in experimental social psychology* (Vol. 21, pp. 181–227). San Diego, CA: Academic Press.

Tesser, A. (2000). On the confluence of self-esteem maintenance mechanisms. *Personality and Social Psychology Review, 4,* 290–299.

Tice, D. M. (1991). Esteem protection or enhancement? Self-handicapping motives and attributions differ by trait self-esteem. *Journal of Personality and Social Psychology, 60,* 711–725.

Tice, D. M. (1993). The social motivations of people with low self-esteem. In R. Baumeister (Ed.), *Self-esteem: The puzzle of low self-regard* (pp. 37–54). Hillsdale, NJ: Erlbaum.

Tice, D. M., & Baumeister, R. F. (1997). Longitudinal study of procrastination, performance, stress, and health: The costs and benefits of dawdling. *Psychological Science, 8,* 454–458.

Tice, D. M., & Bratslavsky, E. (2000). Giving in to feel good: The place of emotion regulation in the context of general self-control. *Psychological Inquiry, 11,* 149–159.

Tice, D. M., Bratslavsky, E., & Baumeister, R. F. (2001). Emotional distress regulation takes precedence over impulse control: If you feel bad, do it! *Journal of Personality and Social Psychology, 80,* 53–67.

Twenge, J. M. (2000). The age of anxiety? The birth cohort change in anxiety and neuroticism, 1952–1993. *Journal of Personality and Social Psychology, 79,* 1007–1021.

Vedhara, K., Hyde, J., Gilchrist, I. D., Tytherleigh, M., & Plummer, S. (2000). Acute stress, memory, attention and cortisol. *Psychoneuroendocrinology, 25,* 535–549.

Vohs, K. D., & Heatherton, T. F. (2000). Self-regulatory failure: A resource-depletion approach. *Psychological Science, 11,* 249–254.

Vohs, K. D., & Heatherton, T. F. (2001). Self-esteem and threats to self: Implications for self-construals and interpersonal perceptions. *Journal of Personality and Social Psychology, 81,* 1103–1118.

Waschull, S. B., & Kernis, M. H. (1996). Level and stability of self-esteem as predictors of children's intrinsic motivation and reasons for anger. *Personality and Social Psychology Bulletin, 22,* 4–13.

White, R. W. (1959). Motivation reconsidered: The concept of competence. *Psychological Review, 66,* 297–333.

Wills, T. A. (1981). Downward comparison principles in social psychology. *Psychological Bulletin, 90,* 245–271.

Wilson, A. E., & Ross, M. (2000). The frequency of temporal-self and social comparisons in people's personal appraisals. *Journal of Personality and Social Psychology, 78,* 928–942.

Wilson, A. E., & Ross, M. (2001). From chump to champ: People's appraisals of their earlier and present selves. *Journal of Personality and Social Psychology, 80,* 572–584.

Wood, J. V., Giordano-Beech, M., & Ducharme, M. J. (1999). Compensating for failure through social comparison. *Personality and Social Psychology Bulletin, 25,* 1370–1386.

JENNIFER CROCKER teaches social psychology at Ohio State University as a professor and Ohio Eminent Scholar. Her research focuses on the setbacks of pursuing self-esteem as a goal, the contingencies of self-worth, and self-esteem in general. She was previously a psychology professor at the University of Michigan.

LORA E. PARK is an associate professor of psychology at the State University of New York at Buffalo. She received her doctoral degree in psychology from the University of Michigan, and her name is now Lora Park Bunting.

EXPLORING THE ISSUE

Is High Self-Esteem Really Beneficial?

Critical Thinking and Reflection

1. Did you find one of the articles more persuasive than the other? Identify a strength and a weakness for each article.
2. A foundational concept in research psychology is "correlation does not imply causation"; this is partially because even if a causal relationship does exist between two variables, it's hard to know which variable is the cause, and which variable is the effect. Do you think that high self-esteem leads to good or bad outcomes, or does success/failure influence one's self-esteem?
3. People who believe that children need high self-esteem are very confident in their opinion, as are people who believe that self-esteem can be too high. Do you think each side of the issue would be open to changing their minds, if the evidence were strong enough? Or do you think people's opinions are so strong that almost nothing would change their minds?
4. Do you, personally, think you have high self-esteem or low self-esteem? Now that you've read both sides of the issue, are you satisfied with your current level of self-esteem? Do you wish it here higher, or lower? Why?
5. If you have children or imagine having them in the future, do you want them to receive a certificate or trophy simply for participating, or do you believe this fosters a sense of spoiled entitlement?

Is There Common Ground?

There are two possible resolutions to this debate. The first is that perhaps a moderate level of self-esteem is the best; this avoids both ends of the extreme. It is reasonable that individuals with very low self-esteem will become depressed and ineffectual. It is also reasonable that individuals with very high self-esteem are arrogant narcissists who do not feel the need to satisfy the needs of anyone but themselves. Thus, moderate self-esteem may be best.

The other possible resolution is that different levels of self-esteem could predict positive outcomes in different contexts. For example, high self-esteem might lead to positive mental health behaviors, whereas low self-esteem might lead to positive physical health behaviors. It is clear that more research is needed to reveal the full and complicated puzzle that is self-esteem.

Donnellan, M. B., Trzesniewski, K. H., Robins, R. W., Moffitt, T. E., & Caspi, A. (2005). Low self-esteem is related to aggression, antisocial behavior, and delinquency. *Psychological Science, 16,* 328–335.

Mann, M., Hosman, C. M. H., Schaalma, H. P., & deVries, N. K. (2004). Self-esteem in a broad-spectrum approach for mental health promotion. *Health Education Research, 19,* 357–372.

Sedikides, C., Rudich, E. A., Gregg, A. P., Kumashiro, M., & Rusubult, C. (2004). Are normal narcissists psychologically healthy? Self-esteem matters. *Personality Processes and Individual Differences, 87,* 400–416. doi: 10.1037/0022-3514.87.3.400

Additional Resources

Baumeister, R. F., Campbell, J. D., Krueger, J. I., & Vohs, K. D. (2003). Does high self-esteem cause better performance, interpersonal success, happiness, or healthier lifestyles? *Psychological Science in the Public Interest, 4,* 1–44.

Internet References . . .

Psychology Today: Self-Esteem

http://www.psychologytoday.com/basics/self-esteem

Self-Confidence

http://www.self-confidence.co.uk/articles/
why-high-self-esteem-is-a-bad-thing/

The Mayo Clinic: Self-Esteem Check

http://www.mayoclinic.org/healthy-living/adult-health/
in-depth/self-esteem/art-20047976

WebMD: Why Self-Esteem Isn't Always Healthy

http://www.webmd.com/balance/news/20080428/
high-self-esteem-isnt-always-healthy

Selected, Edited, and with Issue Framing Material by:
Wind Goodfriend, *Buena Vista University*

ISSUE

Is the Fear of Bullying Justified?

YES: Oyaziwo Aluede et al. from "A Review of the Extent, Nature, Characteristics and Effects of Bullying Behaviour in Schools," *Journal of Instructional Psychology* (2008)

NO: Helene Guldberg, from "Are Children Being Held Hostage by Parental Fears?" *Spiked* (2007)

Learning Outcomes

After reading this issue, you will be able to:

- List and explain at least three negative outcomes of being a bully victim, as discussed in the articles presented.
- List and explain several negative outcomes of being a bully, as discussed in the articles presented.
- Summarize the points made in the article questioning whether fears of bullying are justified.
- Identify some online resources for victims of bullies that offer emotional, psychological, or practical help.

ISSUE SUMMARY

YES: This team of researchers from Nigeria review a long list of negative outcomes both from being the victim of bullying and from being the bully. Negative consequences of being victimized include "physical, academic, social and psychological problems."

NO: Developmental psychologist Helene Guldberg believes that parents' fears of bullying have gone too far. Controlling teachers and parents are restricting children's freedom, teaching them not to trust adults, and preventing children from learning how to resolve conflicts.

In 2010, a journalist named Dan Savage and his partner, Terry Miller, created a video on YouTube called "It Gets Better." In the video, they attempted to present a hopeful message to LGBT (lesbian, gay, bisexual, and transgender) young people that even if they were experiencing bullying right now, they should remain optimistic that their futures held better times. The video was inspired by the high levels of suicides and suicide attempts that LGBT youths go through every year, often as a direct outcome of severe bullying.

The video quickly went viral, and now thousands of people across the United States and around the world have become involved in the "It Gets Better" project. According to the website itgetsbetter.org, the movement has expanded to include 50,000 amateur videos that have a total of over 50 million views on the Internet. Some fans of the original project have created "It Gets Better" videos specifically for other groups, such as people of minority ethnicities, disabilities, or even all children with the common message that bullying and harassment are temporary problems, and that many people who are severely bullied early in life become happy, healthy adults surrounded by a loving and supportive social network.

The "It Gets Better" campaign is just one example of how bullying has become a major focus for parents, educators, the federal government, and—of course—social psychologists. In a subfield of psychology devoted to complicated social interactions, bullying presents an important social phenomenon that is fascinating for both basic and applied research. Almost everyone can identify an emotional memory from his or her childhood in which one's peers exhibited bullying or harassing behavior. However, in spite of the seeming ubiquity of bullying, there is a range of opinions about the effects of this experience on those involved.

To begin, the "yes" side of this debate comes from a team of counseling psychologists who present a summary of literature from 37 previous publications about the pervasive negative outcomes that, they argue, are the direct results of bullying. They first describe characteristics often found in bullies and bully victims, then review the nature of bullying and statistics on how common the phenomenon is, across many different countries and cultures. Their main focus, however, is to list and discuss many negative effects of being either the victim or the perpetrator of bullying, including mental health (such as depression or suicidal attempts, as highlighted above), poor academic performance (due to distraction), and lower self-esteem, just to name a few.

Certainly, the "yes" side of this debate—that the fear of bullying is justified and that a variety of constituencies in the community should be fighting bullying—is the more popular opinion within this controversy. How-

ever, there are scientists and practitioners who believe that the focus on bullying is overblown, a modern version of a social witch hunt, and that everyone is overreacting. The author of the "no" side, Helene Guldberg, is both an online journalist and a doctor of developmental psychology.

Guldberg writes that the massive fear of bullying coming from parents is incapacitating children and preventing them from learning how to explore and navigate social relationships. Constant and smothering supervision from parents, she argues, leads to children who are not left alone to both make friendships (through positive peer social interactions) and learn how to resolve conflict (through negative peer social interactions, such as bullying). She believes that fears about bullying are exaggerated overreactions and that consequential restrictive parenting limits children's opportunities to grow into healthy adults. For example, she states, "Such a strategy is likely to be far more damaging to children than the occasional argument or even kick or punch."

No one wants children to suffer, so the focus on bullying is understandable. The question, however, is whether bullying is really as scary as it seems. Is the fear of bullying justified?

YES ⤶

Oyaziwo Aluede et al.

A Review of the Extent, Nature, Characteristics and Effects of Bullying Behaviour in Schools

School has always been recognized as an institution for the transfer of knowledge and culture to the future generation. It is a dynamic human system dedicated to the nurturing of mutual growth and understanding between children and adults (Schultz, Glass & Kamholtz, 1987; Rutter, 1995).

In schools, the learners are the centre of focus. They are of utmost importance hence, adequate information about the students is necessary for any meaningful learning to take place. For teachers' efforts not to be wasted and for learners to change along with the set goals, such factors that affect learning and teaching, which include child growth, age, heredity, interest, home and social effects and violence in school (including school bullying and peer victimization) need to be addressed.

From the psychological perspective, bullying as a behavioural characteristics can be conceptualized in a number of ways. It can also be taken to be a subset of aggressive behaviours. As with aggressive behaviours generally, bullying intentionally causes hurt to the recipient. This hurt can be both physical and psychological. Bullying behaviour infringes upon the child's right to human dignity, privacy, freedom and security. It has an influence on the victim's physical, emotional, social and educational well being (Wet, 2005).

Bullies frequently target people who are different from themselves and they seek to exploit those differences. They select victims they think are unlikely to retaliate such as persons who are overweight, wear glasses, or have obvious physical differences like big ears or severe acne. Such victims are common subjects of ridicule in the hands of bullies. However, these differences do not necessarily need to be physical, as students who learn at a different pace or are anxious or insecure can also be targets for bullies. Bullies resort to this abusive behaviour as a way of dealing with difficult situations at home such as broken homes, or partial separation from parents. Some bullies may see their behaviours as normal because they grow up from families in which everyone regularly gets angry and shouts.

Whatever the situation or causes, bullies usually pick on others as a way of dealing with their own problems. In some cases, bullies pick on others because they need a victim (someone who seems emotionally or physically weaker), or because they try to gain acceptance and feel more important, popular, or in control. Thus, the thrust of this paper therefore is to bring to further knowledge the concept of bullying, the characteristics of the students who are bullied, the characteristics of the victims, the nature and extent of bullying and the outcome of bullying.

The Concept of Bullying

Bullying is not a new phenomenon among school children. Most adults can remember incidents of bullying in which they were the bullies or the intended victims. Bullying has only received research attention since the early 1970s when Dan Olweus, a Norwegian researcher began to study this area. At that time, strong societal interest in bullying/victim problem emerged in Scandinavia, where bullying was known as "mobbing". Olweus' 1978 book, "Aggression in the Schools—Bullies and Whipping Boys", is considered a landmark and the first systematic study of the phenomenon of bullying (Noelle, 2005).

Bullying can be described as repeated negative events, which over time are directed at special individuals and which are carried out by one or several other people who are stronger than the victim. Negative events can be aggressive physical contact in the form of fights and shoving, verbal threats and mockery, grimacing or cruel gesturing.

Bullying occurs when a person willfully and repeatedly exercises power over another with hostile or malicious intent. A wide range of physical or verbal behaviours

From Adeleke, F., Aluede, O., Afen-Akpaida, J., Omoike, D. (2008). "A Review of the Extent, Nature, Characteristics and Effects of Bullying Behavior in Schools." *Journal of Instructional Psychology,* vol. 35, no. 2, pp. 151–158.

of an aggressive or anti-social nature are encompassed by the term bullying. These include, humiliating, harassing and mobbing (Colvin, Tobin, Beard, Hagan & Sprague, 1998). Bullying may also assume less direct forms (sometimes referred to as "psychological bullying") such as gossiping, spreading rumours, and shunning or exclusion (O'Connel, Pepler & Craig, 1999).

However, the most widely used definition of bullying is that coined by Olweus (1978), which states that a person is being bullied when he or she is exposed repeatedly and over time, to negative actions on the part of one or more other persons. Negative actions are considered to be when someone purposefully inflicts, or tries to inflict injury or discomfort on another person. Negative actions may be both verbal (e.g. threatening, degrading, teasing) and non-verbal (e.g. hitting, kicking, slapping, pushing, vandalizing property, rude gestures, and making faces) (Olweus, 1993). Bullying may be carried out by a single person (the bully) or by a group against a single person (the victim) or by a group.

Langevin (2000) claimed that this definition requires that negative actions must be carried out repeatedly and intentionally to be considered bullying, which excludes occasional and less serious negative action. In order to be considered bullying, there should also be an actual or perceived power imbalance. That is, the person experiencing the negative actions has trouble defending him/herself and is helpless to some degree against the harassing person or persons (Besag, 1991; Rigby & Slee, 1993).

Olweus (1993) opined that another distinction that is sometimes made in defining bullying is that of direct and indirect bullying. Direct bullying is defined as open attacks on the victim, while indirect bullying consists of social isolation and exclusion from the group. Smith and Sharp (1994) submitted that a further criterion is that bullying must be unprovoked on the part of the victim.

The Characteristics of Students Who Are Bullies

There are many common characteristics found in most bullies. Bosworth, Espelage and Simon (2001) opined that most bullies are male, popular, and often athletes. They have excellent social skills, with the ability to attract many followers, and easily manipulate others.

Bullies are psychologically strong and very popular among their peers. However, the peer status is important in terms of boosting their well being. Bullying behaviour is self reinforcing. When students find that putting others down give them approval from their peers, they are likely to do it repeatedly. Sometimes, they can easily butter up

to adults, making them unsuspecting bullies (Bosworth, Espelage & Simon, 2001).

Generally, a bully is someone who teases and intimidates other students, although there are many other ways to bully a fellow student. Many people feel that the typical bully comes from a broken home, but this is not necessarily true. Still, the less supervision a child gets at home, the more likely he is to be a bully. Different studies have proved that most bullies look for a victim who is smaller, younger and weaker. As a practice, bullies have more aggressive attitudes towards their social surroundings and a positive attitude about violence. Furthermore, it has been shown by different surveys that bullies are steered by impulses, they need to dominate others and do not show any empathy for the victim.

Rigby (1996) discussed two possible conceptualizations of the bully. One is a child who is vicious and uncaring, the product of a dysfunctional family. This bully has an aggressive temperament, and he/she is hostile and unempathic in relations with others. The second conceptualization suggests that some bullies are in fact members of a group that builds its strength on harassing vulnerable children who are not members of their group. The bully may or may not be malicious in intent, and the members reassure themselves that no real harm is being done. Rigby (1996) called this type of bully a "passive bully" or "follower".

As for girls, they experience a different form of bullying. Although it is a more indirect form of bullying, social manipulation is very prevalent within females. Social manipulation can include many actions, including spreading gossip, telling lies, betraying trust, passing notes, ignoring the victim, or excluding the victim (Anonymous, 2001; Kenny, McEachan & Aluede, 2005).

The Characteristics of Students Who Are Victims of Bully

Victims of bullying are described as more anxious, careful and insecure compared to other students in general. They are not aggressive but have a negative self image. Olweus (1993) stated that bullying victim often lacks friends in the class and at school. Students exposed to long-term bullying can see the school environment as unfriendly, frightening, and go through a major part of school with anxiety and insecurity. The major dependence which bullying victims feel towards their families can also be explained by their vulnerability and their otherwise insecure situation. With respect to physical attributes, victims are physically weak than non-victims.

Bosworth, Espelage and Simon (2001) asserted that 30% to 40% of bullies show some level of depression, and their bullying is often a cry for help. Most likely the victims will be both less confident and unpopular. Therefore, many victims react by becoming upset or crying as a way of dealing with their anger or fear. Victims have a tendency to be depressed, anxious, shy and lonely (Drake, 2003).

Rubin (2003) maintained that from previous research, victims tend to have a lower self-esteem and a high level of depression. Victims tend to be physically smaller, more sensitive, unhappy, cautious, anxious, quiet and withdrawn than other children (Bryne, 1994). Most victims of bullying can be termed "passive" or "submissive" victims (Olweus, 1994). They are generally insecure and non-assertive, and react by withdrawing and crying when attacked by other students. In this sense, they are vulnerable to being victimized, as bullies know these children will not retaliate. A less common characteristic, the "provocative victim", has also been described. Olweus (1994) classified this type of victim of bullying as a combination of both anxious and aggressive traits, and these students sometimes provoke classmates into victimizing them by their overactive and irritable behaviour.

The Nature of Bullying

Bullying can take many forms and has been categorized in many ways by various researchers. Pearce (1991) identified three different kinds of bullies: the aggressive one, the anxious one and the passive one.

a. the aggressive bully—is aggressive towards everybody, not just the weak. The aggressive bullies are insensitive, domineering, lacking in self-control; but, contrary to the psycho-dynamic notion, they are also high in self-esteem. Furthermore, most bullies would fall into this category.

b. the anxious bully—is more disturbed. They share more of the victim's characteristics, such as low self-esteem, insecurity and loneliness, emotionally unstable and provocative. They are met likely to be victims themselves.

c. the passive bully—is the one who engages in bullying in order to protect himself/herself and to achieve status. A passive bully would be easily dominated and led, would be more sensitive to the sufferings of others but would do nothing about it and also would be reluctant to engage in active bullying.

Langevin (2000) classified bully into four, these include:

a. Physical bullies—these are the easiest to identify. They act out their anger by hitting, shoving, or kicking their chosen target—or by damaging their victim's property.

b. Verbal bullies—they use words to hurt and humiliate their target, through either name—calling, insult or persistent and harsh teasing.

c. Relationship bullies—they spread nasty rumours about their target. This behaviour is predominantly adopted by female bullies.

d. Reactive victims—these are victims of bullying who turn into bullies themselves. Of course, their having been victims of bullying does not excuse their conduct; it only helps to explain it.

Aside the above classifications, other researchers (i.e. Garrity, Jens, Porter, Sager & Short-Camilli, 2001; Rigby, 1996) noted that forms of bullying can be basically categorized into five as follows:

a. Physical aggressive (e.g. pushing, tripping, spitting)

b. Social alienation (e.g. excluding, coercing, other to reject or exclude a person)

c. Verbal aggression (e.g. name calling, taunting, teasing)

d. Intimidation (e.g. threats, intimidating, coercing one to do what they would not ordinarily do)

e. Relational bullying—bullying that damages relationships (e.g. gossiping, spreading rumours, making racial slurs)

Bullying can take the form of direct and indirect, overt or very subtle, and it ranges in severity from mild to severe. There is overlap in the categorizations and again there is no one agreed upon categorization (Rigby, 1996).

The more recent form of bullying is electronic bullying, which is otherwise known as digital bullying. This form of bullying is a new and insidious development. It involves the sending of menacing messages through telephone calls or by Email messages. In addition, youths also create hate-filled web pages about a victim where they include personal information about the victim. This form of bullying is extra-ordinarily damaging to the child who is being victimized by it (Aluede, 2006). Moreover, mobile phones are a popular choice for bullies. They provide bullies with the perfect means of taunting their targets with little fear of being caught. Text messages provide complete anonymity. Many "Pay–As–You–Go" mobile phones can be bought over the counter and do not require proof of identity, nor is there any record kept of the new owner. Calls made from these types of mobile phones are difficult to trace (Anonymous, 2005).

The Extent of Bullying

Bullying among school children occurs worldwide. It takes place in small schools, large schools, single sex, co-educational schools, traditional and progressive schools. It occurs in both primary and secondary schools. The most common form of bullying for both sexes is verbal and includes teasing, harassment and name-calling. It is the most painful form and has the longest-lasting impact. However, extortion, physical violence, nasty rumours, exclusion from the group, damage to property and threats are also regarded as bullying. The playground is the most common place for bullying to occur and most children believe that bullying cannot be stopped.

Bullying in schools across the world is beginning to assume a serious dimension. For example, in Australia, Prof. Ken Rigby reported that one student out of six between the ages of 9 and 17, is affected by bullying at least once a week. In American schools, there are approximately 2.1 million bullies and 2.7 million victims (Lumsdem, 2002).

For instance, in U.S., in a national study, Nansel, Overpeck, Pilla, Ruan, Simons-Morton and Scheidt (2001) found that about 30% of 6th through 10th grade students had been involved in bullying incidents with moderate or frequent regularity. Similar prevalence rates were found in the State of Florida. For example, in a study by Bully Police, USA (n.d.) found that of the 2,701,022 school age children in Florida, approximately 442,157 students representing 16.37% were involved in bullying.

Nansel, Overpeck, Pilla, Ruan, Simons-Morton and Scheidt (2001) added that limited available data show that bullying is much more common among younger teens than older teens. As teens grow older, they are less likely to bully others and to be the targets of bullies.

Rigby and Slee (1991) remarked that bullying occurs more frequently among boys than girls. Teenage boys are much more likely to bully others and also to be the targets of bullies. While both girls and boys say others bully them by making fun of the way they look or talk, boys are more likely to report being hit, slapped or pushed. Teenage girls are more often the targets of rumours and sexual comments.

Also, in a study of fourth-through eighth-graders, above 15% of the respondents reported being severely distressed by bullying and 22% reported academic difficulties stemming from maltreatment by peers (Hoover & Oliver, 1996). Gallagher's study (as cited in Nansel et al, 2001) reported that one out of four children is bullied, and one out of five defined himself/herself as a bully. In all, approximately 282,000 students are physically attacked in secondary schools every month. In the same view, Vail (2002) claimed that many students avoid public areas of the school such as the cafeteria and restrooms in an attempt to elude bullies. For some students, the fear is so great that they avoid school altogether, hence everyday approximately 160,000 students stay home from school because they are afraid of being bullied.

Olweus (1993) opined that teenage boys target boys and girls, teenage girls most often bully other girls, using more subtle and indirect forms of aggression than boys. For example, teenage girls, instead of physically harming others, they are more likely to spread gossip or encourage others to reject or exclude another girl. In addition, a survey published in "Pediatrics in Review" reveals that in Norway, 14% of children are either bullies or victims. In Japan, 15% of primary school pupils say that they are bullied, while in Australia and Spain, the problem prevails among 17% of the students. In Britain, one expert figures that 1.3 million children are involved in bullying.

In Israel, Professor Amos Rolider of Emek Yizre'el College surveyed 2,972 pupils in 21 schools. According to the *Jerusalem Post*, the professor found that "65% complained of being smacked, kicked, pushed or molested by fellow pupils" (Anonymous, 2003). Wet (2005) reported that in 1985, investigation on bullying conducted by the University of California, Los Angeles, it was found that 7% of the youths who took part in the investigation victimized their fellow learners; 9% indicated that they were victims of bullies. Furthermore, 6% indicated that they were victims and bullies. Similarly, in a Norwegian study, in which 568,000 learners participated during 1983–1984, it was found that 9% of the participants were "now and then" "relatively regularly" or "regularly" victims of bullying; 7% were found guilty of bullying (Olweus, 1994).

According to Limber, Flerx, Nation and Melton, 1996 (cited in McEachern, Kenny, Blake & Aluede, 2005), one out of 12 secondary school children in the Netherlands is "very regularly" or "regularly" bullied. Nanse1 et al (2001) found that 60.9% of the 207 participants in a research project in Gauteng indicated that they were bullied during the 2002 school year. Northmore's study (as cited in Wet, 2005) of Johannesburg Centre for School Quality and Improvement (CSQI) points out that 90% of the learners at a Johannesburg school told CSQI that they were bullied in the previous year.

In Nigeria, however, there are little or no adequate statistical facts (as at now) to show the number of students affected by bullying. Nevertheless, Umoh (2000) noted that cases of bullying have been reported in many schools in Nigeria but that the deviant act is not usually given the desirable attention. Bullying has most of the time been ignored by many teachers, counsellors and school administrators because of its silent but adverse effect. Some school personnel even see it as not a serious problem and consequently pay little or no attention to the behaviour. This lukewarm attitude promotes the deviant behaviour and discourages researchers into bullying. This may be responsible for the paucity of literature on bullying among secondary school students in Nigeria (Asonibare, 1998, as cited in Idowu & Yahaya, 2006).

The Effects of Bullying

Bullying can have devastating effects on victims. For the victims of bullying, they go to school everyday fearing harassment, taunting and humiliation. For all potential educators, it is very important to realize that bullying is a problem, so that we can work to prevent it now or in the future (Anonymous, 2005).

There are many repercussions of bullying that are quite shocking. According to Kerlikowske (2003) these include:

1. Children who are bullied are more likely to be depressed; 26% of girls who were frequently bullied reported depression as opposed to 8% of girls who were not. Similarly the boys who were bullied and reported depression were 16% as against 3% who were not.
2. Victims are more likely to be suicidal, with 8% for girls and 4% for boys, compared to 1% overall for non-victims of bullying.
3. Bullies are more likely to carry weapons, with 43% carrying weapons to school at least once a week, compared to 8% who were not carrying weapons.
4. 46% of bullies are more likely to be injured while 16% of bullies are not likely to be injured.
5. As one middle-school student expressed it "there is another kind of violence, and that is violence by talking. It can leave you hurting more than a cut with knife. It can leave you bruised inside" (National Association of Attorneys General, 2000).
6. Students who are targeted by bullies often have difficulty concentrating on their school work, and their academic performance tends to move from "marginal to poor" (Ballard, Tucky & Remley, 1999). Typically, bullied students feel anxious, and this anxiety may in turn produce a variety of physical or emotional ailments.
7. Rates of absenteeism are higher among victimized students than rates among non-bullied peers, as are drop-out rates. Nansel et al (2001) observed that "youths who are bullied generally show higher levels of insecurity, anxiety,

depression, loneliness, unhappiness, physical and mental symptoms, and low-self esteem.
8. Long-term effects on victims—persistent bullying during the school years may have long-term negative effects on the victims many years beyond school (Olweus, 1993). Chronic bullies seem to maintain their behaviours into adulthood thus influencing their ability to develop and maintain positive relationships (Oliver, Hoover & Hazler, 1994).
9. Drake (2003) found that victims of bullies tend to be less popular in school than other students not involved in bullying. As a result of being bullied, 16% boys and 31% girls reported being absent from school in attempt to avoid being victimized (Rigby, 1997).
10. Bullying does not just affect the victim, but it also has consequences for the bully. First, for the victim, bullying can cause physical, academic, social and psychological problems. Some of the physical symptoms include headaches and migraines, skin problems such as eczema, psoriasis, athletes foot, ulcers, sweating, trembling, shaking, palpitations and panic attacks, irritable bowel syndrome, aches and pains in the joints and muscles; and frequent illness such as viral infections and second, for the bully, they are seldom able to conclude friendship, they are often anti-social adults and the bullying is sometimes the first stepping stone to juvenile crime and criminal activities (Aluede, 2006; Wet, 2005).
11. The psychological scars left by bullying often endure for years. For instance, the feelings of isolation and the loss of self-esteem that victims experience seem to last into adulthood (Clarke & Kiselica, 1997).

Conclusion

Bullying is not just isolated behaviour on the part of its perpetrators; instead it is part of a more generally anti-social and rule-breaking (conduct-disordered) behaviour pattern. Therefore, students (particularly boys) who bully others are especially likely to engage in other anti-social/delinquent behaviours such as vandalism, shop lifting, truancy and frequent drug use; and these may continue into young adulthood.

References

Aluede, O. (2006). Bullying in Schools: A form of Child abuse in schools. *Educational Research Quarterly,* 30(1), 37–49.

Anonymous (2001). Bullies and their victims. *Harvard Mental Health Letter*, 4–7. Retrieved on 18th Sept., 2006 from htlp://tcnj.edu/miller8/Bullying.htm.

Anonymous (2003). August 22, Bullying: What can you do about it? *Awake*, pp. 3–11.

Anonymous (2005). *The nature and extent of bullying at school*. Retrieved on September 18, 2006 from http://goliath.ecnext.com/comsite5/bin/pdinventory.

Ballard, M., Tucky, A., & Remley, T.P. Jr. (1999). Bullying and violence: A proposed prevention program, *NASSP Bulletin*, 38–47.

Besag, V. (1991). *Parents and teachers working together*. Essex: Longman Publishers.

Bosworth, K., Espelage, D.L. & Simon, T.R. (2001). Short-term stability and prospective correlates of bullying in middle-school students: An examination of potential demographic, psychosocial, and environmental influences. *Violence and Victims*, 16(4), 411–426.

Bryne, B.J., (1994). Bullies and victims in a school setting with reference to some Dublin Schools. *Irish Journal Psychology*, 15, 574–586.

Clarke, E.A., & Kiselica, M.S. (1997). A systemic counselling approach to the problem of bullying. *Elementary School Guidance and Counselling*, 31, 310–324.

Colvin, G.T., Tobin, T., Beard, K., Hagan, K., & Sprague, L. (1998). The school bully: Assessing the problem, developing interventions, and future research directions. *Journal of Behavioural Education*, 8(3), 293–319.

Drake, J. (2003). Teacher preparation and practices regarding school bullying. *Journal of School Health*, 347–356. Retrieved on September 18, 2006 from http://tcnj.edul-miller8/Bullying.htm.

Garrity, C., Jens, K., Porter, W., Sager, N. & Short-Camilli, C. (2001). *Bully-proofing your school: A comprehensive approach for elementary schools (2nd Ed.)* Longmont, Co.: Sporis West Educational Services.

Hoover, J.H. & Oliver, R. (1996). *The bullying prevention handbook: A guide for principals, teachers and counselors*. Bloomington, Indiana: National Education Service.

Idowu, A.I. & Yahaya, L.A. (2006). Systemic approach as a strategy of handling bullying among secondary school students in Nigeria. *The Counsellor*, 22, 255–262.

Kenny, M., McEachern, A.G. & Aluede, O. (2005). Female bullying: Prevention and counselling intervention, *Journal of Social Sciences, Special Issue*, 8, 13–19.

Kerlikowske, G. (2003). One in six students fall prey to bullies. *Inside School Safety*, 6–9. Retrieved on September 19, 2006 from http://www.tcnj.edu/miller8/Bullying.htm.

Langevin, M. (2000). Teasing and Bullying: Helping children deal with teasing and bullying: for parents, teachers and other adults. Retrieved on September 19, 2006 from http://www.stutterisa.org/CDRom/teasing/tease_bully.htm.

Lumsdem, L. (2002). Preventing Bullying. *Eric Digest*. Retrieved on 18/09/2006 from http://www.ericdigests.org/2003-1/bullying.htm.

McEachern, A.G., Kenny, M., Blake, E. & Aluede, O., (2005). Bullying in schools: International variations. *Journal of Social Sciences, Special Issue*, 51–58.

Nansel, T.R., Overpeck, M., Pilla, R.S., Ruan, W.J., Simons-Morton, & Scheidt, P. (2001). Bullying behaviours among U.S. youth: Prevalence and association with psychosocial adjustment, *Journal of the American Medical Association*, 285(16), 2094–2100.

National Association of Attorneys General (2000). *Bruised inside: What our children say about youth violence, what causes it*. Retrieved on September 18, 2006 from http://library.adoption.com/child-development/preventing-bullyingarticle/3872/l.html.

O'Connel, P., Pepler, D., & Craig, W. (1999). Peer involvement in bullying: Insight and challenges for invention. *Journal of Adolescence*, 22, 437–452.

Oliver, R., Hoover, J.H., & Hazier, R. (1994). The perceived roles of bullying in small-town Midwestern Schools. *Journal of Counselling and Development*, 72(4), 416–419.

Olweus, D. (1978). *Aggression in the schools: Bullying and whipping boys*. Washington, DC: Hemisphere.

Olweus, D. (1994). Annotation: Bullying at school: Basic facts and effects of a school based intervention program. *Journal of Child Psychology and Psychiatry*, 3, 1171–1190.

Pearce, J. (1991). *What can be done about the Bully?* London: Longman. Retrieved on September 19, 2006 from http://info.smkb.ac.il/home.exe/2710/2799.

Rigby, K. & Slee, P.T. (1991). Bullying among Australian school children: Reported behavior and attitudes toward victims. *The Journal of Social Psychology,* 131(5), 615–627.

Rigby, K., & Slee, P.T. (1993). *Children's attitudes towards victim.* In D.P. Tattums (Ed.), *Understanding and managing bullying,* (pp. 119–135). Melbourne: Heinemann Books.

Rigby, K. (1996). *Bullying in Schools: What to do about it.* Victoria, Melbourne: The Australian Council for Educational Research Ltd.

Rigby, K. (1997). What children tell us about bullying in schools. *Children Australia,* 22 (20, 2–34).

Rutter, M. (1995). *Psychosocial disturbances in young people: challenges for prevention.* New York: Cambridge University Press.

Rubin, P. (2003). Study: Bullies and their victims tend to be more violent. *U.S.A. Today.* Retrieved on September 19, 2006 from http://www.tcnj.edu/miller8/Bullying.htm.

Schultz, E.W., Glass, R.M. & Kamholtz, J.D. (1987). School climate: Psychological health and well being in school. *Journal of School Health,* 57, 432–436.

Smith, P.K. & Sharp, S. (1994). *School bullying: Insights and perspectives.* Retrieved on September 20, 2006 from http://www.education.unisa.edu.au/bullying.countering.htm.

Umoh, S.H. (2000). *Managing the problems of the Nigerian adolescents through counselling.* A paper presented at a workshop organized by the Federal Polytechnic, Offa, Kwara State.

Vail, K. (2002). Words that wound. *American School Board Journal,* 37–40. Retrieved on September 19, 2006 from http://www.bullying.com.au/pages/school/bullying.

Wet, C. (2005). *The nature and extent of bullying in Free State secondary schools.* Retrieved on September 18, 2006 from http//www.ericdigests.org/2003-1/bullying.htm.

OYAZIWO ALUEDE is a faculty member at Ambrose Alli University in Ekpoma, Nigeria. His research topics include guidance and counseling.

FAJOJU ADELEKE is a psychologist in Nigeria.

DON OMOIKE is a psychologist in Nigeria; his research surrounds health and fitness.

JUSTINA AFEN-AKPAIDA has a master's in education and was at Ambrose Alli University at the time the article in this volume was published.

Helene Guldberg

 **NO**

Are Children Being Held Hostage by Parental Fears?

A new report calls on parents to let their kids venture out unsupervised. That might be easier if scaremongering officials put a sock in it.

It cannot be easy being a parent today. They get criticised for not giving their children the right kind of love and attention and for not sufficiently protecting them from a never-ending list of risks. And now they are criticised for overanxiously keeping their children tied to their apron strings. Last week, the UK Children's Society published a report, *The Good Childhood Inquiry,* which caused a splash with its claims that children are becoming hostages to parental fears.

The report argues that parents are denying children the freedom to mess around with friends, a freedom that we ourselves once enjoyed. Play is essential for children and young people, the report points out, because it allows them to practice making and consolidating friendships and dealing with conflict. That means being given the space to play *away* from adult supervision. Yet according to research by Play England, a campaign group sponsored by the National Children's Bureau which calls for kids to have access to good and free local play space, in 2003 67 per cent of 8- to 10-year-olds and 24 per cent of 11- to 15-year-olds had never been to the park or the shops on their own.

An NOP survey commissioned by The Children's Society found that 43 per cent of adults thought children should not go out unsupervised until they were 14 years old. Other research has found that in 1970 the average nine-year-old was free to roam 840 metres from his or her front door. By 1997, that had shrunk to 280 metres.

Bob Reitemeier, chief executive of The Children's Society, warned: 'If we go too far down the road of being overprotective and not allowing children to explore, to play, to be up with their peers, but also with children of other ages, then we may be influencing the way in which they look at society and social interaction later on.'

So, in preoccupying themselves with keeping their loved ones safe, are parents denying children the freedom they need to develop and grow up? Quite possibly so. But can we really blame parents for this? As many contributors to *Spiked* have argued, parents are constantly being inundated with warnings about the dreadful things that can happen to their children if they do not keep a watchful eye on them at all times.

Now that there is a growing recognition that parental fears are exaggerated, the finger of blame tends to be pointed at the media—and, of course, the media do have a lot to answer for. No doubt parental fears have been exacerbated by the relentless reporting of the disappearance of Madeleine McCann, and the earlier coverage of the murders of Soham schoolgirls Holly Wells and Jessica Chapman in 2002, and the abduction and killing of Sarah Payne in 2000. Alongside this, there are frequent media reports about an obesity epidemic killing our kids, the dangers of bullying and how older children—'feral teens'—are running riot. All of this no doubt contributes to a sense that the world is a dangerous place for children. However, it is disingenuous to pin all the blame on the media. The government and government-sponsored charities have done far more than their fair share of scaremongering.

Consider the government-sponsored Child Safety Week. As I pointed out on *spiked* in 2001, the message communicated by charities during that year's Child Safety Week was that 'from choking on food or being poisoned by detergents to falling out of windows or drowning in garden ponds . . . your child is at risk, from everything'. Later this month, some of the tips parents will be given by the Child Accident Prevention Trust (CAPT) during Child Safety Week 2007 may be sensible, but they are also patronising. The message of this year's Child Safety Week is 'Safer children, healthier lives. Pass it on'—because of course mums and dads don't know that it is good to keep children safe and healthy. When parents are constantly reminded about how vulnerable children are, it is not

From Helene Guldberg, "Are Children Being Held Hostage by Parental Fears?" *Spiked*, June 11, 2007. http://www.spiked-online.com/newsite/article/3465#.VA99HDfuuSq.

surprising that they lose sight of how resilient, resourceful and capable children could be—if they were given more of a chance to make mistakes and to learn from them.

American social worker and family therapist Michael Ungar, author of *Too Safe for Their Own Good: How Risk and Responsibility Help Teens Thrive*, argues: 'Adults go to great lengths to protect children from the very experiences of failure children *need* to grow up healthy.' From his experience of working with troubled teenagers, Ungar has become convinced that children need to be given more opportunities for risk-taking, as well as more responsibility. The troubled youths he works with, whether they have grown up with many advantages or none, have all told him that they crave adventure and responsibility. 'Both necessarily come with a sizable amount of risk. And both are often in short supply in families and communities dead set on keeping their children too safe for their own good', he argues.

The UK government and various government agencies not only constantly warn parents about the need to prevent accidents—they have also played a key role in undermining, or even breaking down, people's trust in other adults outside of the family. The Safeguarding Vulnerable Groups Bill, for instance, which is currently working its way into law, will make it compulsory for any adult who comes into contact with a child as part of his or her working day to undergo criminal records checks. The message is clear: don't trust any adult, as they may be out to harm or abuse your child. Is it any wonder that parents don't feel confident letting their children play unsupervised in local parks?

Very often today, it is assumed that a parent who *does* let their child go out and about is a bad parent. Simon Knight, a senior community learning and development worker for a Scottish local authority and director of the campaign group Generation Youth Issues, tells me: 'This is the basis on which much government policy is founded. . . . Almost all state-sponsored youth work today is about getting children off the streets. Isn't it ironic? In the name of combating anti-social behaviour, people, in jobs much like my own, are charged with acting like the child catcher in *Chitty Chitty Bang Bang* and tasked with clearing children off the streets—the very place where they learn to be social in the first place.'

On the one hand, youth workers are tasked with clearing kids from public spaces—on the other hand, parents are chastised for not letting their kids go out in public on their own. This says a lot about the screwed-up approach to children today.

Apparently, it is not only adults who pose a risk to children. Other children can destroy lives as well, par-

ents are frequently told. Government officials, teachers' unions, charities and, yes, the media warn about the dangers of bullying—which they claim can damage children for life, giving rise to socially inadequate and depressed adults.

As a consequence of today's bullying obsession, teachers are encouraged to intervene in every little playground spat. More and more everyday childhood activities—from namecalling to group exclusion—are being lumped together with acts of violence as examples of the 'bullying' that is apparently rampant in our schools. The National Association of Head Teachers advises teachers always to take the word of the child claiming to be bullied—partly in order to avoid being sued for not taking action. One of Britain's most expensive state schools, Thomas Deacon City Academy in Peterborough, Cambridgeshire, is even being built without a playground. Staff claim that this will avoid a situation where pupils fall victim to playground bullies. Miles Delap, project manager at the academy, said: 'For a school of this size, a playground would have had to be huge. That would have been almost uncontrollable. We have taken away an uncontrollable space to prevent bullying and truancy.'

It beggars belief. Such is the panic about bullying today that a school is *denying* children the ability to play freely—where they might make friends and develop interpersonal skills—in the name of protecting them from bullies. Such a strategy is likely to be far more damaging to children than the occasional argument or even kick or punch.

Thankfully, not many schools are abandoning breaktime completely. But breaktimes are being eroded in the name of combating bullying. In most schools, adults are put on guard at all times to make sure no children are being picked on. But is it necessarily in children's interest to have adults intervening to help resolve every dispute? By having a zero tolerance approach to bullying, could we be denying children the experiences they need to develop? Peter Blatchford, professor of psychology and education at the Institute of Education in London, points out that some teasing serves a social purpose. He says it helps 'to denote limits . . . define and consolidate friendships, [show] off sharpness in social discourse, and [jostle] for status. Pupils showed that considerable skill could be required in determining what form of teasing was appropriate with particular people.'

The Children's Society inquiry found that in response to the question 'If you need help with a problem, who is the person you are most likely to talk to?', children were most likely to go to their friends (46 per cent), followed by a parent (35 per cent). The report concluded: 'Having friends helps children to develop a sense of identity and social belonging and to learn a sense of "everyday morality" in the way they treat others.' The author of one of the submissions to the inquiry argued that, considering the importance of friendship to children, maybe there should be a re-evaluation of the purpose of education and teacher training in terms of 'the ability to promote co-operation and friendship between students'. This misses the point. Children cannot be taught, in the abstract, about how to make friends. It is through unsupervised play—through conflict and cooperation—that children are given the opportunity to develop friendships and to build up relationships of trust.

Research has shown that there is often *more* conflict between friends than between peers in general. Children use friendship to test boundaries and explore what is appropriate and acceptable behaviour. When I went to pick up my four-year-old niece, Maja, from her nursery during a visit in Norway last week, and asked her if I could meet her best friend, Irene, I was sulkily told no, because they were '*uvenner*' (Norwegian for 'not friends'). Apparently, Irene had thrown two stones at Maja and when Maja picked up a stone to throw back, Irene declared that she no longer wanted to be her friend. Of course Maja thought the whole episode was very unfair, as she hadn't even thrown a stone. Yet by the time I had finished my 10-minute tour of the nursery, Irene had given Maja a bouquet of dandelions and they were best friends again. As her nursery teacher told me, they frequently fall out, but they always make up again.

Children will often end up in disputes with their friends—disputes that can be a lot more upsetting than the tiff between Maja and Irene. But through conflict and argument, they gain a better understanding of what they can expect from each other. So the formation of childhood friendships will inevitably involve both intimacy and trust, as well as tension and conflict.

It is understandable that adults want to intervene when they feel children are misbehaving. But it may not necessarily be the best thing to do in all circumstances. Of course adults need to set boundaries. When a child is clearly being scared witless by other children, adult intervention is necessary. But the boundaries need to be very carefully drawn and applied, if the benefits of play are not to be undermined.

Tim Gill, a writer and consultant on childhood and former director of the UK Children's Play Council, astutely argues: 'One problem for adults is that children's play is not always about nice warm-glow things like building sandcastles, climbing to the top of the spacenet or making chocolate chip cookies. Sometimes it's about destroying someone else's sandcastle, fighting for the right to get to the top of the net or stealing those cookies. . . . Play involves all of the emotions, not just the ones we normally see as positive.'

According to Gill, children can only learn to express feelings and recognise the feelings of others—and understand the difference between mock anger and real anger—'if they are given the chance to practice them. A lot. And much of what looks to adults like bad behaviour is simply children practising, getting the hang of all these skills.' Adults need to appreciate that conflicts of interest are as inevitable in childhood as they are in adulthood. Children are, of course, not as sophisticated in resolving conflicts as adults, and therefore they need the experiences that will help them develop their social skills.

For those concerned about the future wellbeing of today's generation of children, let us stop having a go at parents, castigating them for everything they do. It would be more constructive to counter all of the various initiatives—which are often government-led—which undermine our trust in other adults and children. Free from such scaremongering and hectoring advice and tellings-off from the authorities, parents might learn to trust each other more, and let their children play.

Helene Guldberg is the director and co-founder of *Spiked*, an online publication for current affairs in the United Kingdom, in addition to being a two-time published book author. She received her doctoral degree from the University of Manchester in developmental psychology, and she now teaches developmental psychology with the Open University and CAPA, the United States' study abroad center.

EXPLORING THE ISSUE

Is the Fear of Bullying Justified?

Critical Thinking and Reflection

1. Is it possible that people's opinions about whether bullying is very harmful might be based on their own personal experiences? Think about your own personal history of bullying and relate it to your opinion about the issue.
2. The articles selected for this issue are written by individuals from two different cultures. Is it possible that cultural norms influence the way bullying is perceived? Identify other cultures with which you're familiar and discuss how aspects of that culture may make people from there more or less accepting of bullying.
3. Some people who study bullying break it up into different types or forms, such as physical bullying, verbal bullying, or cyber bullying (such as negative posts on someone's Facebook profile). Do you think that different kinds of bullying are more or less acceptable? Why or why not?

Is There Common Ground?

No one wants to be bullied, and it is likely that everyone would find it uncomfortable even to be the witness to bullying. The disagreement within this controversial issue may be limited to whether bullying is *always* harmful, or whether the negative effects of bullying are the *only* consequences. Both sides of this issue could potentially agree that social relationships, including even the relationship between a bully and his or her victim, are complicated and that different people will react differently.

    Resilience and empathy are logical outcomes to being bullied, harassed, or socially isolated. When bullying is taken to its extreme, it may reach the point of illegal hate crimes. While some people may question the utility of the legal category of behaviors classified as "hate crimes," and while some may believe that children learn lessons from tough situations, almost everyone would likely agree that striving for a world in which all individuals are treated with respect is a noble goal, worthy of pursuit.

Additional Resources

Adams, F. D., & Lawrence, G. J. (2011). Bullying victims: The effects last into college. *American Secondary Education, 40*, 4–13.

Charron, S. (2013, February 3). Being bullied makes you tougher. *The Huffington Post.* Retrieved from http://www.huffingtonpost.ca/sandra-charron/getting-bullied-toughening-up_b_2595912.html

Hoel, H., Faragher, B., & Cooper, C. L. (2004). Bullying is detrimental to health, but all bullying behaviors are not necessarily equally damaging. *British Journal of Guidance & Counselling, 32*, 367–387. doi: 10.1080/03069880410001723594

Sharp, S. (1995). How much does bullying hurt? The effects of bullying on the personal wellbeing and educational progress of secondary aged students. *Educational and Child Psychology, 12*, 81–88.

van Heugten, K. (2013). Resilience as an underexplored outcome of workplace bullying. *Qualitative Health Research, 23*, 291–301.

Internet References . . .

Bully Online

> http://www.bullyonline.org/index.htm

Fear Stops Here

> http://www.fearstopshere.com/

Life After Adult Bullying

http://www.lifeafteradultbullying.com/index.html

Spiked

> http://www.spiked-online.com/

The It Gets Better Project

> http://www.itgetsbetter.org/

Unit 2

UNIT

Close Relationships

A loving, lasting intimate relationship is one of the major life goals for almost everyone, and social psychology has made the scientific study of relationships one of its priorities. Are different sexual choices predictive of long-lasting happiness? What are the origins of sexual orientation, and are people of different sexual orientations really that different from each other? What are the lasting negative effects of social phenomena like homophobia? These are the kinds of questions that social psychology researchers seek to answer; just a few of the controversies within this subfield are addressed here.

Selected, Edited, and with Issue Framing Material by:
Wind Goodfriend, *Buena Vista University*

ISSUE

Is Hookup Culture on College Campuses Bad for Heterosexual Girls?

YES: Amy Julia Becker, from "Hookup Culture Is Good for Women, and Other Feminist Myths," *Christianity Today* (2012)

NO: Timaree Schmit, from "Hookup Culture Can Help Build Stronger Relationships," Original Work (2013)

Learning Outcomes
After reading this issue, you will be able to: • Summarize competing arguments related to hookup culture.   • Evaluate the gender imbalance of this debate and why there is particular focus on the impact on women.   • Evaluate the long-term implications of sexual decision making in college.

ISSUE SUMMARY

YES: Amy Julia Becker argues that hookup culture demeans women. From a Christian perspective, she argues that sex leads to greater life fulfillment when removed from the hookup culture.

NO: Timaree Schmit argues that hookup culture is nothing new and that it can be healthy for people to have different sexual experiences.

Sexual activity occurs on college campuses, and it sometimes occurs with high frequency. Larger schools allow a level of anonymity that students would never have experienced in high school. Sometimes sexual activity is in the context of a long-term, committed relationship. Other times it is in the context of a one-night stand.

Who benefits from a one-night stand? Is it wrong to want one? Is it wrong to enjoy it? Should there be a different answer for males or females, and for heterosexual, gay, lesbian, or bisexual individuals?

Hooking up in college is not something new. However, there are some newer trends in higher education. For example, women are attending in much larger numbers than men. Some colleges have 60 percent or more female students. Add a few other variables to this: (a) most studies show a higher proportion of gay men versus lesbians in the general population; and (b) some men are already in committed relationships at school or at home. On many college campuses, if a woman is looking for a long-term heterosexual relationship, she is finding that the odds are stacked in the men's favor.

What about the women who are not looking for a long-term relationship? What about the pre-med student who does not want a relationship to tie her down when she is ready to leave for medical school? Or the woman who believes that college is the right time to experiment? One college student recently posted many of her sexual experiences online and wrote, "I turn 20 in two weeks. I feel like I should be making a lot more mistakes right now."

Why does this discussion so often focus on the impact on women? There is often an assumption that men prefer hookup culture and women prefer relationships. The theory goes that women are joining hookup culture at their own expense to please men.

How much is hookup culture today different from generations past? Does it diminish a woman's chances of being in a relationship?

Of course the major point of college is the education that is received there. Yet during our time in colleges, relationships are formed, sometimes long-term, and hookups occur. One mother wrote an open letter to the young women attending Princeton University telling them that they would never again be in such a large pool of marriageable, impressive men. They should be using this opportunity to find a husband rather than engage in hookup culture.

Why do women hook up? Is it because they like sex? Or is it because they want to please men? What about when they keep hooking up with the same person, known as friends with benefits? Are they keeping the relationship light to please a man?

We are in an era today in which there is a sex-positive feminism that is captured by *Sex and the City, Girls,* Christina Aguilera, and many others. Do these media depictions of sex-positive women capture a real demographic in American society? If so, how big is it? How overestimated or underestimated is it?

The truth is that during college we learn a great deal more than what comes from the instruction of our professors and the words in our books. We learn a great deal about relationships from the people around us. The general culture influences how the people around us act.

The articles in this essay help us take a better look at the case for or against the impact of hookup culture on heterosexual girls.

YES

Amy Julia Becker

Hookup Culture Is Good for Women, and Other Feminist Myths

According to *Atlantic* essayist Hanna Rosin, we should celebrate that young women are now acting as sexually selfish as their male counterparts.

Pornography. Casual sex. Crude jokes about sex. Hooking up with no strings attached.

Hanna Rosin's most recent *Atlantic* article, "Boys on the Side," describes highly intelligent, career-oriented women engaging in all of these behaviors with a mere shrug of the shoulders. In the minds of many driven young women on college campuses across the country, sexual promiscuity doesn't harm anyone. Hooking up has become the new sexual norm for young adults, and according to this norm, students shy away from committed relationships and instead enjoy one-time sexual encounters with no expectation of further intimacy. And, Rosin argues, the sexual liberation of the 1960s that led to the more recent "hookup culture" on college campuses is good for women—it allows women to enjoy casual sex without being "tied down" by serious commitment.

Rosin initially substantiates this claim through interviews with her subjects. Most women who are engaging in the hookup culture report that they don't want to return to the days of chastity belts or even more traditional dating, and Rosin takes these positive reports as evidence that the hookup culture is not only here to stay but is also good for the women involved. She provides no evidence, however, that women who hookup a lot during their early 20s go on to lead fulfilling lives, and she doesn't offer a counterpoint of women who have opted out of hooking up. Furthermore, Rosin offers a few statistics to demonstrate positive trends nationwide when it comes to sexual mores. The rate of teenage girls having sex has declined from 37 to 27 percent in the past 25 years, for instance. And the rate of rape and sexual assault against females has declined by 70 percent nationally since 1993. Both of these numbers demonstrate significant progress for women. Whether or not the positive statistics correlate to the rise of the hookup culture, however, remains unclear.

Rosin's stance on hookup culture hinges on two assumptions. First, she assumes that economic productivity and personal independence are the twin goals of every modern person. Feminists shouldn't decry the advent of the hookup culture, she argues, because it "is too bound up with everything that's fabulous about being a young woman in 2012—the freedom, the confidence, the knowledge that you can always depend on yourself." Moreover, "[the hookup culture] is not a place where they drown . . . unlike women in earlier ages, they have more-important things on their minds, such as good grades and internships and job interviews and a financial future of their own." Intimacy, family, and community might be desirable, but only after a woman has established herself as an independent financial entity.

Second, though I suspect she would disagree with me here, Rosin's argument assumes that for women to "arrive," they must become *just like men*. She describes sexually aggressive women at a business-school party as ones who "had learned to keep pace with the boys," and later as ones who were "behaving exactly like frat boys." Instead of challenging male behavior that demeans women (and men), Rosin capitulates to it. Instead of arguing for men and women to change culture in such a way that the responsibility for pregnancy and childrearing falls on the shoulders of both parents, she simply heralds women's ability to avoid pregnancy through birth control and abortion. And instead of promoting an understanding of human flourishing that includes relationships with trust, responsibility, and love, she succumbs to a truncated and depleted view of humanity that esteems individual work as the highest goal and self-serving love as the highest love.

From a Christian perspective, it's easy to critique Rosin's argument, one that she explores in her new book, *The End of Men* (a review of which *Christianity Today* will publish online in the coming weeks). Even if they don't always heed it in practice, Christians at least acknowledge the truth and goodness of the biblical view of human sexuality—that both men and women will honor God and find personal fulfillment in engaging in a sexual relationship with one other person within the covenant of marriage. Christians understand relationships as the core of our humanity, beginning with God's relationship within the Trinity, and extending to humans, who are invited into relationship with God but also into interdependent relationships with one another. Marriage, children, and community are viewed not as problems to be delayed until a career is in place, but rather as blessings to be received. And Christians understand love as, at its core, self-sacrificial, modeled after the love of Christ offered to us on the cross.

In Rosin's view, "Feminist progress right now largely depends on the existence of the hookup culture." But women can continue to find their rightful roles in the workplace and within the home without succumbing to the lie that a fulfilling life is one in which financial independence and self-sufficiency are the primary goals.

Instead of assuming that women must become just like the traditional norm of sexually active men, the gospel offers a transformative vision of humanity. And it isn't a picture of the 1950s housewife either. It's a picture that challenges notions of traditional masculinity and femininity, including, but not limited to, the sexual norms for both. Yes, it's a picture that calls for chastity for both men and women outside of marriage. But it's also a picture that holds forth the possibility not of sexual liberation, but of true freedom.

Christians have done plenty of finger-wagging about the state of our nation's sexual culture, for the same reasons that Rosin extols it. But Rosin's posture, and the norm it extols, calls for more than rebuke. Christians have an opportunity to offer a different understanding not only of sex, but of what it means to know abiding joy and peace as a full human being. Let's make sure we can both articulate and live that understanding of sex and humanity in a world starving for true fulfillment.

Amy Julia Becker focuses her writing on faith, family, disability, and ethics. She is identified as a Christian theological conservative and also socially liberal.

Timaree Schmit

 **NO**

Hookup Culture Can Help Build Stronger Relationships

Hookup Culture, if such a thing exists, provides opportunities for young people to be more contemplative and communicative about sexuality, fostering a climate that encourages collaborative, consensual sexual behavior over transactional or predatory behavior. It also holds the possibility of freeing women and men from constraints of traditional gender expectations.

Is Hookup Culture Real?

When a young person says that he or she "hooked up with" someone, this should prompt more questions than commentary. After all, there is no strict definition of the term or even a majority opinion on what, specifically, must happen for a "hook up" to have occurred. Among college students, the phrase can indicate anything from prolonged kissing to oral, vaginal and anal sex. While common, the term is often too vague to be useful.

Researcher Amanda Holman uses the term hookups to refer to sexual behavior that takes place without the expectation of commitment. This is often purported to represent a fundamental change in the dating and sexual patterns of young people from previous generations. However, a comparison of responses to the General Social Survey from 1988–1996 and those of 2002–2010 failed to find evidence this is true. Sociologists Martin Monto and Anna Carey's research found "no evidence that there has been a sea change in the sexual behavior of college students or that there has been a liberalization of attitudes towards sexuality." They found a greater percentage of current college students indicate that they have had sex with a friend within the last year (68% versus 56%) and a larger number report having had sexual activity with a casual partner (44% compared to 34.5%). This degree of change indicates that casual sex was already a common experience and that a significant portion of the population does not engage in commitment-less hookups.

Instead, Hookup Culture is largely a matter of change in conversations about sexual behaviors. Students are more likely to talk with peers about experiences, but use non-specific terms like "hookup" to describe what happened. This intentional vagueness serves several functions. It can retain privacy, diminish embarrassment associated with using more technical or degrading terminology, or deliberately give the impression that a greater or smaller variety of sexual acts occurred.

There is not much research, about whether most young people approve of Hookup Culture or think it is harmless. Qualitative interviews about hooking up find experiences may range from entirely satisfying to devastating. Additionally, there continue to be different social acceptance levels for males and females in terms of frequency of casual sex and number of partners. While traditional sexual gender norms are expanding for both men and women, many of the stigmas and expectations remain. Males are more likely than females to receive social encouragement to seek sexual pleasure, engage in sexual activity without intimacy or commitment and to be sexually involved with multiple partners.

Social Desirability Bias is a major issue when researching sexual behaviors, as respondents often feel pressure to appear 'normal' among their peers or to align their answers with personal ideals about how much and what kind of sex is OK to have. Perhaps young people now, especially young women, are simply more willing to acknowledge sexual activity that occurs outside of a serious relationship than in previous decades. Holman also suggests that young men now may feel pressured to over-report their experiences, thinking that their peers are engaging in more casual sex than they really are. She argues that the vagueness of the term "hookup" cultivates misperceptions about how much sex young people are having, giving the false impression that committed relationships are no longer the most common context for sexual activity.

What Is Wrong with Hookup Culture?

Many discussions about hooking up focus on whether or not it's healthy for young people to have more casual sexual encounters. Some emphasize that Hookup Culture is a result of independent, career-oriented women feeling free to express their sexual desires and seek physical satisfaction without commitment in the way that only men were previously able to do. Others express concern that a climate that encourages strings-free sex will make it harder for young adults to build respectful and loving committed relationships or to say "no" to sex without facing social disapproval.

As for the first claim, longitudinal studies are not yet possible about how Hookup Culture affects women later in life, their relationship outcomes, satisfaction and sense of self. As for the latter claims, we have no evidence either. In fact, rates of sexual assault have dropped dramatically since the 1970s, with evidence that enthusiastic sexual consent may be viewed as more important now than in previous generations. Assessing whether intimacy in relationships is harmed by hooking up is made extra complicated by the variety of other variables of modern life, including: the ubiquity of social media, online dating, and a growing body of research that shows social isolation has increased for all demographics of Americans over the last two decades.

What Might Be Right about Hookup Culture

Among the few facts we can ascertain about Hookup Culture, there are positive signs. Any deconstruction of traditional sexual mores bodes well for those who have been historically subjugated by them. For young women, the probability of negative consequences for engaging in premarital sexual behavior is reduced, including: harassment, ostracism, and the perception that she is no longer marriageable. As marriage becomes less and less vital for a woman's survival and sense of self, Hookup Culture enables those women who want to remain single to do so without sacrificing sexual pleasure, an optional luxury long granted to men.

Hookup Culture also supports the "queering" of restrictive sexual norms. Queer Theory aims to deconstruct restrictive essentialist ideas about men, women and sexual identities. Traditional sexual norms divide identities and behaviors categorically: man and woman, straight and gay, good and bad. Through a queer lens, sexuality is viewed as fluid and existing on a continuum, rather than in dichotomous boxes. According to both feminist and queer thought, someone's sex or gender shouldn't limit their behavioral choices. Since Hookup Culture subverts traditional sexual norms, it serves as a de facto "queering." As it expands the parameters of what is possible sexually, it holds the possibility of adding to the liberation of gay, lesbian and bisexual individuals. For those who are oppressed by a system that says sex is only appropriate for a husband and wife, any opportunity to reexamine these beliefs may hold promise.

Finally, Hookup Culture prioritizes sexual pleasure. Traditional sexual norms emphasize male sexual prowess and female sexual purity. These ideas put unrealistic expectations on young men and discourage them from expressing doubt or seeking information about what is pleasurable to female partners. Females, in contrast, are discouraged from demonstrating familiarity with their turn-ons, or expressing sexual desires. This results in a cycle of sexual encounters where men feel uncomfortable asking for direction and females are unable to ask for what they want. Even in the context of long-term relationships, partners may fear communicating uncommon desires out of fear of rejection or upending stability. The commitment-free nature of a hookup allows for partners to express their sexual needs without fear of judgment or compromising the relationship. Within Hookup Culture, individuals may experience a greater variety of partners and sexual acts, possibly introducing them to a diverse array of sexual pleasures that they can integrate into any future sexual interactions, including those in committed situations. Some authors have described this experimental process as helpful "practice" for more significant relationships.

A young person may choose to stop having sexual relations with a partner who is selfish, unwilling to learn, or otherwise unsatisfying, and focus their energies on partners who are more giving and open to experience. A selfish lover may find their reputation disqualifies them with other possible partners. This encourages a culture of reciprocal, mutually pleasurable sexual experiences.

Hookup Culture will never be acceptable to those who espouse the belief that sex is only appropriate between committed partners. However, there is little evidence that those people will have to change to accommodate those who do not share this belief. The possibility of Hookup Culture is not a replacement of traditional norms, but the addition of new norms with different values.

TIMAREE SCHMIT runs a sex-positive podcast and blogs under the title *Sex with Timaree*. She possesses a doctorate in human sexuality from Widener University.

EXPLORING THE ISSUE

Is Hookup Culture on College Campuses Bad for Heterosexual Girls?

Critical Thinking and Reflection

1. What are some arguments made on each side with which you agree or disagree?
2. What are the strengths and weaknesses of the two positions made in this essay?
3. Pick the side with which you most agree. What are some additional arguments you would make to strengthen the case for or against hookup culture?
4. Think more broadly about hookup culture. Are there ways to look at this as a bad thing for heterosexual girls from a non-Christian perspective? If so, what case would you make? Is there a way to make the case for hookup culture from a religious perspective? If so, what would you say?

Is There Common Ground?

The two authors have opposite views regarding the impact of hookup culture on college campus. However, both, to a certain degree, have the same goal: they want young women to do what is in their best interest. Of course one argument is secular and one is non-secular. Beyond that, there are other reasons that are not necessarily anchored in religious faith: transmission of sexually transmitted diseases, finding the right partner, and other goals. What sort of sexuality education can occur on campus—or off campus—that can help students make sexual decisions that are consistent with their best interest and long-term goals?

Additional Resources

Kathleen A. Bogle, *Hooking Up: Sex, Dating, and Relationships on Campus*, NYU Press (2008)

Donna Freitas, *The End of Sex: How Hookup Culture Is Leaving a Generation Unhappy, Unfulfilled, and Confused about Intimacy*, Basic Books (2013)

Laura Sessions Stepp, *Unhooked: How Young Women Pursue Sex, Delay Love and Lose at Both*, Riverhead Trade (2008)

Internet References . . .

American Psychological Association

http://www.apa.org/monitor/2013/02/ce-corner.aspx

Bacchus Network

http://www.bacchusnetwork.org

Selected, Edited, and with Issue Framing Material by:
Wind Goodfriend, *Buena Vista University*

ISSUE

Are Extremely Homophobic People Secretly Gay?

YES: Henry E. Adams, Lester W. Wright, Jr., and Bethany A. Lohr, from "Is Homophobia Associated with Homosexual Arousal?" *Journal of Abnormal Psychology* (1996)

NO: Mark E. Johnson, Christiane Brems, and Pat Alford-Keating, from "Personality Correlates of Homophobia," *Journal of Homosexuality* (1997)

Learning Outcomes

After reading this issue, you will be able to:

- Define homophobia and explain two different ways to measure it in a research study.
- List and explain two defense mechanisms that could be used if a homosexual person didn't want to acknowledge his or her latent, or secret, desires.
- List and explain three or four other variables that some researchers believe predict levels of homophobia in individuals.

ISSUE SUMMARY

YES: Researchers Adams, Wright, and Lohr present an empirical study which shows that highly homophobic men become sexually aroused when exposed to gay male pornography. They argue that these men are homophobic due to their own secret sexual interests.

NO: Researchers Johnson, Brems, and Alford-Keating find evidence that homophobia is related to many other variables, including gender, age, empathy, religiosity, and coping style.

The website GayHomophobe.com keeps at the top of its main page a huge counter; the counter notes the number of days it's been—they claim—since the last very public and homophobic personality or celebrity was "caught in a gay scandal." The creators of the site then list many prominent individuals they believe fit into this category over the past several years, including U.S. senators, ministers, mayors, and judges. They provide links to explain each case, as well as a star-rating system that denotes if the individual "admitted" to being gay after his or her scandal and whether he or she subsequently started to support gay rights.

In a classic line from Shakespeare's play *Hamlet*, Queen Gertrude appears to not enjoy a play she's watching in which one of the characters represents her. When her son, Hamlet, asks for her opinion of the play, she states, "The lady doth protest too much, methinks." This single line has since been used as an example of a human tendency to be defensive when our own flaws are highlighted. Sometimes we don't want to admit something about ourselves, and it makes us criticize that same phenomenon when we see it in others. While being gay is certainly not a flaw, some people who were raised with anti-gay values may believe it is, and thus be very motivated to deny any homosexual tendencies in themselves.

This denial of something we don't want to admit is something that psychologists have found interesting since the days of Sigmund Freud, who listed and defined several "defense mechanisms," of which denial is one. Defense mechanisms are cognitive tricks we play on ourselves, to avoid feelings of anxiety or trauma. Thus, an alcoholic might deny his or her drinking problem; indeed, admitting the problem is the first step to many drug and alcohol recovery treatment programs. Another defense mechanism identified by Freud is projection, where we not only avoid seeing something within ourselves that's unsettling, but we also tend to see it everywhere else. For example, if a man secretly wanted to cheat on his wife but didn't want to admit it, he might start accusing his wife of flirting with other men. Finally, reaction formation is a defense mechanism in which people do the opposite behaviors of what they really want to do, again to cover up their secret desires. They are, in a word, overcompensating.

All three of these defense mechanisms could potentially explain the ironic phenomenon of people who publicly appear to be extremely against homosexuality or homosexual rights, but then are "caught" engaging in homosexual behaviors. While much of Freudian theory is now considered out of date, or at least not based on much empirical evidence, current social psychologists remain interested in the basic idea of engaging in behaviors that seem to go against one's espoused opinions. Sometimes, explicit attitudes are very poor at predicting behavior, and many social psychologists believe that it's possible to have a major disconnect between one's explicit feelings or attitudes and his or her implicit (or emotional, hidden, or gut-level) feelings or attitudes.

The possibility thus arises that some very public personalities or celebrities may appear to be against homosexuality, but that their motivation for being so vocal is that they are really hiding their true, latent desire to engage in those very behaviors. Thus, the "yes" side of this debate argues that for people who explicitly claim to be extremely homophobic, they may actually have secret gay desires. However, testing this is difficult; certainly, these individuals are not likely to admit it if they do have gay tendencies; the entire point is that they may be trying to cover it up, even to themselves. Researchers Henry Adams, Lester Wright, and Bethany Lohr thus present their creative procedural method to test for secret homosexual desires. In this study, they have male participants watch various types of pornography, including a heterosexual video, a gay male video, and a gay female video. While the participants watch the videos, their physiological sexual arousal is measured. The researchers then compare arousal to the three different videos. Importantly, however, they also compare results between men who claim to be heterosexual but not particularly homophobic to men who also claim to be heterosexual and homophobic. The results are probably easy to predict, given that this article is used to support the "yes" side of this controversial issue.

However, there are many criticisms to the "yes" study presented here. First, the ethical considerations are interesting. Second, they had a relatively small sample of only white men, so it is questionable how generalizable the results may be. Finally, however, the biggest criticism of the study is that there are many, many potential reasons for any given individual to have homophobic attitudes. Thus, the "no" article also presents original data collected by Mark Johnson, Christiane Brems, and Pat Alford-Keating. Here, they argue that levels of homophobia in any given individual can be predicted by a variety of constructs, including sex of the participant (male or female), low empathy and perspective taking, and higher religiosity, among others.

As you read both sides of this debate, consider both the theory and hypotheses behind each study and the procedural methods used. Is one study more convincing than the other? What are the strengths and weaknesses in each?

YES ↵   Henry E. Adams, Lester W. Wright, Jr., and Bethany A. Lohr

Is Homophobia Associated with Homosexual Arousal?

Hostility and discrimination against homosexual individuals are well-established facts (Berrill, 1990). On occasion, these negative attitudes lead to hostile verbal and physical acts against gay individuals with little apparent motivation except a strong dislike (Herek, 1989). In fact, more than 90% of gay men and lesbians report being targets of verbal abuse or threats, and more than one-third report being survivors of violence related to their homosexuality (Fassinger, 1991). Although negative attitudes and behaviors toward gay individuals have been assumed to be associated with rigid moralistic beliefs, sexual ignorance, and fear of homosexuality, the etiology of these attitudes and behaviors remains a puzzle (Marmor, 1980). Weinberg (1972) labeled these attitudes and behaviors *homophobia*, which he defined as the dread of being in close quarters with homosexual men and women as well as irrational fear, hatred, and intolerance by heterosexual individuals of homosexual men and women.

It has been argued that the term *homophobic* may not be appropriate because there is no evidence that homophobic individuals exhibit avoidance of homosexual persons (Bernstein, 1994; Rowan, 1994). Nevertheless, the only necessary requirement for the label of phobia is that phobic stimuli produce anxiety. Whether the individual exhibits avoidance or endures the anxiety often depends on the nature of the stimuli and the environmental circumstances. MacDonald's (1976) suggestions are consistent with this analysis because he defined *homophobia* as anxiety or anticipatory anxiety elicited by homosexual individuals. O'Donahue and Caselles (1993) noted that McDonald's definition parallels the diagnostic criteria of the *Diagnostic and Statistical Manual of Mental Disorders* (*DSM-IV*; American Psychiatric Association, 1994) for simple phobia and captures the negative emotional reactions toward homosexuality that seem to have motivated use of the term.

Although the causes of homophobia are unclear, several psychoanalytic explanations have emerged from the idea of homophobia as an anxiety-based phenomenon. Psychoanalytic theories usually postulate that homophobia is a result of repressed homosexual urges or a form of latent homosexuality. *Latent homosexuality* can be defined as homosexual arousal which the individual is either unaware of or denies (West, 1977). Psychoanalysts use the concept of repressed or latent homosexuality to explain the emotional malaise and irrational attitudes displayed by some individuals who feel guilty about their erotic interests and struggle to deny and repress homosexual impulses. The relationship between homophobia and latent homosexuality has not been empirically investigated and is one of the purposes of the present study.

Specifically, the present study was designed to investigate whether homophobic men show more sexual arousal to homosexual cues than nonhomophobic men. As O'Donahue and Caselles (1993, p. 193) have noted, an investigation of whether those who "aggress against homosexuals become sexually aroused to homosexual stimuli (as certain psychoanalytic theories might predict)" would contribute to our understanding of homophobia. A secondary goal was to evaluate whether homophobic individuals are persons who are more generally hostile or aggressive than nonhomophobic men. The present investigation was designed to evaluate these two hypotheses.

Method

Participants

Caucasian heterosexual male volunteers (n = 64) recruited from the Psychology Department Research Subject Pool at the University of Georgia participated in the study. They were screened during large group testing during which time they completed the modified version of the Kinsey Heterosexual-Homosexual Rating Scale (Kinsey, Pomeroy, & Martin, 1948), the Index of Homophobia (IHP; Hudson & Ricketts, 1980), and the Aggression Questionnaire (Buss

Adams, H. E., Wright, L. W., & Lohr, B. A. (1996). "Is Homophobia Associated with Homosexual Arousal?" *Journal of Abnormal Psychology*, vol. 105, pp. 440–445. Copyright © 1996 American Psychological Association.

& Perry, 1992). They were contacted by telephone at a later date to schedule the laboratory portion of the study. All participants received partial course credit. The mean age of the men was 20.3 years (range = 18 to 31 years).

Screening Measures

Kinsey Heterosexual-Homosexual Rating Scale
A modified version of the Kinsey Heterosexual-Homosexual Rating Scale was used to assess sexual arousal and prior sexual experiences. This version of the Kinsey is a 7-point scale on which individuals separately rated their sexual arousal and experiences from *exclusively homosexual* to *exclusively heterosexual.* Only participants who reported exclusively heterosexual arousal and experiences (i.e., is on both sections) were selected for participation.

IHP
The IHP is the most widely used measure of homophobia (O'Donahue & Caselles, 1993). The items of the IHP assess affective components of homophobia. The scale contains 25 items, and scores range from 0 to 100: 0–25, high-grade nonhomophobic; 26–50, low-grade nonhomophobic; 51–75, low-grade homophobic; and 76–100, high-grade homophobic. The score obtained is a measure of "dread" when placed in close quarters with a homosexual; a low score equals low dread, and a high score equals high dread. Because most of the items contain the terms *comfortable* or *uncomfortable,* dread can be assumed to mean anticipatory anxiety about interacting with a homosexual person. For example, one item states "I would feel nervous being in a group of homosexuals."

The men were divided into two groups on the basis of their scores on the IHP: 0–50 = nonhomophobic men, n = 29, $M = 30.48$; 51–100 = homophobic men, n = 35, $M = 80.40$. This split was necessary because of an inability to find an adequate number of exclusively heterosexual men who scored in the high-grade nonhomophobic range (0–25).

Response Measures

Penile plethysmography
A mercury-in-rubber (MIR) circumferential strain gauge (Bancroft, Jones, & Pullan, 1966) was used to measure erectile responses to the sexual stimuli. When attached, changes in the circumference of the penis caused changes in the electrical resistance of the mercury column, which were detected by a Parks Model 270 Plethysmograph. The pre-amplifier output was channeled into a Grass polygraph. Tumescence responses were recorded on the polygraph and were channeled to an IBM computer. Penile plethys-

mographic responses to sexually explicit stimuli have been shown to discriminate between homosexual and heterosexual men (Tollison, Adams, & Tollison, 1979). Zuckerman (1971) described penile plethysmography as the most specific measure of sexual arousal because significant changes occur only during sexual stimulation and sleep.

Aggression Questionnaire
Buss and Perry's (1992) 29-item scale was used to assess an overall trait of aggression. The men rated each item on a scale of 1 (extremely uncharacteristic of me) to 5 (extremely characteristic of me). Items targeted four aspects of aggression: physical aggression, verbal aggression, anger, and hostility. This overall score of aggression was used as the dependent variable.

Stimulus Materials

The stimuli were 4-minute segments of explicit erotic videotapes depicting consensual adult heterosexual activity, consensual male homosexual activity, and consensual female homosexual activity. The sexual activity in the videos included sexual foreplay (e.g., kissing and undressing), oral-genital contact (e.g., fellatio or cunnilingus), and intercourse (i.e., vaginal penetration, anal penetration, or tribadism in the lesbian film). The lesbian videotape was included because it has been shown to be highly sexually arousing to heterosexual men and is a better discriminator between heterosexual and homosexual men than other stimuli (Mavissikalian, Blanchard, Abel, & Barlow, 1975).

Editor's note: A plethysmograph is an instrument that measures variations in the size of an organ or other body part based on how much blood is present or passing through it. In the present study, a plethysmograph measured the degree of tumescence, or *penile erection,* that participants had while being shown experimental stimuli. Greater tumescence scores indicated a higher degree of engorgement (erection).

Procedure

The procedure was explained to the participant on arrival at the laboratory. He was informed that he could terminate participation at any time, and he signed informed consent. The participant was accompanied to a soundproof chamber, where he was seated in a comfortable reclining chair and was given instructions on the proper placement of the MIR strain gauge. After the experimenter's departure from the experimental chamber into the adjoining equipment room, the participant attached the penile strain gauge. The adjoining equipment room housed the polygraph, the videotape player, an IBM-compatible computer, and the two-way intercom. Once the participant indicated that the apparatus was in place by way of the intercom, a 4-minute baseline was recorded in the absence of any stimuli. Next, the three sexually explicit videos were presented to the participant. Following each videotaped presentation, he rated his level of subjective sexual arousal (i.e., how "turned on" he was) and the degree of penile erection (i.e., from no change to 100% erection) on a scale of 0 to 10. The participant's penile circumference was allowed to return to baseline levels before the next stimulus was presented. The sequence of presentation was counterbalanced across participants to avoid order effects.

Data Reduction

A change score was used to analyze the penile plethysmographic data where the mean penile circumference (in millimeters) in the first second of time was subtracted from subsequent seconds for each video presentation. These scores were divided into six 40-second time blocks. The average change score in penile circumference for each time block was then analyzed.

Results

Penile Plethysmography

The data were analyzed using analysis of variance (ANOVA). Data for each time block for the two groups are presented separately for each stimulus type in Figure 1. For the heterosexual and lesbian videos, both groups showed significant engorgement. For the male homosexual video, results indicate that the homophobic men showed a significant increase in penile circumference to the male homosexual video but that the control men did not.

Another way of evaluating these data is to calculate the percentage of men who demonstrated no significant tumescence (i.e., 0–6 mm), modest tumescence (i.e., > 6–12 mm), and definite tumescence (i.e., > 12 mm) based on their mean tumescence score to the homosexual video. In the homophobic group, 20% showed no significant tumescence, 26% showed moderate tumescence, and 54% showed definite tumescence to the homosexual video; the corresponding percentages in the nonhomophobic group were 66%, 10%, and 24%, respectively.

Subjective Ratings

Subjective estimates of sexual arousal and penile erection were analyzed with a mixed model ANOVA. The main effect of stimulus type was significant, $F(2,124) = 90.93$, $p < .001$, indicating significantly greater arousal and

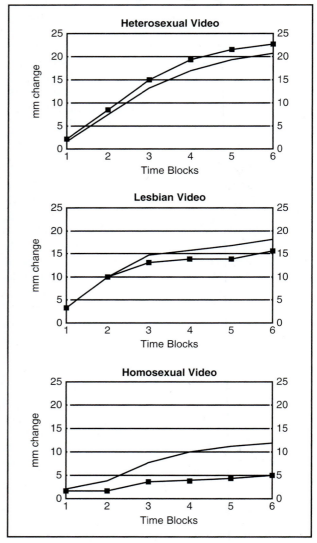

Figure 1

Stimulus presentations by groups across time blocks. The only significant difference between groups is with the homosexual video. The blocked line represents the nonhomophobic group; the solid line represents the homophobic group.

erection ratings to the heterosexual and lesbian videos than to the male homosexual video. These means are shown in Table 1.

Correlation coefficients were computed between the penile response measures and subjective ratings of arousal and erection, as shown in Table 1. These correlations ranged

Table 1

Means and Correlations of Subjective Ratings with Penile Response

| | Arousal | | Erection | |
Video	M	r[A]	M	r
Heterosexual	7.14	.57*	7.10	.64*
Lesbian	6.28	.63*	6.31	.66*
Male homosexual	2.03	.53*	2.79	.64

[a] Subjective ratings were correlated with mean penile response across time blocks.
*p < .01.

Table 2

Correlation Between Subjective Arousal and Subjective Erection Ratings

| | | Video | | |
Group	N	Heterosexual	Lesbian	Male Homosexual
Homophobic	35	.91	.95	.90
Nonhomophobic	29	.93	.94	.78

from .53 to .66 and indicate that participants' ratings were generally in agreement with their penile responses. Correlation coefficients were also computed with subjective ratings of arousal and erection ratings for each group, as shown in Table 2. These correlations are quite high and are all significant at the p < .01 level of confidence, indicating that these two ratings are essentially measuring the same event. The correlation of erection and arousal to the homosexual video in the nonhomophobic group was significantly smaller when compared to other correlations. The decreased consistency between erection and arousal may have been due to the smaller changes in penile responses in this group, making subjective estimates more difficult.

Aggression Questionnaire

A t-test between groups was conducted on the Aggression Questionnaire. The difference between the scores for the homophobic (M = 58.37) and the nonhomophobic men (M = 55.96) was not statistically significant. This result indicates that these groups did not differ in aggression as measured by this questionnaire.

Discussion

The results of this study indicate that individuals who score in the homophobic range and admit negative affect toward homosexuality demonstrate significant sexual arousal to male homosexual erotic stimuli. These individuals were selected on the basis of their report of having only heterosexual arousal and experiences. Furthermore, their

ratings of erection and arousal to homosexual stimuli were low and not significantly different from nonhomophobic men who demonstrated no significant increase in penile response to homosexual stimuli. These data are consistent with various psychoanalytic theories, which have generally explained homophobia as a threat to an individual's own homosexual impulses causing repression, denial, or reaction formation (or all three; West, 1977). Generally, these explanations conceive of homophobia as one type of latent homosexuality where persons either are unaware of or deny their homosexual urges.

The hypothesis that homophobic men are merely aggressive individuals is not supported by the present data. There were no differences in aggression scores between groups as measured by the Aggression Questionnaire. However, this questionnaire is a general measure of aggression and does not address the possibility of situational aggression or hostility where the situation involves homosexuality or interacting with a homosexual person. It is possible that aggressiveness in homophobic individuals is specific to homosexual cues.

These data also indicate that subjective estimates of arousal and erection are largely consistent with physiological indices of penile erections, with correlation coefficients ranging from .53 to .66. Because the relationships between subjective measures of erection and arousal were quite high, ranging from .78 to .95, it is likely that these two estimates are measures of similar or identical events. Most of these latter correlations were in the .90 range with the exception of nonhomophobic individuals' ratings of arousal and erection to homosexual stimuli, which was .78. As noted before, these results were probably due to the small penile responses to this stimulus, making subjective estimates more difficult and less consistent.

A major difficulty in this area of research is in defining and measuring homophobia. For example, with the scale used in the present study, we found it difficult to find heterosexual men who scored in the high-grade nonhomophobic range (0–25). The issue of whether homophobia is specific to men or may also occur in women has not been addressed systematically, nor is it clear whether homophobic women may show sexual arousal to erotic lesbian stimuli. With answers to these and similar issues, a clearer understanding of the nature of homophobia will be possible.

References

American Psychiatric Association. (1994). *Diagnostic and statistical manual of mental disorders* (4th ed.). Washington, DC: Author.

Bancroft, J. H., Jones, H. G. & Pullan, B. R. (1966). A simple transducer for measuring penile erection with comments on its use in the treatment of sexual disorders. *Behaviour Research and Therapy, 4,* 230–241.

Bernstein, G. S. (1994). A reply to Rowan. *Behavior Therapist, 17,* 185–186.

Berrill, K. T. (1990). Anti-gay violence and victimization in the United States: An overview. *Journal of Interpersonal Violence, 5,* 274–294.

Buss, A. H. & Perry, M. (1992). The aggression questionnaire. *Journal of Personality and Social Psychology, 63,* 452–459.

Fassinger, R. (1991). The hidden minority: Issues and challenges in working with lesbian women and gay men. *Counseling Psychologist, 19,* 157–176.

Herek, G. M. (1989). Hate crimes against lesbians and gay men: Correlates and gender differences. *American Psychologist, 44,* 948–955.

Hudson, W. W. & Ricketts, W. A. (1980). A strategy for the measurement of homophobia. *Journal of Homosexuality, 5,* 356–371.

Kinsey, A. C., Pomeroy, W. B. & Martin, C. E. (1948). *Sexual behavior in the human male.* Philadelphia: W. B. Saunders.

MacDonald, A. P. Jr. (1976). Homophobia: Its roots and meanings. *Homosexual Counseling Journal, 3,* 23–33.

Marmor, J. (1980). Overview: The multiple roots of homosexual behavior. In J. Marmor (Ed.), *Homosexual behavior—A modern reappraisal* (pp. 3–22). New York: Basic Books.

Mavissikalian, N., Blanchard, E. D., Abel, G. G. & Barlow, D. H. (1975). Responses to complex erotic stimuli in homosexual and heterosexual males. *British Journal of Psychiatry, 126,* 252–257.

O'Donahue, W. & Caselles, C. E. (1993). Homophobia: Conceptual, definitional, and value issues. *Journal of Psychopathology and Behavioral Assessment, 15,* 177–195.

Rowan, A. (1994). Homophobia: A new diagnosis for DSM-V? *Behavior Therapist, 17,* 183–184.

Tollison, C. D., Adams, H. E., & Tollison, J. W. (1979). Cognitive and physiological indices of sexual arousal in homosexual, bisexual, and heterosexual males. *Journal of Behavioral Assessment, 1,* 305–314.

Weinberg, G. (1972). *Society and the healthy homosexual.* New York: St. Martin's Press.

West, D. J. (1977). *Homosexuality re-examined.* Minneapolis: University of Minnesota Press.

Zuckerman, M. (1971). Physiological measures of sexual arousal in the human. *Psychological Bulletin, 75,* 297–329.

HENRY E. ADAMS obtained his PhD in clinical psychology at Louisiana State University, then served as professor of psychology at the University of Georgia for 36 years. He was a distinguished scientist, clinician, forensic specialist, professor, and author of various textbooks, books, and journal articles. Before his death on October 16, 2000, he served as the founding editor of *Journal of Psychotherapy and Behavioral Assessment,* was the editor of *The Comprehensive Handbook of Psychopathology,* and was a consultant for the American Psychological Association in addition to the National Veterans Association Hospital.

LESTER W. WRIGHT, JR. serves as an associate professor of clinical psychology at Western Michigan University. He conducts research on deviant behavior and human sexuality, the interaction between sexual behavior and anxiety, and the psychophysiological assessment of sexual arousal.

BETHANY A. LOHR teaches psychology at the Harold Abel School of Social and Behavioral Sciences at Capella University. She earned her PhD in psychology from the University of Georgia.

Mark E. Johnson, Christiane Brems, and Pat Alford-Keating

 **NO**

Personality Correlates of Homophobia

Despite the fact that as early as 1975 the American Psychological Association (APA) asserted that homosexuality is neither a mental illness nor a personality trait that results in impairment of vocational capabilities, emotional adjustment, or judgment (Congor, 1975), pervasive negative attitudes about homosexuality have continued in our society. Many heterosexual individuals have continued to view their gay peers as a threat and approach them with fear and prejudice (Coleman, 1982; Herek, 1984; Moss, 1992; Wallick, Cambre, & Townsend, 1993).

The prejudice and fear thus expressed has received numerous labels including homosexphobia, heterosexism, homoerotophobia, and homophobia (see Herek, 1984, for a review of these terms). Since homophobia was identified as a personality trait with deleterious effects for at least one portion of society (Fein & Nuehring, 1981), the social psychology literature has proliferated with the development of various scales measuring homophobia (e.g., Aguero, Bloch, & Byrne, 1984; Bouton, Gallaher, Garlinghouse, Leal, Rosenstein, & Young, 1987; Lumby, 1976; Millham, San Miguel, & Kellogg, 1976), as well as with attempts to identify predictors of this biased attitude.

Variables that have been identified as being consistently correlated with homophobia include gender (cf. Kite, 1984, for a meta-analysis; Young, Gallaher, Marriott, & Kelly, 1993), sexism (e.g., Stark, 1991), sex-role (e.g., Black & Stevenson, 1984), racism (e.g., Ficarrotto, 1990), and authoritarianism (e.g., Greendlinger, 1985). One variable that has received some attention but has remained somewhat less conclusive in its relationship with homophobia is religiosity (Hansen, 1982; Hellman, Green, Gray, & Williams, 1981; Kunkel & Temple, 1992; Wylie & Forest, 1992).

Variables that appear conceptually correlated but have not received attention in the research literature despite a call for additional research exploring possible antecedents of homosexuality by APA's Committee on Lesbian and Gay Concerns (1991) are empathy and coping styles. As both of these variables have been identified as being related to various interpersonal processes that express sensitivity, altruism, or caring (e.g., Brems, 1989;

Schutz, 1962), they appear quite relevant in the exploration of homophobia.

It was the purpose of the current study to engage in an exploration of three personality variables that, although likely to be correlated with homophobia, have either never been studied in this context or have produced inconsistent findings. Specifically, with three separate samples of respondents, empathy, religiosity, and coping styles were explored in their relationship with homophobia. Given the research evidence in the literature that gender is related to homophobia, particularly in college age samples, gender was controlled for across all analyses. Further, based on the findings that individuals' levels of homophobia change over time, respondents' age was assessed and controlled for.

Method

Overall Sample

The overall sample included 411 women and 303 men who identified themselves as exclusively heterosexual. They ranged in age from 18 to 53 ($M = 21.29$; $SD = 5.51$; Mdn = 19). The majority (80.8%) were European American, all had at least a high-school degree, and most were single (83.3%).

Participants for Part One—Empathy

Participants in the empathy aspect of the study were 133 female and 120 male college students, whose ages ranged from 18 to 47 years ($M = 20.4$; $SD = 3.79$; Mdn = 19). Of the participants, 46% were Freshmen, 32% Sophomores, 12% Juniors, and 10% Seniors. Ethnic distribution was relatively typical of the region with 3.2% African Americans, 4.3% Asian Americans, 1.0% Hispanics, 7.1% Native Americans, 81% European Americans, and 4% other.

Participants for Part Two—Religiosity

Participants participating in the religiosity aspect of the study were 143 female and 78 male college students

From Mark E. Johnson, Christiane Brems, and Pat Alford-Keating (1997). "Personality Correlates of Homophobia," *Journal of Homosexuality*, vol. 34, no. 1, pp. 57–69, DOI: 10.1300/J082v34n01_05.

whose ages ranged from 18 to 41 years ($M = 20.7, SD = 4.3$, Mdn = 19). Of these participants, 39% were Freshmen, 35% Sophomores, 12% Juniors, and 14% Seniors. Ethnic composition of this sample was 6.3% African Americans, 3.6% Asian Americans, 1.0% Hispanics, 7.2% Native Americans, 78.3% European Americans, and 3.2% other.

Participants for Part Three—Coping Styles

Participants participating in the coping styles aspect of the study were 115 female and 125 male college students, ranging in age from 18 to 53 years ($M = 22.75, SD = 7.47$, Mdn = 19). Of these participants, 40% were Freshmen, 32% Sophomores, 23% Juniors, and 5% Seniors. Ethnicity of participants was 4.6% African American, 2.5% Asian American, 1.3% Hispanic, 5.4% Native American, 82.9% White, and 3.3% other.

Instruments

Homophobia Attitude Scale (HAS; Aguero, Bloch, & Byrne, 1984). This instrument was designed to assess an individual's attitudes and beliefs about gays. It consists of 11 items to which a participant responds on a 5-point Likert scale ranging from *agree not strongly* (1), to *agree very strongly* (5). The instrument yields an overall homophobia score, with higher scores indicating greater degrees of homophobia. The instrument was factor-analytically validated by the original authors and yielded two minimally intercorrelated ($r = .18$) factors. The first factor, consisting of eight items, is labeled Affective and is interpreted as the respondent's personal affective response to gays. The second factor, consisting of three items, is labeled Beliefs and is interpreted as reflective of the respondent's personal belief that homosexuality is learned and hence gays can change their sexual orientation. Internal consistency for the Affective Factor was .76 and for the Beliefs Factor, .69.

Interpersonal Reactivity Index (IRI; Davis, 1980). This instrument consists of 28 items scored on a 5-point Likert scale ranging from *disagree strongly* (1) to *agree strongly* (5) and is designed to assess four separate aspects of empathy. These aspects are Perspective Taking (PT), the ability to adopt others' point of view; Empathic Concern (EC), the level of other-oriented feelings of sympathy and concern; Fantasy (FS), the ability to put oneself into the feelings and actions of fictitious characters; and Personal Distress (PD), feelings of personal anxiety and unease in intense situations. Higher scores on PT, EC, and FS indicate greater levels of empathy, whereas higher scores on PD indicate higher levels of personal distress that result in lesser ability to empathize in a healthy or constructive manner. All

subscales have satisfactory internal consistency and test-retest reliability (.71 to .77 and .62 to .71, respectively).

Shepherd Scale (SS; Basset, 1981). This instrument was developed to assess level of religiosity and consists of 38 items to which a respondent answers on a 4-point scale ranging from *not true* (1) to *true* (4). Two factors are derived from the scale. The Beliefs subscale assesses the degree to which respondents hold religious beliefs and the Walk subscale measures the degree of adherence to these religious beliefs. A third scale, Total Religiosity, is calculated by summing all responses. For all scales, higher scores indicate higher levels of religious beliefs. Reliability and validity indices are reported to be adequate (Basset, 1981). In the current sample, reliability coefficients for the Beliefs and Walk subscales and the total score were .93, .93, and .96, respectively.

FIRO-Cope (Schutz, 1962). This instrument was designed to measure a person's coping styles. It describes six situations with five possible responses to each situation. For each situation, respondents are asked to rank order the five possible responses from *most likely* (1) to *least likely* (5) according to how likely they would be to respond in the described manner. Each choice reflects one of five coping mechanisms: denial, isolation, projection, regression, and turning against self. For each of the coping styles, the ranks given to the respective responses to each of the six situations are summed to provide a total score for each coping style. For each coping style, lower scores indicate greater likelihood to use it. Psychometric data for the FIRO-Cope are not available but the instrument nevertheless has enjoyed consistent use in research and clinical settings (cf. Brems & Johnson, 1989).

Procedure

All participants completed the research protocol in a group setting. After having provided informed consent, they responded to the questionnaire which always consisted of a demographic data form, Homophobia Attitude Scale, and relevant personality characteristics scale (i.e., the Interpersonal Reactivity Index in Part One; the Shepherd Scale in Part Two; the FIRO-Cope in Part Three). Order of the HAS and personality characteristics scale was counterbalanced to prevent possible order effect.

Design and Analyses

Preliminary analyses. Before the main analyses were calculated it was deemed important to validate the factor structure of the HAS. A principal components factor analysis was calculated using varimax rotation. Findings from this analysis determined the dependent variables derived from the HAS.

Table 1

Factor Analysis Results for the Homophobia Attitude Scale

Item	Physical Proximity	Human Rights	Beliefs
1	.868	.243	−.117
2	−.131	−.349	.735
3	.894	.166	−.099
4	.800	.316	−.187
5	−.045	−.015	.806
6	−.172	−.079	.737
7	.134	.798	.012
8	.275	.530	−.082
9	.375	.717	−.151
10	.381	.650	−.255
11	.040	.651	−.146
Eigenvalue	4.60	1.42	1.12
% Variance	41.9%	13.0%	10.2%
Internal Consistency	.89	.77	.69

To determine whether age and gender were related to homophobia and whether their effects had to be partialled out when computing the main analyses, preliminary statistical analyses were conducted. First, to assess differences in homophobia between women and men, the scores from the factorially derived HAS subscales and the HAS total score were used as dependent variables in multivariate and univariate analyses of variance with Gender as independent variable. Second, the HAS total and subscale scores were also correlated with age. All preliminary analyses were based on the total sample of 714 respondents.

Main analyses. Partial correlations (controlling for variance contributed by age and gender) were calculated between the HAS scores and the relevant personality characteristics scores using the respective participant portion of the total sample.

Results

Preliminary Analyses

Factor analysis of the HAS. Principal components factor analysis utilizing varimax rotation and a scree test identified three subscales with eigenvalues above 1.00. Of these subscales, one conformed to the Beliefs Factor identified by Aguero, Bloch, and Byrne (1984). The other two factors were comprised of three and five items respectively that were identified by Aguero, Bloch, and Byrne (1984) as items of one factor, namely, the Affective Factor. These two identified subfactors of the original Affective Factor were labeled Physical Proximity and Human Rights to reflect their item content. Table 1 provides factor loadings, eigenvalues, and internal consistency coefficients for the three factors of the HAS.

Gender differences. The MANOVA using gender as the independent variable and the three HAS subscales as dependent variables, was statistically significant, $F(3, 710) = 15.09$, $p < .001$. Univariate analyses revealed significant differences between the genders on all three factors, Physical Proximity, Human Rights, and Beliefs, $F(1, 712) = 37.18$, $p < .001$, $F(1, 712) = 31.33$, $p < .001$, $F(1, 712) = 13.38$, $p < .001$, respectively. Men scored higher on Proximity and Rights, whereas women scored higher on Beliefs. Similarly, the ANOVA using the total HAS score as dependent variable was significant, $F(1, 712) = 31.56$, $p < .001$, with men scoring higher than women. Means and standard deviations are shown in Table 2.

Relationship with age. Results of partial correlations, controlling for gender, revealed that age was significantly correlated to the HAS total score, $r(706) = −.242$, $p < .001$, and the Beliefs, Physical Proximity, and Human Rights, $r(706) = .095$, $p < .005$; $r(706) = −.313$, $p < .001$; $r(706) = −.158$, $p < .001$, respectively. These results reveal that as age increases, homophobia decreases and belief that homosexuality has a genetic basis increases.

Main Analyses

Part One—Empathy. Partial correlations between the HAS scales and the Interpersonal Reactivity Inventory subscales revealed that Perspective Taking and Empathic Concern were related to various aspects of homophobia. Specifically, PT and EC were significantly and negatively correlated with the total HAS score and the Human Rights subscales, and PT with the Proximity subscale. These findings indicate that as empathy increases along the two dimensions of PT and EC, homophobia decreases. No other IRI subscale resulted in significant correlations. All

Table 2

Means and Standard Deviations for the HAS Subscales and Total Score by Gender

| | HAS Total | HAS Subscale Scores | | |
	Score	Proximity	Rights	Beliefs
Gender				
Female				
Mean	27.53	8.71	10.57	8.24
SD	5.76	3.44	3.66	2.52
Male				
Mean	30.15	10.30	12.33	7.52
SD	6.69	3.45	4.74	2.72

Table 3

Partial Correlations Controlling for Gender and Age Between Personality Characteristics and Homophobia

| | Total | Subscale Scores | | |
	Score	Proximity	Rights	Beliefs
Empathy				
Personal Distress	.084	.027	.048	.079
Perspective Taking	−.191***	−.141*	−.211***	.081
Fantasy	−.093	−.057	−.094	.014
Empathic Concern	−.195***	−.074	−.174**	−.070
Religiosity				
Total	.129*	.260***	.131*	−.266***
Beliefs	.096	.237***	.093	−.252***
Walk	.139*	.250***	.144**	−.250***
Coping Style				
Denial	−.096	−.065	−.157**	.090
Isolation	−.094	−.028	−.030	−.117*
Projection	−.006	.005	.029	−.056
Regression	.021	−.001	−.029	.082
Turning Against Self	.163**	.095	.209***	−.060

*$p < .05$; **$p < .01$; *** $p < .001$

second order partial correlations (controlled for age and gender; $n = 253$) are displayed in Table 3.

Part Two—Religiosity. Partial correlations between the Shepherd total score and subscales and the HAS total score and subscales revealed significant and negative relationships between all religiosity indices and homophobia. Specifically, all three scales derived from the Shepherd Scale correlated significantly with the Beliefs and Physical Proximity subscales of the HAS. These results indicate that as level of religiosity increases, homophobia increases, and belief that homosexuality has a genetic basis decreases. All

second order partial correlations (controlled for age and gender; $n = 221$) are displayed in Table 3.

Part Three—Coping Styles. Three of the five FIRO-Cope scales were correlated with homophobia. Specifically, denial was negatively related to the human rights subscale, isolation was negatively related to beliefs that homosexuality is genetic, and turning against self was positively related to total HAS scores and the human rights subscale. Because lower scores on the FIRO-Cope subscales indicate greater use of that defense, these findings suggest that the greater one's use of denial and the more one uses isolation from others, the greater the homophobia, and the more one turns against oneself, the less the homophobia. All second order partial correlations (controlled for age and gender; $n = 240$) are displayed in Table 3.

Discussion

Using a college student population, this study was designed to investigate the relationship between homophobia and three personality variables, empathy, religiosity, and coping style, and, secondarily, the relationship between homophobia and gender and age. Validating many previous studies (e.g., Kite, 1984; Reiter, 1991), preliminary analyses revealed that gender was related to homophobia. Specifically, the current results reveal that men and women differ in their affective responses to and beliefs about gays, with women being less homophobic than men, having a less negative response to gays with regard to their own level of discomfort while being close to them, and expressing more willingness to grant human rights to gay individuals. Men reported not only less comfort around and less willingness to grant human rights to gays, but also expressed weaker beliefs than women about homosexuality having a genetic basis, instead believing that homosexuality was a lifestyle choice that can be altered through therapy.

Age was significantly correlated with homophobia, regardless of gender of the participant, revealing that older respondents were less homophobic than younger respondents. Younger participants endorsed higher levels of discomfort when being in the physical proximity of gays and less willingness to grant human rights. They were less likely to rate homosexuality as having a genetic basis and more likely to view it as a lifestyle choice that can be altered. Given the cross-sectional nature of the sample, it is not clear whether this correlation reflects a change in homophobia across an individual's life span or a more general, previously hypothesized (Black & Stevenson, 1984), trend in the population toward less prejudice against gays. It should also be noted that the distribution of ages in the current sample was skewed toward younger participants; the results may have been somewhat different had there been a wider range of ages.

The primary results from this study revealed significant relationships between homophobia and all three personality variables of empathy, religiosity, and coping styles. Relative to empathy, findings from this study suggest that certain components of empathy are significantly related to attitudes about homosexuality. Specifically, both empathic concern (affective form of empathy) *and* perspective taking (cognitive form of empathy) were sig-

nificantly related to overall levels of homophobia as well as to willingness to grant gays human rights; perspective taking was also related to physical proximity. No form of empathy was significantly related to beliefs about the origins of homosexuality.

These findings suggest that higher levels of empathy are related to less biased attitudes and behaviors (i.e., less homophobia, less human rights violation) but not necessarily to beliefs. In other words, although more empathic individuals may be less likely than less empathic individuals to discriminate against gays with regard to their overall attitudes and behaviors toward them, they are no more or less likely to hold genetic views about the development or origins of homosexuality than less empathic persons. This finding is interesting in that it appears that empathic individuals experience less homophobia toward gay individuals regardless of perceived origins of their homosexuality. This response style of the more empathic person suggests that for her or him the perceived reason why someone behaves or believes the way they do is not important; she or he still responds to others neither prejudicially nor inappropriately. It would appear that such an approach reflects the essence of empathy and lack of bias or prejudice.

Results further revealed that religiosity overall, as well as religious beliefs and religion-consistent behavior in particular, were related to higher levels of homophobia in general and greater discomfort around gays, less willingness to grant gays human rights, and less holding of genetic views about the origin of homosexuality, in particular. This finding of bias against gays by more religious persons is consistent with previous literature. The prejudice expressed by religious individuals toward gays was consistent across all interpersonal realms, extending from behavior, to attitudes and beliefs.

Relative to coping styles, it was revealed that individuals who tend to use denial and to isolate or turn away from others were more homophobic. Individuals were less homophobic if they used more defenses that indicated a turning against self approach. This finding is intuitively correct as it suggests that individuals who turn against themselves are less likely to search for negative traits in others and to tread on others' rights. Persons, however, who live with more denial tend to be more likely to look for causes and negativity outside of themselves and hence are more likely to discriminate and respond prejudicially in a manner that violates others' rights. Finally, individuals who turn away from others in an attempt to cope tend to have a less realistic and more self-absorbed way of looking at the world that results in idiosyncratically flavored beliefs about others.

Several limitations must be acknowledged and considered when interpreting these results. First, the current findings and conclusions are based on a large sample of college students. It may be that education plays a role in people's attitudes about homosexuality. Hence, replication with less educated participants than the ones included in this study would lend further support to the relationships of gender, age, empathy, religiosity, and coping style with homosexuality. Second, with the large number of statistical analyses conducted, the likelihood of a Type I error is increased. Next, given the correlational nature of this study, conclusions cannot be drawn regarding whether any of these variables necessarily caused the individual's attitudes toward gays. Because more clear-cut establishment of causal relationships would have strong implications for how to deal with homophobic attitudes in society and about toward whom to target interventions to decrease such homophobia, additional research in this area is warranted. It should also be noted that even the largest correlation between the variables only accounted for 9.8% of the variance. Clearly, homophobia is a complicated personality variable with numerous antecedents and correlates. The current study investigated several possible variables that were found to be correlated with homophobia; however, many other variables no doubt exist that will account for additional variance, perhaps even more than the ones included in this study.

These limitations notwithstanding, the current study provided empirical evidence that gender, age, empathy, religiosity, and coping style are five variables that can serve to predict a person's attitudes, beliefs, feelings, and behaviors with regard to homosexuality.

References

Aguero, J. E., Bloch, L., & Byrne, D. (1984). The relationships among sexual beliefs, attitudes, experience, and homophobia. *Journal of Homosexuality*, *10*, 95–107.

Basset, R. L. (1981). The Shepherd Scale: Separating the sheep from the goats. *Journal of Theology and Psychology*, *9*, 335–351.

Black, K. N., & Stevenson, M. R. (1984). The relationship of self-reported sex-role characteristics and attitudes toward homosexuality. *Journal of Homosexuality*, *10*, 83–93.

Bouton, R., Gallaher, P., Garlinghouse, P., Leal, T., Rosenstein, L., & Young, R. K. (1987). Scales for measuring fear of AIDS and homophobia. *Journal of Personality Assessment*, *51*, 606–614.

Brems, C. (1989). Dimensionality of empathy and its correlates. *Journal of Psychology*, *123*, 329–337.

Brems, C., & Johnson, M. E. (1989). Coping styles and problem-solving appraisal: Influence of sex-role and gender. *Journal of Psychology*, *123*, 187–194.

Committee on Lesbian and Gay Concerns. (1991). *Bias in psychotherapy with lesbians and gay men*. Washington, DC: American Psychological Association.

Coleman, E. (1982). Developmental stages of the coming out process. *Journal of Homosexuality*, *7*, 41–43.

Congor, J. (1975). Proceedings of the American Psychological Association for the year 1974: Minutes of the Annual Meeting of the Council of Representatives. *American Psychologist*, *30*, 620–651.

Davis, M. H. (1980). A multidimensional approach to individual differences in empathy. *JSAS Catalog of Selected Documents in Psychology*, *10*, 85.

Fein, S. B., & Nuehring, E. M. (1981). Intrapsychic effects of stigma: A process of breakdown and reconstruction of social reality. *Journal of Homosexuality*, *7*, 3–13.

Ficarrotto, T. J. (1990). Racism, sexism, and erotophobia: Attitudes of heterosexuals toward homosexuals. *Journal of Homosexuality*, *19*(1), 111–116.

Greendlinger, V. (1985). Authoritarianism as a predictor of response to heterosexual and homosexual erotica. *The High School Journal*, *68*, 183–186.

Hansen, G. L. (1982). Androgyny, sex-role orientation, and homosexism. *Journal of Psychology*, *112*, 39–45.

Hellman, R. E., Green, R., Gray, J. L., & Williams, K. (1981). Childhood sexual identity, childhood religiosity, and homophobia as influences in the development of transsexualism, homosexuality, and heterosexuality. *Archives of General Psychiatry*, *38*, 910–915.

Herek, G. M. (1984). Beyond homophobia: A social psychological perspective on attitudes toward lesbians and gay men. *Journal of Homosexuality*, *10*, 1–19.

Kite, M. E. (1984). Sex differences in attitudes toward homosexuals: A meta-analytic review. *Journal of Homosexuality*, *10*, 69–80.

Kunkel, L. E., & Temple, L. L. (1992). Attitudes toward AIDS and homosexuals: Gender, marital status, and religion. *Journal of Applied Social Psychology*, *22*, 1030–1040.

Lumby, M. E. (1976). Homophobia: The quest for a valid scale. *Journal of Homosexuality, 2,* 39–47.

Millham, J., San Miguel, C. L., & Kellogg, R. (1976). A factor-analytic conceptualization of attitudes toward male and female homosexuals. *Journal of Homosexuality, 2,* 3–10.

Moss, D. (1992). Introductory thoughts: Hating in the first person plural: The example of homophobia. *American Imago, 49,* 277–291.

Reiter, L. (1991). Developmental origins of antihomosexual prejudice in heterosexual men and women. *Clinical Social Work Journal, 19,* 163–175.

Schutz, W. (1962). *FIRO-Cope.* Los Angeles: Consulting Psychologists Press.

Stark, L. P. (1991). Traditional gender role beliefs and individual outcomes: An exploratory analysis. *Sex Roles, 24,* 639–650.

Wallick, M. M., Cambre, K. M., & Townsend, M. H. (1993). Freshman students' attitudes toward homosexuality. *Academic Medicine, 68,* 357–358.

Wylie, L., & Forest, J. (1992). Religious fundamentalism, right-wing authoritarianism, and prejudice. *Psychological Reports, 71,* 1291–1298.

Young, R. K., Gallaher, P. E., Marriott, S., & Kelly, J. (1993). Reading about AIDS and cognitive coping style: Their effects on fear of AIDS and homophobia. *Journal of Applied Social Psychology, 23,* 911–924.

MARK JOHNSON teaches psychology at Pacific University in Oregon, where his research specializes in HIV/AIDS, rural health care disparities, clinical and research ethics, substance abuse, and the concessions of conducting research ethically. Before working at Pacific University, he was a psychology professor at the University of Alaska Anchorage.

CHRISTIANE BREMS is a psychology professor at Pacific University in Oregon. Her research interests include clinical and research ethics, disease prevention and health promotion, and rural health care disparities and challenges.

PAT ALFORD-KEATING is a licensed psychologist at Psych-Wellness in Redondo Beach, California. She specializes in group psychotherapy, LGBT support, writer's block therapy, hypnotherapy, and treatment for anxiety, relationship issues, and issues related to identifying as LGBT.

EXPLORING THE ISSUE

Are Extremely Homophobic People Secretly Gay?

Critical Thinking and Reflection

1. The "yes" side of this debate argues that people who don't want to admit that they're gay sometimes seem the most homophobic. Can you think of anyone you know, either personally or a public figure, who you think might provide evidence of this hypothesis?
2. Some people have criticized the Adams et al. study for being unethical. The concern is that the participants may have become uncomfortable with the fact that they became aroused after watching gay pornography. What are your thoughts on the ethics of this experiment? Do you believe it should have passed a university ethics committee? Do you think the participants may have had any long-term negative effects?
3. Can you think of other examples of celebrities or public figures who have appeared to be very much against a particular issue, but then got "caught" engaging in that very behavior?
4. The "no" side of this debate listed several variables they believe predict homophobia, such as age, religiosity, and level of empathy. Are there additional variables you believe should be added to this list? Why do you think they are potentially tied to levels of homophobia?

Is There Common Ground?

This controversy is a good example of a false dichotomy, in that the two apparent sides of the debate are not mutually exclusive. People who believe that extreme homophobia *could* be caused by latent or secret homosexual desires are unlikely to believe that this is the *only* variable that predicts homophobia. In a similar way, people who believe there are many predictors of homophobia are unlikely to believe that latent homosexual tendencies are *never* relevant to someone's motivation to be anti-gay.

Support for the ability for the two sides to come together lies in the "no" article, where the authors even included use of denial as a predictor—and found that denial and homophobia are, in fact, positively correlated. It is important to understand all of the possible causes of homophobia, so that this particular form of prejudice can be battled just as strongly as racism, sexism, ageism, and the other forms of discrimination studied by social psychology.

Additional Resources

Bering, J. (2009, January 30). Single, angry, straight male . . . seeks same? *Scientific American.* Retrieved from http://www.scientificamerican.com/blog/post/single-angry-straight-male/.

Eguchi, S. (2006). Social and internalized homophobia as a source of conflict: How can we improve the quality of communication? *The Review of Communication, 6,* 348–357.

MacDonald, A. P. (1976). Homophobia: Its roots and meanings. *Homosexual Counseling Journal, 3,* 23–33.

MacInnis, C. C., & Hodson, G. (2013). Is homophobia associated with an implicit same-sex attraction? *Journal of Sex Research, 50,* 777–785. doi:10.1080/00224499.2012.690111

Meier, B. P., Robinson, M. D., Gaither, G. A., & Heinert, N. J. (2006). A secret attraction or defensive loathing? Homophobia, defense, and implicit cognition. *Journal of Research in Personality, 40,* 377–394.

Internet References . . .

GayHomophobe.com

> http://gayhomophobe.com/

LGBTQIA Healthcare Guild

> http://healthcareguild.com/homophobia_and_
> heterosexism.html

National Organization for Men Against Sexism

> http://site.nomas.org/

Social(In)Queery

> http://socialinqueery.com/

Understanding Prejudice: Heterosexism

> http://www.understandingprejudice.org/links/
> hetero.htm

Unit 3

UNIT

Gender and Sexism

*A*nother major topic in the field of social psychology is that of stereotypes, prejudice, and discrimination. In this unit, the controversies surround issues of one form of prejudice, that of sexism, as well as other relevant issues in the world of gender. With relatively rapid changes in the last 50 years regarding roles that women are undertaking in society, the prevalence of GLTBQI individuals and the prominence of issues regarding their civil rights, and tough decisions parents are having to make regarding how to raise their children in an increasingly complicated world, this unit highlights just a few relevant and current controversies.

Selected, Edited, and with Issue Framing Material by:
Wind Goodfriend, *Buena Vista University*

ISSUE

Are Male Teens More Aggressive Than Female Teens?

YES: Lori Rose Centi, from "Teenage Boys: From Sweet Sons to Narcissistic Teens," *The Washington Times* (2012)

NO: Frances McClelland Institute, from "Aggression Among Teens: Dispelling Myths About Boys and Girls," *Research Link* (2009)

Learning Outcomes

After reading this issue, you will be able to:

- Describe the overall findings from each article that either support or do not support gender differences with regard to aggression in teens.
- Decide for yourself if the research presented is compelling enough to help you decide which side of the issue you are on.

ISSUE SUMMARY

YES: Lori Rose Centi addresses the differences in male and female brain development, and how gray and white matter in the brain can impact adolescent behaviors. She also discusses other brain changes that may contribute to males being more impulsive and less careful than their female peers.

NO: The Frances McClelland Institute shares a fact sheet which dispels "myths" about the differences in male and female teens. It reports on a meta-analysis of 148 studies and the resulting major findings. Different types of aggression are defined and discussed.

Research on aggression and adolescents suggests that aggressive acts are neither uncommon nor restricted to a certain demographic. School bullying and aggression cut across all economic, cultural, ethnic, and gender boundaries. The reported rates of bullying and aggression for the United States suggest that a significant number of adolescents have either been a victim of school aggression or have bullied others themselves. This is a concern because aggression is associated with a host of behavioral, social, and emotional adjustment difficulties.

In order to answer the question "Are male teens more aggressive than female teens?" it is important to understand what we mean by "aggression." Social scientists define aggression as behavior intended to hurt, harm, or injure another person. However, research has demonstrated that children engage in a variety of forms of aggressive behavior. The most important distinction for classification purposes is whether aggression is physical or relational in form.

Physical, or direct, aggression consists of behaviors that harm another through damage to one's physical well-being. Physical aggression among adolescents has received considerable attention from researchers. Some have argued that there is a general tendency for physical violence to worsen over time, with behaviors like minor aggression giving way to more serious behaviors, including assault and robbery. Other research has shown that, among boys, early physical aggression predicts an elevated risk of physical violence in adolescence as well as nonviolent forms of delinquency.

Relational, or indirect, aggression includes behaviors that harm others through damage to relationships or feelings of friendship, acceptance, or social inclusion. Existing evidence suggests that relational aggression, like physical aggression, can result in emotional harm to victims. Outcomes include a range of psychosocial problems including lower social and emotional adjustment, poorer relationships with peers, and more loneliness. An added concern among some researchers who study relational aggression is the potential for retaliatory violence by those who have been victimized. Research has shown that a majority of females use relational aggression to secure their social status and maintain social harmony.

In general, convention states that males tend to employ more physical aggression, while females are more likely to use relational aggression. However, recent research suggests that it is not always appropriate to categorize aggression types by gender. Several studies have found that male and female teens appear to use a complex combination of both physical and relational aggression.

In addition to the aggression issue, be mindful of the age group on which these selections focus. Adolescence is a time of physical, developmental, social, and emotional change. Adolescents often feel out of control and overwhelmed by daily living. Remember when you were a teenager? Were you ever a victim or perpetrator of physical or relational aggression? Who were more aggressive, males or females? Which one of these views best reflects your experiences?

The question remains: Are male teens more aggressive than female teens? As you read the following two selections, keep in mind the different types of aggression.

YES ↵

Lori Rose Centi

Teenage Boys: From Sweet Sons to Narcissistic Teens

Huntingdon, PA—January 8, 2012—Teenage boys can be an enigma to their mothers, who are often perplexed by the way their sweet young boys have seemingly morphed overnight into moody, narcissistic young teenagers.

A plethora of images fill a mother's mind when considering her teenage son and his behaviors. Some of the images may be of laughing and talking together, enjoying time outdoors, or pleasant family time playing cards or board games. Other images may not be as positive.

These less than positive experiences, involving some recalcitrant behaviors, uncharacteristic outbursts, demands for more freedom and fewer rules, may not completely be the teen's fault. In other words, his growing, developing brain may be at "fault," but he as a person is not completely to blame. Recent research conducted on the development of the male and female brains, beginning in infancy and often continuing to age 20, have corroborated many psychiatrists' (and parents') previous assertions with physiological findings.

These findings may help parents to not only understand their teenage sons better, but also to advocate for the enhancement of education geared toward reaching both sexes more effectively. It may also make parents of teens feel less frustration and more empathy for their growing, often misunderstood, sons.

Many friends and colleagues have expressed confusion about the differences between their male and female children, especially during the teen years. Comments, such as "He is so immature compared to her," and "He seems to be unable to control his anger at times, while she just cries," are commonly heard in the parenting realm. Now, at least, the research has revealed valid, solid reasons for the sometimes churlish, impulsive behavior exhibited by our male offspring.

"Adolescence is a period of rapid changes. Between the ages of 12 and 17, for example, a parent ages as much as 20 years." Author unknown.

The National Institutes of Health released a report on "Male/Female Difference Offers Insight into Brain Development" stating "there are gender differences in the trajectory of gray matter maturation in adolescent girls and boys that may have lasting effects on the brain." Male adolescent brains have more gray matter than female brains. Gray matter is sometimes called "thinking matter."

However, developing female brains have more white matter, responsible for connecting various parts of the brain than their male counterparts. So, in spite of this seeming "advantage," boys are actually at a disadvantage because the information acquired usually cannot be fully processed due to the inability of their brains to make adequate connections.

Perhaps the actual physiology of male and female teens' brains is the most revealing aspect of the studies. The cortex, which contains both gray and white matter, is the part of the brain responsible for thinking, perceiving, and processing language. More specifically, the prefrontal cortex, a portion of the brain right behind the forehead, is one of the last areas of the brain to mature in males. This part of the brain is necessary for "good judgment, controlling impulses, solving problems, setting goals, organizing and planning, and other skills that are essential to adults," according to "The Amazing Adolescent Brain," compiled by Dr. Linda Burgess Chamberlain, Ph.D., MPH.

In addition to the physiology of the brain, a teen's gender and hormones affect his or her developing brain in myriad ways. It may also help you to understand why your son spends hours on video games that involve more violence than you and your husband have allowed him to see in his short lifetime. In addition, you may now understand why your son grunts or mutters incomprehensible words while his fingers rapidly press buttons on his game controller.

Hormones contribute greatly to the differences in male and female brain development. The hippocampus, which helps to move newly acquired information into long-term storage in the brain, responds to the primary female hormone, estrogen. As a result, the hippocampus grows and matures much faster in teenage girls than in teenage boys. This cerebral advantage allows girls to do better in social settings and causes them to show emotions more freely than boys.

Conversely, the amygdala and the hypothalamus are affected by male sex hormones and, consequently, grow larger in teenage males. Both of these parts of the brain are involved in responding to frightening and/or dangerous situations. These brain functions are exhibited by boys' greater enjoyment of physically challenging sports and being more aggressive in some settings than females.

It also may, in part, explain their need for excitement, whether literal or virtual. (Hence, those video games.) Researchers also contend that this aspect of brain development makes males less able to sit still for long periods of time. For that reason, males often learn better while moving around in a learning environment.

The greatest difference between the male and female adolescent brains, however, appears to be the delayed development of the prefrontal cortex.

Mark Weist, Ph.D., professor of psychology at the University of South Carolina and the father of three boys and two girls, concurs that male brains take longer to mature.

"Compared to teenage girls, teenage males have less developed brain functions in the frontal lobe region, associated with more impulsive behavior and less careful processing of information."

Unfortunately for males, brain development often continues into the early to mid-20s. This puts them at a higher risk for engaging in dangerous, superfluous behaviors that could cause them to make poor decisions. If drug or alcohol use is involved, brain development may also be adversely affected.

So how can parents and/or family members assist teenage boys though this difficult time? One thing that experts recommend is encouraging your son, family member, etc., to become actively involved in athletic endeavors, artistic activities (such as theatrical productions), and outdoor recreation. Being physically and mentally involved in activities that allow teens to move around while learning is especially beneficial to males. These kinds of activities are also both mentally and physically stimulating, so they aid in the development of the brain as well.

In addition, parents should also remember that because the prefrontal cortex is still developing in male teens, it is wise to give them simple instructions, rather than overwhelming them with information. Also, the information should be given in a step-by-step fashion.

It is helpful to give your teenager a planner to help him organize his homework and extra-curricular activities. Ask him to be responsible and listen to the teacher or coach's instructions, then write the instructions in the planner. This will help to reinforce the information that has been conveyed to him.

Neuroscientists stress that both male and female teenagers are often sleep-deprived due to a biological tendency to become drowsy later at night than adults. Sleep deprivation can exacerbate teenagers' tendencies to make poor decisions or to act impulsively. Parents should encourage their teenagers to get a minimum of nine hours of sleep per night. Getting extra sleep on weekends is also beneficial.

During the teen years of rapid growth and change, teenagers need family togetherness and ties that only you can give him or her. Family dinners and discussions are as important to his development into a person of good character and responsibility as any facet of his educational process.

"Even as kids reach adolescence, they need more than ever for us to watch over them. Adolescence is not about letting go. It's about hanging on during a very bumpy ride," according to Ron Taffel, renowned child development expert.

LORI ROSE CENTI is a writer and a teacher on the postsecondary level.

Frances McClelland Institute    **NO**

Aggression Among Teens: Dispelling Myths About Boys and Girls

A new study dispels the popular belief that girls are more likely than boys to hurt other children through gossip, rumor, and social rejection. While boys do tend to hit, push, and call their peers names more than girls do, they are just as likely as girls to hurt other kids socially.

Background

Why study aggression in children and adolescents? Such behaviors are associated with maladjustment—that is, difficulties coping with problems and social relationships. For over 100 years, scientists have studied children who physically and verbally attack other kids, what we now call "direct" aggression. Since most people previously thought that physical attacks were typical of boys, researchers often left girls out of their studies. In addition, in the last 20 years, girls have been linked with social or "indirect" aggression—that is, they hurt other girls through talking badly about them and keeping them out of their social group. Over time, a belief has grown that social aggression is a female form of aggression. But new evidence shows that boys hurt their peers socially, too. . . .

The study also dispelled another myth, that girls tend not to be physically aggressive. This myth may exist because public opinion is more likely to approve the use of direct aggression by boys than by girls. But even though boys use direct aggression more than girls, girls are directly aggressive, too.

Implications

- We need to study direct and social aggression, but not because one is a male form and the other female. Both forms of aggression affect both genders, and boys and girls who engage in aggression are equally likely to experience maladjustment.
- To understand whether aggression causes poor adjustment, or vice versa, we need to do longitudinal studies. We must look at aggressive kids over time to see which condition—aggression or maladjustment—comes before the other.

- People who work with aggressive children can look for signs of delinquent behavior, attention problems, depression, or anxiety. Indirectly aggressive children are as much at risk for problems as directly aggressive children.
- Researchers can look at the source of perceptions of aggression. Do they arise in adult or children's minds?

THIS RESEARCH BRIEF SUMMARIZES THE FOLLOWING REPORT:

Card, N. A., Stucky, B. D., Sawalani, G. M., & Little, T. D. (2008). Direct and indirect aggression during childhood and adolescence: A meta-analytic review of gender differences, intercorrelations, and relations to maladjustment. *Child Development, 79,* 1185–1229.

SUGGESTED CITATION FOR THIS RESEARCH LINK:

Van Campen, K. S., & Card, N. A. (2009). Aggression Among Teens: Dispelling Myths About Boys and Girls (Frances McClelland Institute for Children, Youth, and Families Research Link Vol. 1, No. 2). Tucson, AZ: The University of Arizona.

About the Study

A recent meta-analysis examined 148 studies that consisted of almost 74,000 children. The goal of the meta-analysis, which examined direct and social forms of aggression, was to understand three things:

1. Are direct and social aggression more common among boys or among girls, and how large are these gender differences?

2. To what extent are children who are directly aggressive also socially aggressive, and vice versa?
3. How much does aggressive behavior explain the likelihood that a child will suffer from problems such as depression or delinquency? . . .

Finding 1

Boys tend to engage in hitting and punching more than girls, but girls do physically hurt others to a moderate degree. For example:

- Imagine a school with 100 boys and 100 girls, and 100 children are directly aggressive and 100 are not.
- Of these 100 aggressive children, about 65 would be boys and 35 would be girls.
- So even though direct aggression is nearly twice as common among boys than girls, there are still a lot of girls who use direct aggression.

Boys and girls are equally likely to use social aggression. For example:

- Imagine again a school with 100 boys and 100 girls, and 100 children are indirectly aggressive and 100 are not.
- Of these 100 indirectly aggressive children, about 51 would be girls and 49 would be boys.
- The amount of difference in social aggression between boys and girls is so small that it is not meaningful.

Finding 2

Physically and socially aggressive behaviors tend to be used together. For example:

- Imagine again a school of 200 children and that 100 of them are directly aggressive and 100 are indirectly aggressive.
- Because there is overlap between the two forms, about 85 or 90 children use both direct and social aggression.
- But because the two forms are not perfectly overlapping, there is a large number—about 20 to 30—who use only one form or the other.
- So, although most aggressive children will use both types, some will only use one form or the other.

Finding 3

Both direct and social aggression are related to behavioral problems, but to different types. For example:

- There is a *strong* link between direct aggression and problems we can see in a child. That is, children who hit and punch tend to misbehave and act impulsively more so than children who gossip and hurt others socially.
- Directly aggressive children are also more likely to have poor relations with their peers than other children.
- There is a *moderate* link between social aggression and problems that are harder to see. That is, children who are indirectly aggressive are more likely to suffer from depression and anxiety than other children.
- Children who use direct aggression show low prosocial behavior (e.g., helping, sharing, cooperating), while children who use social aggression show high rates of acting prosocially toward others.
- No matter which type of aggression they use, girls and boys experience poor adjustment in the same ways. This finding contradicts previous beliefs that boys who gossip and spread rumors and girls who hit and punch are especially likely to have poor adjustment.

Misperceptions of Aggression in Girls

The myth that girls tend to be more socially aggressive than boys is strong among teachers, parents, and even some researchers. These adults may set social expectations for girls early in life that are hard to shake. Recent movies and books that depict girls as mean and hurtful maintain these stereotypes. According to the meta-analysis, teachers and parents were more likely to say that girls were more socially aggressive than boys. Meanwhile, peers and research observers were likely to view boys and girls as equally socially aggressive.

> "These findings challenge the popular belief that social aggression is a female form of aggression," says Noel A. Card, assistant professor of Family Studies and Human Development at The University of Arizona and the study's lead author.

Frances McClelland Institute for Children, Youth, and Families serves as a catalyst for cross-disciplinary research on children, youth, and families at the University of Arizona.

EXPLORING THE ISSUE

Are Male Teens More Aggressive Than Female Teens?

Critical Thinking and Reflection

1. What evidence did each article present for whether the authors believe there are gender differences in aggressive behavior among teens?
2. Identify some limitations in each article regarding the participants, methods, and overall generalizability to the entire teen population. Given these limitations, can you think of ways to improve these studies and build on the research?

Is There Common Ground?

Both articles examined gender differences in aggression among teenage males and females. However, neither of the articles mentioned the ethnic or cultural background. Whether this was omitted for the purposes of condensing the articles or it was just left out, could this information explain some of the findings? How might ethnic or cultural background influence aggression in each gender? What about teens in rural versus urban areas?

Both sets of researchers utilized children from elementary school as part of their study, partly to examine patterns of aggression based on earlier experiences and behavior patterns at a younger age into adolescence. How might the results of their findings be different if only adolescents had been used? Although information regarding the behaviors from childhood to adolescents is important, is it possible that these behaviors may change as the adolescents move further away from their preadolescent years?

Can you think of ways in which the research presented and other research like it will contribute to school-age children (elementary through high school)? What is the significance of knowing whether gender differences exist with regards to these possible contributions of the research?

Additional Resources

Karriker-Jaffe, K. J., Foshee, V. A., Ennett, S. T., & Suchindran, C. (2008). The Development of Aggression During Adolescence: Sex Differences in Trajectories of Physical and Social Aggression Among Youth in Rural Areas. *Journal of Abnormal Child Psychology*, 36(8), pp. 1227–1236. doi: 10.1007/s10802-008-9245-5. Retrieved on April 24, 2011, from www.ncbi.nlm.nih.gov/pmc /articles/PMC2773662/.

The authors report findings in the study that support that male teens tend to be more physically aggressive than female teens.

National Youth Violence Prevention Resource Center. (2002). Facts for Teens: Aggression. Retrieved on April 24, 2011, from http://herkimercounty.org/content /departments/View/11:field=services;/content /DepartmentServices/View/68:field=documents; /content/Documents/File/123.PDF

This website offers information about different types of aggression and explains some of the contributing factors to aggression in adolescents and how this might relate to earlier childhood.

Nichols, T. R., Graber, J. A., Brooks-Gunn, J., & Botvin, G. J. (2006). Sex Differences in Overt Aggression and Delinquency Among Urban Minority Middle School Students. *Applied Developmental Psychology*, 27, pp. 78–91. doi: 10.1016/j.appdev.2005.12.006. Retrieved on April 24, 2011, from www.med.cornell. edu/ipr/PDF/Nichols-et-al-2006-JADP.pdf

This article describes a longitudinal study that examined minority male and female adolescents' aggressive behavior with relation to precursors such as family disruption, anger, and self-control.

Internet References . . .

Global Post

http://everydaylife.globalpost.com/aggressive
-behavior-teenagers-2848.html

Scientific American

http://www.scientificamerican.com/article
.cfm?id=bitch-evolved-girls-cruel

Selected, Edited, and with Issue Framing Material by:
Wind Goodfriend, *Buena Vista University*

ISSUE

Should Parents Be Allowed to Choose the Sex of Their Children?

YES: Z. O. Merhi and L. Pal, from "Gender 'Tailored' Conceptions: Should the Option of Embryo Gender Selection Be Available to Infertile Couples Undergoing Assisted Reproductive Technology?" *Journal of Medical Ethics* (2008)

NO: American College of Obstetricians and Gynecologists, Committee on Ethics, from "Sex Selection," *Obstetrics & Gynecology* (2007)

Learning Outcomes

After reading this issue, you will be able to:

- Explain the relation between sex of a child and gender of a child.
- Determine whether the question of parental selection of their child's sex is a social or an ethical issue.
- Determine the question of parental selection of their child's sex is a question of parental rights or children's rights.
- Understand is the position taken by the American College of Obstetricians and Gynecologists' Committee on Ethics.

ISSUE SUMMARY

YES: Physicians Z. O. Merhi and L. Pal discuss the conditions under which selection of the sex of a child does not breach any ethical considerations in family planning among infertile couples.

NO: The American College of Obstetricians and Gynecologists' Committee on Ethics supports the practice of offering patients procedures for the purpose of preventing serious sex-linked genetic diseases, but opposes sex selection for personal and family reasons.

The potency of sex and gender as explanations for differences between males and females escalates early in life. By early childhood, a host of differences are observed between boys and girls as children internalize a sense of themselves and others as gendered. Concern has been raised about inequities and deficits resulting from the effects of sex and gender. All of these concerns are compounded by issues of preference for, and ability to select prenatally, a particular sex. Even before conception many people think about the sex of their child—which sex they want. For some, the decision even to carry a fetus to term can be influenced by gender. Research has con-

sistently documented the preference and desire for sons in America and in other cultures. In many cultures, such as India and China, maleness means social, political, and economic entitlement. Men are expected to support their parents in their old age. Moreover, men remain with their family throughout life; women, upon marriage, become part of the husband's family. Thus, women are traditionally seen as a continuing economic burden on the family—particularly in the custom of large dowry payments at weddings. In some cultures, if a bride's family cannot pay the demanded dowry, the brides are often killed (usually by burning). Although dowries and dowry deaths are illegal, the laws are rarely enforced. In such cultures, there is an expressed desire for male children and an urgency to select fetal sex. In contrast to this pattern, a recent 2010 study based on data from several health and demographic surveys, by Kana Fuse, published in *Demographic Research*, suggests that in some developing countries there has been a shift in attitudes toward a preference for balance (i.e., sons and daughters), with some countries showing a preference for daughters. In general, Fuse found that the preference for daughters is strongest in Latin America and the Caribbean (with the exception of Bolivia) and in some Southeast Asian countries. Southern Asia, Western Asia, and Northern Africa show a preference for sons, which was also the pattern in 16 of the 28 countries sub-Saharan Africa studied with the remaining countries showing a daughter preference. Thus, it appears that there may be much more heterogeneity currently in preferences for the sex of children than in the past.

Recently, sex-determination technology is most commonly used to assay the sex of fetuses, although in many cultures the use of such technology has been banned. When the fetus is determined to be female, abortion often follows because of cultural pressures to have sons. Such sex-determination practices have led to many more male than female infants being born. The gap grows even wider because of a high childhood death rate of girls, often from neglect or killing by strangulation, suffocation, or poisoning. Furthermore, women are blamed for the birth of a female child and are often punished for it (even though, biologically, it is the male's sperm, carrying either X or Y chromosomes, that determines sex). Research shows that in contemporary America, 78 percent of adults prefer their firstborn to be a boy. Moreover, parents are more likely to continue having children if they have all girls versus if they have all boys. Faced with having only one child, many Americans prefer a boy.

The issue of prenatal sex selection can be considered within the larger context of the "sexual revolution" and the burgeoning expansion in reproductive technologies. As a child, my peers and I would taunt each other with the saying, "First comes love, then comes marriage, then comes [name] with a baby carriage." Such childhood teasing reflected the cultural understanding that the order of things was love, marriage, and then children (with heterosexuality assumed). This is no longer the case. Sexual activity, without a reproductive goal, at earlier ages, parenthood without marriage, and the increase in the number of same-sex parents challenge much of what we understand about relationships and parenting. Additionally, discussions of the desired sex of one's child, along with the possibility of prenatal fetal sex selection, become even

more real given all the reproductive technologies that are readily available. These include the use of sperm donors, *in vitro* fertilization, artificial insemination, and surrogate mothers, to the more controversial techniques of artificial wombs and cloning.

The availability of sex-selection technology in the last quarter of the twentieth century has been met with growing interest and widespread willingness to make use of the technology. Available technologies for sex selection include preconception, preimplantation, and postconception techniques. Preconception selection techniques include folkloric approaches like intercourse timing, administering an acid or alkaline douche, and enriching maternal diets with potassium or calcium/magnesium, all thought to create a uterine environment conducive to producing male or female fetuses. There are also sperm-separating technologies whereby X- and Y-bearing sperm are separated, and the desired sperm are artificially inseminated into the woman, increasing the chance of having a child of the chosen sex. Preimplantation technologies identify the sex of embryos as early as 3 days after fertilization. For sex-selection purposes, the choice of an embryo for implantation is based on sex. Postconception approaches use prenatal diagnostic technologies to determine the sex of the fetus. The three most common technologies are amniocentesis (available after the 20th week of pregnancy), chorionic villus sampling (available earlier but riskier), and ultrasound (which can determine sex as early as 12 weeks but is not 100 percent accurate). The American demand for social acceptance of sex-selection technologies has increased in the past decade. Preconception selection techniques are becoming quite popular in the United States, and preimplantation technologies (though more expensive) are also more frequently used. It has become more and more socially accepted to use prenatal diagnostic technologies to determine fetal sex. But incidence rates for sex-selective abortions are difficult to obtain. There is mixed opinion about the frequency of sex-selective abortions, tinged by political controversy.

In the following selections, physicians Merhi and Pal argue that a desire for gender balance in the family is ethical. In contrast, the American College of Obstetricians and Gynecologists' Committee on Ethics asserts that fetal sex selection is always unethical, except in the case of preventing sex-linked genetic diseases. They suggest that parents are really not interested in the genitalia that their infants are born with. What they are really choosing is an "ideal," defined by gender role expectations: a boy dad can play ball with or a girl who can wear mom's wedding gown when she marries.

YES ↵

Z. O. Merhi and L. Pal

Gender "Tailored" Conceptions: Should the Option of Embryo Gender Selection Be Available to Infertile Couples Undergoing Assisted Reproductive Technology?

Preimplantation genetic diagnosis (PGD) was introduced at the beginning of the 1990s as an adjunct to the prenatal diagnostic armamentarium, allowing for genetic diagnoses earlier in the gestational period. This diagnostic option allows couples the opportunity of reaching decisions regarding terminating a genetically compromised fetus earlier in the course of the pregnancy, thus minimising the psychological stress as well as medical risks associated with terminations performed at more advanced gestations. Since its inception, PGD testing has been utilised for evaluation of a spectrum of inherited diseases (e.g., cystic fibrosis, sickle cell disease, hemophilia A and B, Lesch-Nyhan syndrome, thalassemia, Duchenne muscular dystrophy, and recently, Marfan's syndrome) allowing parents to avoid the lengthy, fearful wait for results of traditional testing (e.g., amniocentesis, chorionic villous sampling) while their pregnancy continues to progress. However, the application of PGD has raised multiple ethical issues, many of which were addressed by the President's Council on Bioethics in a recent paper in which the council sought to improve the application of PGD. One of the thorniest issues currently being confronted is the use of PGD for gender selection.

The methods used for preconception gender selection have evolved over time. An influence of coital timing on the gender of the conceptus was proposed by Shettles, who described an exaggerated motility by the smaller Y-bearing sperm in the mid cycle cervical mucus, and hypothesised that there would be male offspring dominance if the timing of coitus was proximate to ovulation. The length of the follicular phase of the menstrual cycle (i.e., period of maturation of the ovarian follicle and the contained egg therein), risk modifications by changing vaginal PH, possible effects of ionic concentrations in the woman's body, susceptible to dietary modifications and pre-fertilisation separation of X-bearing from Y-bearing spermatozoa, have all been stated to demonstrate varying degrees of success in gender determination. However, while some of these methodologies offer successes greater than predicted by the "toss of a coin," the results remain far from "guaranteed."

Among the prominent motivations driving a demand for preconception gender selection is the desire for children of the culturally preferred gender, and to achieve gender balance within a given family. Recently, an interest in PGD testing for the purpose of "gender selection" for social reasons seems to be escalating, although no concrete data are available. This use of PGD for "family tailoring" has engendered debate and controversy. While the acceptability of PGD for traditional medical indications is generally condoned, utilisation of this modality for non-medical purpose has generated ethical concerns. The American College of Obstetricians and Gynecologists has taken a clear stance on this issue as reflected in the following committee opinion, "The committee rejects the position that gender selection should be performed on demand. . . ." Additionally, the American Society of Reproductive Medicine states that "in patients undergoing IVF, PGD used for gender selection for non-medical reasons holds some risk of gender bias, harm to individuals and society, and inappropriateness in the use and allocation of limited medical resources." An introspective assessment of the published literature on clinical practices suggests that, while the stance of the principal governing bodies on the issue of PGD for gender selection is unambiguous, the actual practice of the technology of "gender tailoring on demand" is not uncommon. In fact, a recent survey of IVF clinics in the United States, an access to and provision of PDG services for sex selection was acknowledged by as many as

From *Journal of Medical Ethics*, vol. 34, 2008, pp. 590–593. Copyright © 2008 by Institute of Medical Ethics. Reprinted by permission of BMJ Publishing Group via Rightslink.

42% of the providers of assisted reproductive technique (ART) services; furthermore, beyond these geographical boundaries, the literature is replete with documentation of couples undergoing ART specifically wishing for family completion and/or balancing requesting that embryo(s) of a preferred gender be utilised for transfer.

Acknowledging the contrasting stance of the licensing and governing bodies on ethical concerns related to a wider availability and access to gender selection option versus the prevalent practices (as mentioned above), the authors herein attempt to explore whether the explicit utilisation of PGD for the purpose of gender selection by the infertile couple already undergoing a medically indicated ART procedure encroaches on breach of basic dictates of medical ethics.

It is currently not the "standard of care" (an individualised paradigm of diagnostic and treatment plan that an appropriately trained clinician is expected to pursue in the care of an individual patient) to perform PGD in the absence of a medical indication. However, "standards of care" should remain receptive to evolving scientific data, both that which supports and that which stands in opposition to changes in the standard. Accordingly, the opportunity to explore ethical arguments for and against the utilisation of PGD for gender selection by infertile couples undergoing ART is undertaken in this paper. This process might enable the patient and the provider to make informed and rational decisions when considering PGD utilisation for such a non-medical indication.

Beneficence and Non-Maleficence

Within the context of beneficence-based clinical judgment, a physician's inherent obligation towards his/her patient (i.e., the potential benefits of PGD) *must* be balanced against the risks of the proposed technique. For the infertile patients undergoing ART, and therefore already anticipating a procedure with some treatment related inherent risks, that is, minimal and yet real risks of anaesthesia, infection, bleeding, and ovarian hyperstimulation syndrome (a potentially lethal complication of attempts at inducing multiple ovulation), PGD for targeted genetic anomalies has been shown to improve ART outcomes (i.e., successful pregnancy following treatment), and to significantly reduce the risk of aneuploidy and miscarriage rates in a high-risk population. We believe, that in this patient population, use of additional gene probes per request, that is, for sex chromosomes, would not in any way jeopardise the principle of beneficence.

The limiting factor within this prototype of allowing PGD for gender selection "on request" will be the availability of an adequate number of cleaving embryos. A small yet real possibility does exist for a failure to achieve an embryo transfer either because of evidence of aneuploidy in the entire cohort of the tested embryos, a scenario that can be easily conjured for an older woman, or because of a procedure-related embryo loss due to the mechanisms used to create an opening in the zona pellucida (a membrane surrounding the egg) for the explicit purpose of removing a cell from the dividing embryo for PGD. The proposed benefits of PGD for the sole intention of gender selection in a patient undergoing ART must be thus balanced against the small yet real risks of embryo loss, and even failure to achieve an embryo transfer, as well as the incremental costs incurred (approximately $2500 per cycle above the costs of approximately $7500–$10000 for the IVF cycle and related procedures). To date, there are no reports of increased identifiable problems (fetal malformations or others) attributable to the embryo biopsy itself. On the contrary, data suggest that PGD for aneuploidy screening may significantly reduce the risk of spontaneous abortions and of aneuploidies in the offspring of women undergoing IVF, particularly so in the reproductively aging patient population.

The principle of beneficence is maintained in offering PGD to couples undergoing ART (the analysis of risks and benefits being based on the physician's assessment, and the risks being primarily confined to the embryo, and not to the patient). However, the same may not hold for otherwise fertile couples. In that case, the female partner would be subjected to medically unindicated risks as well as substantial financial costs ($10000–$15000), driven solely by a desire for a child of the preferred gender. Such couples may represent a "vulnerable population" whose vulnerability lies within a potential, enticed by a promise of a child of the preferred gender, for making impetuous decisions regarding an expensive and medically non-indicated intervention that has an uncommon, yet real potential for health hazard. For the fertile population, this desire may lead them to "medicalise" the spontaneous procreative process, transforming it into a controlled and expensive process.

While the authors believe that the principles of beneficence and non-maleficence are upheld within the context of allowing couples anticipating undergoing ART for the management of infertility, we believe that the medical community needs to pause and ponder on any potential for generation of *unwanted surplus embryos* of the undesired sex prior to declaring this as an "acceptable practice." Aspects for further "beneficence" may be appreciated within the folds of this latter concern as couples may consider donation of discard embryos of the non-desired gender to the less fortunate infertile patients. These plausible scenarios must be discussed at length with any couple wishing to discuss the possibility of embryo gender selection while undergoing a medically indicated IVF.

In contrast to an infertile patient anticipating undergoing medically indicated IVF and requesting embryo gender selection, a similar request from an otherwise fertile couple merits additional consideration. A decision to discard embryos of an undesired gender may be less onerous to a reproductively competent individual, although data in support of such a conjecture are lacking. Whether or not this concern regarding abandonment of the "unwanted" embryos is legitimate depends on the perception of the status accorded to the embryos. Although debatable, some would agree that since embryos are too rudimentary in the developmental paradigm to have "interests," there is simply no basis upon which to grant the embryos "rights." Additionally, the ethical principle of non-maleficence is not violated since this principle is directed to "people" rather than "tissues." Future debates on this particular concern might be needed to settle this issue.

To summarise, the performance of PGD per request specifically for gender selection in an infertile couple already planning to undergo ART for medical indications may not breach the principle of beneficence nor hold undue harm for the patient. However, the principles of justice and autonomy must also be considered.

Justice

The principle of justice requires an equitable distribution of the benefits as well as the burdens associated with an intervention. While at one end of the spectrum, this concept addresses the concern of societal gender imbalance resulting from utilisation of PGD for gender selection, at the other extreme, there may be concerns of gender imbalance in relation to socioeconomic strata, as an economic differential in the utilisation of ART services is well recognised.

Concerns are voiced regarding a potential of PGD, if deemed acceptable for the explicit purpose of sex selection, for disrupting the societal gender balance. Indeed, examples of gender preferences abound in existing communities and societies. For example, in certain regions of China, termination of pregnancies, infanticide, and inferior medical care for baby girls have created a shift in the population to a ratio of approximately 1.5 to 1 favouring males. Gender preference for the firstborn can thus overwhelmingly favour male gender, particularly

if "one child per family" population policies continue to be implemented. Similarly, a preference for male offspring is recognised in other regions across the globe including India and the Middle East. In contrast, in Nigeria, anecdotal tradition suggests that although a son is beneficial for propagating the family's name, a female infant is preferentially hoped for, as a daughter holds promise for eventual financial gains at the time of marriage. Similarly, in Haiti, a female firstborn is welcomed as a potential caregiver to the future siblings (personal communication).

It is important to appreciate that concerns voiced by the community regarding a potential for creating a gender differential across global regions if PGD for sex selection while undergoing a medically indicated IVF indeed achieves wider acceptability, while not unreasonable, appear based on "snap shot" views of cultural preferences. One is reassured by results of a recent cross-sectional web-based survey of 1197 men and women aged 18–45 years in the United States which revealed that the majority of those surveyed were unlikely to utilise "sperm sorting," an already existing, cheaper and less invasive technology, as a means for preferential preconception gender selection (sperm sorting employs flow cytometric separation of the 2.8% heavier "X chromosome" from the relatively lighter "Y chromosome" bearing sperm, thus providing an "X" [destined to contribute to a female fetus] or "Y" [destined to create a male fetus] enriched sperm sample for subsequent utilisation for artificial insemination or ART). Given the lack of enthusiasm for this simpler modality for preconception gender selection (an intervention that involves no risks to the patient or the embryos), at the population level, individuals are even less likely to opt for a more aggressive approach, that is, proceeding with ART and PGD, just for gender selection reasons. Similarly, a study from England on 809 couples revealed that gender selection is unlikely to lead to a serious distortion of the sex ratio in Britain and other Western societies. Yet another survey performed on a sample of German population (1094 men and women aged 18–45 years were asked about their gender preferences and about selecting the sex of their children through flow cytometric separation of X- and Y-bearing sperm followed by intrauterine insemination), revealed that the majority did not seem to care about the sex of their offspring and only a minority expressed a desire for gender selection. These authors concluded that preconception gender selection is unlikely to cause a severe gender imbalance in Germany. Similar conclusions, that is, the lack of an overwhelming interest in preconception gender selection were deduced in a survey of infertile Hungarian couples with regard to utilisation of sperm sorting for gender selection. These data are thus reassuring and suggest that, at least in the developed world, even if given access to technology facilitating preferential gender selection, and subsequently while undergoing a medically indicated IVF, use of such methods is not likely to significantly impact on the natural sex ratio within the communities. It needs to be appreciated however, that surveys generated within the industrialised nations are not representative of global perceptions regarding access to and utilisation of similar technology for ensuring conception of progeny of a preferred gender.

Another concern regarding the possibility of breaching the principle of justice is the ART-related cost as well as the additional expenditure related to the use of PGD. The financial burden is likely to preclude a section of the infertile population from using this service, hence holding the potential for a breach in the principle of justice. However, given that utilisation of PGD for gender selection may be limited secondary to financial constraints, such a differential would render significant shifts in population gender distribution very unlikely (like in ART, the issue of social and economic differences pose a distributive bias here that is beyond the scope of our paper).

Given the lack of information regarding the magnitude of utilisation of technologies for gender selection (PGD or sperm sorting) within societies, it may not be unreasonable to suppose that PGD would not be accessible to large enough numbers of people to make a real difference in the population gender balance. A potential donation of the undesired embryos by couples who opt to utilise PGD for gender selection is likely to negate any concerns regarding eventual disturbance of the sex ratio, enhance the balance towards "beneficence" by offering a possibility of parenthood to those who would otherwise not be able to afford the cost associated with ART and thus address some concerns regarding the principle of "justice" voiced earlier.

To summarise, although the existing literature touches upon aspects of preferential and differential biases in terms of gender preferences in the various communities around the world, data specifically addressing this aspect in infertile couples undergoing medically indicated ART are nonexistent, and voice a need to more formally assess the use of preconception gender selection technologies globally, so as to fully evaluate the impact of these practices on the principle of justice. It follows that performing PGD for gender selection might be consistent with substantive justice–based considerations until more thorough analysis for societal disruptive imbalance of the sexes has been performed.

Patient Autonomy

The freedom to make reproductive decisions is recognised as a fundamental moral and legal right that should not be denied to any couple, unless an exercise of that right would cause harm to them or to others. Access to and use of contraceptive choices, recognition of a woman's right to request for a termination of an unplanned and/or undesired pregnancy, and an emerging acceptance of an individual's right to determine his or her sexual orientation reflect evolving social and societal perceptions as relates to "reproductive autonomy, the authors believe that utilisation of PGD for the purpose of gender selection by infertile couples already undergoing ART may be incorporated within this paradigm of "reproductive autonomy." Across the societies, while parental autonomy in shaping the social identity of their progeny (behaviour, education, attire, . . . etc.) is an acceptable norm, this debate proposes that, in defined clinical situations, allowing parents to shape the genetic identity of a much-desired child will be within the purview of patient autonomy.

It is of interest that most of the ethical debates around use of PGD for gender selection stem from concerns regarding termination of pregnancies. Opponents to use of PGD for gender selection project that acceptability of such a practice will add yet another indication to justifying pregnancy termination, namely termination of a conceptus of an undesired gender. This latter concern however pales against the escalating requests for "selective reduction" of fetuses (a procedure in which one or more fetuses in a multiple pregnancy is/are destroyed in an attempt to allow the remaining embryo/s a better chance to achieve viability as well as minimise health risks to the mother) resulting from ART, driven by patients' "demands" for transfer of surplus embryos so as to ensure "success," albeit at escalating health risks for the mother and the fetus(es). If indeed a request for "selective reduction" of fetuses by an infertile couple is an acceptable exercise of parental autonomy, the authors put forth that compliance with a request for "gender selection" by an infertile couple undergoing ART be viewed in a similar vein.

By the same token of parental autonomy, the couple has to assume all responsibility of consequences resulting from such a decision, including a possibility of not achieving an embryo transfer secondary to failure of embryos to demonstrate ongoing development following the biopsy, a possibility of all embryos being of the less desired gender, as well as of the child of the desired gender failing to conform to their expectations! Extensive counselling of the couple must therefore be an integral part of the consenting process, if couples and practitioners are considering utilisation of such procedure.

Conclusion

While concerns regarding a potential for breach of ethical principles related to a generalised acceptance of such a practice are real, this paper attempts to evaluate the integrity of principles of ethics within the context of acceptability and use of PGD for the purpose of gender selection, exclusively in patients undergoing ART for the management of infertility. The authors believe that given the current prevalence of such practices despite a stance to the contrary taken by the licensing bodies, the needs and desires of an individual seeking care within the context of the overall society's perspective be considered; this extrapolation seems not to breach the basic four principles of ethics, nor does it hold harm for the patient/embryos. Accessibility of PGD for gender selection to couples undergoing ART for management of infertility is unlikely to influence the gender balance within this society and is very distant from being in the "bright-line" areas described by the President's Council on Bioethics.

Z. O. Merhi is on the staff of Maimonides Medical Center, Brooklyn, New York, specializing in gynecology and obstetrics.

American College of Obstetricians and Gynecologists

 **NO**

Sex Selection

Sex selection is the practice of using medical techniques to choose the sex of offspring. Patients may request sex selection for a number of reasons. Medical indications include the prevention of sex-linked genetic disorders. In addition, there are a variety of social, economic, cultural, and personal reasons for selecting the sex of children. In cultures in which males are more highly valued than females, sex selection has been practiced to ensure that offspring will be male. A couple who has one or more children of one sex may request sex selection for "family balancing," that is, to have a child of the other sex.

Currently, reliable techniques for selecting sex are limited to postfertilization methods. Postfertilization methods include techniques used during pregnancy as well as techniques used in assisted reproduction before the transfer of embryos created in vitro. Attention also has focused on preconception techniques, particularly flow cytometry separation of X-bearing and Y-bearing spermatozoa before intrauterine insemination or in vitro fertilization (IVF).

In this Committee Opinion, the American College of Obstetricians and Gynecologists' Committee on Ethics presents various ethical considerations and arguments relevant to both prefertilization and postfertilization techniques for sex selection. It also provides recommendations for health care professionals who may be asked to participate in sex selection.

Indications

The principal medical indication for sex selection is known or suspected risk of sex-linked genetic disorders. For example, 50% of males born to women who carry the gene for hemophilia will have this condition. By identifying the sex of the preimplantation embryo or fetus, a woman can learn whether or not the 50% risk of hemophilia applies, and she can receive appropriate prenatal counseling. To ensure that surviving offspring will not have this condition, some women at risk for transmitting hemophilia choose to abort male fetuses or choose not to transfer male embryos. Where the marker or gene for a sex-linked

genetic disorder is known, selection on the basis of direct identification of affected embryos or fetuses, rather than on the basis of sex, is possible. Direct identification has the advantage of avoiding the possibility of aborting an unaffected fetus or deciding not to transfer unaffected embryos. Despite the increased ability to identify genes and markers, in certain situations, sex determination is the only current method of identifying embryos or fetuses potentially affected with sex-linked disorders.

Inevitably, identification of sex occurs whenever karyotyping is performed. When medical indications for genetic karyotyping do not require information about sex chromosomes, the prospective parent(s) may elect not to be told the sex of the fetus.

Other reasons sex selection is requested are personal, social, or cultural in nature. For example, the prospective parent(s) may prefer that an only or first-born child be of a certain sex or may desire a balance of sexes in the completed family.

Methods

A variety of techniques are available for sex identification and selection. These include techniques used before fertilization, after fertilization but before embryo transfer, and, most frequently, after implantation.

Prefertilization

Techniques for sex selection before fertilization include timing sexual intercourse and using various methods for separating X-bearing and Y-bearing sperm. No current technique for prefertilization sex selection has been shown to be reliable. Recent attention, however, has focused on flow cytometry separation of X-bearing and Y-bearing spermatozoa as a method of enriching sperm populations for insemination. This technique allows heavier X-bearing sperm to be separated; therefore, selection of females alone may be achieved with increased probability. More research is needed to determine whether any of these techniques can be endorsed in terms of reliability or safety.

Postfertilization and Pretransfer

Assisted reproductive technologies, such as IVF, make possible biopsy of one or more cells from a developing embryo at the cleavage or blastocyst stage. Fluorescence in situ hybridization can be used for analysis of chromosomes and sex selection. Embryos of the undesired sex can be discarded or frozen.

Postimplantation

After implantation of a fertilized egg, karyotyping of fetal cells will provide information about fetal sex. This presents patients with the option of terminating pregnancies for the purpose of sex selection.

Ethical Positions of Other Organizations

Many organizations have issued statements concerning the ethics of health care provider participation in sex selection. The ethics committee of the American Society for Reproductive Medicine maintains that the use of preconception sex selection by preimplantation genetic diagnosis for nonmedical reasons is ethically problematic and "should be discouraged." However, it issued a statement in 2001 that if prefertilization techniques, particularly flow cytometry for sperm sorting, were demonstrated to be safe and efficacious, these techniques would be ethically permissible for family balancing. Because a preimplantation genetic diagnosis is physically more burdensome and necessarily involves the destruction and discarding of embryos, it was not considered similarly permissible for family balancing.

The Programme of Action adopted by the United Nations International Conference on Population and Development opposed the use of sex selection techniques for any nonmedical reason. The United Nations urges governments of all nations "to take necessary measures to prevent . . . prenatal sex selection."

The International Federation of Gynecology and Obstetrics rejects sex selection when it is used as a tool for sex discrimination. It supports preconception sex selection when it is used to avoid sex-linked genetic disorders.

The United Kingdom's Human Fertilisation and Embryology Authority Code of Practice on preimplantation genetic diagnosis states that "centres may not use any information derived from tests on an embryo, or any material removed from it or from the gametes that produced it, to select embryos of a particular sex for nonmedical reasons."

Discussion

Medical Testing Not Expressly for the Purpose of Sex Selection

Health care providers may participate unknowingly in sex selection when information about the sex of a fetus results from a medical procedure performed for some other purpose. For example, when a procedure is done to rule out medical disorders in the fetus, the sex of a fetus may become known and may be used for sex selection without the health care provider's knowledge.

The American College of Obstetricians and Gynecologists' Committee on Ethics maintains that when a medical procedure is done for a purpose other than obtaining information about the sex of a fetus but will reveal the fetus's sex, this information should not be withheld from the pregnant woman who requests it. This is because this information legally and ethically belongs to the patient. As a consequence, it might be difficult for health care providers to avoid the possibility of unwittingly participating in sex selection. To minimize the possibility that they will unknowingly participate in sex selection, physicians should foster open communication with patients aimed at clarifying patients' goals. Although health care providers may not ethically withhold medical information from patients who request it, they are not obligated to perform an abortion, or other medical procedure, to select fetal sex.

Medical Testing Expressly for the Purpose of Sex Selection

With regard to medical procedures performed for the express purpose of selecting the sex of a fetus, the following four potential ethical positions are outlined to facilitate discussion:

Position 1: Never participate in sex selection. Health care providers may never choose to perform medical procedures with the intended purpose of sex selection.

Position 2: Participate in sex selection when medically indicated. Health care providers may choose to perform medical procedures with the intended purpose of preventing sex-linked genetic disorders.

Position 3: Participate in sex selection for medical indications and for the purpose of family balancing. Health care providers may choose to perform medical procedures for sex selection when the patient has at least one child and desires a child of the other sex.

Position 4: Participate in sex selection whenever requested. Health care providers may choose to perform medical procedures for the purpose of sex selection whenever the patient requests such procedures.

The committee shares the concern expressed by the United Nations and the International Federation of Gynecology and Obstetrics that sex selection can be motivated by and reinforce the devaluation of women. The committee supports the ethical principle of equality between the sexes.

The committee rejects, as too restrictive, the position that sex selection techniques are always unethical (position 1). The committee supports, as ethically permissible, the practice of sex selection to prevent serious sex-linked genetic disorders (position 2). However, the increasing availability of testing for specific gene mutations is likely to make selection based on sex alone unnecessary in many of these cases. For example, it supports offering patients using assisted reproductive techniques the option of pre-implantation genetic diagnosis for identification of male sex chromosomes if patients are at risk for transmitting Duchenne's muscular dystrophy. This position is consistent with the stance of equality between the sexes because it does not imply that the sex of a child itself makes that child more or less valuable.

Some argue that sex selection techniques can be ethically justified when used to achieve a "balance" in a family in which all current children are the same sex and a child of the opposite sex is desired (position 3). To achieve this goal, couples may request 1) sperm sorting by flow cytometry to enhance the probability of achieving a pregnancy of a particular sex, although these techniques are considered experimental; 2) transferring only embryos of one sex in assisted reproduction after embryo biopsy and preimplantation genetic diagnosis; 3) reducing, on the basis of sex, the number of fetuses in a multifetal pregnancy; or 4) aborting fetuses that are not of the desired sex. In these situations, individual parents may consistently judge sex selection to be an important personal or family goal and, at the same time, reject the idea that children of one sex are inherently more valuable than children of another sex.

Although this stance is, in principle, consistent with the principle of equality between the sexes, it nonetheless raises ethical concerns. First, it often is impossible to ascertain patients' true motives for requesting sex selection procedures. For example, patients who want to abort female fetuses because they value male offspring more than female offspring would be unlikely to espouse such

beliefs openly if they thought this would lead physicians to deny their requests. Second, even when sex selection is requested for nonsexist reasons, the very idea of preferring a child of a particular sex may be interpreted as condoning sexist values and, hence, create a climate in which sex discrimination can more easily flourish. Even preconception techniques of sex selection may encourage such a climate. The use of flow cytometry is experimental, and preliminary reports indicate that achievement of a female fetus is not guaranteed. Misconception about the accuracy of this evolving technology coupled with a strong preference for a child of a particular sex may lead couples to terminate a pregnancy of the "undesired" sex.

The committee concludes that use of sex selection techniques for family balancing violates the norm of equality between the sexes; moreover, this ethical objection arises regardless of the timing of selection (i.e., preconception or postconception) or the stage of development of the embryo or fetus.

The committee rejects the position that sex selection should be performed on demand (position 4) because this position may reflect and encourage sex discrimination. In most societies where sex selection is widely practiced, families prefer male offspring. Although this preference sometimes has an economic rationale, such as the financial support or physical labor male offspring traditionally provide or the financial liability associated with female offspring, it also reflects the belief that males are inherently more valuable than females. Where systematic preferences for a particular sex dominate, there is a need to address underlying inequalities between the sexes.

Summary

The committee has sought to assist physicians and other health care providers facing requests from patients for sex selection by calling attention to relevant ethical considerations, affirming the value of equality between the sexes, and emphasizing that individual health care providers are never ethically required to participate in sex selection. The committee accepts, as ethically permissible, the practice of sex selection to prevent sex-linked genetic disorders. The committee opposes meeting other requests for sex selection, such as the belief that offspring of a certain sex are inherently more valuable. The committee opposes meeting requests for sex selection for personal and family reasons, including family balancing, because of the concern that such requests may ultimately support sexist practices.

Medical techniques intended for other purposes have the potential for being used by patients for sex selection without the health care provider's knowledge or consent. Because a patient is entitled to obtain personal medical information, including information about the sex of her fetus, it will sometimes be impossible for health care professionals to avoid unwitting participation in sex selection.

AMERICAN COLLEGE OF OBSTETRICIANS AND GYNECOLOGISTS is a nonprofit organization of women's health care physicians advocating the highest standards of practice, continuing member education, and public awareness of women's health care issues.

EXPLORING THE ISSUE

Should Parents Be Allowed to Choose the Sex of Their Children?

Critical Thinking and Reflection

1. What assumptions about sex and gender underlie the desire to have boy or girl children?
2. Is fetal sex selection ever ethical? Does the method used to make the selection affect your answer to this question?
3. Is using sex-selection as a "small family planning tool" an acceptable use of sex-selection technologies?
4. Are sex differences located in biology and/or culture?
5. Can children's gender roles be redefined?

Is There Common Ground?

A primary focus of critics' concern about sex-selection technologies (and cultural biases toward males) is their impact on population sex ratios. A skewed sex ratio, they fear, will cause dire consequences for a society, particularly for heterosexual mating (although it is ironic that the same class of reproductive technological advances not only facilitates sex selection but also makes reproduction less reliant on conventional heterosexual mating). But what about social concerns about sex selection? How will the increasing frequency of the use of sex-selection technologies impact families? How will it affect gender assumptions and sex discrimination? Is the acceptability of sex selection conditional? If Americans were not as biased toward having just boys or just girls, and therefore the population sex ratio would not be threatened, would sex selection be acceptable to control the birth order of the sexes, to ensure a mixture of boys and girls, or to have an only child of a certain desired sex? Sex selection technology might reduce overpopulation by helping families who already have a child of one sex "balance" their family with a second child of the other sex, rather than continue to have children "naturally" until they get the sex they want. Is using sex-selection as a "small family planning tool" an acceptable use of sex-selection technologies? Many feel that using sex selection to balance a family is not sexist. But others argue that it is sexist because it promotes gender stereotyping, which undermines equality between the sexes. Some feminists argue that sex selection for any reason, even family balancing, perpetuates gender roles and thus the devalua-

tion of women. Some people in the disabilities rights movement have joined with this perspective, suggesting that if it is permissible to select against female embryos (is sex per se a genetic "abnormality"?), then so is it permissible to select against embryos with genetic abnormalities of all types; and who is to define what is "abnormal"—height, IQ? Then the door is open to increasing discrimination against people with disabilities. Should abortions solely for the purpose of sex selection be allowed? This is a profound dilemma for many pro-choice feminists for whom a woman's right to choose an abortion for any reason but are opposed to gross sex discrimination in the form of sex-selective abortions (usually of female fetuses). It is interesting to note that when parents choose to abort based on fetal sex in an effort to "balance" their family, sex selection is regarded as more acceptable than when only female fetuses are aborted because of a preference for males.

Additional Resources

K. M. Boyd, Medical Ethics: Principles, Persons, and Perspectives: From Controversy to Conversation, *Journal of Medical Ethics, 31* (2005).

J. Hughes, "Sex Selection and Women's Reproductive Rights," Institute for Ethics and Emerging Technologies. Retrieved May 10, 2007, from http://ieet.org/index.php/ieet/more/hughes20070510/

The Future of Children. http://www.futureofchildren.org/

Susan M. Wolf, *Feminism and Bioethics: Beyond Reproduction* (New York: Oxford University Press, 1996).

Internet References . . .

Center for Young Women's Health

http://www.youngwomenshealth.org/
healthy_relat.html

Educational Communications Board

http://www.ecb.org/guides/dating.htm

Enough Is Enough

http://www.protectkids.com/effects/

**Gender and Communication Section of the
International Association for Media and
Communication Research**

http://iamcr.org/s-wg/cctmc/gco

Men Against Violence

http://www.menagainstviolence.org/

**National Online Resource Center on
Violence Against Women**

http://www.vawnet.org/

Same-Sex Dating Violence

http://brown.edu/Student_Services/Health_Services/
Health_Education/sexual_assault_&_dating_
violence/dating_violence_in_LGBTQ_communities
.php

Unit 4

UNIT

Race and Intergroup Relations

*W*hile Unit 3 focused on gender and sexism, this unit takes a parallel approach with a focus on racism. However, this unit also addresses intergroup relations from a more global, abstract perspective as well. Our world has a lasting history of conflict, war, and genocide resulting from negative intergroup relations. Perhaps one of social psychology's most noble—and more challenging—goals is to understand the origins and outcomes of group-based prejudice.

Selected, Edited, and with Issue Framing Material by:
Wind Goodfriend, *Buena Vista University*

ISSUE

Is Racism a Permanent Feature of American Society?

YES: Derrick Bell, from *Faces at the Bottom of the Well: The Permanence of Racism*, Basic Books (1993)

NO: Russell Niele, from "'Postracialism': Do We Want It?" *Princeton Alumni Weekly* (2010)

Learning Outcomes

After reading this issue, you will be able to:

- Develop a sophisticated understanding of the influence of racism in the development of American society.
- Develop a conceptual distinction between discrimination and racism.
- Comprehend different forms of racism, including individual and institutional racism.
- Understand the reification of racism.
- Explain Niele's idea of a post-racist society.
- Understand why Niele promotes meritocracy as a goal.

ISSUE SUMMARY

YES: Derrick Bell, a prominent African American scholar and authority on civil rights and constitutional law, argues that the prospects for achieving racial equality in the United States are "illusory" for blacks.

NO: Russell Niele, a lecturer in politics at Princeton, works for the Executive Precept Program sponsored by Princeton's James Madison Program. He has written on affirmative action and the origins of an urban black underclass. Niele argues that American society is moving toward a meritocracy, which is post-racist (not post-racial). For him, race, ethnicity, and religious identity are less determinant than they were in earlier American history.

The persistence of ideological and institutional racism within the United States has given rise to a debate over the prospects for ridding American society of this glaring contradiction. On one side of this debate are those who believe that a proper examination of the American experience and the treatment of African Americans and other peoples of color throughout history lead to the conclusion that racism is unlikely to be eroded in this country and will continue to challenge the American creed. The other side comprises those who advance the more optimistic view concerning race relations within the United States.

Members of this camp claim that the destructive impact of racism is declining in this country, and that any lagging progress of African Americans is due to factors other than racial discrimination.

Racist ideology has been employed throughout the nation's history in attempts to justify institutional policies and practices such as slavery and segregation. Despite the substantial efforts of supporters of a racially egalitarian society, the reification of racism is a continuing reality of this nation.

Derrick Bell is a proponent of the thesis that racism is a permanent feature of American society. His classic proposition is supported by an analysis of some of the most important aspects of African Americans' historical development. Bell reminds us that despite the fact of significant progress for some blacks of the United States, the legacy of slavery has left a significant portion of the race "with life-long poverty and soul-devastating despair. . . ."

Bell believes that race consciousness is so embedded in whites that it is virtually impossible to rise above it. He argues that "few whites are able to identify with blacks as a group" and tend to view them through "comforting racial stereotypes." Bell cites a number of examples of the destructive impact of racial bonding among whites upon blacks' efforts to progress within society. He points out that even poor whites have tended to support institutions such as slavery and segregation rather than coalescing with blacks to fight against common class-based social disadvantages such as unemployment and poverty. Given this record of race relations, it is impossible for Bell to accept the claim that racism has been largely overcome in the United States. To the contrary, he feels strongly that a critical and proper examination of the history of black–white relations supports the conclusion that racism is a permanent feature of American society.

In the YES selection, Bell argues that "Black people will never gain full equality in this country." For him the legacy of institutional discrimination that was reflected in slavery continues through the exclusionary policies of racial segregation that has left blacks "at the bottom of the well." Additionally, Bell views certain roles that blacks play in the society, such as the scapegoat, as contributing to the permanence of racism. Who will play these roles? He also views the color-coded perceptions and behaviors that dominate social interaction between the "races" as so culturally imbedded as to be virtually impossible to overcome.

In the NO selection, Russell Niele does not agree with Bell that racism is a permanent strain of the fabric of American society. Niele believes that America is moving toward a meritocracy based on talent and hard work, which neutralizes racism. Thus, he opposes Bell's position that racism is a permanent feature of American society. Niele views American society as post-racist. Traditional forms of identity, in his view, are less determinant of opportunity for social advancement today than they were in earlier American history. He cites progress within the institutions of society that have been achieved by blacks and other minorities as strong evidence of a post-racist America.

The reader would benefit from expanding his or her perspective for dealing with the issue to include ideas and concepts dealing with social and cultural values. This is a debate in itself. That is, do structural conditions such

as racism, discrimination, and lack of opportunity lead to inequality and poverty? Or, is poverty attributed to individual factors including socialization and value formation? Bell makes a structural argument to explain the permanence of racism. Niele cites Harvard sociologist, William Julius Wilson's thesis of the declining significance of race, which is reflected in more opportunities for formal education, including higher education leading to significant social and economic advantages. Nieie places more emphasis on the individual, hence his argument for meritocracy.

Racism has played a major role in the formation and ongoing development of the American society. Given this existential reality, it is not difficult to understand that some observers and analysts of American race relations, when confronted with the inequality that persists between blacks and whites in society, would blame this phenomenon on racial discrimination. Those who support this argument view racism as a continuing and permanent reality of American society.

In developing their views on this issue, students may consider a 2008 racial controversy started by white radio talk show host Don Imus' on-air comments about the predominantly black Rutgers University women's basketball team is instructive. The host referred to the team as "nappy-headed hoes" and "jigaboos." Is this an example of media perpetuated racism? Does it contribute to the continuity and perhaps permanence of racism in American culture? Moreover, increasingly popular talk radio, which at times promotes public hatred of minority groups, is at the center of the controversy. Students may want to use additional talk radio examples in their discussion of the permanence of racism and the persistence of discrimination.

American presidents who have addressed the state of race relations in the United States have tended to state some variant of the following assessment: we have made significant progress but that we have a long way to go. Even President Obama, the nation's first African American president, acknowledges that substantial racial progress has been made in the United States. His election is a testament to this fact. However, he does not embrace the claim that the United States has become a post-racial society, that is, a society where racial egalitarianism is the organizing principle of race relations. Considering this point, students are reminded that the idea of meritocracy has been more of an ideal than a reality for the African American experience. Prior the civil rights era, the nation was challenged to apply the meritocratic ideal. Americans continue to struggle to achieve the vision of an egalitarian society.

YES

Derrick Bell

Faces at the Bottom of the Well: The Permanence of Racism

Divining Our Racial Themes

In these bloody days and frightful nights when an urban warrior can find no face more despicable than his own, no ammunition more deadly than self-hate and no target more deserving of his true aim than his brother, we must wonder how we came so late and lonely to this place.

—Maya Angelou

When I was growing up in the years before the Second World War, our slave heritage was more a symbol of shame than a source of pride. It burdened black people with an indelible mark of difference as we struggled to be like whites. In those far-off days, survival and progress seemed to require moving beyond, even rejecting slavery. Childhood friends in a West Indian family who lived a few doors away often boasted—erroneously as I later learned—that their people had never been slaves. My own more accurate—but hardly more praiseworthy—response was that my forebears included many free Negroes, some of whom had Choctaw and Blackfoot Indian blood.

In those days, self-delusion was both easy and comforting. Slavery was barely mentioned in the schools and seldom discussed by the descendants of its survivors, particularly those who had somehow moved themselves to the North. Emigration, whether from the Caribbean islands or from the Deep South states, provided a geographical distance that encouraged and enhanced individual denial of our collective, slave past. We sang spirituals but detached the songs from their slave origins. As I look back, I see this reaction as no less sad, for being very understandable. We were a subordinate and mostly shunned portion of a society that managed to lay the onus of slavery neatly on those who were slaves while simultaneously exonerating those who were slaveholders. All things considered, it seemed a history best left alone.

Then, after the Second World War and particularly in the 1960s, slavery became—for a few academics and some militant Negroes—a subject of fascination and a sure means of evoking racial rage as a prelude to righteously repeated demands for "Freedom Now!" In response to a resurrection of interest in our past, new books on slavery were written, long out-of-print volumes republished. The new awareness reached its highest point in 1977 with the television version of Alex Haley's biographical novel, *Roots*. The highly successful miniseries informed millions of Americans—black as well as white—that slavery in fact existed and that it was awful. Not, of course, as awful as it would have been save for the good white folks the television writers had created to ease the slaves' anguish, and the evil ones on whose shoulders they placed all the guilt. Through the magic of literary license, white viewers could feel revulsion for slavery without necessarily recognizing American slavery as a burden on the nation's history, certainly not a burden requiring reparations in the present.

Even so, under pressure of civil rights protests, many white Americans were ready to accede to, if not applaud, Supreme Court rulings that the Constitution should no longer recognize and validate laws that kept in place the odious badges of slavery.

As a result, two centuries after the Constitution's adoption, we did live in a far more enlightened world. Slavery was no more. Judicial precedent and a plethora of civil rights statutes formally prohibited racial discrimination. Compliance was far from perfect, but the slavery provisions in the Constitution[1] did seem lamentable artifacts of a less enlightened era.

But the fact of slavery refuses to fade, along with the deeply embedded personal attitudes and public policy assumptions that supported it for so long. Indeed, the racism that made slavery feasible is far from dead in the last decade of twentieth-century America; and the civil rights gains, so hard won, are being steadily eroded. Despite undeniable progress for many, no African Americans are insulated from incidents of racial discrimination. Our careers, even our lives, are threatened because of our color. Even the most successful of us are haunted by the plight of our less fortunate brethren who struggle for existence in what some social scientists call the "underclass." Burdened with life-long poverty and soul-devastating despair, they live beyond the pale of the American dream. What we designate as "racial progress" is not a solution to that problem. It is a regeneration of the problem in a particularly perverse form.

According to data compiled in 1990 for basic measures of poverty, unemployment, and income, the slow advances African Americans made during the 1960s and 1970s have definitely been reversed. The unemployment rate for blacks is 2.5 times the rate for whites. Black per-capita income is not even two thirds of the income for whites; and blacks, most of whom own little wealth or business property, are three times more likely to have income below the poverty level than whites. If trends of the last two decades are allowed to continue, readers can safely—and sadly—assume that the current figures are worse than those cited here.[2]

Statistics cannot, however, begin to express the havoc caused by joblessness and poverty: broken homes, anarchy in communities, futility in the public schools. All are the bitter harvest of race-determined unemployment in a society where work provides sustenance, status, and the all-important sense of self-worth. What we now call the "inner city" is, in fact, the American equivalent of the South African homelands. Poverty is less the source than the status of men and women who, despised because of their race, seek refuge in self-rejection. Drug-related crime, teenaged parenthood, and disrupted and disrupting family life all are manifestations of a despair that feeds on self. That despair is bred anew each day by the images on ever-playing television sets, images confirming that theirs is the disgraceful form of living, not the only way people live.

Few whites are able to identify with blacks as a group—the essential prerequisite for feeling empathy with, rather than aversion from, blacks' self-inflicted suffering, as expressed by the poet Maya Angelou in this introduction's epigraph. Unable or unwilling to perceive that "there but for the grace of God, go I," few whites are ready to actively promote civil rights for blacks. Because of an irrational but easily roused fear that any social reform will unjustly benefit blacks, whites fail to support the programs this country desperately needs to address the ever-widening gap between the rich and the poor, both black and white.

Lulled by comforting racial stereotypes, fearful that blacks will unfairly get ahead of them, all too many whites respond to even the most dire reports of race-based disadvantage with either a sympathetic headshake or victim-blaming rationalizations. Both responses lead easily to the conclusion that contemporary complaints of racial discrimination are simply excuses put forward by people who are unable or unwilling to compete on an equal basis in a competitive society.

For white people who both deny racism and see a heavy dose of the Horatio Alger myth as the answer to blacks' problems, how sweet it must be when a black person stands in a public place and condemns as slothful and unambitious those blacks who are not making it. Whites eagerly embrace black conservatives' homilies to self-help, however grossly unrealistic such messages are in an economy where millions, white as well as black, are unemployed and, more important, in one where racial discrimination in the workplace is as vicious (if less obvious) than it was when employers posted signs "no negras need apply."

Whatever the relief from responsibility such thinking provides those who embrace it, more than a decade of civil rights setbacks in the White House, in the courts, and in the critical realm of media-nurtured public opinion has forced retrenchment in the tattered civil rights ranks. We must reassess our cause and our approach to it, but repetition of time-worn slogans simply will not do. As a popular colloquialism puts it, it is time to "get real" about race and the persistence of racism in America.

To make such an assessment—to plan for the future by reviewing the experiences of the past—we must ask whether the formidable hurdles we now face in the elusive quest for racial equality are simply a challenge to our commitment, whether they are the latest variation of the old hymn "One More River to Cross." Or, as we once again gear up to meet the challenges posed by these unexpected new setbacks, are we ignoring a current message with implications for the future which history has already taught us about the past?

Such assessment is hard to make. On the one hand, contemporary color barriers are certainly less visible as a result of our successful effort to strip the law's endorsement from the hated Jim Crow signs. Today one can travel for thousands of miles across this country and never see a public facility designated as "Colored" or "White." Indeed, the very absence of visible signs of discrimination creates an atmosphere of racial neutrality and encourages whites to believe that racism is a thing of the past. On the other hand, the general use of so-called neutral standards to continue exclusionary practices reduces the effectiveness of traditional civil rights laws, while rendering discriminatory actions more oppressive than ever. Racial bias in the pre-*Brown* era was stark, open, unalloyed with hypocrisy and blank-faced lies.

We blacks, when rejected, knew who our enemies were. They were not us! Today, because bias is masked in unofficial practices and "neutral" standards, we must wrestle with the question whether race or some individual failing has cost us the job, denied us the promotion, or prompted our being rejected as tenants for an apartment. Either conclusion breeds frustration and alienation—and a rage we dare not show to others or admit to ourselves.

Modern discrimination is, moreover, not practiced indiscriminately. Whites, ready and willing to applaud, even idolize black athletes and entertainers, refuse to hire, or balk at, working with blacks. Whites who number individual blacks among their closest friends approve, or do not oppose, practices that bar selling or renting homes or apartments in their neighborhoods to blacks they don't know. Employers, not wanting "too many of them," are willing to hire one or two black people, but will reject those who apply later. Most hotels and restaurants who offer black patrons courteous—even deferential—treatment, uniformly reject black job applicants, except perhaps for the most menial jobs. When did you last see a black waiter in a really good restaurant?

Racial schizophrenia is not limited to hotels and restaurants. As a result, neither professional status nor relatively high income protects even accomplished blacks from capricious acts of discrimination that may reflect either individual "preference" or an institution's bias. The motivations for bias vary; the disadvantage to black victims is the same.

Careful examination reveals a pattern to these seemingly arbitrary racial actions. When whites perceive that it will be profitable or at least cost-free to serve, hire, admit, or otherwise deal with blacks on a nondiscriminatory basis, they do so. When they fear—accurately or not—that there may be a loss, inconvenience, or upset to themselves or other whites, discriminatory conduct usually follows. Selections and rejections reflect preference as much as prejudice. A preference for whites makes it harder to prove the discrimination outlawed by civil rights laws. This difficulty, when combined with lackluster enforcement, explains why discrimination in employment and in the housing market continues to prevail more than two decades after enactment of the Equal Employment Opportunity Act of 1965 and the Fair Housing Act of 1968.

Racial policy is the culmination of thousands of these individual practices. Black people, then, are caught in a double bind. We are, as I have said, disadvantaged unless whites perceive that nondiscriminatory treatment for us will be a benefit for them. In addition, even when nonracist practices might bring a benefit, whites may rely

on discrimination against blacks as a unifying factor and a safety valve for frustrations during economic hard times.

Almost always, the injustices that dramatically diminish the rights of blacks are linked to the serious economic disadvantage suffered by many whites who lack money and power. Whites, rather than acknowledge the similarity of their disadvantage, particularly when compared with that of better-off whites, are easily detoured into protecting their sense of entitlement vis-à-vis blacks for all things of value. Evidently, this racial preference expectation is hypnotic. It is this compulsive fascination that seems to prevent most whites from even seeing—much less resenting—the far more sizable gap between their status and those who occupy the lofty levels at the top of our society.

Race consciousness of this character, as Professor Kimberlè Crenshaw suggested in 1988 in a pathbreaking *Harvard Law Review* article, makes it difficult for whites "to imagine the world differently. It also creates the desire for identification with privileged elites. By focusing on a distinct, subordinate 'other,' whites include themselves in the dominant circle—an arena in which most hold no real power, but only their privileged racial identity."

The critically important stabilizing role that blacks play in this society constitutes a major barrier in the way of achieving racial equality. Throughout history, politicians have used blacks as scapegoats for failed economic or political policies. Before the Civil War, rich slave owners persuaded the white working class to stand with them against the danger of slave revolts—even though the existence of slavery condemned white workers to a life of economic privation. After the Civil War, poor whites fought social reforms and settled for segregation rather than see formerly enslaved blacks get ahead. Most labor unions preferred to allow plant owners to break strikes with black scab labor than allow blacks to join their ranks. The "them against us" racial ploy—always a potent force in economic bad times—is working again: today whites, as disadvantaged by high-status entrance requirements as blacks, fight to end affirmative action policies that, by eliminating class-based entrance requirements and requiring widespread advertising of jobs, have likely helped far more whites than blacks. And in the 1990s, as through much of the 1980s, millions of Americans—white as well as black—face steadily worsening conditions: unemployment, inaccessible health care, inadequate housing, mediocre education, and pollution of the environment. The gap in national incomes is approaching a crisis as those in the top fifth now earn more than their counterparts in the bottom four fifths combined. The conservative guru Kevin

Phillips used a different but no less disturbing comparison: the top two million income earners in this country earn more than the next one hundred million.

Shocking. And yet conservative white politicians are able to gain and hold even the highest office despite their failure to address seriously any of these issues. They rely instead on the time-tested formula of getting needy whites to identify on the basis of their shared skin color, and suggest with little or no subtlety that white people must stand together against the Willie Hortons, or against racial quotas, or against affirmative action. The code words differ. The message is the same. Whites are rallied on the basis of racial pride and patriotism to accept their often lowly lot in life, and encouraged to vent their frustration by opposing any serious advancement by blacks. Crucial to this situation is the unstated understanding by the mass of whites that they will accept large disparities in economic opportunity in respect to other whites as long as they have a priority over blacks and other people of color for access to the few opportunities available.

This "racial bonding" by whites means that black rights and interests are always vulnerable to diminishment if not to outright destruction. The willingness of whites over time to respond to this racial rallying cry explains—far more than does the failure of liberal democratic practices (re black rights) to coincide with liberal democratic theory—blacks' continuing subordinate status. This is, of course, contrary to the philosophy of Gunnar Myrdal's massive midcentury study *The American Dilemma*. Myrdal and two generations of civil rights advocates accepted the idea of racism as merely an odious holdover from slavery, "a terrible and inexplicable anomaly stuck in the middle of our liberal democratic ethos." No one doubted that the standard American policy making was adequate to the task of abolishing racism. White America, it was assumed, *wanted* to abolish racism.[3]

Forty years later, in *The New American Dilemma*, Professor Jennifer Hochschild examined what she called Myrdal's "anomaly thesis," and concluded that it simply cannot explain the persistence of racial discrimination. Rather, the continued viability of racism demonstrates "that racism is not simply an excrescence on a fundamentally healthy liberal democratic body, but is part of what shapes and energizes the body." Under this view, "liberal democracy and racism in the United States are historically, even inherently, reinforcing; American society as we know it exists only because of its foundation in racially based slavery, and it thrives only because racial discrimination continues. The apparent anomaly is an actual symbiosis."

The permanence of this "symbiosis" ensures that civil rights gains will be temporary and setbacks inevitable.

Consider: In this last decade of the twentieth century, color determines the social and economic status of all African Americans, both those who have been highly successful and their poverty-bound brethren whose lives are grounded in misery and despair. We rise and fall less as a result of our efforts than in response to the needs of a white society that condemns all blacks to quasi citizenship as surely as it segregated our parents and enslaved their forebears. The fact is that, despite what we designate as progress wrought through struggle over many generations, we remain what we were in the beginning: a dark and foreign presence, always the designated "other." Tolerated in good times, despised when things go wrong, as a people we are scapegoated and sacrificed as distraction or catalyst for compromise to facilitate resolution of political differences or relieve economic adversity.

We are now, as were our forebears when they were brought to the New World, objects of barter for those who, while profiting from our existence, deny our humanity. It is in the light of this fact that we must consider the haunting questions about slavery and exploitation contained in Professor Linda Myers's *Understanding an Afrocentric World View: Introduction to an Optimal Psychology*, questions that serve as their own answers.

We simply cannot prepare realistically for our future without assessing honestly our past. It seems cold, accusatory, but we must try to fathom with her "the mentality of a people that could continue for over 300 years to kidnap an estimated 50 million youth and young adults from Africa, transport them across the Atlantic with about half dying unable to withstand the inhumanity of the passage, and enslave them as animals."

As Professor Myers reminds us, blacks were not the only, and certainly not America's most, persecuted people. Appropriately, she asks about the mindset of European Americans to native Americans. After all, those in possession of the land were basically friendly to the newcomers. And yet the European Americans proceeded to annihilate almost the entire race, ultimately forcing the survivors onto reservations after stealing their land. Far from acknowledging and atoning for these atrocities, American history portrays whites as the heroes, the Indian victims as savage villains. "What," she wonders, "can be understood about the world view of a people who claim to be building a democracy with freedom and justice for all, and at the same time own slaves and deny others basic human rights?"

Of course, Americans did not invent slavery. The practice has existed throughout recorded history, and Professor Orlando Patterson, a respected scholar, argues impressively that American slavery was no worse than that practiced in other parts of the world.[4] But it is not comparative slavery policies that concern me. Slavery is, as an example of what white America has done, a constant reminder of what white America might do.

We must see this country's history of slavery, not as an insuperable racial barrier to blacks, but as a legacy of enlightenment from our enslaved forebears reminding us that if they survived the ultimate form of racism, we and those whites who stand with us can at least view racial oppression in its many contemporary forms without underestimating its critical importance and likely permanent status in this country.

To initiate the reconsideration, I want to set forth this proposition, which will be easier to reject than refute: *Black people will never gain full equality in this country. Even those herculean efforts we hail as successful will produce no more than temporary "peaks of progress," short-lived victories that slide into irrelevance as racial patterns adapt in ways that maintain white dominance. This is a hard-to-accept fact that all history verifies. We must acknowledge it, not as a sign of submission, but as an act of ultimate defiance.*

We identify with and hail as hero the man or woman willing to face even death without flinching. Why? Because, while no one escapes death, those who conquer their dread of it are freed to live more fully. In similar fashion, African Americans must confront and conquer the otherwise deadening reality of our permanent subordinate status. Only in this way can we prevent ourselves from being dragged down by society's racial hostility. Beyond survival lies the potential to perceive more clearly both a reason and the means for further struggle.

In this book, Geneva Crenshaw, the civil rights lawyer—protagonist of my earlier *And We Are Not Saved: The Elusive Quest for Racial Justice*, returns in a series of stories that offer an allegorical perspective on old dreams, long-held fears, and current conditions. The provocative format of story, a product of experience and imagination, allows me to take a new look at what, for want of a better phrase, I will call "racial themes." Easier to recognize than describe, they are essentials in the baggage of people subordinated by color in a land that boasts of individual freedom and equality. Some of these themes—reliance on law, involvement in protests, belief in freedom symbols—are familiar and generally known. Others—the yearning for a true homeland, the rejection of racial testimony, the temptation to violent retaliation—are real but seldom revealed. Revelation does not much alter the mystique of interracial romance or lessen its feared consequences. Nor does the search ever end for a full understanding of why blacks are and remain this country's designated scapegoats. . . .

The goal of racial equality is, while comforting to many whites, more illusory than real for blacks. For too long, we have worked for substantive reform, then settled for weakly worded and poorly enforced legislation, indeterminate judicial decisions, token government positions, even holidays. I repeat. If we are to seek new goals for our struggles, we must first reassess the worth of the racial assumptions on which, without careful thought, we have presumed too much and relied on too long.

Let's begin.

Notes

1. According to William Wiecek, ten provisions in the Constitution directly or indirectly provided for slavery and protected slave owners.
2. Not all the data are bleak. While the median family income for black families declined in the 1970s and 1980s, the proportion of African American families with incomes of $35,000 to $50,000 increased from 23.3 to 27.5 percent. The proportion with incomes above $50,000 increased by 38 percent, from 10.0 to 13.8 percent. The overall median income for blacks declined though: while the top quarter made progress, the bottom half was sliding backward, and the proportion of blacks receiving very low income (less than $5,000) actually increased.
3. According to Myrdal, the "Negro problem in America represents a moral lag in the development of the nation and a study of it must record nearly everything which is bad and wrong in America. . . . However, . . . not since Reconstruction has there been more reason to anticipate fundamental changes in American race relations, changes which will involve a development toward the American ideals."
4. He suggests: "The dishonor of slavery . . . came in the primal act of submission. It was the most immediate human expression of the inability to defend oneself or to secure one's livelihood. . . . The dishonor the slave was compelled to experience sprang instead from that raw, human sense of debasement inherent in having no being except as an expression of another's being."

DERRICK BELL is a visiting professor of law at New York University School of Law. He is the author of many books including *Faces at the Bottom of the Well: The Permanence of Racism* (Basic Books, 1992) and the classic *Race, Racism and American Law* (Aspen Publishers Inc., 2000).

Russell Niele

 **NO**

"Postracialism": Do We Want It?

I often have asked students in my politics precept classes to perform the following thought experiment. "You're going to die tomorrow and will be reincarnated the next day. God offers you two choices. Either you will be reborn into a white working-class family in a lower-middle-income, white-ethnic community in Brooklyn, or you will be reborn into an upper-middle-class, black professional family, living in an upper-middle-class neighborhood in Forest Hills, Queens. You will not remember your present incarnation and have no reason to maintain any continuity with it. Which rebirth do you choose?"

Some readers may be surprised to learn that 90 to 100 percent of students of all races to whom I have posed this question say they would rather be reborn into the upper-middle-class black professional family living in an affluent neighborhood than into the white working-class family living in more modest circumstances. White skin color may still have its privileges in America, but they seem to these post-civil-rights-era students much less important than class advantages.

The most nuanced and perceptive answer I ever got to the question came from a black female student: "If I knew that I would have the same academic talent that I have now," the student explained, "I would choose the poor white family. Having white skin still has many advantages, and it is easy to get a high-paying job in this country if you are smart in school." But, she continued, if she were an average or below-average student, she'd prefer to be born into the rich black family—because affluence brings many advantages, and it's difficult for mediocre students to find lucrative jobs regardless of their race.

This student didn't know it, but she was reflecting what labor economists and other social scientists have been saying for many years: Since the middle of the last century, America has been experiencing a "declining significance of race"—the title of a book by Harvard sociologist William Julius Wilson—and a corresponding rise in the significance to social and economic advancement of formal education and developed cognitive skills. While these latter factors are related in important ways to family and neighborhood background, they also are tied intimately to individual talent and temperament. America has become a very kind place to the academically talented, hardworking, and ambitious students of all races and ethnicities—that is, the sorts of people who wind up at places like Princeton.

Which brings up the case of Barack Obama. What better example is there of how far talent, ambition, hard work, and a focus on what one wants to achieve in life can take you today in America than Barack Obama's meteoric career as Ivy League student, *Harvard Law Review* editor, community organizer, law school professor, local politician, U.S. senator, best-selling author, and ultimately president of the United States? I have serious problems with many of Obama's stated views. But it is clear that Obama is a man of great talent, oratorical and otherwise, and that his success in so many fields of endeavor and his ability to do so well among white voters in the 2008 election are the culmination of a long-term trend in America toward greater appreciation of merit, regardless of one's ethnicity, gender, or race.

When one considers that 63 percent of respondents in a 1958 Gallup poll said that if their political party "nominated a generally well-qualified man for president and he happened to be a Negro" they would not vote for him, one gets a sense of how far America has advanced along the meritocratic path. While many black voters—and some guilt-ridden whites—no doubt voted for Obama because of his race, his impressive showing among white independents and young people clearly was based on the perception that he was a fresh voice and a gifted speaker with many talents of intellect and temperament that would make for an effective national leader.

The Obama success has provoked the claim that we have entered an era of a "postracial America." At first blush the phrase strikes me as Utopian silliness, since it ignores the inevitable intergroup tensions and hostilities that are inextricably a part of any multiracial, multiethnic, multireligious society. Nevertheless, insofar as "postracial" conveys the idea not of utopian transformation but of the more modest claim that the many racial, ethnic, and religious identity groups to which Americans belong are considerably less important than they once were in determining success in America, the phrase conveys an important truth.

Race, ethnicity, and religious identity clearly are less important determinants of who gets ahead in the United States today than was the case in the long period of WASP ascendancy—hence my students' preference for being born into a well-to-do black family over a poor white one. Barack Obama's election is only the latest development in a long evolutionary process that accelerated after the Second World War, by which members of various minority groups have ascended to positions of power and influence. It is an important milestone—like the election of John Kennedy as the first Catholic president—though it is not the Holy Grail.

To use an older phrase of classical liberalism, it is part of an important and much-welcomed trend in which careers are increasingly "open to the talents." The widespread belief in this principle is one reason so many Americans continue to oppose race- and ethnicity-based preferences in employment and other areas of American life, and why a majority of the members of the U.S. Supreme Court have been eager to invalidate most such policies through the vehicle of the 14th Amendment's equal-protection clause.

But for many there is a sinister undertone to the phrase "postracial." Michael Eric Dyson *93, for instance, has said that while it surely is good that America should seek to become "postracist," it is not good to strive to become "post-racial"—at least if that means people must abandon their cherished racial and ethnic identities to become full Americans. Here I find myself in agreement with my fellow Princetonian (though I have disagreed sharply with Dyson on many other issues concerning race). *E pluribus unum* ("out of many, one") is one of America's foundational ideals, affirming two equally important principles: We must show respect for particularized diversities (the *pluribus)*, while at the same time affirming the importance of participation in a more encompassing civic and political realm (the *unum*) in which those diversities are transcended, without being destroyed.

This means that it is OK to have what older theorists of assimilation called "layered identities," so that Irish-Americans, Italian-Americans, Chinese-Americans, African-Americans, Mormon Americans, Jewish Americans, and all those who cherish their "hyphenated and hybrid attachments" can be no less Americans than WASP Americans or those who have no group identity other than their American nationality. While all individuals and groups in the United States are called upon to affirm certain basic tasks and ideals—like respecting democracy and the rule of law, seeing to it that their children become educated and learn English, respecting the Constitution—the idea of liberty in America generally has encompassed the notion that outside the limited civic and political realm where we share a national identity, people are free to seek happiness and fulfillment in their particularized communities. A "postracial America" for many would mean the destruction of these communal attachments and hybrid identities, the toleration of which, I believe, has contributed to America's relative success in assimilating the diverse peoples of the globe.

The Harvard philosopher Horace Kallen, who wrote in the period between the two world wars, had many wise things to say on these matters. Resisting the extreme Anglo-Saxon assimilationists of his day who enjoined against "hyphenated Americanism" and who reached menacing proportions in the 3-million-strong Ku Klux Klan of the 1920s, Kallen, a Jew, spoke of America as a "multiplicity within unity" of peoples from many diverse ethnic and religious communities. It was within these "organic" communities, Kallen wrote, that we nurture our "preferences of the herd type in which the individual feels freest and most at ease," and it was important for the well-being of everyone, he believed, that citizens not be required to abandon these communal attachments to become fully American.

Around the same time Kallen was defending hyphenated Americanism, the historian Marcus Hansen was fleshing out his law of immigrant succession: What the second generation often tries to forget about its ancestral roots, subsequent generations desperately try to recover and preserve. Hansen and Kallen understood that we all crave a sense of belonging and place, and that America offers the cherished freedom for people to mold and select their own place-defining narratives.

Today, in a "postracist" (but not "post-racial") America, this freedom has become more appealing than ever. Its presence is one reason America remains a magnet for diverse peoples around the world. Together with "careers open to the talents" and our open-market system, it is a freedom we all must seek to preserve. . . .

Russell Niele is a lecturer in politics at Princeton University. He has written numerous articles on social policy including affirmative action and the emergence of the urban black underclass.

EXPLORING THE ISSUE

Is Racism a Permanent Feature of American Society?

Critical Thinking and Reflection

1. What is the historical influence of racism on American society?
2. What is the difference between discrimination and racism?
3. Explain the various forms of racism and employ contemporary examples.
4. What is the reification of racism? Offer some examples.
5. What does Niele mean by a post-racist society?
6. What is a meritocracy? What is Niele's argument in favor of it? Is a true meritocracy possible in the United States?

Is There Common Ground?

The struggle to overcome racism has persisted from the Civil War to the present. Racism has consistently challenged major American values including racial equality and meritocracy. Despite the gains of the civil rights movement and changing attitudes on race, it is clear that racism has not vanished. Will racism ever go away? Both Bell and Niele would agree that there has been significant progress in race relations including a decline in racism. Neither of these authors goes so far as to suggest that we are on the threshold of eliminating racism in America. However, the debate over such a policy goal within society serves to illuminate the salience of "race" and the establishment of distinct color-coded racial categories in influencing the development of social relations within modern societies such as the United States and South Africa. In this regard, students should recognize that racism has developed new and different, more covert forms within society. This is a critical point in one's exploration of the permanence of racism.

Additional Resources

Almaguer, Tomas. 1994. *Racial Fault Lines: The Historical Origins of White Supremacy in California* (University of California Press).

Banfield, Edward. 1970. *The Unheavenly City* (Little, Brown).

Blackmon, Douglas A. 2008. *Slavery by Another Name: The Re-Enslavement of Black Americans from the Civil War to World War II* (Doubleday).

Bonilla-Silva, Eduardo. 2001. *White Supremacy and Racism in the Post Civil Rights Era* (Rienner).

Bonilla-Silva, Eduardo. 2003. *Racism Without Racists: Color-Blind Racism and the Persistence of Racial Inequality in the United States* (Rowman & Littlefield).

Bulmer, Martin and John Solomos, eds. 1999. *Racism* (Oxford Press).

Cox, Oliver Cromwell. 1848. *Caste, Class and Race: A Study in Social Dynamics* (Modern Reader Paperbacks).

Crouch, Stanley. 1997. *The All-American Skin Game, or, The Decoy of Race* (New York, NY: Vintage Books).

Douglas, Herbert. 2005. "Migration and Adaptations of African American Families Within Urban America," in *Minority Voices: Linking Personal Ethnic History and the Sociological Imagination Relations* by John Myers (Allyn & Bacon).

Frazier, E. Franklin. 1939. *The Negro Family in the United States* (University of Chicago Press).

Harrison, Lawrence E. 1992. *Who Prospers? How Cultural Values Shape Economic and Political Success* (Basic Books).

Jaspin, Elliot. 2007. *Buried in the Bitter Waters: The Hidden History of Racial Cleansing in America* (Basic Books, 2007).

Jordan, Winthrop. 1968. *White Over Black*: *American Attitudes Toward the Negro, 1550–1812* (The University of North Carolina Press).

Kelley, Robin. 1997. *Yo' Mama's Disfunktional: Fighting the Culture Wars in Urban America* (Beacon).

Lewis, Oscar. 1966. *La Vida: A Puerto Rican Family in the Culture of Poverty, San Juan and New York* (Random House).

Lipsitz, George. 2006. *The Possessive Investment in Whiteness: How White People Profit from Identity Politics* (Temple University Press).

Lipsitz, George. 2011. *How Racism Takes Place* (Temple University Press).

Loewen, James W. 2006. *Sundown Towns: A Hidden Dimension of American Racism* (Touchstone).

Myrdal, Gunnar. 1944. *An American Dilemma* (Harper).

Pfaelzer, Jean. 2007. *Driven Out: The Forgotten War against Chinese Americans* (Random House).

Rhoden, William. 2006. *Forty Million Dollar Slaves: The Rise, Fall, and Redemption of the Black Athlete* (Crown Publishers).

Royster, Deidre. 2003. *Race and the Invisible Hand: How White Networks Exclude Black Men from Blue-Collar Jobs* (University of California Press).

Sports Illustrated. 1968. "The Black Athlete—A Shameful Story." Documents racism in professional and collegiate sports during the 1950s and 1960s. (29: July, 1–5).

Washington, Harriet, A. 2008a. *Medical Apartheid: The Dark History of Medical Experimentation on Black Americans from Colonial Times to the Present* (Doubleday).

Washington, Harriet, A. 2008b. "Apology Shines Light on Racial Schism in Medicine." *The New York Times* (July).

Wilson, William Julius. 1978. *The Declining Significance of Race: Blacks and Changing American Institutions* (University of Chicago Press).

Wilson, William Julius. 1990. *The Truly Disadvantaged* (University of Chicago Press).

Internet References . . .

Amnesty International

http://www.amnesty.org/

Southern Poverty Law Center (SPLC)

http://www.splcenter.org/

Understanding Prejudice: Forms of Racism

http://www.understandingprejudice.org/apa/english/page10.htm

Working Against Racism (WAR)

http://www.workingagainstracism.org/

Selected, Edited, and with Issue Framing Material by:
Wind Goodfriend, *Buena Vista University*

ISSUE

Is Race Prejudice a Product of Group Position?

YES: Herbert Blumer, from "Race Prejudice as a Sense of Group Position," *The Pacific Sociological Review* (1958)

NO: Gordon W. Allport, from "The Young Child," Basic Books (1979)

Learning Outcomes

After reading this issue, you will be able to:

- Gain a proper understanding of the group position thesis.
- Properly understand how the group position thesis is employed to explain race prejudice.
- Identify and explain the central thesis that Allport advances to explain how prejudice is acquired.
- Understand the relationship between the acquisition of a racial identity and race prejudice.
- Explain the distinction between individual prejudice and institutional prejudice.
- Apply the group position thesis to the examination of critical issues of race relations, including racial stratification, racial conflict, and segregation.
- Understand the psychological and sociological approaches to explain prejudice.

ISSUE SUMMARY

YES: Herbert Blumer, a sociologist, asserts that prejudice exists in a sense of group position rather than as an attitude based on individual feelings. The collective process by which a group comes to define other racial groups is the focus of Blumer's position.

NO: Gordon W. Allport, a psychologist, makes the case that prejudice is the result of a three-stage learning process.

The nature of prejudice is a critical focus of research concerning intergroup relations. Where does prejudice come from? How and under what circumstances do we acquire it? What are its characteristics? Is prejudice an individual personality trait or, is it a product of structural factors such as group position or economic factors? Ill feelings and overt hostility can reflect prejudice, but so can quiet benign beliefs. The many theories that explain prejudice can be categorized into those that attribute prejudice to individual personality, and those that see prejudice resulting from larger structural factors.

Herbert Blumer begins his group position argument in the context of dominant-subordinate group analysis. Members of the dominant group will, in addition to feelings of superiority, "feel a proprietary claim to certain areas of privilege and advantage." Suspicions of subordinate group members exist because of a fear that the minority group "harbors design on the prerogatives of the dominant race." Although Blumer uses psychological concepts such as feelings, superiority, and distinctiveness, his focus is not on the individual. Rather it rests on the process of image formation. Image formation takes place in the public domain including newspapers, film, and other media. "Careless ignorance of the facts" is often part of the image formation. Surely Blumer believes that prejudice is learned. Nevertheless, his analysis transcends mere "learning."

The analysis of the collective process through which one group defines another involves a historical analysis. Group position is formed in a process defined by the dominant group and redefines subordinate groups. Hence, attitudes are formed from the dominant group perspective.

When the position of the dominant group is challenged, race prejudice emerges. According to Blumer, this may occur in different ways. For example, it may be an affront to feelings or an attempt to transgress racial boundaries. Reaction to interracial marriage or the racial integration of a neighborhood may provoke a "defensive reaction" on the part of the dominant group. Generalizations of the minority group often lead to fear. Disturbed feelings are marked by hostility. Thus, Blumer suggests that race prejudice becomes a protective device. Prejudice is associated with the belief that gains for other (racial and ethnic) groups will result in losses for one's own—a zero sum game.

Examining how prejudice is learned, Gordon Allport stresses the first six years of a child's life, especially the role of the parents in transferring ideas as creating an atmosphere in which the child "develops prejudice as his style of life." The psychological factors exhibited during childrearing, including how the child is disciplined, loved, and threatened, translate into fear or hatred that may ultimately be directed at minorities. A rigid home environment in which parents exercise strict control is more likely to lead to prejudice among the children than a less rigid upbringing. Tolerance results from a less strict childrearing style.

Allport explains that there are three stages of learning prejudice. In the first stage, the pregeneralized learning period, the child learns linguistic categories before he/she is ready to apply them. For example, ethnic and racial slurs are not yet applied to specific groups. Nevertheless, the categories are learned. The second stage in learning prejudice, the period of total rejection, occurs when children connect the labels of groups to be rejected with the individuals in minority groups. For example, Allport argues, by the fifth grade, children tend to choose their own racial group. However, as children grow older and mature, they lose the tendency to overgeneralize about minorities. The third stage, differentiation, sets in often during the later years of high school. By then, the "escape clauses" or exceptions to stereotypes are incorporated

into the individual's attitude. So, the limited early learning experiences are replaced by the wider experiences that come with adolescence.

The NO selection by Allport is part of his more comprehensive social psychological account of how prejudice is learned. The emphasis on personality traits formed during early childhood contrasts with Blumer's group position thesis.

Film and other components of popular culture have tended to stereotyped images of African Americans and other minorities throughout much of American history. D. W. Griffith's controversial film, *Birth of a Nation*, illustrates this tendency to stereotype blacks and other minorities. The film, originally *The Clansmen*, presented to the country's dominant white population an image of emancipated blacks with exaggerated physical features and association with negative behavioral patterns. The stereotyped images of black men included an alleged desire for white women, and the threat that they represented in that regard. In the Jim Crow America that evolved after Reconstruction, many whites formed such images of blacks derived from available popular cultural images.

Both Blumer and Allport associate prejudice with attitudes of individuals, whether the cause is psychological or sociological. Beyond individual prejudice is institutional prejudice, which, along with institutional discrimination, cannot be ignored in the study of prejudice. For example, institutional racism was the law of the land before the 1954 *Brown* decision. The "separate but equal" doctrine stemming from the landmark *Plessy* case enabled institutions such as schools to discriminate. Institutional prejudice was a "normal" part of American culture and reflected the negative stereotyping of blacks. One of the consequences of institutional prejudice led to self-segregation. Although the country has moved away from legal segregation, the latent effect of institutional prejudice today leads to self-segregation.

Given the history of the persistence of prejudice and the discrimination that flows from it, it is difficult to envision a society in which the vestiges of prejudice are eliminated. The persistence of prejudice is a continuing challenge to the diverse American society due to the social conflict that it has been generating. So students are challenged to develop strategies through which prejudice can be confronted. Overcoming prejudice is vital to the achievement of a more cohesive and unified America in the future.

Herbert Blumer

Race Prejudice as a Sense of Group Position

In this paper I am proposing an approach to the study of race prejudice different from that which dominates contemporary scholarly thought on this topic. My thesis is that race prejudice exists basically in a sense of group position rather than in a set of feelings which members of one racial group have toward the members of another racial group. This different way of viewing race prejudice shifts study and analysis from a preoccupation with feelings as lodged in individuals to a concern with the relationship of racial groups. It also shifts scholarly treatment away from individual lines of experience and focuses interest on the collective process by which a racial group comes to define and redefine another racial group. Such shift, I believe, will yield a more realistic and penetrating understanding of race prejudice.

There can be little question that the rather vast literature on race prejudice is dominated by the idea that such prejudice exists fundamentally as a feeling or set of feelings lodged in the individual. It is usually depicted as consisting of feelings such as antipathy, hostility, hatred, intolerance, and aggressiveness. Accordingly, the task of scientific inquiry becomes two-fold. On one hand, there is a need to identify the feelings which makeup race prejudice—to see how they fit together and how they are supported by other psychological elements, such as mythical beliefs. On the other hand, there is need of showing how the feeling complex has come into being. Thus, some scholars trace the complex feelings back chiefly to innate dispositions; some trace it to personality composition, such as authoritarian personality; and others regard the feelings of prejudice as being formed through social experience. However different may be the contentions regarding the makeup of racial prejudice and the way in which it may come into existence, these contentions are alike in locating prejudice in the realm of individual feeling. This is clearly true of the work of psychologists, psychiatrists, and social psychologists, and tends to be predominantly the case in the work of sociologists.

Unfortunately, this customary way of viewing race prejudice overlooks and obscures the fact that race prejudice is fundamentally a matter of relationship between racial groups. A little reflective thought should make this very clear. Race prejudice presupposes, necessarily, that racially prejudiced individuals think of themselves as belonging to a given racial group. It means, also, that they assign to other racial groups those against whom they are prejudiced. Thus, logically and actually, a scheme of racial identification is necessary as a framework for racial prejudice. Moreover, such identification involves the formation of an image or a conception of one's own racial group and of another racial group, inevitably in terms of the relationship of such groups. To fail to see that racial prejudice is a matter (a) of the racial identification made of oneself and of others, and (b) of the way in which the identified groups are conceived in relation to each other, is to miss what is logically and actually basic. One should keep clearly in mind that people necessarily come to identify themselves as belonging to a racial group; such identification is not spontaneous or inevitable but a result of experience. Further, one must realize that the kind of picture which a racial group forms of itself and the kind of picture which it may form of others are similarly products of experience. Hence, such pictures are variable, just as the lines of experience which produce them are variable.

The body of feelings which scholars, today, are so inclined to regard as constituting the substance of race prejudice is actually a resultant of the way in which given racial groups conceive of themselves and of others. A basic understanding of race prejudice must be sought in the process by which racial groups form images of themselves and of others. This process, as I hope to show, is fundamentally *a collective process*. It operates chiefly through the public media in which individuals who are accepted as the spokesmen of a racial group characterize publicly another racial group. To characterize another racial group is, by opposition, to define one's own group. This is equivalent to placing the two groups in relation to each other, or

From Blumer, H. (1958). "Race Prejudice as a Sense of Group Position." *The Pacific Sociological Review,* vol. 1, no. 1 (Spring 1958), pp. 3–7. Copyright © 1958 Pacific Sociological Association.

defining their positions *vis-à-vis* each other. It is the *sense of social position* emerging from this collective process of characterization which provides the basis of race prejudice. The following discussion will consider important facets of this matter.

I would like to begin by discussing several of the important feelings that enter into race prejudice. This discussion will reveal how fundamentally racial feelings point to and depend on a positional arrangement of the racial groups. In this discussion I will confine myself to such feelings in the case of a dominant racial group.

There are four basic types of feelings that seem to be always present in race prejudice in the dominant group. They are (1) a feeling of superiority, (2) a feeling that the subordinate race is intrinsically different and alien, (3) a feeling of proprietary claim to certain areas of privilege and advantage, and (4) a fear and suspicion that the subordinate race harbors designs on the prerogatives of the dominant race. A few words about each of these four feelings will suffice.

In race prejudice there is a self-assured feeling on the part of the dominant racial group of being naturally superior or better. This is commonly shown in a disparagement of the qualities of the subordinate racial group. Condemnatory or debasing traits, such as laziness, dishonesty, greediness, unreliability, stupidity, deceit, and immorality, are usually imputed to it. The second feeling, that the subordinate race is an alien and fundamentally different stock, is likewise always present. "They are not of our kind" is a common way in which this is likely to be expressed. It is this feeling that reflects, justifies, and promotes the social exclusion of the subordinate racial group. The combination of these two feelings of superiority and of distinctiveness can easily give rise to feelings of aversion and even antipathy. But in themselves they do not form prejudice. We have to introduce the third and fourth types of feeling.

The third feeling, the sense of proprietary claim, is of crucial importance. It is the feeling on the part of the dominant group of being entitled to either exclusive or prior rights in many important areas of life. The range of such exclusive or prior claims may be wide, covering the ownership of property such as choice lands and sites; the right to certain jobs, occupations, or professions; the claim to certain kinds of industry or lines of business; the claim to certain positions of control and decision-making as in government and law; the right to exclusive membership in given institutions such as schools, churches, and recreational institutions; the claim to certain positions of social prestige and to the display of the symbols and accoutrements of these positions; and the claim to certain areas

of intimacy and privacy. The feeling of such proprietary claims is exceedingly strong in race prejudice. Again, however, this feeling even in combination with the feeling of superiority and the feeling of distinctiveness does not explain race prejudice. These three feelings are present frequently in societies showing no prejudice, as in certain forms of feudalism, in caste relations, in societies of chiefs and commoners, and under many settled relations of conquerors and conquered. Where claims are solidified into a structure which is accepted or respected by all, there seems to be no group prejudice.

The remaining feeling essential to race prejudice is a fear or apprehension that the subordinate racial group is threatening, or will threaten, the position of the dominant group. Thus, acts or suspected acts that are interpreted as an attack on the natural superiority of the dominant group, or an intrusion into their sphere of group exclusiveness, or an encroachment on their area of proprietary claim are crucial in arousing and fashioning race prejudice. These acts mean "getting out of place."

It should be clear that these four basic feelings of race prejudice definitely refer to a positional arrangement of the racial groups. The feeling of superiority places the subordinate people *below;* the feeling of alienation places them *beyond;* the feeling of proprietary claim excludes them from the prerogatives of position; and the fear of encroachment is an emotional recoil from the endangering of group position. As these features suggest, the positional relation of the two racial groups is crucial in race prejudice. The dominant group is not concerned with the subordinate group as such but it is deeply concerned with its position *vis-à-vis* the subordinate group. This is epitomized in the key and universal expression that a given race is all right in "its place." The sense of group position is the very heart of the relation of the dominant to the subordinate group. It supplies the dominant group with its framework of perception, its standard of judgment, its patterns of sensitivity, and its emotional proclivities.

It is important to recognize that this sense of group position transcends the feelings of the individual members of the dominant group, giving such members a common orientation that is not otherwise to be found in separate feelings and views. There is likely to be considerable difference between the ways in which the individual members of the dominant group think and feel about the subordinate group. Some may feel bitter and hostile, with strong antipathies, with an exalted sense of superiority and with a lot of spite; others may have charitable and protective feelings, marked by a sense of piety and tinctured by benevolence; others may be condescending and reflect mild contempt; and others may be disposed to politeness and considerateness with no feelings of truculence. These are only a few of many different patterns of feeling to be found among members of the dominant racial group. What gives a common dimension to them is a sense of the social position of their group. Whether the members be humane or callous, cultured or unlettered, liberal or reactionary, powerful or impotent, arrogant or humble, rich or poor, honorable or dishonorable—all are led, by virtue of sharing the sense of group position, to similar individual positions.

The sense of group position is a general kind of orientation. It is a general feeling without being reducible to specific feelings like hatred, hostility, or antipathy. It is also a general understanding without being composed of any set of specific beliefs. On the social psychological side it cannot be equated to a sense of social status as ordinarily conceived, for it refers not merely to vertical positioning but to many other lines of position independent of the vertical dimension. Sociologically it is not a mere reflection of the objective relations between racial groups. Rather, it stands for "what ought to be" rather than for "what is." It is a sense of where the two racial groups *belong*.

In its own way, the sense of group position is a norm and imperative—indeed a very powerful one. It guides, incites, cows, and coerces. It should be borne in mind that this sense of group position stands for and involves a fundamental kind of group affiliation for the members of the dominant racial group. To the extent they recognize or feel themselves as belonging to that group they will automatically come under the influence of the sense of position held by that group. Thus, even though given individual members may have personal views and feelings different from the sense of group position, they will have to conjure with the sense of group position held by their racial group. If the sense of position is strong, to act contrary to it is to risk a feeling of self-alienation and to face the possibility of ostracism. I am trying to suggest, accordingly, that the locus of race prejudice is not in the area of individual feeling but in the definition of the respective positions of the racial groups.

The source of race prejudice lies in a felt challenge to this sense of group position. The challenge, one must recognize, may come in many different ways. It may be in the form of an affront to feelings of group superiority; it may be in the form of attempts at familiarity or transgressing the boundary line of group exclusiveness; it may be in the form of encroachment at countless points of proprietary claim; it may be a challenge to power and privilege; it may take the form of economic competition. Race prejudice is a defensive reaction to such challenging of the sense of group position. It consists of the disturbed

feelings, usually of marked hostility, that are thereby aroused. As such, race prejudice is a protective device. It functions, however shortsightedly, to preserve the integrity and the position of the dominant group.

It is crucially important to recognize that the sense of group position is not a mere summation of the feelings of position such as might be developed independently by separate individuals as they come to compare themselves with given individuals of the subordinate race. The sense of group position refers to the position of group to group, not to that of individual to individual. Thus, *vis-à-vis* the subordinate racial group the unlettered individual with low status in the dominant racial group has a sense of group position common to that of the elite of his group. By virtue of sharing this sense of position such an individual, despite his low status, feels that members of the subordinate group, however distinguished and accomplished, are somehow inferior, alien, and properly restricted in the area of claims. He forms his conception as a representative of the dominant group; he treats individual members of the subordinate group as representative of that group.

An analysis of how the sense of group position is formed should start with a clear recognition that it is an historical product. It is set originally by conditions of initial contact. Prestige, power, possession of skill, numbers, original self-conceptions, aims, designs, and opportunities are a few of the factors that may fashion the original sense of group position. Subsequent experience in the relation of the two racial groups, especially in the area of claims, opportunities, and advantages, may mould the sense of group position in many diverse ways. Further, the sense of group position may be intensified or weakened, brought to sharp focus or dulled. It may be deeply entrenched and tenaciously resist change for long periods of time. Or it may never take root. It may undergo quick growth and vigorous expansion or it may dwindle away through slow-moving erosion. It may be firm or soft, acute or dull, continuous or intermittent. In short, viewed comparatively, the sense of group position is very variable.

However variable its particular career, the sense of group position is clearly formed by a running process in which the dominant racial group is led to define and redefine the subordinate racial group and the relations between them. There are two important aspects of this process of definition that I wish to single out for consideration.

First, the process of definition occurs obviously through complex interaction and communication between the members of the dominant group. Leaders, prestige bearers, official, group agents, dominant individuals, and ordinary laymen present to one another characterizations of the subordinate group and express their feelings and ideas on the relations. Through talk, tales, stories, gossip, anecdotes, messages, pronouncements, news accounts, orations, sermons, preachments and the like definitions are presented and feelings are expressed. In this usually vast and complex interaction separate views run against one another, influence one another, modify each other, incite one another, and fuse together in new forms. Correspondingly, feelings which are expressed meet, stimulate each other, feed on each other, intensify each other, and emerge in new patterns. Currents of view and currents of feeling come into being; sweeping along to positions of dominance and serving as polar points for the organization of thought and sentiment. If the interaction becomes increasingly circular and reinforcing, devoid of serious inner opposition, such currents grow, fuse, and become strengthened. It is through such a process that a collective image of the subordinate group is formed and a sense of group position is set. The evidence of such a process is glaring when one reviews the history of any racial arrangement marked by prejudice.

Such a complex process of mutual interaction with its different lines and degrees of formation gives the lie to the many schemes which would lodge the cause of race prejudice in the makeup of the individual—whether in the form of innate disposition, constitutional makeup, personality structure, or direct personal experience with members of the other race. The collective image and feelings in race prejudice are forged out of a complicated social process in which the individual is himself shaped and organized. The scheme, so popular today, which would trace race prejudice to a so-called authoritarian personality shows a grievous misunderstanding of the simple essentials of the collective process that leads to a sense of group position.

The second important aspect of the process of group definition is that it is necessarily concerned with *an abstract image* of the subordinate racial group. The subordinate racial group is defined as if it were an entity or whole. This entity or whole—like the Negro race, or the Japanese, or the Jews—is necessarily an abstraction, never coming within the perception of any of the senses. While actual encounters are with individuals, the picture formed of the racial group is necessarily of a vast entity which spreads out far beyond such individuals and transcends experience with such individuals. The implications of the fact that the collective image is of an abstract group are of crucial significance. I would like to note four of these implications.

First, the building of the image of the abstract group takes place in the area of the remote and not of the near. It is not the experience with concrete individuals in daily association that gives rise to the definitions of the extended, abstract group. Such immediate experience is usually regulated and orderly. Even where such immediate experience is disrupted the new definitions which are formed are limited to the individuals involved. The collective image of the abstract group grows up not by generalizing from experiences gained in close, first-hand contacts but through the transcending characterizations that are made of the group as an entity. Thus, one must seek the central stream of definition in those areas where the dominant group as such is characterizing the subordinate group as such. This occurs in the "public arena" wherein the spokesmen appear as representatives and agents of the dominant group. The extended public arena is constituted by such things as legislative assemblies, public meetings, conventions, the press, and the printed word. What goes on in this public arena attracts the attention of large numbers of the dominant group and is felt as the voice and action of the group as such.

Second, the definitions that are forged in the public arena center, obviously, about matters that are felt to be of major importance. Thus, we are led to recognize the crucial role of the "big event" in developing a conception of the subordinate racial group. The happening that seems momentous, that touches deep sentiments, that seems to raise fundamental questions about relations, and that awakens strong feelings of identification with one's racial group is the kind of event that is central in the formation of the racial image. Here, again, we note the relative unimportance of the huge bulk of experiences coming from daily contact with individuals of the subordinate group. It is the events seemingly loaded with great collective significance that are the focal points of the public discussion. The definition of these events is chiefly responsible for the development of a racial image and of the sense of group position. When this public discussion takes the form of a denunciation of the subordinate racial group, signifying that it is unfit and a threat, the discussion becomes particularly potent in shaping the sense of social position.

Third, the major influence in public discussion is exercised by individuals and groups who have the public ear and who are felt to have standing, prestige, authority, and power. Intellectual and social elites, public figures of prominence, and leaders of powerful organizations are likely to be the key figures in the formation of the sense of group position and in the characterization of the subordinate group. It is well to note this in view of the not infrequent tendency of students to regard race prejudice as growing out of the multiplicity of experiences and attitudes of the bulk of the people.

Fourth, we also need to perceive the appreciable opportunity that is given to strong interest groups in directing the lines of discussion and setting the interpretations that arise in such discussion. Their self-interests may dictate the kind of position they wish the dominant racial group to enjoy. It may be a position which enables them to retain certain advantages, or even more to gain still greater advantages. Hence, they may be vigorous in seeking to manufacture events to attract public attention and to set lines of issue in such a way as to predetermine interpretations favorable to their interests. The role of strongly organized groups seeking to further special interest is usually central in the formation of collective images of abstract groups. Historical records of major instances of race relations, as in our South, or in South Africa, or in Europe in the case of the Jew, or on the West Coast in the case of the Japanese show the formidable part played by interest groups in defining the subordinate racial group.

I conclude this highly condensed paper with two further observations that may throw additional light on the relation of the sense of group position to race prejudice. Race prejudice becomes entrenched and tenacious to the extent the prevailing social order is rooted in the sense of social position. This has been true of the historic South in our country. In such a social order race prejudice tends to become chronic and impermeable to change. In other places the social order may be affected only to a limited extent by the sense of group position held by the dominant racial group. This I think has been true usually in the case of anti-Semitism in Europe and this country. Under these conditions the sense of group position tends to be weaker and more vulnerable. In turn, race prejudice has a much more variable and intermittent career, usually becoming pronounced only as a consequence of grave disorganizing events that allow for the formation of a scapegoat.

This leads me to my final observation which in a measure is an indirect summary. The sense of group position dissolves and race prejudice declines when the process of running definition does not keep abreast of major shifts in the social order. When events touching on relations are not treated as "big events" and hence do not set crucial issues in the arena of public discussion; or when the elite leaders or spokesmen do not define such big events vehemently or adversely; or where they define them in the direction of racial harmony; or when there is a paucity of strong interest groups seeking to build up a strong adverse image for special advantage—under such conditions the sense of group position recedes and race prejudice declines.

The clear implication of my discussion is that the proper and the fruitful area in which race prejudice should be studied is the collective process through which a sense of group position is formed. To seek, instead, to understand it or to handle it in the arena of individual feeling and of individual experience seems to me to be clearly misdirected.

HERBERT BLUMER (1900–1987) was a former professional football player who became a sociology professor at the University of Chicago and the University of California, Berkeley. He helped to establish symbolic interactionism as a major paradigm in sociology.

Gordon W. Allport    **NO**

The Young Child

How is prejudice learned? We have opened our discussion of this pivotal problem by pointing out that the home influence has priority, and that the child has excellent reasons for adopting his ethnic attitudes ready-made from his parents. We likewise called attention to the central role of identification in the course of early learning. In the present chapter we shall consider additional factors operating in preschool years. The first six years of life are important for the development of all social attitudes, though it is a mistake to regard early childhood as alone responsible for them. A bigoted personality may be well under way by the age of six, but by no means fully fashioned.

Our analysis will be clearer if at the outset we make a distinction between *adopting* prejudice and *developing* prejudice. A child who adopts prejudice is taking over attitudes and stereotypes from his family or cultural environment. . . . Parental words and gestures, along with their concomitant beliefs and antagonisms, are transferred to the child. He adopts his parents' views. . . .

But there is also a type of training that does not transfer ideas and attitudes directly to the child, but rather creates an atmosphere in which he *develops* prejudice as his style of life. In this case the parents may or may not express their own prejudices (usually they do). What is crucial, however, is that their mode of handling the child (disciplining, loving, threatening) is such that the child cannot help acquire suspicions, fears, hatreds that sooner or later may fix on minority groups.

In reality, of course, these forms of learning are not distinct. Parents who *teach* the child specific prejudices are also likely to *train* the child to develop a prejudiced nature. Still it is well to keep the distinction in mind, for the psychology of learning is so intricate a subject that it requires analytical aids of this type.

Child Training

We consider now the style of child training that is known to be conducive to the *development* of prejudice. (We shall disregard for the time being the learning of specific attitudes toward specific groups.)

One line of proof that a child's prejudice is related to the manner of his upbringing comes from a study of Harris, Gough, and Martin.[1] These investigators first determined the extent to which 240 fourth-, fifth-, and sixth-grade children expressed prejudiced attitudes toward minority groups. They then sent questionnaires to the mothers of these children, asking their views on certain practices in child training. Most of these were returned with the mothers' replies. The results are highly instructive. Mothers of prejudiced children, *far more often* than the mothers of unprejudiced children, held that

> Obedience is the most important thing a child can learn.
>
> A child should never be permitted to set his will against that of his parents.
>
> A child should never keep a secret from his parents.
>
> "I prefer a quiet child to one who is noisy."
>
> (In the case of temper tantrums) "Teach the child that two can play that game, by getting angry yourself."

In the case of sex-play (masturbation) the mother of the prejudiced child is much more likely to believe she should punish the child; the mother of the unprejudiced child is much more likely to ignore the practice.

All in all, the results indicate that pervasive family atmospheres do definitely slant the child. Specifically, a home that is suppressive, harsh, or critical—where the parents' word is law—is more likely to prepare the groundwork for group prejudice.

It seems a safe assumption that the mothers who expressed their philosophies of child training in this questionnaire actually carried out their ideas in practice. If so, then we have strong evidence that children are more likely to be prejudiced if they have been brought up by mothers who insist on obedience, who are suppressive of the child's impulses, and who are sharp disciplinarians.

What does such a style of child training do to a child? For one thing it puts him on guard. He has to watch his impulses carefully. Not only is he punished for them when they counter the parents' convenience and rules, as they frequently do, but he feels at such times that love is withdrawn from him. When love is withdrawn he is alone, exposed, desolate. Thus he comes to watch alertly for signs of parental approval or disapproval. It is they who have power, and they who give or withhold their conditional love. Their power and their will are the decisive agents in the child's life.

What is the result? First of all, the child learns that power and authority dominate human relationships—not trust and tolerance. The stage is thus set for a hierarchical view of society. Equality does not really prevail. The effect goes even deeper. The child mistrusts his impulses: he must not have temper tantrums, he must not disobey, he must not play with his sex organs. He must fight such evil in himself. Through a simple act of projection . . . the child comes to fear evil impulses in others. They have dark designs; their impulses threaten the child; they are not to be trusted.

If this style of training prepares the ground for prejudice, the opposite style seems to predispose toward tolerance. The child who feels secure and loved whatever he does, and who is treated not with a display of parental power (being punished usually through shaming rather than spanking), develops basic ideas of equality and trust. Not required to repress his own impulses, he is less likely to project them upon others, and less likely to develop suspicion, fear, and a hierarchical view of human relationships.[2]

While no child is always treated according to one and only one pattern of discipline or affection, we might venture to classify prevailing home atmospheres according to the following scheme:

Permissive treatment by parents

Rejective treatment

   suppressive and cruel (harsh, fear-inspiring)

   domineering and critical (overambitious parents nagging and dissatisfied with the child as he is)

Neglectful

Overindulgent

Inconsistent (sometimes permissive, sometimes rejective, sometimes overindulgent)

Although we cannot yet be dogmatic about the matter, it seems very likely that rejective, neglectful, and inconsistent styles of training tend to lead to the development of prejudice.[3] Investigators have reported how impressed they are by the frequency with which quarrelsome or broken homes have occurred in the childhood of prejudiced people.

> Ackerman and Jahoda made a study of anti-Semitic patients who were undergoing psychoanalysis. Most of them had had an unhealthy homelife as children, marked by quarreling, violence, or divorce. There was little or no affection or sympathy between the parents. The rejection of the child by one or both parents was the rule rather than the exception.[4]

These investigators could not find that specific parental indoctrination in anti-Semitic attitudes was a necessary element. It is true that the parents, like the children, were anti-Semitic, but the authors explain the connection as follows:

> In those cases where parents and children are anti-Semitic, it is more reasonable to assume that the emotional predispositions of the parents created a psychological atmosphere conducive to the development of similar emotional dispositions in the child, than to maintain the simple imitation hypothesis.[5]

In other words, prejudice was not *taught* by the parent but was *caught* by the child from an infected atmosphere.

Another investigator became interested in paranoia. Among a group of 125 hospital patients suffering from fixed delusional ideas, he found that the majority had a predominantly suppressive and cruel upbringing. Nearly three-quarters of the patients had parents who were either suppressive and cruel or else domineering and overcritical. Only seven percent came from homes that could be called permissive.[6] Thus many paranoias in adult years can be traceable to a bad start in life. We cannot, of course, equate paranoia and prejudice. Yet the rigid categorizing indulged in by the prejudiced person, his hostility, and his inaccessibility to reason are often much like the disorder of a paranoiac.

Without stretching the evidence too far, we may at least make a guess: children who are too harshly treated, severely punished, or continually criticized are more likely to develop personalities wherein group prejudice plays a prominent part. Conversely, children from more relaxed and secure homes, treated permissively and with affection, are more likely to develop tolerance.

Fear of the Strange

Let us return again to the question whether there is an inborn source of prejudice. . . . [We] reported that as soon as infants are able (perhaps at six months of age) to distinguish between familiar and unfamiliar persons, they sometimes show anxiety when strangers approach. They do so especially, if the stranger moves abruptly or makes a "grab" for the child. They may show special fear if the stranger wears eyeglasses, or has skin of an unfamiliar color, or even if his expressive movements are different from what the child is accustomed to. This timidity usually continues through the preschool period—often beyond. Every visitor who has entered a home where there is a young child knows that it takes several minutes, perhaps several hours, for the child to "warm up" to him. But usually the initial fear gradually disappears.

We reported also an experiment where infants were placed alone in a strange room with toys. All of the children were at first alarmed and cried in distress. After a few repetitions they became entirely habituated to the room and played as if at home. But the biological utility of the initial fear reaction is obvious. Whatever is strange is a potential danger, and must be guarded against until one's experience assures one that no harm is lurking.

The almost universal anxiety of a child in the presence of strangers is no more striking than his rapid adaptability to their presence.

> In a certain household a Negro maid came to work. The young children in the family, aged three and five, showed fear and for a few days were reluctant to accept her. The maid stayed with the family for five or six years and came to be loved by all. Several years later, when the children were young adults, the family was discussing the happy period of Anna's services in the household. She had not been seen for the past ten years, but her memory was affectionately held. In the course of the conversation it came out that she was colored. The children were utterly astonished. They insisted that they had never known this fact, or had completely forgotten it if they ever knew it.

Situations of this type are not uncommon. Their occurrence makes us doubt that instinctive fear of the strange has any necessary bearing upon the organization of permanent attitudes.

Dawn of Racial Awareness

The theory of "home atmosphere" is certainly more convincing than the theory of "instinctive roots." But neither theory tells us just when and how the child's ethnic ideas begin to crystallize. Granted that the child possesses relevant emotional equipment, and that the family supplies a constant undertone of acceptance or rejection, anxiety or security, we still need studies that will show how the child's earliest sense of group differences develops. An excellent setting for such a study is a biracial nursery school.

In investigations conducted in this setting, it appears that the earliest age at which children take any note of race is two and a half.

> One white child of this age, sitting for the first time beside a Negro child, said, "Dirty face." It was an unemotional remark, prompted only by his observing a wholly dark-skinned visage—for the first time in his life.

The purely sensory observation that some skins are white, some colored, seems in many cases to be the first trace of racial awareness. Unless there is the quiver of fear of the strange along with this observation, we may say that race difference at first arouses a sense of curiosity and interest—nothing more. The child's world is full of fascinating distinctions. Facial color is simply one of them. Yet we note that even this first perception of racial difference may arouse associations with "clean" and "dirty."

The situation is more insistent by the age of three and a half or four. The sense of dirt still haunts the children. They have been thoroughly scrubbed at home to eradicate dirt. Why then does it exist so darkly on other children? One colored boy, confused concerning his membership, said to his mother, "Wash my face clean; some of the children don't wash well, especially colored children."

> A first grade teacher reports that about one white child in ten refuses to hold hands during games with the solitary Negro child in the classroom. The reason apparently is not "prejudice" in any deep-seated sense. The rejective white children merely complain that Tom has dirty hands and face.

Dr. Goodman's nursery school study shows one particularly revealing result. Negro children are, by and large, "racially aware" earlier than are white children.[7] They tend to be confused, disturbed, and sometimes excited by the problem. Few of them seem to know that they are Negroes. (Even at the age of seven one little Negro girl said to a white playmate, "I'd hate to be colored, wouldn't you?")

The interest and disturbance take many forms. Negro children ask more questions about racial differences; they may fondle the blond hair of a white child; they are often rejective toward Negro dolls. When given a white and Negro doll to play with, they almost uniformly prefer the white doll; many slap the Negro doll and call it dirty or ugly. As a rule, they are more rejective of Negro dolls than are white children. They tend to behave self-consciously when tested for racial awareness. One Negro boy, being shown two baby dolls alike save for color, is asked, "Which one is most like you when you were a baby?"

> Bobby's eyes move from brown to white; he hesitates, squirms, glances at us sidewise—and points to the white doll. Bobby's perceptions relevant to race, feeble and sporadic though they are, have some personal meaning—some ego-reference.

Especially interesting is Dr. Goodman's observation that Negro children tend to be fully as active as white children at the nursery school age. They are on the whole more sociable—particularly those who are rated as high on "racial awareness." A larger proportion of the Negro children are rated as "leaders" in the group. Although we cannot be certain of the meaning of this finding, it may well come from the fact that Negro children are more highly stimulated by the dawning awareness of race. They may be excited by a challenge they do not fully understand, and may seek reassurance through activity and social contacts for the vague threat that hangs over them. The threat comes not from nursery school, where they are secure enough, but from their first contacts with the world outside and from discussions at home, where their Negro parents cannot fail to talk about the matter.

What is so interesting about this full-scale activity at the nursery school age is its contrast to the adult demeanor of many Negroes who are noted for their poise, passivity, apathy, laziness—or whatever the withdrawing reaction may be called. . . . [We] noted that the Negro's conflicts sometimes engender a quietism, a passivity. Many people hold that this "laziness" is a biological trait of Negroes—but in the nursery school we find flatly contradictory evidence. Passivity, when it exists as a Negro attribute, is apparently a learned mode of adjustment. The assertive reaching out of the four-year-old for security and acceptance is ordinarily doomed to failure. After a period of struggle and suffering the passive mode of adjustment may set in.

Why is there, even in the dawning race awareness of four-year-olds, a nebulous sense of inferiority associated with dark skin? A significant part of the answer lies in the similarity between dark pigmentation and dirt. A third of Dr. Goodman's children (both Negro and white) spoke of this matter. Many others no doubt had it in their minds,

but did not happen to mention it to the investigators. An additional part of the answer may lie in those subtle forms of learning—not yet fully understood—whereby value-judgments are conveyed to the child. Some parents of white children may, by word or act, have conveyed to their children a vague sense of their rejection of Negroes. If so, the rejection is still only nascent in the four-year-old, for in virtually no case could the investigators find anything they were willing to label "prejudice" at this age level. Some of the Negro parents, too, may have conveyed to their children a sense of the handicaps of people with black skin, even before the children themselves knew their own skin was black.

The initial damage of associated ideas seems inescapable in our culture. Dark skin suggests dirt—even to a four-year-old. To some it may suggest feces. Brown is not the aesthetic norm in our culture (in spite of the popularity of chocolate). But this initial disadvantage is by no means insuperable. Discriminations in the realm of color are not hard to learn: a scarlet rose is not rejected because it is the color of blood, nor a yellow tulip because it is the color of urine.

To sum up: four-year-olds are normally interested, curious, and appreciative of differences in racial groups. A slight sense of white superiority seems to be growing, largely because of the association of white with cleanness—cleanliness being a value learned very early in life. But contrary associations can be, and sometimes are, easily built up.

> One four-year-old boy was taken by train from Boston to San Francisco. He was enchanted by the friendly Negro porter. For fully two years thereafter he fantasied that he was a porter, and complained bitterly that he was not colored so that he could qualify for the position.

Linguistic Tags: Symbols of Power and Rejection

Earlier we discussed the immensely important role of language in building fences for our mental categories and our emotional responses. This factor is so crucial that we return to it again—as it bears on childhood learning.

In Goodman's study it turned out that fully half the nursery school children knew the word "nigger." Few of them understood what the epithet culturally implies. But they knew that the word was potent. It was forbidden, taboo, and always fetched some type of strong response from the teachers. It was therefore a "power word." Not infrequently in a temper tantrum a child would call his teacher (whether white or colored) a "nigger" or a "dirty nigger." The term expressed an emotion—nothing more. Nor did it always express anger—sometimes merely excitement. Children wildly racing around, shrieking at play might, in order to enhance their orgies, yell "nigger, nigger, nigger." As a strong word it seemed fit to vocalize the violent expenditure of energy under way.

One observer gives an interesting example of aggressive verbalization during wartime play:

> Recently, in a waiting room, I watched three youngsters who sat at a table looking at magazines. Suddenly the smaller boy said: "Here's a soldier and an airplane. He's a Jap." The girl said: "No, he's an American." The little fellow said: "Get him, soldier. Get the Jap." The older boy added, "And Hitler too." "And Mussolini," said the girl. "And the Jews," said the big boy. Then the little fellow started a chant, the others joining in: "The Japs, Hitler, Mussolini, and the Jews! The Japs, Hitler, Mussolini, and the Jews!"[8] It is certain that these children had very little understanding of their bellicose chant. The names of their enemies had an expressive but not a denotative significance.

One little boy was agreeing with his mother, who was warning him never to play with niggers. He said, "No, Mother, I never play with niggers. I only play with white and black children." This child was developing aversion to the term "nigger," without having the slightest idea what the term meant. In other words, the aversion is being set up prior to acquiring a referent.

Other examples could be given of instances where words appear strong and emotionally laden to the child (goy, kike, dago). Only later does he attach the word to a group of people upon whom he can visit the emotions suggested by the word.

We call this process "linguistic precedence in learning." The emotional word has an effect prior to the learning of the referent. Later, the emotional effect becomes attached to the referent.

Before a firm sense of the referent is acquired, the child may go through stages of puzzlement and confusion. This is particularly true because emotional epithets are most likely to be learned when some exciting or traumatic experience is under way. Lasker gives the following example:

> Walking across the playground, a settlement worker found a little Italian boy crying bitterly. She asked him what was the matter. "Hit by Polish boy," the little man repeated several times.

Inquiry among the bystanders showed that the offender was not Polish at all. Turning again to her little friend, she said, "You mean, hit by a big naughty boy." But he would not have it thus and went on repeating that he had been hit by a Polish boy. This struck the worker as so curious that she made inquiries of the little fellow's family. She learned that he lived in the same house with a Polish family and that the Italian mother, by constantly quarreling with her Polish neighbor, had put into the heads of her children the notion that "Polish" and "bad" were synonymous terms.[9]

When this lad finally learns who Poles are, he already will have a strong prejudice against them. Here is a clear case of linguistic precedence in learning.

Children sometimes confess their perplexity concerning emotional tags. They seem to be groping for proper referents. Trager and Radke, from their work with kindergarten, first- and second-grade children, give several examples:[10]

Anna   When I was coming out of the dressing room, Peter called me a dirty Jew.

Teacher   Why did you say that, Peter?

Peter (earnestly)   I didn't say it for spite. I was only playing.

Johnny (helping Louis pull off his leggings)   A man called my father a goy.

Louis   What's a goy?

Johnny   I think everybody around here is a goy. But not me. I'm Jewish.

> On being called a "white cracker" by a Negro boy in the class, the teacher said to her class, "I am puzzled by the meaning of two words. Do you know what 'white cracker' means?"
>
> A number of vague answers were received from the children, one being "You're supposed to say it when you're mad."

Even while the child is having difficulty with words, they have a great power over him. To him they are often a type of magic, of verbal realism. . . .

> A little boy in the South was playing with the child of the washerwoman. Everything was going smoothly until a neighbor white child called over the fence, "Look out, you'll catch it."
>
> "Catch what?" asked the first white child.
> "Catch the black. You'll get colored too."

Just this assertion (reminding the child, no doubt, of expressions such as "catch the measles") frightened him. He deserted his colored companion then and there, and never played with him again.

Children often cry if they are called names. Their self-esteem is wounded by any epithet: naughty, dirty, harum-scarum, nigger, dago, Jap, or what not. To escape this verbal realism of early childhood, they often reassure themselves, when they are a little older, with the self-restorative jingle: Sticks and stones may break my bones, but names can never hurt me. But it takes a few years for them to learn that a name is not a thing-in-itself. As we saw earlier verbal realism may never be fully shaken off. The rigidity of linguistic categories may continue in adult thinking. To some adults "communist" or "Jew" is a dirty word—and a dirty thing—an indissoluble unity, as it may be to a child.

The First Stage in Learning Prejudice

Janet, six years of age, was trying hard to integrate her obedience to her mother with her daily social contacts. One day she came running home and asked, "Mother, what is the name of the children I am supposed to hate?"

Janet's wistful question leads us into a theoretical summary of the present chapter.

Janet is stumbling at the threshold of some abstraction. She wishes to form the right category. She intends to oblige her mother by hating the right people when she can find out who they are.

In this situation we suspect the preceding stages in Janet's developmental history:

1. She identifies with the mother, or at least she strongly craves the mother's affection and approval. We may imagine that the home is not "permissive" in atmosphere, but somewhat stern and critical. Janet may have found that she must be on her toes to please her parent. Otherwise she will suffer rejection or punishment. In any event, she has developed a habit of obedience.
2. While she has apparently no strong fear of strangers at the present time, she has learned to be circumspect. Experiences of insecurity with people outside the family circle may be a factor in her present effort to define her circle of loyalties.
3. She undoubtedly has gone through the initial period of curiosity and interest in racial and ethnic differences. She knows now that human beings are clustered into groups—that there are important distinctions if only

she can identify them. In the case of Negro and white the visibility factor has helped her. But then she discovered that subtler differences were also important; Jews somehow differed from gentiles; wops from Americans; doctors from salesmen. She is now aware of group differences, though not yet clear concerning all the relevant cues.
4. She has encountered the stage of linguistic precedence in learning. In fact, she is now in this stage. She knows that group X (she knows neither its name nor its identity) is somehow hate-worthy. She already has the emotional meaning but lacks the referential meaning. She seeks now to integrate the proper content with the emotion. She wishes to define her category so as to make her future behavior conform to her mother's desires. As soon as she has the linguistic tag at her command, she will be like the little Italian boy for whom "Polish" and "bad" were synonymous terms.

Up to the present, Janet's development marks what we might call the first stage of ethnocentric learning. Let us christen it the period of *pregeneralized* learning. This label is not altogether satisfactory, but none better describes the potpourri of factors listed above. The term draws attention primarily to the fact that the child has not yet generalized after the fashion of adults. He does not quite understand what a Jew is, what a Negro is, or what his own attitude toward them should be. He does not know even what *he* is—in any consistent sense. He may think he is an American only when he is playing with his toy soldiers (this type of categorizing was not uncommon in wartime). It is not only in ethnic matters that thoughts are prelogical from an adult point of view. A little girl may not think that her mother is her mother when the latter is working at the office; and may not regard her mother as an officeworker when she is at home tending the family.[11]

The child seems to live his mental life in specific contexts. What exists here and now makes up the only reality. The strange-man-who-knocks-at-the-door is something to be feared. It does not matter if he is a delivery man. The Negro boy at school is dirty. He is not a member of a race.

Such independent experiences in concrete procession seem to furnish the child's mind. His pregeneralized thinking (from the adult's point of view) has sometimes been labeled "global," or "syncretistic," or "prelogical."[12]

Now the place of linguistic tags in the course of mental development is crucial. They stand for adult abstractions, for logical generalizations of the sort that mature adults accept. The child learns the tags before he is fully ready to apply them to the adult categories. They prepare him for prejudice. But the process takes time. Only after much fumbling—in the manner of Janet and other children described in this chapter—will the proper categorizing take place.

The Second Stage in Learning Prejudice

As soon as Janet's mother gives a clear answer to Janet, she will in all probability enter a second period of prejudice—one that we may call the period of *total rejection.* Suppose the mother answers, "I told you not to play with Negro children. They are dirty; they have diseases; and they will hurt you. Now don't let me catch you at it." If Janet by now has learned to distinguish Negroes from other groups, even from the dark-skinned Mexican children, or Italians—in other words, if she now has the adult category in mind—she will undoubtedly reject all Negroes, in all circumstances, and with considerable feeling.

The research of Blake and Dennis well illustrates the point.[13] It will be recalled that these investigators studied Southern white children in the fourth and fifth grades (ten- and eleven-year-olds). They asked such questions as, "Which are more musical—Negroes or white people?" "Which are more clean?"—and many questions of a similar type. These children had, by the age of ten, learned to reject the Negro category *totally.* No favorable quality was ascribed to Negroes more often than to whites. In effect, whites had all the virtues; Negroes, none.

While this totalized rejection certainly starts earlier (in many children it will be found by the age of seven or eight), it seems to reach its ethnocentric peak in early puberty. First- and second-grade children often elect to play with, or sit beside, a child of different race or ethnic membership. This friendliness usually disappears in the fifth grade. At that time children choose their own group almost exclusively. Negroes select Negroes, Italians select Italians, and so on.[14]

As children grow older, they normally lose this tendency to total rejection and overgeneralization. Blake and Dennis found that in the 12th grade the white youth ascribed several favorable stereotypes to Negroes. They considered them more musical, more easygoing, better dancers.

The Third Stage

Thus, after a period of *total rejection,* a stage of *differentiation* sets in. The prejudices grow less totalized. Escape clauses are written into the attitude in order to make it more

rational and more acceptable to the individual. One says, "Some of my best friends are Jews." Or, "I am not prejudiced against Negroes—I always loved my black Mammy." The child who is first learning adult categories of rejection is not able to make such gracious exceptions. It takes him the first six to eight years of his life to learn total rejection, and another six years or so to modify it. The actual adult creed in his culture is complex indeed. It allows for (and in many ways encourages) ethnocentrism. At the same time, one must give lip service to democracy and equality, or at least ascribe some good qualities to the minority group and somehow plausibly justify the remaining disapproval that one expresses. It takes the child well into adolescence to learn the peculiar double-talk appropriate to prejudice in a democracy.

Around the age of eight, children often *talk* in a highly prejudiced manner. They have learned their categories and their totalized rejection. But the rejection is chiefly verbal. While they may damn the Jews, the wops, the Catholics, they may still *behave* in a relatively democratic manner. They may play with them even while they talk against them. The "total rejection" is chiefly a verbal matter.

Now when the teaching of the school takes effect, the child learns a new verbal norm: he must talk democratically. He must profess to regard all races and creeds as equal. Hence, by the age of 12, we may find *verbal* acceptance, but *behavioral* rejection. By this age the prejudices have finally affected conduct, even while the verbal, democratic norms are beginning to take effect.

The paradox, then, is that younger children may talk undemocratically, but behave democratically, whereas children in puberty may talk (at least in school) democratically but behave with true prejudice. By the age of 15, considerable skill is shown in imitating the adult pattern. Prejudiced talk and democratic talk are reserved for appropriate occasions, and rationalizations are ready for whatever occasions require them. Even conduct is varied according to circumstances. One may be friendly with a Negro in the kitchen, but hostile to a Negro who comes to the front door. Double-dealing, like double-talk, is hard to learn. It takes the entire period of childhood and much of adolescence to master the art of ethnocentrism.

Notes and References

1. D. B. Harris, H. G. Gough, W. E. Martin. Children's ethnic attitudes: II, Relationship to parental beliefs concerning child training. *Child Development,* 1950, 21, 169–181.
2. These two contrasting styles of child training are described more fully by D. P. Ausubel in *Ego*

Development and the Personality Disorders. New York: Grune & Stratton, 1952.

3. The most extensive evidence is contained in researches conducted at the University of California. See: T. W. Adorno, Else Frenkel-Brunswik, D. J. Levinson, R. N. Sanford, *The Authoritarian Personality,* New York: Harper, 1950; also, Else Frenkel-Brunswik, Patterns of social and cognitive outlook in children and parents, *American Journal of Orthopsychiatry,* 1951, 21, 543–558.

4. N. W. Ackerman and Marie Jahoda. *Anti-Semitism and Emotional Disorder.* New York: Harper, 1950, 45.

5. *Ibid.,* 85.

6. H. Bonner. Sociological aspects of paranoia. *American Journal of Sociology,* 1950, 56, 255–262.

7. Mary E. Goodman. *Race Awareness in Young Children.* Cambridge: Addison-Wesley, 1952. Other studies have confirmed the fact that Negro children are race-aware before white children: e.g., Ruth Horowitz, Racial aspects of self-identification in nursery school children, *Journal of Psychology,* 1939, 7, 91–99.

8. Mildred M. Eakin. *Getting Acquainted with Jewish Neighbors.* New York: Macmillan, 1944.

9. B. Lasker. *Race Attitudes in Children.* New York: Henry Holt, 1929, 98.

10. Helen G. Trager and Marian Radke. Early childhood airs its views. *Educational Leadership,* 1947, 5, 16–23.

11. E. L. Hartley, M. Rosenbaum, and S. Schwartz. Children's perceptions of ethnic group membership. *Journal of Psychology,* 1948, 26, 387–398.

12. *Cf.* H. Werner. *Comparative Psychology of Mental Development.* Chicago: Follett, 1948. J. Piaget. *The Child's Conception of the World.* New York: Harcourt, Brace, 1929, 236. G. Murphy. *Personality.* New York: Harper, 1947, 336.

13. R. Blake and W. Dennis. The development of stereotypes concerning the Negro. *Journal of Abnormal and Social Psychology,* 1943, 38, 525–531.

14. J. H. Criswell. A sociometric study of race cleavage in the classroom. *Archives of Psychology,* 1939, No. 235.

GORDON W. ALLPORT (1897–1967) was a social psychologist and author of *The Nature of Prejudice* (1954).

EXPLORING THE ISSUE

Is Race Prejudice a Product of Group Position?

Critical Thinking and Reflection

1. What is Blumer's group position thesis?
2. Illustrate the relationship between group position and the acquisition of race prejudice with examples.
3. How does Allport explain prejudice?
4. How are racial identity and race prejudice related?
5. What is the distinction between individual prejudice and institutional prejudice?
6. To what issues of race relations can the group position thesis be applied? Explain.
7. Compare and contrast the psychological approach to prejudice with the sociological approach?

Is There Common Ground

Allport and Blumer both are involved in research to determine how prejudice is acquired. Clearly, there is no one theory that offers a complete explanation of prejudice. However, when we consider theories together or debate differing positions advanced in this issue, we gain insight and understanding. The basic dilemma is whether or not prejudice results from personality traits best revealed through psychological theories, or whether prejudice is more social and cultural, reflecting Blumer's idea of group position. Utilizing both approaches will help us see how social learning takes place. At this point, we can ask another question concerning the relationship between attitudes and behavior.

To study race prejudice is to consider the role of attitudes and individual feelings in one's life. Still unclear to us is the relationship of attitudes to behavior. Does race prejudice lead to discriminatory practice? Does the prejudiced person behave differently from the nonprejudiced person?

Additional Resources

Adorno, Theodore. 1950. *The Authoritarian Personality* (Harper & Row).

Allport, Gordon. 1979. *The Nature of Prejudice* (Perseus).

Ausdale, Van Debra and Joe Feagin. 2001. *The First R: How Children Learn Race and Racism* (Rowman & Littlefield Publishers).

Clark, Kenneth. 1963. *Prejudice and Your Child* (Beacon Press).

Doob, Christopher Bates. 1996. *Racism: An American Cauldron* (HarperCollins).

Duckett, John. 1992. "Psychology and Prejudice: A Historical Analysis and Integrative Framework," *American Psychologist*.

Jacobs, Bruce A. 1999. *Race Manners: Navigating the Minefield between Black and White Americans* (Arcade).

Pettigrew, Thomas. 1980. "Prejudice," in Stephen Thernstrom, ed., *Harvard Encyclopedia of Ethnic Groups* (Harvard University Press).

Porter, Judith. 1971. *Black Child, White Child: The Development of Racial Attitudes* (Harvard University Press).

Sinkler, George. 1972. *The Racial Attitudes of American Presidents: From Abraham Lincoln to Theodore Roosevelt* (Anchor).

Williams, Patricia. 1995. *The Rooster's Egg: On the Persistence of Prejudice* (Harvard University Press).

Documentary Films

Elliot, Jane. 1995. *Blue-Eyed* (California Newsreel).

Griffith, D. W. 1915. *The Birth of a Nation* (Epoch Producing Co.).

Riggs, Marlon. 1987. *Ethnic Notions* (California Newsreel).

Riggs, Marlon. 1991. *Color Adjustment* (California Newsreel).

Wah, L. M. 1994. *The Color of Fear* (Stir Fry Productions).

Internet References . . .

Reducing Stereotype Threat

http://www.reducingstereotypethreat.org/

Teaching Tolerance

http://www.tolerance.org/

Understanding Prejudice

http://www.understandingprejudice.org/

Selected, Edited, and with Issue Framing Material by:
Wind Goodfriend, *Buena Vista University*

ISSUE

Is the Emphasis on a Color-Blind Society an Answer to Racism?

YES: Ward Connerly, from "Don't Box Me In," *National Review* (2001)

NO: Eduardo Bonilla-Silva, from *Racism without Racists: Color-Blind Racism and the Persistence of Racial Inequality in the United States,* Rowman & Littlefield (2003)

Learning Outcomes

After reading this issue, you will be able to:

- Develop an accurate conceptualization of what it means to be color-blind.
- Identify and explain the significant components of the color-blind ideology.
- Develop an informed understanding of the goals being pursued by advocates of a color-blind society.
- Comprehend the challenges that must be overcome in order to create a color-blind society.
- Identify and explain the functions of racial classification within American society.
- Identify and explain negative impacts of color-blind ideology when applied to minority communities.
- Apply color-blind ideology to contemporary society.

ISSUE SUMMARY

YES: Ward Connerly is a strong critic of all attempts at racial classification and believes that in order to achieve a racially egalitarian, unified American society, the government and private citizens must stop assigning people to categories delineated by race. To achieve this goal, Mr. Connerly is supporting the enactment of a "Racial Privacy Initiative."

NO: Eduardo Bonilla-Silva argues that "regardless of whites' sincere fictions, racial considerations shade almost everything in America" and, therefore, color-blind ideology is a cover for the racism and inequality that persist within contemporary American society.

Skin color has played a pivotal role in determining the legal and social status of individuals and groups throughout American history. Slavery within the United States developed as a racial institution in which blackness defined one's status as a bonded person and the distinction between black and white facilitated the establishment of the social controls necessary to maintain the effectiveness of this mode of economic production. The miscegenation among blacks and whites during the Slave Era resulted in the production of persons of biracial identities, octoroons and quadroons, and these interracial groups were components of a racial hierarchy based upon skin color. The status of the free African Americans of this period was above that of the slaves but below the biracial groups, thus reflecting the color-based status differentiations that informed the social structure of antebellum American society.

In the wake of the Civil War and Reconstruction, racial segregation emerged as the defining mode of race relations within the United States. The Segregation Era was defined by a color–caste system of race relations that was designed to promote the overt exclusion of blacks from meaningful institutional participation and power within society in order to maintain white dominance within society. Signs that read "whites only" and "colored" were quite common throughout this period and defined employment opportunities available to members of the two races and the access of blacks to housing, schools, and other public accommodations that were available within the society.

The *de jure* segregation of American society persisted until it was overtaken by the civil rights movement of the 1960s, but *de facto* segregation remains a prominent feature of the social order of the United States, despite the reforms of the last half-century. Baby boomers within today's African American and white populations bear memories of being socialized and conditioned by the restraining values of this color–caste system of race relations.

Despite the efforts of Martin Luther King and other supporters of civil rights and social justice for African Americans and others of color, the United States is still a nation within which color-consciousness and color-coded decision making are broadly prevalent. The American language and culture are laden with color-coded references such as whites/people of color, black neighborhood/white neighborhood, chocolate cities/vanilla suburbs, and many others. Even within the growing Latino population the tendency to apply color-coding to identify people is prevalent. Despite this fact, in the media and elsewhere there is a tendency to assign Latinos collectively a "brown" identity.

In June 1994, the publishers of *Time magazine* were so confident that the American public would respond to color-coded communications that they darkened the image of O.J. Simpson appearing on one of its covers. This dramatized the image of the sinister black male stereotype and crime. This color-coded presentation is a contradiction of the publishers' claim to be race-neutral. Although part of the culture advances the idea of color-blindness,

with *Time magazine* we see a mainstream publication's use of color to distinguish and define racial differences. This is an obvious contradiction as relates to the color-blind thesis. This interesting paradox has the guise of appearing to be race-neutral. Some observers like Bonilla-Silva argue that color-blindness is a new form of racism—that is, on the one hand, there is a denial of race differences, but on the other, there is a perpetuation of racial stereotypes.

Ward Connerly strongly argues in favor of the promise of a color-blind society. For him, America is becoming increasingly homogeneous where race is concerned and racial discrimination is seen as irrelevant today. Connerly is representative of African Americans who view color-based policies such as affirmative action as obscuring the fact that their success is based on merit, rather than skin color. He embraces the idea that America is increasingly an equal opportunity society.

In contrast, Eduardo Bonilla-Silva views color-blind ideology as a fiction and a new manifestation of racism. For him, the question remains, how do whites explain the contradiction between the notion of a color-blind society and the color-coded inequality that persists in America? For Bonilla-Silva, it is color-blind racism, the new racial ideology. He asks, if all of the society is color-blind, to whom do African Americans and other racial minorities assert their grievances over disadvantage?

Students should be aware that the promotion of a color-blind ideology as social reform raises significant questions. Given the reality of a color-conscious American culture that has lasted for nearly four centuries, how plausible is the achievement of this goal? Is the color-blind thesis as benign as it appears? What is the potential impact of color-blind ideology on black identity? Red? Yellow? Brown? Does color-blind ideology serve as a mask for white privilege? Does the promotion of color-blind ideology undermine civil rights and social justice organization and advocacy? These are among the salient questions that confront this issue.

YES ↵

Ward Connerly

Don't Box Me In

A few weeks ago, I was having dinner with a group of supporters following a lecture. One of those in attendance was a delightful woman who applauded my efforts to achieve a colorblind government. She strongly urged me to stay the course, promised financial support for my organization—the American Civil Rights Institute—and proclaimed that what we are doing is best for the nation.

Then, an odd moment occurred, when she said, "What you're doing is also best for your people." I flinched, took a couple of bites of my salad, and gathered my thoughts. I thought: *"My people"? Anyone who knows me knows that I abhor this mindset. But this dear lady doesn't know all my views or the nuances of race. She has innocently wandered into a racial thicket and doesn't have a clue that she has just tapped a raw nerve. Do I risk offending her by opening this issue for discussion? Do I risk losing her financial support by evidencing my distaste for what she has said? Perhaps it would be best to ignore the moment and let my staff follow up in pursuit of her support.*

I concluded that the situation demanded more of me than to believe that she was incapable of understanding what troubled me about her comment. So, I did what comes naturally in such situations—I politely confronted her. "What did you mean when you referred to 'my people' a moment ago?" I asked. "The black race," she responded. "What is your 'race'?" I asked. She said, "I'm Irish and German." I plowed ahead. "Would it affect your concept of my 'race' if I told you that one of my grandparents was Irish and American Indian, another French Canadian, another of African descent, and the other Irish? Aren't they all 'my people'? What about my children? They consist of my ingredients as well as those of their mother, who is Irish. What about my grandchildren, two of whom have a mother who is half Vietnamese?" The lady was initially awestruck. But that exchange produced one of the richest conversations about race I have ever had.

This discussion is one that an increasing number of Americans are having across our nation. It is one that many more would *like* to have. Thanks to the race questions placed in the 2000 Census, a great number of

people are beginning to wonder about this business of their "race."

From its inception, America has promised equal justice before the law. The Declaration of Independence and the Constitution stand as monuments to the Founders' belief that we can fashion a government of colorblind laws, a unified nation without divisible parts. Unfortunately, they had to compromise on that vision from the beginning. To create a government, they had to protect the international slave trade until 1808. After that time, with the slave trade forever banned, they hoped and believed the slave system would wither away.

In a second concession of their principles to material interests, the Founders also agreed to count slaves as only three-fifths of a person. This compromise stemmed not from a belief that slaves were less than human; rather, slaveowning states wanted to count slaves as whole persons in deciding how large their population was, but not count them at all in deciding how much the states would pay in taxes. The infamous three-fifths compromise was the unfortunate concession.

To distinguish slaves from non-slaves, governments established various race classifications. Unfortunately, these classifications continued long after the Civil War amendments formally repudiated them. After all, once everyone was free to enjoy all the privileges and immunities of American citizenship, there was no longer a need to classify people by race. In hindsight, we recognize that, after nearly a century of race classifications imposed by the state, these classifications had become part of the way average Americans saw themselves, as well as others. Over the next half-century, scientists began to recognize that these race classifications don't exist in nature. We had created them, to justify an inhuman system.

Even as science reached these conclusions, however, these classifications played ever more important roles in American life. Poll taxes and literacy tests; separate bathroom facilities, transportation, water fountains, neighborhoods—the entire Jim Crow system relied on these state-imposed race classifications. And with science unable to distinguish a black person from a non-black person, the government relied on the infamous "one-drop rule": If you have just one drop of "black blood," you're black.

Although the Supreme Court struck down the "separate but equal" legal structure, the Court failed to eliminate the race classifications that sustained all the forms of segregation and discrimination the Court was trying to eliminate. We have seen the actual expansion of the groups being classified. On some level, though, I'm sure we really do want to become "one nation . . . indivisible." Witness the tenfold increase in "multiracial" families since 1967. In its decision that year—aptly named *Loving v. Virginia*—the Supreme Court ruled that anti-miscegenation laws (those forbidding people of different races to marry) were unconstitutional. While it took some time for us to shed the taboos against interracial dating and marriage, today there are more "multiracial" children born in California than there are "black" children. When Benjamin Bratt and Julia Roberts began dating, no one cared that they were an interracial couple. So too with Maury Povich and Connie Chung. Love has become colorblind.

The time has come for America to fulfill the promise of equal justice before the law and for the nation to renounce race classifications. To that end, I am preparing to place the Racial Privacy Initiative (RPI) before California voters on the March 2002 ballot. This initiative would prohibit governments in California from classifying individuals by race, color, ethnicity, or national origin. Much to my surprise, just submitting RPI to the state in preparation for gathering signatures has generated controversy. The American Civil Liberties Union has called it a "racist" initiative, and various proponents of race preferences have said it will "turn back the clock on civil rights."

In drafting RPI, we have exempted medical research and have proposed nothing that would prevent law-enforcement officers from identifying particular individuals, so long as those methods are already lawful. To guarantee that laws against discrimination are enforced, we have exempted the Department of Fair Employment and Housing from the provisions of RPI for ten years.

Getting the government out of the business of classifying its citizens and asking them to check these silly little race boxes represents the next step in our nation's long journey toward becoming one nation. Getting rid of these boxes will strike a blow against the overbearing race industry that has grown like Topsy in America. It will help free us from the costly and poisonous identity politics and the racial spoils system that define our political process. It will clip the wings of a government that has become so intrusive that it classifies its citizens on the basis of race, even when citizens "decline to state." Enacting the Racial Privacy Initiative is the most significant step we can take to bring Americans together.

I ask all Americans who share the goal of a united America to join in this endeavor to fulfill our Founders' promise of colorblind justice before the law. For my part, I just don't want to be boxed in.

WARD CONNERLY is a political activist and conservative commentator. He is best identified with Proposition 209, a California ballot initiative in opposition to affirmative action programs.

Eduardo Bonilla-Silva

 **NO**

Racism without Racists: Color-Blind Racism and the Persistence of Racial Inequality in the United States

The Strange Enigma of Race in Contemporary America

> There is a strange kind of enigma associated with the problem of racism. No one, or almost no one, wishes to see themselves as racist; still, racism persists, real and tenacious.
>
> —Albert Memmi, *Racism*

Racism without "Racists"

Nowadays, except for members of white supremacist organizations, few whites in the United States claim to be "racist." Most whites assert they "don't see any color, just people"; that although the ugly face of discrimination is still with us, it is no longer the central factor determining minorities' life chances; and, finally, that like Dr. Martin Luther King Jr., they aspire to live in a society where "people are judged by the content of their character, not by the color of their skin." More poignantly, most whites insist that minorities (especially blacks) are the ones responsible for whatever "race problem" we have in this country. They publicly denounce blacks for "playing the race card," for demanding the maintenance of unnecessary and divisive race-based programs, such as affirmative action, and for crying "racism" whenever they are criticized by whites. Most whites believe that if blacks and other minorities would just stop thinking about the past, work hard, and complain less (particularly about racial discrimination), then Americans of all hues could "all get along."

But regardless of whites' "sincere fictions," racial considerations shade almost everything in America. Blacks and dark-skinned racial minorities lag well behind whites in virtually every area of social life; they are about three times more likely to be poor than whites, earn about 40 percent less than whites, and have about a tenth of the net worth that whites have. They also receive an inferior education compared to whites, even when they attend integrated institutions. In terms of housing, black-owned units comparable to white-owned ones are valued at 35 percent less. Blacks and Latinos also have less access to the entire housing market because whites, through a variety of exclusionary practices by white realtors and homeowners, have been successful in effectively limiting their entrance into many neighborhoods. Blacks receive impolite treatment in stores, in restaurants, and in a host of other commercial transactions. Researchers have also documented that blacks pay more for goods such as cars and houses than do whites. Finally, blacks and dark-skinned Latinos are the targets of racial profiling by the police that, combined with the highly racialized criminal court system, guarantees their overrepresentation among those arrested, prosecuted, incarcerated, and if charged for a capital crime, executed. Racial profiling in the highways has become such a prevalent phenomenon that a term has emerged to describe it: driving while black. In short, blacks and most minorities are, "at the bottom of the well."

How is it possible to have this tremendous degree of racial inequality in a country where most whites claim that race is no longer relevant? More important, how do whites explain the apparent contradiction between their professed color blindness and the United States' color-coded inequality? I contend that whites have developed powerful explanations—which have ultimately become justifications—for contemporary racial inequality that exculpate them from any responsibility for the status of people of color. These explanations emanate from a new racial ideology that I label *color-blind racism*. This ideology, which acquired cohesiveness and dominance in the late 1960s, explains contemporary racial inequality as the outcome of nonracial dynamics. Whereas Jim Crow racism explained blacks' social standing as the result of their biological and moral inferiority, color-blind racism avoids such facile arguments. Instead, whites rationalize minorities' contemporary status as the product of market dynamics, naturally occurring phenomena, and blacks' imputed cultural limitations. For instance, whites can attribute Latinos' high poverty rate to a relaxed work ethic ("the Hispanics are mañana, mañana, mañana—tomorrow, tomorrow, tomorrow") or residential segregation as the result of natural tendencies among groups ("Does a cat and a dog mix? I can't see it. You can't drink milk and scotch. Certain mixes don't mix.").

Color-blind racism became the dominant racial ideology as the mechanisms and practices for keeping blacks and other racial minorities "at the bottom of the well" changed. I have argued elsewhere that contemporary racial inequality is reproduced through "new racism" practices that are subtle, institutional, and apparently nonracial. In contrast to the Jim Crow era, where racial inequality was enforced through overt means (e.g., signs saying "No Niggers Welcomed Here" or shotgun diplomacy at the voting booth), today racial practices operate in "now you see it, now you don't" fashion. For example, residential segregation, which is almost as high today as it was in the past, is no longer accomplished through overtly discriminatory practices. Instead, covert behaviors such as not showing all the available units, steering minorities and whites into certain neighborhoods, quoting higher rents or prices to minority applicants, or not advertising units at all are the weapons of choice to maintain separate communities. In the economic field, "smiling face" discrimination ("We don't have jobs now, but please check later"), advertising job openings in mostly white networks and ethnic newspapers, and steering highly educated people of color into poorly remunerated jobs or jobs with limited opportunities for mobility are the new ways of keeping minorities in a secondary position. Politically, although the Civil Rights struggles have helped remove many of the obstacles for the electoral participation of people of color, "racial gerrymandering, multimember legislative districts, election runoffs, annexation of predominantly white areas, at-large district elections, and anti–single-shot devices (disallowing concentrating votes in one or two candidates in cities using at-large elections) have become standard practices to disenfranchise" people of color. Whether in banks, restaurants, school admissions, or housing transactions, the maintenance of white privilege is done in a way that defies facile racial readings. Hence, the contours of color-blind racism fit America's "new racism" quite well.

Compared to Jim Crow racism, the ideology of color blindness seems like "racism lite." Instead of relying on name calling (niggers, Spics, Chinks), color-blind racism otherizes softly ("these people are human, too"); instead of proclaiming God placed minorities in the world in a servile position, it suggests they are behind because they do not work hard enough; instead of viewing interracial marriage as wrong on a straight racial basis, it regards it as "problematic" because of concerns over the children, location, or the extra burden it places on couples. Yet this new ideology has become a formidable political tool for the maintenance of the racial order. Much as Jim Crow racism served as the glue for defending a brutal and overt system of racial oppression in the pre–Civil Rights era, color-blind racism serves today as the ideological armor for a covert and institutionalized system in the post–Civil Rights era. And the beauty of this new ideology is that it aids in the maintenance of white privilege without fanfare, without naming those who it subjects and those who it rewards. It allows a President to state things such as, "I strongly support diversity of all kinds, including racial diversity in higher education," yet, at the same time, to characterize the University of Michigan's affirmation action program as "flawed" and "discriminatory" against whites. Thus whites enunciate positions that safeguard their racial interests without sounding "racist." Shielded by color blindness, whites can express resentment toward minorities; criticize their morality, values, and work ethic; and even claim to be the victims of "reverse racism." This is the thesis I will defend to explain the curious enigma of "racism without racists."

Whites' Racial Attitudes in the Post–Civil Rights Era

Since the late 1950s surveys on racial attitudes have consistently found that fewer whites subscribe to the views associated with Jim Crow. For example, whereas the majority of whites supported segregated neighborhoods, schools, transportation, jobs, and public accommodations in the 1940s, less than a quarter indicated they did in the 1970s. Similarly, fewer whites than ever now seem to subscribe to stereotypical views of blacks. Although the number is still high (ranging from 20 percent to 50 percent, depending on the stereotype), the proportion of whites who state in surveys that blacks are lazy, stupid, irresponsible, and violent has declined since the 1940s.

These changes in whites' racial attitudes have been explained by the survey community and commentators in four ways. First, are the *racial optimists*. This group of analysts agrees with whites' common sense on racial matters and believes the changes symbolize a profound transition in the United States. Early representatives of this view were Herbert Hyman and Paul B. Sheatsley, who wrote widely influential articles on the subject in *Scientific American*. In a reprint of their earlier work in the influential collection edited by Talcott Parsons and Kenneth Clark, *The Negro American,* Sheatsley rated the changes in white attitudes as "revolutionary" and concluded,

> The mass of white Americans have shown in many ways that they will not follow a racist government and that they will not follow racist leaders. Rather, they are engaged in the painful task of adjusting to an integrated society. It will not be easy for most, but one cannot at this late date doubt the basic commitment. In their hearts they know that the American Negro is right.

In recent times, Glenn Firebaugh and Kenneth Davis, Seymour Lipset, and Paul Sniderman and his coauthors, in particular, have carried the torch for racial optimists. Firebaugh and Davis, for example, based on their analysis of survey results from 1972 to 1984, concluded that the trend toward less antiblack prejudice was across the board. Sniderman and his coauthors, as well as Lipset, go a step further than Firebaugh and Davis because they have openly advocated color-blind politics *as the* way to settle the United States' racial dilemmas. For instance, Sniderman and Edward Carmines made this explicit appeal in their recent book, *Reaching Beyond Race,*

> To say that a commitment to a color-blind politics is worth undertaking is to call for a politics centered on the needs of those most in need. It is not to argue for a politics in which race is irrelevant, but in favor of one in which race is relevant so far as it is a gauge of need. Above all, it is a call for a politics which, because it is organized around moral principles that apply regardless of race, can be brought to bear with special force on the issue of race.

The problems with this optimistic interpretation are twofold. First, as I have argued elsewhere, relying on questions that were framed in the Jim Crow era to assess whites' racial views today produces an artificial image of progress. Since the central racial debates and the language used to debate those matters have changed, our analytical focus ought to be dedicated to the analysis of the new racial issues. Insisting on the need to rely on old questions to keep longitudinal (trend) data as the basis for analysis will, by default, produce a rosy picture of race relations that misses what is going on on the ground. Second, and more important, because of the change in the normative climate in the post–Civil Rights era, analysts must exert extreme caution when interpreting attitudinal data, particularly when it comes from single-method

research designs. The research strategy that seems more appropriate for our times is mixed research designs (surveys used in combination with interviews, ethnosurveys, etc.), because it allows researchers to cross-examine their results.

A second, more numerous group of analysts exhibit what I have labeled elsewhere as the *racial pesoptimist* position. Racial pesoptimists attempt to strike a "balanced" view and suggest that whites' racial attitudes reflect progress and resistance. The classical example of this stance is Howard Schuman. Schuman has argued for more than thirty years that whites' racial attitudes involve a mixture of tolerance and intolerance, of acceptance of the principles of racial liberalism (equal opportunity for all, end of segregation, etc.) and a rejection of the policies that would make those principles a reality (from affirmative action to busing).

Despite the obvious appeal of this view in the research community (the appearance of neutrality, the pondering of "two sides," and this view's "balanced" component), racial pesoptimists are just closet optimists. Schuman, for example, has pointed out that, although "White responses to questions of principle are . . . more complex than is often portrayed . . . they nevertheless do show in almost every instance a positive movement over time." Furthermore, it is his belief that the normative change in the United States is real and that the issue is that whites are having a hard time translating those norms into personal preferences.

A third group of analysts argues that the changes in whites' attitudes represent the emergence of a *symbolic racism*. This tradition is associated with the work of David Sears and his associate, Donald Kinder. They have defined symbolic racism as "a blend of anti-black affect and the kind of traditional American moral values embodied in the Protestant Ethic." According to these authors, symbolic racism has replaced biological racism as the primary way whites express their racial resentment toward minorities. In Kinder and Sanders's words:

> A new form of prejudice has come to prominence, one that is preoccupied with matters of moral character, informed by the virtues associated with the traditions of individualism. At its center are the contentions that blacks do not try hard enough to overcome the difficulties they face and that they take what they have not earned. Today, we say, prejudice is expressed in the language of American individualism.

Authors in this tradition have been criticized for the slipperiness of the concept "symbolic racism," for claiming that the blend of antiblack affect and individualism is new, and for not explaining why symbolic racism came about. The first critique, developed by Howard Schuman, is that the concept has been "defined and operationalized in complex and varying ways." Despite this conceptual slipperiness, indexes of symbolic racism have been found to be in fact different from those of old-fashioned racism and to be strong predictors of whites' opposition to affirmative action. The two other critiques, made forcefully by Lawrence Bobo, have been partially addressed by Kinder and Sanders in their recent book, *Divided by Color.* First, Kinder and Sanders, as well as Sears, have made clear that their contention is not that this is the first time in history that antiblack affect and elements of the American Creed have combined. Instead, their claim is that this combination has become *central* to the new face of racism. Regarding the third critique, Kinder and Sanders go at length to explain the transition from old-fashioned to symbolic racism. Nevertheless, their explanation hinges on arguing that changes in blacks' tactics (from civil disobedience to urban violence) led to an onslaught of a new form of racial resentment that later found more fuel in controversies over welfare, crime, drugs, family, and affirmative action. What is missing in this explanation is a materially based explanation for why these changes occurred. Instead, their theory of prejudice is rooted in the "process of socialization and the operation of routine cognitive and emotional psychological processes."

Yet, despite its limitations, the symbolic racism tradition has brought attention to key elements of how whites explain racial inequality today. Whether this is "symbolic" of antiblack affect or not is beside the point and hard to assess, since as a former student of mine queried, "How does one test for the unconscious?"

The fourth explanation of whites' contemporary racial attitudes is associated with those who claim that whites' racial views represent a *sense of group position.* This position, forcefully advocated by Lawrence Bobo and James Kluegel, is similar to Jim Sidanius's "social dominance" and Mary Jackman's "group interests" arguments. In essence, the claim of all these authors is that white prejudice is an ideology to defend white privilege. Bobo and his associates have specifically suggested that because of socioeconomic changes that transpired in the 1950s and 1960s, *a laissez-faire racism* emerged that was fitting of the United States' "modern, nationwide, postindustrial free labor economy and polity." Laissez-faire racism "encompasses an ideology that blames blacks themselves for their poorer relative economic standing, seeing it as the function of perceived cultural inferiority."

Some of the basic arguments of authors in the symbolic and modern racism traditions and, particularly, of the laissez-faire racism view are fully compatible with my color-blind racism interpretation. As these authors, I argue that color-blind racism has rearticulated elements of traditional liberalism (work ethic, rewards by merit, equal opportunity, individualism, etc.) for racially illiberal goals. I also argue like them that whites today rely more on cultural rather than biological tropes to explain blacks' position in this country. Finally, I concur with most analysts of post–Civil Rights' matters in arguing that whites do not perceive discrimination to be a central factor shaping blacks' life chances.

Although most of my differences with authors in the symbolic racism and laissez-faire traditions are methodological, I have one central theoretical disagreement with them. Theoretically, most of these authors are still snarled in the prejudice problematic and thus interpret actors' racial views as *individual psychological* dispositions. Although Bobo and his associates have a conceptualization that is closer to mine, they still retain the notion of prejudice and its psychological baggage rooted in interracial hostility. In contrast, my model is not anchored in actors' affective dispositions (although affective dispositions may be manifest or latent in the way many express their racial views). Instead, it is based on a materialist interpretation of racial matters and thus sees the views of actors as corresponding to their systemic location. Those at the bottom of the racial barrel tend to hold oppositional views and those who receive the manifold wages of whiteness tend to hold views in support of the racial status quo. Whether actors express "resentment" or "hostility" toward minorities is largely irrelevant for the maintenance of white privilege. As David Wellman points out in his *Portraits of White Racism,* "[p]rejudiced people are not the only racists in America."

Key Terms: Race, Racial Structure, and Racial Ideology

One reason why, in general terms, whites and people of color cannot agree on racial matters is because they conceive terms such as "racism" very differently. Whereas for most whites racism is prejudice, for most people of color racism is systemic or institutionalized. Although this is not a theory book, my examination of color-blind racism has etched in it the indelible ink of a "regime of truth" about how the world is organized. Thus, rather than hiding my theoretical assumptions, I state them openly for the benefit of readers and potential critics.

The first key term is the notion of *race.* There is very little formal disagreement among social scientists in accepting the idea that race is a socially constructed category. This means that notions of racial difference are human creations rather than eternal, essential categories. As such, racial categories have a history and are subject to change. And here ends the agreement among social scientists on this matter. There are at least three distinct variations on how social scientists approach this constructionist perspective on race. The first approach, which is gaining popularity among white social scientists, is the idea that because race is socially constructed, it is not a fundamental category of analysis and praxis. Some analysts go as far as to suggest that because race is a constructed category, then it is not real and social scientists who use the category are the ones who make it real.

The second approach, typical of most sociological writing on race, gives lip service to the social constructionist view—usually a line in the beginning of the article or book. Writers in this group then proceed to discuss "racial" differences in academic achievement, crime, and SAT scores as if they were truly racial. This is the central way in which contemporary scholars contribute to the propagation of racist interpretations of racial inequality. By failing to highlight the social dynamics that produce these racial differences, these scholars help reinforce the racial order.

The third approach, and the one I use in this book, acknowledges that race, as other social categories such as class and gender, is constructed but insists that it has a *social reality*. This means that after race—or class or gender—is created, it produces real effects on the actors racialized as "black" or "white." Although race, as other social constructions, is unstable, it has a "changing same" quality at its core.

In order to explain how a socially constructed category produces real race effects, I need to introduce a second key term, the notion of *racial structure*. When race emerged in human history, it formed a social structure (a racialized social system) that awarded systemic privileges to Europeans (the peoples who became "white") over non-Europeans (the peoples who became "nonwhite"). Racialized social systems, or white supremacy for short, became global and affected all societies where Europeans extended their reach. I therefore conceive a society's racial structure as *the totality of the social relations and practices that reinforce white privilege*. Accordingly, the task of analysts interested in studying racial structures is to uncover the particular social, economic, political, social control, and ideological mechanisms responsible for the reproduction of racial privilege in a society.

But why are racial structures reproduced in the first place? Would not humans, after discovering the folly of racial thinking, work to abolish race as a category as well as a practice? Racial structures remain in place for the same reasons that other structures do. Since actors racialized as "white"—or as members of the dominant race—receive material benefits from the racial order, they struggle (or passively receive the manifold wages of whiteness) to maintain their privileges. In contrast, those defined as belonging to the subordinate race or races struggle to change the status quo (or become resigned to their position). Therein lies the secret of racial structures and racial inequality the world over. They exist because they benefit members of the dominant race.

If the ultimate goal of the dominant race is to defend its collective interests (i.e., the perpetuation of systemic white privilege), it should surprise no one that this group develops rationalizations to account for the status of the various races. And here I introduce my third key term, the notion of *racial ideology*. By this I mean *the racially based frameworks used by actors to explain and justify* (dominant race) or *challenge* (subordinate race or races) *the racial status quo*. Although all the races in a racialized social system have the *capacity* of developing these frameworks, the frameworks of the dominant race tend to become the master frameworks upon which *all* racial actors ground (for or against) their ideological positions. Why? Because as Marx pointed out in *The German Ideology*, "the ruling *material* force of society, is at the same time its ruling *intellectual* force." This does not mean that ideology is almighty. In fact, ideological rule is always partial. Even in periods of hegemonic rule, such as the current one, subordinate racial groups develop oppositional views. However, it would be foolish to believe that those who rule a society do not have the power to at least color (pun intended) the views of the ruled.

Racial ideology can be conceived for analytical purposes as comprising the following elements: common frames, style, and racial stories. The frames that bond together a particular racial ideology are rooted in the group-based conditions and experiences of the races and are, at the symbolic level, the representations developed by these groups to explain how the world is or ought to be. And because the group life of the various racially defined groups is based on hierarchy and domination, the ruling ideology expresses as "common sense" the interests of the dominant race, while oppositional ideologies attempt to challenge that common sense by providing alternative frames, ideas, and stories based on the experiences of subordinated races.

Individual actors employ these elements as "building blocks . . . for manufacturing versions on actions, self, and social structures" in communicative situations. The looseness of the elements allows users to maneuver within various contexts (e.g., responding to a race-related survey, discussing racial issues with family, or arguing about affirmative action in a college classroom) and produce various accounts and presentations of self (e.g., appearing ambivalent, tolerant, or strong minded). This loose character enhances the legitimating role of racial ideology because it allows for accommodation of contradictions, exceptions, and new information. As Jackman points out about ideology in general: "Indeed, the strength of an ideology lies in its loose-jointed, flexible application. *An ideology is a political instrument, not an exercise in personal logic:* consistency is rigidity, the only pragmatic effect of which is to box oneself in."

Before I can proceed, two important caveats should be offered. First, although whites, because of their privileged position in the racial order, form a social group (the dominant race), they are fractured along class, gender, sexual orientation, and other forms of "social cleavage." Hence, they have multiple and often contradictory interests that are not easy to disentangle and that predict *a priori* their mobilizing capacity (Do white workers have more in common with white capitalists than with black workers?). However, because all actors awarded the dominant racial position, regardless of their multiple structural locations (men or women, gay or straight, working class or bourgeois) benefit from what Mills calls the "racial contract," *most* have historically endorsed the ideas that justify the racial status quo.

Second, although not every single member of the dominant race defends the racial status quo or spouts color-blind racism, *most* do. To explain this point by analogy, although not every capitalist defends capitalism (e.g., Frederick Engels, the coauthor of *The Communist Manifesto,* was a capitalist) and not every man defends patriarchy (e.g., *Achilles Heel* is an English magazine published by feminist men), *most* do in some fashion. In the same vein, although some whites fight white supremacy and do not endorse white common sense, *most* subscribe to substantial portions of it in a casual, uncritical fashion that helps sustain the prevailing racial order. . . .

If instead one regards racial ideology as in fact changing, the reliance on questions developed to tackle issues from the Jim Crow era will produce an artificial image of progress and miss most of whites' contemporary racial nightmares.

Despite my conceptual and methodological concerns with survey research, I believe well-designed surveys are still useful instruments to glance at America's racial reality. Therefore, I report survey results from my own research projects as well as from research conducted by other scholars whenever appropriate. My point, then, is not to deny attitudinal change or to condemn to oblivion survey research on racial attitudes, but to understand whites' new racial beliefs and their implications as well as possible. . . .

One Important Caveat

The purpose of this book is not to demonize whites or label them "racist." Hunting for "racists" is the sport of choice of those who practice the "clinical approach" to race relations—the careful separation of good and bad, tolerant and intolerant Americans. Because this book is anchored in a structural understanding of race relations, my goal is to uncover the collective practices (in this book, the ideological ones) that help reinforce the contemporary racial order. Historically, many good people supported slavery and Jim Crow. Similarly, most color-blind whites who oppose (or have serious reservations about) affirmative action, believe that blacks' problems are mostly their own doing, and do not see anything wrong with their own white lifestyle are good people, too. The analytical issue, then, is examining how many whites subscribe to an ideology that ultimately helps preserve racial inequality rather than assessing how many hate or love blacks and other minorities.

. . . Since color-blind racism is the dominant racial ideology, its tentacles have touched us all and thus most readers will subscribe to some—if not most—of its tenets, use its style, and believe many of its racial stories. Unfortunately, there is little I can do to ease the pain of these readers, since when one writes and exposes an ideology that is at play, its supporters "get burned," so to speak. For readers in this situation (good people who may subscribe to many of the frames of color blindness), I urge a personal and political movement away from claiming to be "non-racist" to becoming "antiracist." Being an antiracist begins with understanding the institutional nature of racial matters and accepting that all actors in a racialized society are affected *materially* (receive benefits or disadvantages) and *ideologically* by the racial structure. This stand implies taking responsibility for your unwilling participation in these practices and beginning a new life committed to the goal of achieving real racial equality. The ride will be rough, but after your eyes have been opened, there is no point in standing still.

EDUARDO BONILLA-SILVA is a professor of sociology at Texas A&M University and the author of several books on race and ethnicity including *Racism without Racists* (Rowman & Littlefield, 2003).

EXPLORING THE ISSUE

Is the Emphasis on a Color-Blind Society an Answer to Racism?

Critical Thinking and Reflection

1. Define color-blind ideology.
2. What are the significant components of the color-blind ideology?
3. What are the goals of the proponents of America assuming a color-blind identity?
4. What are the challenges of creating a color-blind society? Explain.
5. How does Ward Connerly view racial classification? What are the functions of this classification?
6. What are the limits of color-blind ideology for racial minorities?
7. Locate contemporary examples to apply color-blind ideology.

Is There Common Ground?

The YES and NO selections by Connerly and Bonilla-Silva are reflective of the profound and persistent influence of racism in the historical development of American society. Both of these writers are focused on the question, how do we overcome racism in society? Given its troubled racial history, is a color-blind transformation of American society possible? One of the highlights of the civil rights movement was the speech delivered by Dr. Martin Luther King, Jr., during the March on Washington of August 1963. King notes that since color-conscious practices are the source of black disadvantage, policies that address these problems should be color-conscious. Exhibiting the soaring oratory to which the nation and world had become accustomed, this drum major of civil rights advocacy espoused a profound vision of an American future in which people are not judged by the color of their skins, but, rather, by the content of their character as they seek civil rights, equity, and respect for their humanity and human dignity within society. King's words have been used by both sides of the color-blind issue. Connerly would argue that if King were alive today, he would support the color-blind thesis. Bonilla-Silva, on the other hand, would argue that King would never recognize the current color-blind ideology as a basis for racial progress because of persistent race prejudice and discrimination within society. Does color-blind mean blind to racism? Is a color-blind vision utopian, or is it a pragmatic, achievable vision for the American future?

Additional Resources

Bonilla-Silva, Eduardo. 2003. *Racism without Racists: Color-Blind Racism and the Persistence of Racial Inequality in the United States* (Rowman & Littlefield).

Brodkin, Karen. 1999. *How Did Jews Become White Folks and What That Says About Race in America* (Rutgers University Press).

Cose, Ellis. 1998. *Color Blind: Seeing Beyond Race in a Race Obsessed World* (Harper Perennial).

Cuomo, Chris J. and Kim Q. Hall. 1999. *Whiteness: Feminist Philosophical Reflections* on *Who Is White?: Latinos, Asians, and the Black/Nonblack Divide* (Rowman & Littlefield Publishers).

Dobratz, Betty A. and Stephanie Shanks-Meile. 1997. *White Power, White Pride!: The White Separatist Movement in the United States* (Twayne Publishers).

Goldfield, D. R. 1990. *Black, White, and Southern: Race Relations and Southern Culture, 1940 to the Present* (Louisiana State University Press).

Guglielmo, Jennifer and Salvatore Salerno. 2003. *Are Italians White?: How Race Is Made in America* (Routledge).

Ignatiev, Noel. 2008. *How the Irish Became White* (Routledge).

King, Martin Luther. 1964. *Why We Can't Wait* (Harper Collins).

King, Martin Luther. 1967. *Where Do We Go from Here: Chaos or Community?* (Harper & Row).

King, Martin Luther. 1987. *Stride Toward Freedom* (Harper Collins).

Leonardo, Zeus. 2009. *Race, Whiteness, and Education* (Routledge).

Lovato, Robert. 2006. "A New Vision of Immigration." *The Nation* (March 6).

Mann, Coramae, Marjorie Zatz, and Nancy Rodriguez. 2006. *Images of Color, Images of Crime: Readings* (Oxford University Press).

Roediger, David. 2002. *Colored White: Transcending the Racial Past* (University of California Press).

Russell-Brown, Katheryn K. 2008. *The Color of Crime: Racial Hoaxes, White Fear, Black Protectionism, Police Harassment, and Other Macroaggressions* (New York University Press).

"The Obama Era: Post Racial or Most Racial?" 2011. The American Civil Rights Coalition (June). www .acrc1.org/media/The_Obama_Era_Post_Racial_or_ Most_Racial-5[2].pdf

Walker, Samuel, Cassia Spohn, and Miriam DeLeon. 2011. *The Color of Justice: Race, Ethnicity and Crime In America*, 5th ed. (Wadsworth Publishing).

Williams, Patricia. 1997. *Seeing a Color Blind Future* (Farrar, Straus and Giroux).

Wise, Tim. 2009. *Between Barack and a Hard Place: Racism and White Denial in the Age of Obama* (City Lights Publisher).

Wright, Lawrence. 1999. "One Drop of Blood." *The New Yorker* (July 12).

Yancey, George. 2006. *Beyond Racial Gridlock: Embracing Mutual Responsibility* (IVP Books).

Internet References . . .

American Civil Rights Coalition

http://www.acrc1.org/media/

American Civil Rights Institute

http://www.acri.org/

Journal of Blacks in Higher Education

http://www.jbhe.com/

Selected, Edited, and with Issue Framing Material by:
Wind Goodfriend, *Buena Vista University*

ISSUE

Does the Implicit Association Test (IAT) Measure Racial Prejudice?

YES: Shankar Vedantam, from "See No Bias," *The Washington Post* (2005)

NO: Amy Wax and Philip E. Tetlock, from "We Are All Racists at Heart," *The Wall Street Journal* (2005)

Learning Outcomes
After reading this issue, you will be able to:
• Understand the definition of implicit racial prejudice with regard to the Implicit Association Test.
• Discuss whether implicit racial prejudice results in discriminatory behavior.

ISSUE SUMMARY

YES: The performance of most white Americans on the Implicit Association Test reflects hidden or "implicit" racial prejudice. Since implicit prejudice can result in discriminatory behavior toward African Americans, it is appropriate to consider scores on the Implicit Association Test to be a form of racial prejudice.

NO: Most white Americans are aware of the negative stereotypes of African Americans that exist in American society, even though they may not believe those stereotypes to be true. So the performance of whites on the Implicit Association Test likely reflects their knowledge of these negative stereotypes, rather than true racial prejudice.

Since its introduction in 1998, the Implicit Association Test (IAT) has become one of the most well-known tests in social psychology. The test requires individuals to make a series of split-second judgments about stimuli that appear on a computer screen. The results of these judgments determine whether particular concepts have largely positive or negative associations. (If you are unfamiliar with the test, it may be helpful for you to take the online test for yourself at https://implicit.harvard.edu/implicit/). These associations are generally referred to as "implicit" associations because individuals may often be unaware of the nature of these associations.

There are many different versions of the IAT, which measures the implicit associations among many different types of concepts. However, the IAT is most frequently used to measure implicit prejudice. Implicit prejudice is generally considered to be an automatic, often unconscious, negative attitude toward a group, which can potentially influence how people react toward members of that group. Many social psychologists would contend that the performance of whites on the IAT is evidence of implicit racial prejudice against African Americans.

In the first selection, journalist Shankar Vedantam describes the research of Mahzarin Banaji and Anthony Greenwald, the two social psychologists who created the IAT. While Banaji and Greenwald believe that IAT scores should be interpreted with great caution, they contend that IAT scores may nonetheless reflect implicit racial prejudice. Also, there is significant evidence that implicit prejudice, as assessed by measures like the IAT, may result in discriminatory behavior. Since implicit prejudice can result in negative behavior toward African Americans, it is appropriate to consider an individual's score on the IAT to be a form of racial prejudice.

Amy Wax and Philip Tetlock argue that while the IAT does demonstrate that white Americans associate negative concepts with African Americans, these associations do not reflect true racial prejudice. Rather, these negative associations may simply reflect an awareness of the negative stereotypes of African Americans that exist in American culture. Since awareness of these stereotypes does not necessarily reflect the endorsement of prejudicial beliefs, it would be inappropriate to describe these associations as racial prejudice.

YES

Shankar Vedantam

See No Bias

At 4 o'clock on a recent wednesday afternoon, a 34-year-old white woman sat down in her Washington office to take a psychological test. Her office decor attested to her passion for civil rights—as a senior activist at a national gay rights organization, and as a lesbian herself, fighting bias and discrimination is what gets her out of bed every morning. A rainbow flag rested in a mug on her desk.

The woman brought up a test on her computer from a Harvard University Web site. It was really very simple: All it asked her to do was distinguish between a series of black and white faces. When she saw a black face she was to hit a key on the left, when she saw a white face she was to hit a key on the right. Next, she was asked to distinguish between a series of positive and negative words. Words such as "glorious" and "wonderful" required a left key, words such as "nasty" and "awful" required a right key. The test remained simple when two categories were combined: The activist hit the left key if she saw either a white face or a positive word, and hit the right key if she saw either a black face or a negative word.

Then the groupings were reversed. The woman's index fingers hovered over her keyboard. The test now required her to group black faces with positive words, and white faces with negative words. She leaned forward intently. She made no mistakes, but it took her longer to correctly sort the words and images.

Her result appeared on the screen, and the activist became very silent. The test found she had a bias for whites over blacks.

"It surprises me I have any preferences at all," she said. "By the work I do, by my education, my background. I'm progressive, and I think I have no bias. Being a minority myself, I don't feel I should or would have biases."

Although the activist had initially agreed to be identified, she and a male colleague who volunteered to take the tests requested anonymity after seeing their results. The man, who also is gay, did not show a race bias. But a second test found that both activists held biases against homosexuals—they more quickly associated words such as "humiliate" and "painful" with gays and words such as "beautiful" and "glorious" with heterosexuals.

If anything, both activists reasoned, they ought to have shown a bias in favor of gay people. The man's social life, his professional circle and his work revolve around gay culture. His home, he said, is in Washington's "gayborhood."

"I'm surprised," the woman said. She bit her lip. "And disappointed."

Mahzarin Banaji will never forget her own results the First Time She Took a Bias Test, now widely known as the Implicit Association Test. But whom could she blame? After all, she'd finally found what she was looking for.

Growing up in India, Banaji had studied psychophysics, the psychological representation of physical objects: A 20-watt bulb may be twice as bright as a 10-watt bulb, for example, but if the two bulbs are next to each another, a person may guess the difference is only 5 watts. Banaji enjoyed the precision of the field, but she realized that she found people and their behavior toward one another much more interesting. The problem was that there was no accurate way to gauge people's attitudes. You had to trust what they told you, and when it came to things such as prejudice—say, against blacks or poor people—people usually gave politically correct answers. It wasn't just that people lied to psychologists—when it came to certain sensitive topics, they often lied to themselves. Banaji began to wonder: Was it possible to create something that could divine what people really felt—even if they weren't aware of it themselves?

The results of one of Banaji's experiments as a young scholar at Yale University encouraged her. She and her colleagues replicated a well-known experiment devised by psychologist Larry Jacoby. Volunteers were first shown a list of unfamiliar names such as Sebastian Weisdorf. The volunteers later picked out that name when asked to identify famous people from a list of famous and unknown names. Because they had become familiar with the name, people mistakenly assumed Sebastian Weisdorf was a famous man. The experiment showed how subtle cues can cause errors without people's awareness.

Banaji and her colleagues came up with a twist. Instead of Sebastian Weisdorf, they asked, what if the name was Sally Weisdorf? It turned out that female names were less likely to elicit the false-fame error; volunteers did not say Sally Weisdorf was a famous woman. Women, it appeared, had to be more than familiar to be considered famous. Banaji had stumbled on an indirect measure of gender bias.

She began scouting for other techniques. In 1994, Anthony Greenwald, Banaji's PhD adviser and later her collaborator, came up with a breakthrough. Working out of the University of Washington, Greenwald drew up a list of 25 insect names such as wasp, cricket and cockroach, 25 flower names such as rose, tulip and daffodil, and a list of pleasant and unpleasant words. Given a random list of these words and told to sort them into the four groups, it was very easy to put each word in the right category. It was just as easy when insects were grouped with unpleasant words and flowers were grouped with pleasant words.

But when insects were grouped with pleasant words, and flowers with unpleasant words, the task became unexpectedly difficult. It was harder to hold a mental association of insects with words such as "dream," "candy" and "heaven," and flowers with words such as "evil," "poison" and "devil." It took longer to complete the task.

Psychologists have long used time differences to measure the relative difficulty of tasks. The new test produced astonishing results. Greenwald took the next step: Instead of insects and flowers, he used stereotypically white-sounding names such as Adam and Chip and black-sounding names such as Alonzo and Jamel and grouped them with the pleasant and unpleasant words. He ran the test on himself.

"I don't know whether to tell you I was elated or depressed," he says. "It was as if African American names were insect names and European American names were flower names. I had as much trouble pairing African American names with pleasant words as I did insect names with pleasant words."

Greenwald sent Banaji the computer test. She quickly discovered that her results were similar to his. Incredulous, she reversed the order of the names in the test. She switched the left and right keys. The answer wouldn't budge.

"I was deeply embarrassed," she recalls. "I was humbled in a way that few experiences in my life have humbled me."

The Implicit Association Test is designed to examine which words and concepts are strongly paired in people's minds. For example, "lightning" is associated with "thunder," rather than with "horses," just as "salt" is associated

with "pepper," "day" with "night." The reason Banaji and Greenwald still find it difficult to associate black faces with pleasant words, they believe, is the same reason it is harder to associate lightning with horses than with thunder. Connecting concepts that the mind perceives as incompatible simply takes extra time. The time difference can be quantified and, the creators of the test argue, is an objective measure of people's implicit attitudes.

For years, Banaji had told students that ugly prejudices were not just in other people but inside themselves. As Banaji stared at her results, the cliche felt viscerally true.

In time, other experiments would support the idea that these tests were more than just an interesting exercise: The tests were better predictors of many behaviors than people's explicit opinions were. They predicted preferences on matters of public policy—even ideological affiliations. Banaji and others soon developed tests for bias against gays, women and foreigners. The bias tests, which have now been taken by more than 2 million people, 90 percent of them American, and used in hundreds of research studies, have arguably revolutionized the study of prejudice. In their simplicity, the tests have raised provocative questions about this nation's ideal of a meritocracy and the nature of America's red state/blue state political divide. Civil rights activists say the tests have the potential to address some of the most corrosive problems of American society; critics, meanwhile, have simultaneously challenged the results and warned they could usher in an Orwellian world of thought crimes. Banaji has received death threats from supremacist groups; sensing that the tests can detect secrets, officials from the Central Intelligence Agency have made discreet inquiries.

The results of the millions of tests that have been taken anonymously on the Harvard Web site and other sites hint at the potential impact of the research. Analyses of tens of thousands of tests found 88 percent of white people had a pro-white or anti-black implicit bias; nearly 83 percent of heterosexuals showed implicit biases for straight people over gays and lesbians; and more than two-thirds of non-Arab, non-Muslim volunteers displayed implicit biases against Arab Muslims.

Overall, according to the researchers, large majorities showed biases for Christians over Jews, the rich over the poor, and men's careers over women's careers. The results contrasted sharply with what most people said about themselves—that they had no biases. The tests also revealed another unsettling truth: Minorities internalized the same biases as majority groups. Some 48 percent of blacks showed a pro-white or anti-black bias; 36 percent of Arab Muslims showed an anti-Muslim bias; and 38 percent of gays and lesbians showed a bias for straight people over homosexuals.

"The Implicit Association Test measures the thumb-print of the culture on our minds," says Banaji, one of three researchers who developed the test and its most ardent proponent. "If Europeans had been carted to Africa as slaves, blacks would have the same beliefs about whites that whites now have about blacks."

As the tests have been refined, replicated and reinterpreted over the past decade, they have challenged many popular notions—beginning with the increasingly common assertion that discrimination is a thing of the past.

The research has also upset notions of how prejudice can best be addressed. Through much of the 20th century, activists believed that biases were merely errors of conscious thought that could be corrected through education. This hopeful idea is behind the popularity of diversity training. But Banaji suggests such training relies on the wrong idea of how people form biases.

There is likely a biological reason people so quickly make assumptions—good or bad—about others, Banaji says. The implicit system is likely a part of the "primitive" brain, designed to be reactive rather than reasoned. It specializes in quick generalizations, not subtle distinctions. Such mental shortcuts probably helped our ancestors survive. It was more important when they encountered a snake in the jungle to leap back swiftly than to deduce whether the snake belonged to a poisonous species. The same mental shortcuts in the urban jungles of the 21st century are what cause people to form unwelcome stereotypes about other people, Banaji says. People revert to the shortcuts simply because they require less effort. But powerful as such assumptions are, they are far from permanent, she says. The latest research, in fact, suggests these attitudes are highly malleable.

Such reassurance has not assuaged test takers, who are frequently shocked by their results. The tests are stupid, and the results are wrong, some say. People have argued that the tests are measures of only hand-eye coordination or manual dexterity. Some have complained about which groups are assigned to the left- and right-hand keys, and about how the computer switches those categories. None of these factors has any real impact on the results, but Banaji believes the complaints are a sign of embarrassment. Americans find evidence of implicit bias particularly galling, Banaji theorizes, because more than any other nation, America is obsessed with the ideal of fairness. Most of the people approached for this article declined to participate. Several prominent politicians, Republican and Democrat, declined to take the tests for this article. The aide to one senator bristled, "You think he is a racist!"

But the tests do not measure actions. The race test, for example, does not measure racism as much as a race bias. Banaji is the first to say people ought to be judged by how they behave, not how they think. She tells incredulous volunteers who show biases that it does not mean they will always act in biased ways—people can consciously override their biases. But she also acknowledges a sad finding of the research: Although people may wish to act in egalitarian ways, implicit biases are a powerful predictor of how they actually behave.

People who find their way to the Harvard Web site that hosts the Implicit Association Test are asked a few questions about themselves. The tests are anonymous, but volunteers are asked about their sex, race and whether they consider themselves liberal or conservative.

The voluntary questionnaires have allowed Banaji and her colleagues to arrive at one of the most provocative conclusions of the research: Conservatives, on average, show higher levels of bias against gays, blacks and Arabs than liberals, says Brian Nosek, a psychologist at the University of Virginia and a principal IAT researcher with Greenwald and Banaji. In turn, bias against blacks and Arabs predicts policy preferences on affirmative action and racial profiling. This suggests that implicit attitudes affect more than snap judgments—they play a role in positions arrived at after careful consideration.

Brian Jones, a Republican National Committee spokesman, says the findings are interesting in an academic context but questions whether they have much relevance in the real world. "It's interesting to ponder how people implicitly make decisions, but ultimately we live in a world where explicit thoughts and actions are the bottom line," he says. Volunteers drawn to the tests were not a random sample of Americans, Jones adds, cautioning against reading too much into the conclusions.

Though it's true that about two-thirds of test takers lean liberal, Banaji says, the sample sizes are so large that randomness is not a serious concern. And Andy Poehlman, a graduate student at Yale, has tracked 61 academic studies using the IAT to explore how implicit attitudes predict people's actions.

When volunteers who took the race bias test were given the option to work with a white or black partner, one study found, those with the strongest implicit bias scores on the test tended to choose a white partner. Another study found that volunteers with lower bias scores against gays were more willing to interact with a stranger holding a book with an obviously gay theme. A third experiment found that when volunteers were told that another person was gay, those whose scores indicated more bias against gays were more likely to avoid eye contact and show other signs of unfriendliness. A study in Germany by psychologist Arnd Florack found that volunteers whose results suggested more bias against Turks—an immigrant group—were more likely to find a Turkish suspect guilty when asked to make a judgment about criminality in an ambiguous situation.

In another study by psychologist Robert W. Livingston at the University of Wisconsin, Poehlman says, volunteers were given details of a crime in which a Milwaukee woman had been assaulted, suffered a concussion and required several stitches. In this case, Poehlman says, some volunteers were told the perpetrator had been proven to be David Edmonds from Canada. Others were told the guilty perpetrator was Juan Luis Martinez from Mexico. Volunteers were asked what length of sentence was appropriate for the crime: Bias scores against Hispanics on the implicit tests tended to predict a longer sentence for the Mexican.

An implicit attitude "doesn't control our behavior in a be-all and end-all kind of way, but it flavors our behavior in a pretty consistent way," says Poehlman.

In perhaps the most dramatic real-world correlate of the bias tests, economists at the Massachusetts Institute of Technology and the University of Chicago recently sent out 5,000 résumés to 1,250 employers who had help-wanted ads in Chicago and Boston. The résumés were culled from Internet Web sites and mailed out with one crucial change: Some applicants were given stereotypically white-sounding names such as Greg; others were given black-sounding names such as Tyrone.

Interviews beforehand with human resources managers at many companies in Boston and Chicago had led the economists to believe that black applicants would be more likely to get interview calls: Employers said they were hungry for qualified minorities and were aggressively seeking diversity. Every employer got four résumés: an average white applicant, an average black applicant, a highly skilled white applicant and a highly skilled black applicant.

The economists measured only one outcome: Which résumés triggered callbacks?

To the economists' surprise, the résumés with white-sounding names triggered 50 percent more callbacks than résumés with black-sounding names. Furthermore, the researchers found that the high-quality black résumés drew no more calls than the average black résumés. Highly skilled candidates with white names got more calls than average white candidates, but lower-skilled candidates with white names got many more callbacks than even highly skilled black applicants.

"Fifty percent? That's huge," says Sendhil Mullainathan, an economist who led the study and who recently moved to Harvard to work with Banaji. Human resources managers were stunned by the results, he says. Explicit bias, says Mullainathan, can occur not only without the intent to discriminate, but despite explicit desires to recruit minorities. Implicit attitudes need only sway a few decisions to have large impact, he says. For example, if implicit bias caused a recruiter to set one résumé aside, it could be just one of 100 decisions the recruiter made that day. Collectively, however, such decisions can have dramatically large consequences.

Banaji says that researchers have shown the implicit tests are measuring more than mere awareness of bias, through studies that cancel out the effects of familiarity.

"Is the IAT picking up something about the culture?" Banaji asks. "Yes, but it is picking up that aspect of the culture that has gotten into your brain and mind."

On the race test, for example, a sophisticated brain-imaging study showed that implicit bias tests can predict fear responses among volunteers. Banaji and New York University neural scientist Elizabeth Phelps had white volunteers take the implicit race bias test and then undergo sophisticated brain scans called fMRIs, which measure instantaneous changes in brain activity. Those with the most bias on the implicit tests showed the most activity in the brain area called the amygdala, when photos of black faces, obtained from college yearbooks, were flashed before their eyes. The amygdala is part of the primitive brain involved with fear responses.

But the critics persist. Philip Tetlock, a professor of organizational behavior in the business school at the University of California at Berkeley, and Ohio State University psychology professor Hal Arkes argue that Jesse Jackson might score poorly on the test. They cite the civil rights leader's statement a decade ago that there was nothing more painful at that stage of his life "than to walk down the street and hear footsteps and start thinking about robbery. Then look around and see somebody white and feel relieved."

If a prominent black civil rights leader could hold such a bias, Tetlock and Arkes ask, what do bias scores really mean? Whatever the IAT is measuring, Tetlock and Arkes argue, it is not what people would call discrimination—no one would dream of accusing Jesse Jackson of harboring feelings of hostility toward African Americans.

Banaji says Tetlock and Arkes are relying on an outmoded notion of discrimination. The IAT research shows that hostility is not needed for discrimination to occur. Women and minorities can just as easily harbor biases, absorbed from the larger culture, that can lead them to discriminate against people like themselves.

Tetlock says he thinks the IAT research project is drawing conclusions much more sweeping than are justified.

"One of the key points in contention is not a psychological point, it is a political point," says Tetlock. "It is where we are going to set our threshold of proof for saying something represents prejudice. My view is the implicit prejudice program sets the threshold at a historical low."

By the standards of slavery and segregation, the critics argue, delays in mental associations are trivial. "We've come a long way from Selma, Alabama, if we have to calibrate prejudice in milliseconds," says Tetlock.

But the biases that the tests uncover are not trivial, Banaji counters. Their consequences, while subtler, could be devastating. In settings such as the criminal justice system, she argues, lives may hang in the balance.

In their most controversial argument, Tetlock and Arkes asked whether some implicit biases might simply be politically incorrect truths. By comparing national statistics of violent crime against census figures of different ethnic groups, the researchers argued it was more likely for a violent crime to be perpetrated by an African American man than a white man. Would it not therefore be rational, they asked, for people to hold biases against blacks?

Even here, however, rationality did not appear to be the prime mover, Banaji argues. Even if whites and blacks committed crimes at exactly the same rate, Banaji says, people would assign greater weight to the black crimes. This phenomenon is known as an illusory correlation: Aberrational behavior by a member of a minority group is not only given greater prominence in the mind but is also more easily associated with the entire group, rather than just the individual. "When in-groups do bad things, we think it is individual behavior or circumstance," says Jerry Kang, a UCLA law professor who is interested in policy applications of the research. "I screw up because it is a bad day; others screw up because they are incompetent."

***

SHANKAR VEDANTAM is a writer and journalist for *The Washington Post*.

Amy Wax and Philip E. Tetlock    **NO**

We Are All Racists at Heart

It was once easy to spot a racial bigot: The casual use of the n-word, the sweeping hostility, and the rigid unwillingness to abandon vulgar stereotypes left little doubt that a person harbored prejudice toward blacks as a group. But 50 years of survey research has shown a sharp decline in overt racial prejudice. Instead of being a cause for celebration, however, this trend has set off an ever more strident insistence in academia that whites are pervasively biased.

Some psychologists went low-tech: They simply expanded the definition of racism to include any endorsement of politically conservative views grounded in the values of self-reliance and individual responsibility. Opposition to busing, affirmative action or generous welfare programs were tarred as manifestations of "modern" or symbolic racism.

Others took a high-tech path: Racists could be identified by ignoring expressed beliefs and tapping into the workings of the unconscious mind. Thus was born the so-called "implicit association test." The IAT builds on the fact that people react faster to the word "butter" if they have just seen the word "bread" momentarily flashed on a screen. The quicker response suggests that the mind closely associates those concepts. Applying this technique, researchers such as Mahzarin Banaji of Harvard have found that people recognize "negative" words such as "angry," "criminal" or "poor" more quickly after being momentarily exposed to a black (as opposed to a white) face. And this effect holds up for the vast majority of white respondents—and sometimes even for majorities of blacks.

What do investigators conclude from their findings that "blackness" often primes bad associations and "whiteness" good ones? According to some, it shows that prejudice permeates our unconscious minds and is not just confined to the 10% of hard-core bigots. Know it or not, we are all vessels of racial bias. From this sweeping conclusion, based on a small if intriguing scientific finding, social scientists, legal scholars, opinion leaders and "diversity experts" leap from thought to conduct and from unconscious association to harmful actions. Because most of us are biased, these individuals claim, we can safely assume that every aspect of social life—every school, institution, organization and workplace—is a bastion of discrimination. The most strenuous measures, whether they be diversity programs, bureaucratic oversight, accountability or guilt-ridden self-monitoring, cannot guarantee a level playing field.

What is wrong with this picture? In the first place, split-second associations between negative stimuli and minority group images don't necessarily imply unconscious bias. Such associations may merely reflect awareness of common cultural stereotypes. Not everyone who knows the stereotypes necessarily endorses them.

Or the associations might reflect simple awareness of the social reality: Some groups are more disadvantaged than others, and more individuals in these groups are likely to behave in undesirable ways. Consider the two Jesses—Jackson and Helms. Both know that the black family is in trouble, that crime rates in this community are far too high, and that black educational test scores are too low. That common awareness might lead to sympathy, to indifference, or to hostility. Because the IAT can distinguish none of these parameters, both kinds of Jesses often get similar, failing scores on tests of unconscious association.

Measures of unconscious prejudice are especially untrustworthy predictors of discriminatory behavior. MIT psychologist Michael Norton has recently noted that there is virtually no published research showing a systematic link between racist attitudes, overt or subconscious, and real-world discrimination. A few studies show that openly-biased persons sometimes favor whites over blacks in simulations of job hiring and promotion. But no research demonstrates that, after subtracting the influence of residual old-fashioned prejudice, split-second reactions in the laboratory predict real-world decisions. On the contrary, the few results available suggest that persons who are "high bias" on subconscious criteria are no more likely than others to treat minorities badly and may sometimes even favor them.

There is likewise no credible proof that actual business behavior is pervasively influenced by unconscious racial prejudice. This should not be surprising. Demonstrating racial bias is no easy matter because there is often no straightforward way to detect discrimination of any kind, let alone discrimination that is hidden from those doing the deciding. As anyone who has ever tried a job-discrimination case knows, showing that an organization is systematically skewed against members of one group requires a benchmark for how each worker would be treated if race or sex never entered the equation. This in turn depends on defining the standards actually used to judge performance, a task that often requires meticulous data collection and abstruse statistical analysis.

Assuming everyone is biased makes the job easy: The problem of demonstrating actual discrimination goes away and claims of discrimination become irrefutable. Anything short of straight group representation—equal outcomes rather than equal opportunity—is "proof" that the process is unfair.

Advocates want to have it both ways. On the one hand, any steps taken against discrimination are by definition insufficient, because good intentions and traditional checks on workplace prejudice can never eliminate unconscious bias. On the other, researchers and "diversity experts" purport to know what's needed and do not hesitate to recommend more expensive and strenuous measures to purge pervasive racism. There is no more evidence that such efforts dispel supposed unconscious racism than that such racism affects decisions in the first place.

But facts have nothing to do with it. What began as science has morphed into unassailable faith. However we think, feel or act, and however much apparent progress has been made, there is no hope for us. We are all racists at heart.

Amy Wax is a professor of law at the University of Pennsylvania Law School. She has authored over 20 publications on topics including social welfare law and the relationships among the family, the workplace, and labor markets.

Philip E. Tetlock is a professor of organizational behavior at the University of California, Berkeley. He also currently holds the Lorraine Tyson Mitchell Chair in leadership and communication. He is the author of dozens of publications, including nine books. He has also won numerous awards for his research that explores the role of psychological processes in political science.

EXPLORING THE ISSUE

Does the Implicit Association Test (IAT) Measure Racial Prejudice?

Critical Thinking and Reflection

1. If you have already taken the IAT, consider how you felt about your performance. Were you disappointed or upset by your score? Do you think that your score reflected something important about your own attitudes and beliefs?
2. Why do you think that so many whites have negative implicit associations toward African Americans? What is the source of these negative associations?
3. Do you think implicit prejudice results in discriminatory behavior? If so, how might you combat this form of discrimination?

Is There Common Ground?

The Implicit Association Test is probably the most controversial measure within all of social psychology. Extremely popular within some circles for measuring "implicit" attitudes, some researchers view it at creative and extremely useful for measuring prejudices that individuals may not want to admit—even to themselves. Critics of the IAT are not necessarily arguing that it is entirely useless; instead, they are warning that interpretations of the results should be made with caution. Results may not indicate endorsement or agreement with stereotypes or prejudice, but simply knowledge of those stereotypes instead. This is one explanation for why some minority group members appear to provide results indicating that they are prejudiced against their own group. However, IAT proponents argue that this result really indicates "internalized prejudice" and can be interpreted as indicating unconscious negative views. The common ground here may not be how to interpret results from an IAT test, but instead that—at the very least—the IAT reveals some interesting individual differences that could predict certain patterns of behavior.

Additional Resources

Greenwald, A. G., McGhee, D. E., & Schwartz, J. K. L. (1998). Measuring individual differences in implicit cognition: The implicit association test. *Journal of Personality & Social Psychology, 74,* 1464–1480.

Nosek, B. A., & Hansen, J. J. (2008). The associations in our heads belong to us: Searching for attitudes and knowledge in implicit evaluation. *Cognition and Emotion, 22,* 553–594.

Nosek, B. A., & Hansen, J. J. (2008). Personalizing the Implicit Association Test increases explicit evaluation of the target concepts. *European Journal of Psychological Assessment, 25,* 226–236.

Internet References . . .

American Psychological Association: The IAT

http://www.apa.org/monitor/2008/07-08/psychometric.aspx

Project Implicit

http://projectimplicit.net/index.html

Project Implicit: Take a Test

https://implicit.harvard.edu/implicit/takeatest.html

Selected, Edited, and with Issue Framing Material by:
Wind Goodfriend, *Buena Vista University*

ISSUE

Do Whites Associate Privilege with Their Skin Color?

YES: Paul Kivel, from *Uprooting Racism: How White People Can Work for Racial Justice* New Society Publishers (1995)

NO: Tim Wise, from "The Absurdity (and Consistency) of White Denial: What Kind of Card Is Race?" counterpunch.org (2006)

Learning Outcomes

After reading this issue, you will be able to:

- Comprehend how white skin privilege is concretely manifested within society according to Kivel and Wise.
- Critically examine how skin color has been fundamental to the determination of racial identity in American culture.
- Establish the relationship between white skin privilege and racial discrimination.
- Critically examine the evidence that is presented in support of the claim of white skin privilege.
- Examine the contribution of white skin privilege to the existence of disadvantaged minorities in the United States.
- Explain the difficulties many whites face in accepting the contention that white skin privilege is a fact of life in America.
- Explain the meaning and function of the "race card."

ISSUE SUMMARY

YES: Paul Kivel, a teacher, writer, and antiviolence/antiracist activist, asserts that many benefits accrue to whites solely on the basis of skin color. These benefits range from economic to political advantages and so often include better residential choice, police protection, and education opportunities.

NO: Tim Wise, an author of two books on race, argues that whites do not acknowledge privilege. Instead, whites are often convinced that the race card is "played" by blacks to gain their own privilege, something that whites cannot do. Hence, whites simply do not see discrimination and do not attach privilege to their skin color.

W. E. B. DuBois has reminded us of the centrality of skin color when he noted that issues of color would dominate human relations of the twentieth century. In the United States, African American children tend to exhibit a keen understanding of the impact of color in race relations when they repeat the following line from blues singer Big Bill Broonzy's 1951 composition, "Black, Brown, and White":

> If you're white, you're alright!
> If you're brown, stick around!
> And, if you're black, get back!

These lines were uttered routinely by black American children during their developmental years during the Jim Crow era. It reminds us of the salience of skin color for racial identity.

There is a consensus view among scholars that racial distinctions were not a primary factor influencing human relations in the premodern world. The more substantial influence of race within society tends to be a more recent phenomenon influencing modern cultures and civilizations, especially institutional arrangements such as slavery and segregation. So, the issue of white skin privilege falls in the larger context of race identity in American history.

The history of race relations within the United States is properly examined by employing a white super-ordination black-subordination paradigm. Many Americans have grown accustomed to blacks occupying the lower strata of American class structure. Some Americans tend to view this pattern of race relations as normal. Whites who are accustomed to the social reality, which has been presented here, are challenged to rationalize their position within society. Denial of the existence of privilege is a significant component of this rationalization.

Clearly, the formation of racial consciousness and its impact upon society are vital areas of scholarly investigation in a world characterized by nations of increasing racial/ethnic diversity. Naomi Zack, in *Thinking about Race*, explains the rise of whiteness studies in perspective. Most recent immigration and demographic trends have led to what has been called "the browning of America." A significant increase in Latino and Asian immigration, along with white–nonwhite intermarriage, symbolizes the decrease in the number of whites as a majority. Many scholars see this browning as having the effect of stimulating an increase of white self-awareness.

Throughout the world, although whites do not constitute a majority, they are a dominant group (people who have the most wealth, power, and possessions). This is an important sociological consideration. The reality of privilege is so embedded within dominant group status that to recognize and admit its reality is alien to most whites. Whites are often asked to think about race from a minority point of view. Throughout one's years of formal education, there is an emphasis upon tolerance and understanding, which enable dominant-group whites to appreciate minority-group experiences. Despite the built-in limitations of viewing things from the point of view of another race, color shifting can enable one to view one's own race differently.

Paul Kivel sees race privilege as white, middle-class privilege. It is not something to be earned; it is viewed as a birthright. It comes with economic, social, and political benefits. Tim Wise, in contrast, argues that whites are oblivious to the notion of skin privilege. Further, he uses the white allegation of "playing the race card," which is directed at blacks, to demonstrate that whites do not think that skin privilege exists.

Many Americans believe that white skin privilege is a myth. It is common for such persons to assert that if such a privilege existed in the past, it would have been overtaken by the reforms of the civil rights era and the color-blind, race-neutral (deracialized) environment that has resulted from these developments. Such observers of current social trends tend to cite the significant expansion of the African American middle class, the more visible presence of blacks and other people of color within American institutions, most especially within the professions, and the increasing profile of black and minority athletes in support of their claim.

These assertions of racial progress, while valid, do not answer the question of whether or not white skin privilege exists. There is copious empirical evidence that significant inequity in such vital areas as wealth, income, education, employment, etc., exists between whites and people of color, especially blacks and Latinos. Both groups are disproportionately represented within the lower strata of the class structure. How does one explain this persistent advantage of whites over others? Is it due to white intellectual superiority? Can it be explained by the assertion that whites are more industrious and motivated? Or, is white skin privilege part of it?

The emerging body of literature on whiteness studies raises questions of privilege in the context of being white. Wise links this with white denial of racism and a "blaming the victim" attitude of blacks. He writes that blacks use racism as a crutch for their own inadequacies. In contrast, Kivel's straightforward presentation lists how whites benefit directly from color. He does not consider denial of racism and neither does he view playing the race card as a factor in white privilege.

This issue will challenge students in several ways. First, the notion of white privilege should expand the boundaries of the discussion of race relations. Second, unlike most issues in this edition, the positions elicited are not strongly opposite to each other. By using Kivel and Wise's concepts, the student will need to deconstruct the concepts and challenge both pieces. Kivel and Wise both write about white privilege and their ideas overlap. At the same time, Wise interprets the attitude held by whites that there is no such thing as white skin privilege. Historically, since race in the United States has been divided into black or white—one had to be either—a black person was defined as someone having black ancestors. The increasing diversity of the American population has rendered traditional race and ethnic categories, regardless of how familiar they are, inadequate. Expanded populations of Asians, Hispanics, and Middle Easterners, for example, challenge the traditional black–white dichotomy employed in research on race relations. The historical mixing of the races that occurred in the United States resulted in the rule of hypo-descent, or "the one drop rule," and rigidly enforced the black–white dichotomy. Intermarriage across racial lines is undermining the black–white dichotomy in research.

Why, in the American experience, did mixed-race people become categorized as black? How would you define whiteness? Why do blacks and whites have such divergent views on racial matters? Is the emphasis on examining white privilege another way to argue for minorities and against the majority group? Is white skin privilege a functional form of discrimination?

YES

Paul Kivel

Uprooting Racism: How White People Can Work for Racial Justice

White Benefits, Middle-Class Privilege

It is not necessarily a privilege to be white*, but it certainly has its benefits. That's why so many of us gave up our unique histories, primary languages, accents, distinctive dress, family names and cultural expressions. It seemed like a small price to pay for acceptance in the circle of whiteness. Even with these sacrifices it wasn't easy to pass as white if we were Italian, Greek, Irish, Jewish, Spanish, Hungarian, or Polish. Sometimes it took generations before our families were fully accepted, and then usually because white society had an even greater fear of darker skinned people.

Privileges are the economic "extras" that those of us who are middle class and wealthy gain at the expense of poor and working class people of all races. Benefits, on the other hand, are the advantages that all white people gain at the expense of people of color regardless of economic position. Talk about racial benefits can ring false to many of us who don't have the economic privileges that we see many in this society enjoying. But just because we don't have the economic privileges of those with more money doesn't mean we haven't enjoyed some of the benefits of being white.

We can generally count on police protection rather than harassment. Depending on our financial situation, we can choose where we want to live and choose neighborhoods that are safe and have decent schools. We are given more attention, respect and status in conversations than people of color. We see people who look like us in the media, history books, news and music in a positive light. (This is more true for men than for women, more

true for the rich than the poor.) We have more recourse to, and credibility within, the legal system (again taking into account class and gender). Nothing that we do is qualified, limited, discredited or acclaimed simply because of our racial background. We don't have to represent our race, and nothing we do is judged as a credit to our race, or as confirmation of its shortcomings or inferiority. There are always mitigating factors, and some of us have these benefits more than others. All else being equal, it pays to be white. We will be accepted, acknowledged and given the benefit of the doubt. Since all else is not equal we each receive different benefits or different levels of the same benefits from being white.

These benefits start early. Most of them apply less to white girls than white boys, but they are still substantial. Others will have higher expectations for us as children, both at home and at school. We will have more money spent on our education, we will be called on more in school, we will be given more opportunity and resources to learn. We will see people like us in the textbooks, and if we get into trouble adults will expect us to be able to change and improve, and therefore will discipline or penalize us less or differently than children of color.

These benefits continue today and work to the direct economic advantage of every white person in the United States. First of all, we will earn more in our lifetime than a person of color of similar qualifications. We will be paid $1.00 for every $.60 that a person of color makes. We will advance faster and more reliably as well.

There are historically derived economic benefits too. All the land in this country was taken from Native Americans. Much of the infrastructure of this country was built by slave labor, incredibly low-paid labor, or by prison labor

---

*I draw on important work on privilege done by Peggy McIntosh, "White Privilege and Male Privilege: A Personal Account of Coming to See Correspondences through Work in Women's Studies," Center for Research on Women, Wellesley College, MA 02181 (1988), as well as material from *Helping Teens Stop Violence*, Allan Creighton with Paul Kivel, Hunter House, Alameda CA (1992).

---

performed by men and women of color. Much of the housecleaning, childcare, cooking and maintenance of our society has been done by low-wage earning women of color. Further property and material goods were appropriated by whites through the colonization of the West and Southwest throughout the 19th century, through the internment of Japanese Americans during World War II, through racial riots against people of color in the 18th, 19th and 20th centuries, and through an ongoing legacy of legal manipulation and exploitation. Today men and women and children of color still do the hardest, lowest paid, most dangerous work throughout the country. And we white people, again depending on our relative economic circumstances, enjoy plentiful and inexpensive food, clothing and consumer goods because of that exploitation.

We have been taught history through a white-tinted lens which has minimized our exploitation of people of color and extolled the hardworking, courageous qualities of white people. For example, many of our foreparents gained a foothold in this country by finding work in such trades as railroads, streetcars, construction, shipbuilding, wagon and coach driving, house painting, tailoring, longshore work, brick laying, table waiting, working in the mills, furriering or dressmaking. These were all occupations that Blacks, who had begun entering many such skilled and unskilled jobs, were either excluded from or pushed out of in the 19th century. Exclusion and discrimination, coupled with immigrant mob violence against Blacks in many northern cities (such as the anti-black draft riots of 1863), meant that recent immigrants had economic opportunities that Blacks did not. These gains were consolidated by explicitly racist trade union practices and policies which kept Blacks in the most unskilled labor and lowest paid work.

It is not that white Americans have not worked hard and built much. We have. But we did not start out from scratch. We went to segregated schools and universities built with public money. We received school loans, V.A. loans, housing and auto loans when people of color were excluded or heavily discriminated against. We received federal jobs, military jobs and contracts when only whites were allowed. We were accepted into apprenticeships, training programs and unions when access for people of color was restricted or nonexistent.

Much of the rhetoric against more active policies for racial justice stem from the misconception that we are all given equal opportunities and start from a level playing field. We often don't even see the benefits we have received from racism. We claim that they are not there.

Think about your grandparents and parents and where they grew up and lived as adults. What work did

they do? What are some of the benefits that have accrued to your family because they were white?

Look at the following benefits checklist. Put a check beside any benefit that you enjoy that a person of color of your age, gender and class probably does not. Think about what effect not having that benefit would have had on your life. (If you don't know the answer to any of these questions, research. Ask family members. Do what you can to discover the answers.)

White Benefits Checklist

- My ancestors were legal immigrants to this country during a period when immigrants from Asia, South and Central America or Africa were restricted.
- My ancestors came to this country of their own free will and have never had to relocate unwillingly once here.
- I live on land that formerly belonged to Native Americans.
- My family received homesteading or landstaking claims from the federal government.
- I or my family or relatives receive or received federal farm subsidies, farm price supports, agricultural extension assistance or other federal benefits.
- I lived or live in a neighborhood that people of color were discriminated from living in.
- I lived or live in a city where red-lining discriminates against people of color getting housing or other loans.
- I or my parents went to racially segregated schools.
- I live in a school district or metropolitan area where more money is spent on the schools that white children go to than on those that children of color attend.
- I live in or went to a school district where children of color are more likely to be disciplined than white children, or more likely to be tracked into nonacademic programs.
- I live in or went to a school district where the textbooks and other classroom materials reflected my race as normal, heroes and builders of the United States, and there was little mention of the contributions of people of color to our society.
- I was encouraged to go on to college by teachers, parents or other advisors.
- I attended a publicly funded university, or a heavily endowed private university or college, and/or received student loans.
- I served in the military when it was still racially segregated, or achieved a rank where there were few people of color, or served in a combat situation where there were large numbers of people of color in dangerous combat positions.

- My ancestors were immigrants who took jobs in railroads, streetcars, construction, shipbuilding, wagon and coach driving, house painting, tailoring, longshore work, brick laying, table waiting, working in the mills, furriering, dressmaking or any other trade or occupation where people of color were driven out or excluded.
- I received job training in a program where there were few or no people of color.
- I have received a job, job interview, job training or internship through personal connections of family or friends.
- I worked or work in a job where people of color made less for doing comparable work or did more menial jobs.
- I have worked in a job where people of color were hired last, or fired first.
- I work in a job, career or profession, or in an agency or organization in which there are few people of color.
- I received small business loans or credits, government contracts or government assistance in my business.
- My parents were able to vote in any election they wanted without worrying about poll taxes, literacy requirements or other forms of discrimination.
- I can always vote for candidates who reflect my race.
- I live in a neighborhood that has better police protection, municipal services and is safer than that where people of color live.
- The hospital and medical services close to me or which I use are better than that of most people of color in the region in which I live.
- I have never had to worry that clearly labeled public facilities, such as swimming pools, restrooms, restaurants and nightspots were in fact not open to me because of my skin color.
- I see white people in a wide variety of roles on television and in movies.
- My race needn't be a factor in where I choose to live.
- My race needn't be a factor in where I send my children to school.
- I don't need to think about race and racism everyday. I can choose when and where I want to respond to racism.

What feelings come up for you when you think about the benefits that white people gain from racism? Do you feel angry or resentful? Guilty or uncomfortable? Do you want to say "Yes, but . . . "?

Again, the purpose of this checklist is not to discount what we, our families and foreparents, have achieved. But we do need to question any assumptions we retain that everyone started out with equal opportunity.

You may be thinking at this point, "If I'm doing so well how come I'm barely making it?" Some of the benefits listed previously are money in the bank for each and every one of us. Some of us have bigger bank accounts—much bigger. According to 1989 figures, 1 percent of the population controls about 40 percent of the wealth of this country (*New York Times,* April 17, 1995 "Gap in Wealth in United States called Widest in West"). In 1992, women generally made about 66 cents for every dollar that men made (Women's Action Coalition p. 59).

Benefits from racism are amplified or diminished by our relative privilege. People with disabilities, people with less formal education, and people who are lesbian, gay or bi-sexual are generally discriminated against in major ways. All of us benefit in some ways from whiteness, but some of us have cornered the market on significant benefits from being white to the exclusion of the rest of us.

The opposite of a benefit is a disadvantage. People of color face distinct disadvantages many of which have to do with discrimination and violence. If we were to talk about running a race for achievement and success in this country, and white people and people of color lined up side by side as a group, then every white benefit would be steps ahead of the starting line and every disadvantage would be steps backwards from the starting line before the race even began.

The disadvantages of being a person of color in the United States today include personal insults, harassment, discrimination, economic and cultural exploitation, stereotypes and invisibility, as well as threats, intimidation and violence. Not every person of color has experienced all the disadvantages described below, but they each have experienced some of them, and they each experience the vulnerability to violence that being a person of color in this country entails.

Institutional racism is discussed in detail in parts five, six, and seven. But the personal acts of harassment and discrimination experienced directly from individual white people can also take a devastating toll. People of color never know when they will be called names, ridiculed or have comments made to them or about them by white people they don't know. They don't know when they might hear that they should leave the country, go home or go back to where they came from. Often these comments are made in situations where it isn't safe to confront the person who made the remark.

People of color also have to be ready to respond to teachers, employers or supervisors who have stereotypes, prejudices or lowered expectations about them. Many have been discouraged or prevented from pursuing academic or work goals or have been placed in lower vocational levels because of their racial identity. They have to be prepared for receiving less respect, attention or response from a doctor, police officer, court official, city official or other professional. They are not unlikely to be mistrusted or accused of stealing, cheating or lying, or to be stopped by the police because of their racial identity. They may also experience employment or housing discrimination or know someone who has.

There are cultural costs as well. People of color see themselves portrayed in degrading, stereotypical and fear-inducing ways on television and in the movies. They may have important religious or cultural holidays which are not recognized where they work or go to school. They have seen their religious practices, music, art, mannerisms, dress and other customs distorted, "borrowed," ridiculed, exploited or otherwise degraded by white people.

If they protest they may be verbally attacked by whites for being too sensitive, too emotional or too angry. Or they may be told they are different from other people of their racial group. Much of what people of color do, or say, or how they act in racially mixed company is judged as representative of their race.

On top of all this they have to live with the threat of physical violence. Some are the survivors of racial violence or have had close friends or family who are. People of color experience the daily toll of having to plan out how they are going to respond to racist comments and racial discrimination whenever it might occur.

In the foot race referred to above for jobs, educational opportunities or housing, each of these disadvantages would represent a step backward from the starting line *before the race even started*.

Although all people of color have experienced some of the disadvantages mentioned above, other factors make a difference in how vulnerable a person of color is to the effects of racism. Economic resources help buffer some of the more egregious effects of racism. Depending upon where one lives, women and men from different racial identities are treated differently. Discrimination varies in form and ranges from mild to severe depending on one's skin color, ethnicity, level of education, location, gender, sexual orientation, physical ability, age and how these are responded to by white people and white-run institutions.

Is it hard for you to accept that this kind of pervasive discrimination still occurs in this country? Which of the above statements is particularly hard to accept?

There is ample documentation for each of the effects of racism on people of color listed above. In many work-shops we do a stand-up exercise using a list of disadvantages for people of color to respond to. Those of us who are white are often surprised and disturbed about how many people of color stand when asked if they have experienced these things.

Most of us would like to think that today we have turned the tide and people of color have caught up with white people. We would like to believe (and are often told by other white people) that they enjoy the same opportunities as the rest of us. If we honestly add up the benefits of whiteness and the disadvantages of being a person of color, we can see that existing affirmative action programs don't go very far toward leveling the playing field.

The benefits of being white should be enjoyed by every person in this country. No one should have to endure the disadvantages that people of color experience. In leveling the playing field we don't want to hold anyone back. We want to push everyone forward so that we all share the benefits.

When we talk about the unequal distribution of benefits and disadvantages, we may feel uncomfortable about being white. We did not choose our skin color. Nor are we guilty for the fact that racism exists and that we have benefitted from it. We are responsible for acknowledging the reality of racism and for the daily choices we make about how to live in a racist society. We are only responsible for our own part, and we each have a part.

Sometimes, to avoid accepting our part, we want to shoot the bearer of bad news. Whether the bearer is white or a person of color, we become angry at whoever points out a comment or action that is hurtful, ignorant or abusive. We may accuse the person of being racist. This evasive reaction creates a debate about who is racist, or correct, or good, or well-intentioned, not about what to do about racism. It is probably inevitable that, when faced with the reality of the benefits and the harm of racism, we will feel defensive, guilty, ashamed, angry, powerless, frustrated or sad. These feelings are healthy and need to be acknowledged. Because they are uncomfortable we are liable to become angry at whoever brought up the subject.

Acknowledge your feelings and any resistance you have to the information presented above. . . . Yes, it is hard and sometimes discouraging. For too long we have ignored or denied the realities of racism. In order to make any changes, we have to start by facing where we are and making a commitment to persevere and overcome the injustices we face.

We can support each other through the feelings. We need a safe place to talk about how it feels to be white and know about racism. It is important that we turn to other white people for this support. Who are white people you can talk with about racism?

When people say, "We all have it hard," or "Everyone has an equal opportunity," or "People of color just want special privileges," how can you use the information in this book to respond? What might be difficult about doing so? What additional information or resources will you need to be able to do this with confidence? How might you find those resources?

PAUL KIVEL is a teacher, writer, and anti-racist social activist. He is the author of *Uprooting Racism: How White People Can Work for Racial Justice* (New Society Publishers, 1995).

Tim Wise  **NO**

The Absurdity (and Consistency) of White Denial: What Kind of Card Is Race?

Recently, I was asked by someone in the audience of one of my speeches, whether or not I believed that racism—though certainly a problem—might also be something conjured up by people of color in situations where the charge was inappropriate. In other words, did I believe that occasionally folks play the so-called race card, as a ploy to gain sympathy or detract from their own shortcomings? In the process of his query, the questioner made his own opinion all too clear (an unambiguous yes), and in that, he was not alone, as indicated by the reaction of others in the crowd, as well as survey data confirming that the belief in black malingering about racism is nothing if not ubiquitous.

It's a question I'm asked often, especially when there are several high-profile news events transpiring, in which race informs part of the narrative. Now is one of those times, as a few recent incidents demonstrate: Is racism, for example, implicated in the alleged rape of a young black woman by white members of the Duke University lacrosse team? Was racism implicated in Congresswoman Cynthia McKinney's recent confrontation with a member of the Capitol police? Or is racism involved in the ongoing investigation into whether or not Barry Bonds—as he is poised to eclipse white slugger Babe Ruth on the all-time home run list—might have used steroids to enhance his performance?*

Although the matter is open to debate in any or all of these cases, white folks have been quick to accuse blacks who answer in the affirmative of playing the race card, as if their conclusions have been reached not because of careful consideration of the facts as they see them, but rather, because of some irrational (even borderline paranoid) tendency to see racism everywhere. So too, discussions over immigration, "terrorist" profiling, and Katrina and its aftermath often turn on issues of race, and so give rise to the charge that as regards these subjects, people of color are "overreacting" when they allege racism in one or another circumstance.

Asked about the tendency for people of color to play the "race card," I responded as I always do: First, by noting that the regularity with which whites respond to charges of racism by calling said charges a ploy, suggests that the race card is, at best, equivalent to the two of diamonds. In other words, it's not much of a card to play, calling into question why anyone would play it (as if it were really going to get them somewhere). Secondly, I pointed out that white reluctance to acknowledge racism isn't new, and it isn't something that manifests only in situations where the racial aspect of an incident is arguable. Fact is, whites have always doubted claims of racism at the time they were being made, no matter how strong the evidence, as will be seen below. Finally, I concluded by suggesting that whatever "card" claims of racism may prove to be for the black and brown, the denial card is far and away the trump, and whites play it regularly: a subject to which we will return.

Turning Injustice into a Game of Chance: The Origins of Race as "Card"

First, let us consider the history of this notion: namely, that the "race card" is something people of color play so as to distract the rest of us, or to gain sympathy. For most Americans, the phrase "playing the race card" entered the national lexicon during the O.J. Simpson trial. Robert Shapiro, one of Simpson's attorneys famously claimed, in the aftermath of his client's acquittal, that co-counsel Johnnie Cochran had "played the race card, and dealt it from the bottom of the deck." The allegation referred to Cochran's bringing up officer Mark Fuhrman's regular use of the "n-word" as potentially indicative of his propensity to frame Simpson. To Shapiro, whose own views of his client's innocence apparently shifted over time, the issue of race had no place in the trial, and even if Fuhrman was a racist, this fact had no bearing on whether or not O.J. had killed his ex-wife and Ron Goldman. In other words, the idea that O.J. had been framed because of racism made no sense and to bring it up was to interject race into an arena where it was, or should have been, irrelevant.

That a white man like Shapiro could make such an argument, however, speaks to the widely divergent way in which whites and blacks view our respective worlds. For people of color—especially African Americans—the idea that racist cops might frame members of their community is no abstract notion, let alone an exercise in irrational conspiracy theorizing. Rather, it speaks to a social reality about which blacks are acutely aware. Indeed, there has been a history of such misconduct on the part of law enforcement, and for black folks to think those bad old days have ended is, for many, to let down their guard to the possibility of real and persistent injury.[1]

So if a racist cop is the lead detective in a case, and the one who discovers blood evidence implicating a black man accused of killing two white people, there is a logical alarm bell that goes off in the head of most any black person, but which would remain every bit as silent in the mind of someone who was white. And this too is understandable: for most whites, police are the helpful folks who get your cat out of the tree, or take you around in their patrol car for fun. For us, the idea of brutality or misconduct on the part of such persons seems remote, to the point of being fanciful. It seems the stuff of bad TV dramas, or at the very least, the past—that always remote place to which we can consign our national sins and predations, content all the while that whatever demons may have lurked in those earlier times have long since been vanquished.

To whites, blacks who alleged racism in the O.J. case were being absurd, or worse, seeking any excuse to let a black killer off the hook—ignoring that blacks on juries vote to convict black people of crimes every day in this country. And while allegations of black "racial bonding" with the defendant were made regularly after the acquittal in Simpson's criminal trial, no such bonding, this time with the victims, was alleged when a mostly white jury found O.J. civilly liable a few years later. Only blacks can play the race card, apparently; only they think in racial terms, at least to hear white America tell it.

Anything but Racism: White Reluctance to Accept the Evidence

Since the O.J. trial, it seems as though almost any allegation of racism has been met with the same dismissive reply from the bulk of whites in the U.S. According to national surveys, more than three out of four whites refuse to believe that discrimination is any real problem in America.[2] That most whites remain unconvinced of racism's salience—with as few as six percent believing it to be a "very serious problem," according to one poll in the mid 90s[3]—suggests that racism-as-card makes up an awfully weak hand. While folks of color consistently articulate their belief that racism is a real and persistent presence in their own lives, these claims have had very little effect on white attitudes. As such, how could anyone believe that people of color would somehow pull the claim out of their hat, as if it were guaranteed to make white America sit up and take notice? If anything, it is likely to be ignored, or even attacked, and in a particularly vicious manner.

That bringing up racism (even with copious documentation) is far from an effective "card" to play in order to garner sympathy, is evidenced by the way in which few people even become aware of the studies confirming its existence. How many Americans do you figure have even heard, for example, that black youth arrested for drug possession for the first time are incarcerated at a rate that is forty-eight times greater than the rate for white youth, even when all other factors surrounding the crime are identical?[4]

How many have heard that persons with "white sounding names," according to a massive national study, are fifty percent more likely to be called back for a job interview than those with "black sounding" names, even when all other credentials are the same?[5]

How many know that white men with a criminal record are slightly more likely to be called back for a job interview than black men without one, even when the men are equally qualified, and present themselves to potential employers in an identical fashion?[6]

How many have heard that according to the Justice Department, black and Latino males are three times more likely than white males to have their vehicles stopped and searched by police, even though white males are over four times more likely to have illegal contraband in our cars on the occasions when we are searched?[7]

How many are aware that black and Latino students are about half as likely as whites to be placed in advanced or honors classes in school, and twice as likely to be placed in remedial classes? Or that even when test scores and prior performance would justify higher placement, students of color are far less likely to be placed in honors classes?[8] Or that students of color are 2–3 times more likely than whites to be suspended or expelled from school, even though rates of serious school rule infractions do not differ to any significant degree between racial groups?[9]

Fact is, few folks have heard any of these things before, suggesting how little impact scholarly research on the subject of racism has had on the general public, and how difficult it is to make whites, in particular, give the subject a second thought.

Perhaps this is why, contrary to popular belief, research indicates that people of color are actually reluctant to allege racism, be it on the job, or in schools, or anywhere else. Far from "playing the race card" at the drop of a hat, it is actually the case (again, according to scholarly investigation, as opposed to the conventional wisdom of the white public), that black and brown folks typically "stuff" their experiences with discrimination and racism, only making an allegation of such treatment after many, many incidents have transpired, about which they said nothing for fear of being ignored or attacked.[10] Precisely because white denial has long trumped claims of racism, people of color tend to underreport their experiences with racial bias, rather than exaggerate them. Again, when it comes to playing a race card, it is more accurate to say that whites are the dealers with the loaded decks, shooting down any evidence of racism as little more than the fantasies of unhinged blacks, unwilling to take personal responsibility for their own problems in life.

Blaming the Victims for White Indifference

Occasionally, white denial gets creative, and this it does by pretending to come wrapped in sympathy for those who allege racism in the modern era. In other words, while steadfastly rejecting what people of color say they experience—in effect suggesting that they lack the intelligence and/or sanity to accurately interpret their own lives—such commentators seek to assure others that whites really do care about racism, but simply refuse to pin the label on incidents where it doesn't apply. In fact, they'll argue, one of the reasons that whites have developed compassion fatigue on this issue is precisely because of the overuse of the concept, combined with what we view as unfair reactions to racism (such as affirmative action efforts which have, ostensibly, turned us into the victims of racial bias). If blacks would just stop playing the card where it doesn't belong, and stop pushing for so-called preferential treatment, whites would revert back to our prior commitment to equal opportunity, and our heartfelt concern about the issue of racism.

Don't laugh. This is actually the position put forward recently by James Taranto of the *Wall Street Journal,* who in January suggested that white reluctance to embrace black claims of racism was really the fault of blacks themselves, and the larger civil rights establishment.[11] As Taranto put it: "Why do blacks and whites have such divergent views on racial matters? We would argue that it is because of the course that racial policies have taken over the past forty years." He then argues that by trying to bring about racial equality—but failing to do so because of "aggregate differences in motivation, inclination and aptitude" between different racial groups—policies like affirmative action have bred "frustration and resentment" among blacks, and "indifference" among whites, who decide not to think about race at all, rather than engage an issue that seems so toxic to them. In other words, whites think blacks use racism as a crutch for their own inadequacies, and then demand programs and policies that fail to make things much better, all the while discriminating against them as whites. In such an atmosphere, is it any wonder that the two groups view the subject matter differently?

But the fundamental flaw in Taranto's argument is its suggestion—implicit though it may be—that prior to the creation of affirmative action, white folks were mostly on board the racial justice and equal opportunity train, and were open to hearing about claims of racism from persons of color. Yet nothing could be further from the truth. White denial is not a form of backlash to the past forty years of civil rights legislation, and white indifference to claims of racism did not only recently emerge, as if from a previous place where whites and blacks had once seen the world similarly. Simply put: whites in every generation have thought there was no real problem with racism, irrespective of the evidence, and in every generation we have been wrong.

Denial as an Intergenerational Phenomenon

So, for example, what does it say about white rationality and white collective sanity, that in 1963—at a time when in retrospect all would agree racism was rampant in the United States, and before the passage of modern civil rights legislation—nearly two-thirds of whites, when polled, said they believed blacks were treated the same as whites in their communities—almost the same number as say this now, some forty-plus years later? What does it suggest about the extent of white folks' disconnection from the real world, that in 1962, eighty-five percent of whites said black children had just as good a chance as white children to get a good education in their communities?[12] Or that in May, 1968, seventy percent of whites said that blacks were treated the same as whites in their communities, while only seventeen percent said blacks were treated "not very well" and only 3.5 percent said blacks were treated badly?[13]

What does it say about white folks' historic commitment to equal opportunity—and which Taranto would have us believe has only been rendered inoperative because of affirmative action—that in 1963, three-fourths of white Americans told *Newsweek,* "The Negro is moving too fast" in his demands for equality?[14] Or that in October 1964, nearly two-thirds of whites said that the Civil Rights Act should be enforced gradually, with an emphasis on persuading employers not to discriminate, as opposed to forcing compliance with equal opportunity requirements?[15]

What does it say about whites' tenuous grip on mental health that in mid-August 1969, forty-four percent of whites told a Newsweek/Gallup National Opinion Survey that blacks had a better chance than they did to get a good paying job—two times as many as said they would have a worse chance? Or that forty-two percent said blacks had a better chance for a good education than whites, while only seventeen percent said they would have a worse opportunity for a good education, and eighty percent saying blacks would have an equal or better chance? In that same survey, seventy percent said blacks could have improved conditions in the "slums" if they had wanted to, and were more than twice as likely to blame blacks themselves, as opposed to discrimination, for high unemployment in the black community.[16]

In other words, even when racism was, by virtually all accounts (looking backward in time), institutionalized, white folks were convinced there was no real problem. Indeed, even forty years ago, whites were more likely to think that blacks had better opportunities, than to believe the opposite (and obviously accurate) thing: namely, that whites were advantaged in every realm of American life.

Truthfully, this tendency for whites to deny the extent of racism and racial injustice likely extends back far before the 1960s. Although public opinion polls in previous decades rarely if ever asked questions about the extent of racial bias or discrimination, anecdotal surveys of white opinion suggest that at no time have whites in the U.S. ever thought blacks or other people of color were getting a bad shake. White Southerners were all but convinced that their black slaves, for example, had it good, and had no reason to complain about their living conditions or lack of freedoms. After emancipation, but during the introduction of Jim Crow laws and strict Black Codes that limited where African Americans could live and work, white newspapers would regularly editorialize about the "warm relations" between whites and blacks, even as thousands of blacks were being lynched by their white compatriots.

From Drapetomania to Victim Syndrome—Viewing Resistance as Mental Illness

Indeed, what better evidence of white denial (even dementia) could one need than that provided by "Doctor" Samuel Cartwright, a well-respected physician of the 19th century, who was so convinced of slavery's benign nature, that he concocted and named a disease to explain the tendency for many slaves to run away from their loving masters. Drapetomania, he called it: a malady that could be cured by keeping the slave in a "child-like state," and taking care not to treat them as equals, while yet striving not to be too cruel. Mild whipping was, to Cartwright, the best cure of all. So there you have it: not only is racial oppression not a problem; even worse, those blacks who resist it, or refuse to bend to it, or complain about it in any fashion, are to be viewed not only as exaggerating their condition, but indeed, as mentally ill.[17]

And lest one believe that the tendency for whites to psychologically pathologize blacks who complain of racism is only a relic of ancient history, consider a much more recent example, which demonstrates the continuity of this tendency among members of the dominant racial group in America.

A few years ago, I served as an expert witness and consultant in a discrimination lawsuit against a school district in Washington State. Therein, numerous examples of individual and institutional racism abounded: from death threats made against black students to which the school district's response was pitifully inadequate, to racially disparate "ability tracking" and disciplinary action. In preparation for trial (which ultimately never took place as the district finally agreed to settle the case for several million dollars and a commitment to policy change), the school system's "psychological experts" evaluated dozens of the plaintiffs (mostly students as well as some of their parents) so as to determine the extent of damage done to them as a result of the racist mistreatment. As one of the plaintiff's experts, I reviewed the reports of said psychologists, and while I was not surprised to see them downplay the damage done to the black folks in this case, I was somewhat startled by how quickly they went beyond the call of duty to actually suggest that several of the plaintiffs exhibited "paranoid" tendencies and symptoms of borderline personality disorder. That having one's life threatened might make one a bit paranoid apparently never entered the minds of the white doctors. That facing racism on a regular basis might lead one to act out, in a way these "experts" would then see as a personality disorder, also seems to have escaped them. In this way, whites have continued to see mental illness behind black claims of victimization, even when that victimization is blatant.

In fact, we've even created a name for it: "victimization syndrome." Although not yet part of the DSM-IV (the diagnostic manual used by the American Psychiatric Association so as to evaluate patients), it is nonetheless a malady from which blacks suffer, to hear a lot of whites tell it. Whenever racism is brought up, such whites insist that blacks are being encouraged (usually by the civil rights establishment) to adopt a victim mentality, and to view themselves as perpetual targets of oppression. By couching their rejection of the claims of racism in these terms, conservatives are able to parade as friends to black folks, only concerned about them and hoping to free them from the debilitating mindset of victimization that liberals wish to see them adopt.

Aside from the inherently paternalistic nature of this position, notice too how concern over adopting a victim mentality is very selectively trotted out by the right. So, for example, when crime victims band together—and even form what they call victim's rights groups—no one on the right tells them to get over it, or suggests that by continuing to incessantly bleat about their kidnapped child or murdered loved one, such folks are falling prey to a victim mentality that should be resisted. No indeed: crime victims are venerated, considered experts on proper crime policy (as evidenced by how often their opinions are sought out on the matter by the national press and politicians), and given nothing but sympathy.

Likewise, when American Jews raise a cry over perceived anti-Jewish bigotry, or merely teach their children (as I was taught) about the European Holocaust, replete with a slogan of "Never again!" none of the folks who lament black "victimology" suggests that we too are wallowing in a victimization mentality, or somehow at risk for a syndrome of the same name.

In other words, it is blacks and blacks alone (with the occasional American Indian or Latino thrown in for good measure when and if they get too uppity) that get branded with the victim mentality label. Not quite drapetomania, but also not far enough from the kind of thinking that gave rise to it: in both cases, rooted in the desire of white America to reject what all logic and evidence suggests is true. Further, the selective branding of blacks as perpetual victims, absent the application of the pejorative to Jews or crime victims (or the families of 9/11 victims or other acts of terrorism), suggests that at some level white folks simply don't believe black suffering matters. We refuse to view blacks as fully human and deserving of compassion as we do these other groups, for whom victimization has been a reality as

well. It is not that whites care about blacks and simply wish them not to adopt a self-imposed mental straightjacket; rather, it is that at some level we either don't care, or at least don't equate the pain of racism even with the pain caused by being mugged, or having your art collection confiscated by the Nazis, let alone with the truly extreme versions of crime and anti-Semitic wrongdoing.

See No Evil, Hear No Evil, Wrong as Always

White denial has become such a widespread phenomenon nowadays, that most whites are unwilling to entertain even the mildest of suggestions that racism and racial inequity might still be issues. To wit, a recent survey from the University of Chicago, in which whites and blacks were asked two questions about Hurricane Katrina and the governmental response to the tragedy. First, respondents were asked whether they believed the government response would have been speedier had the victims been white. Not surprisingly, only twenty percent of whites answered in the affirmative. But while that question is at least conceivably arguable, the next question seems so weakly worded that virtually anyone could have answered yes without committing too much in the way of recognition that racism was a problem. Yet the answers given reveal the depths of white intransigence to consider the problem a problem at all.

So when asked if we believed the Katrina tragedy showed that there was a lesson to be learned about racial inequality in America—any lesson at all—while ninety percent of blacks said yes, only thirty-eight percent of whites agreed.[18] To us, Katrina said nothing about race whatsoever, even as blacks were disproportionately affected; even as there was a clear racial difference in terms of who was stuck in New Orleans and who was able to escape; even as the media focused incessantly on reports of black violence in the Superdome and Convention Center that proved later to be false; even as blacks have been having a much harder time moving back to New Orleans, thanks to local and federal foot-dragging and the plans of economic elites in the city to destroy homes in the most damaged (black) neighborhoods and convert them to non-residential (or higher rent) uses.

Nothing, absolutely nothing, has to do with race nowadays, in the eyes of white America writ large. But the obvious question is this: if we have never seen racism as a real problem, contemporary to the time in which the charges are being made, and if in all generations past we were obviously wrong to the point of mass delusion in thinking this way, what should lead us to conclude that now, at long last, we've become any more astute at discerning social reality than we were before? Why should we trust our own perceptions or instincts on the matter, when we have run up such an amazingly bad track record as observers of the world in which we live? In every era, black folks said they were the victims of racism and they were right. In every era, whites have said the problem was exaggerated, and we have been wrong.

Unless we wish to conclude that black insight on the matter—which has never to this point failed them—has suddenly converted to irrationality, and that white irrationality has become insight (and are prepared to prove this transformation by way of some analytical framework to explain the process), then the best advice seems to be that which could have been offered in past decades and centuries: namely, if you want to know about whether or not racism is a problem, it would probably do you best to ask the folks who are its targets. They, after all, are the ones who must, as a matter of survival, learn what it is, and how and when it's operating. We whites on the other hand, are the persons who have never had to know a thing about it, and who—for reasons psychological, philosophical and material—have always had a keen interest in covering it up.

In short, and let us be clear on it: race is not a card. It determines whom the dealer is, and who gets dealt.

Notes

*Personally, I have no idea whether or not Barry Bonds has used anabolic steroids during the course of his career, nor do I think the evidence marshaled thus far on the matter is conclusive, either way. But I do find it interesting that many are calling for the placement of an asterisk next to Bonds' name in the record books, especially should he eclipse Ruth, or later, Hank Aaron, in terms of career home runs. The asterisk, we are told, would differentiate Bonds from other athletes, the latter of which, presumably accomplished their feats without performance enhancers. Yet, while it is certainly true that Aaron's 755 home runs came without any form of performance enhancement (indeed, he, like other black ball-players had to face overt hostility in the early years of their careers, and even as he approached Ruth's record of 714, he was receiving death threats), for Ruth, such a claim would be laughable. Ruth, as with any white baseball player from the early 1890s to 1947, benefited from the "performance enhancement" of not having to compete against black athletes, whose abilities often far surpassed their own. Ruth didn't have to face black pitchers, nor vie for batting titles against black home run sluggers. Until white fans demand an asterisk next to the names of every one of their white baseball heroes—Ruth, Cobb, DiMaggio, and Williams, for starters—who played under apartheid rules, the demand for such

a blemish next to the name of Bonds can only be seen as highly selective, hypocritical, and ultimately racist. White privilege and protection from black competition certainly did more for those men's game than creotine or other substances could ever do for the likes of Barry Bonds.

1. There is plenty of information about police racism, misconduct and brutality, both in historical and contemporary terms, available from any number of sources. Among them, see Kristian Williams, *Our Enemies in Blue*. Soft Skull Press, 2004. . . .
2. *Washington Post*. October 9, 1995: A22.
3. Ibid.
4. "Young White Offenders Get Lighter Treatment," 2000. *The Tennessean*. April 26: 8A.
5. Bertrand, Marianne and Sendhil Mullainathan, 2004. "Are Emily and Greg More Employable Than Lakisha and Jamal? A Field Experiment in Labor Market Discrimination." June 20.
6. Pager, Devah. 2003. "The Mark of a Criminal Record." *American Journal of Sociology*. Volume 108: 5, March: 937–75.
7. Matthew R. Durose, Erica L. Schmitt and Patrick A. Langan, *Contacts Between Police and the Public: Findings from the 2002 National Survey*. U.S. Department of Justice (Bureau of Justice Statistics), April 2005.
8. Gordon, Rebecca. 1998. *Education and Race*. Oakland: Applied Research Center: 48–49; Fischer, Claude S. et al., 1996. *Inequality by Design: Cracking the Bell Curve Myth*. Princeton, NJ: Princeton University Press: 163; Steinhorn, Leonard and Barabara Diggs-Brown, 1999. *By the Color of Our Skin: The Illusion of Integration and the Reality of Race*. NY: Dutton: 95–96.
9. Skiba, Russell J. et al., *The Color of Discipline: Sources of Racial and Gender Disproportionality in School Punishment*. Indiana Education Policy Center, Policy Research Report SRS1, June 2000; U.S. Centers for Disease Control and Prevention, *Youth Risk Behavior Surveillance System: Youth 2003*, Online Comprehensive Results, 2004.
10. Terrell, Francis and Sandra L. Terrell, 1999. "Cultural Identification and Cultural Mistrust: Some Findings and Implications," in *Advances in African American Psychology*, Reginald Jones, ed., Hampton VA: Cobb & Henry; Fuegen, Kathleen, 2000. "Defining Discrimination in the Personal/Group Discrimination Discrepancy," *Sex Roles: A Journal of Research*. September; Miller, Carol T. 2001. "A Theoretical Perspective on Coping With Stigma," *Journal of Social Issues*. Spring; Feagin, Joe, Hernan Vera and Nikitah Imani, 1996. *The Agony of Education: Black Students in White Colleges and Universities*. NY: Routledge.

11. Taranto, James. 2006. "The Truth About Race in America—IV," Online Journal (*Wall Street Journal*), January 6.
12. The Gallup Organization, *Gallup Poll Social Audit, 2001. Black-White Relations in the United States, 2001 Update*, July 10: 7–9.
13. The Gallup Organization, *Gallup Poll*, #761, May, 1968.
14. "How Whites Feel About Negroes: A Painful American Dilemma," *Newsweek*, October 21, 1963: 56.
15. The Gallup Organization, *Gallup Poll #699*, October, 1964.
16. Newsweek/Gallup Organization, *National Opinion Survey*, August 19, 1969.
17. Cartwright, Samuel. 1851. "Diseases and Peculiarities of the Negro Race," *DeBow's Review*. (Southern and Western States: New Orleans), Volume XI.
18. Ford, Glen and Peter Campbell, 2006. "Katrina: A Study-Black Consensus, White Dispute," *The Black Commentator*, Issue 165, January 5.

Tim Wise is the author of *White Like Me: Reflections on Race from a Privileged Son* (Soft Skull Press, 2005) and director of the newly formed Association for White Anti-Racist Education (AWARE) in Nashville, Tennessee.

EXPLORING THE ISSUE

Do Whites Associate Privilege with Their Skin Color?

Critical Thinking and Reflection

1. How is white skin privilege manifested within American society?
2. What role does skin color play in the acquisition of one's racial identity?
3. How is white skin privilege related to racial discrimination?
4. What is the evidence of white skin privilege?
5. Has white skin privilege contributed to the existence of disadvantaged minorities? How has this contributed to racial stratification, poverty, and inequality?
6. Why do most whites resist the claim of white skin privilege?
7. What is the "race card"? What is its meaning and function?

Is There Common Ground?

Wise and Kivel recognize that a macro-level analysis of the white skin privilege issue reveals that whites are in an advantageous position over blacks and other racial minorities in society. Their socioeconomic status is higher, and institutional placement, power, and influence tend to be higher for whites. Both Wise and Kivel are also interested in overcoming the impact of white skin privilege in American diverse society. They both recognize differences in real-life experiences of whites and minorities such as racial profiling. Wise cites several surveys to indicate white reluctance to acknowledge racism. Essentially, he argues that blacks and whites see the world differently. The white assertion that blacks play the race card is noted in many examples including the relationship between the police and both the black and white communities. Distrust of the police among blacks is more than conventional wisdom; it is a reflection of real-life experiences. At the same time, whites' view of the police reflects a different real-life experience, which Wise sees as white privilege. However, many do not recognize this as privilege. Thus, the idea of white privilege is difficult, if not impossible, for most whites to recognize because for centuries the culture has associated race with minority blacks in the United States. White privilege is taken for granted by whites, many of whom tend to see their life experiences as universally normal.

Additional Resources

Barnes, Annie S. 2000. *Everyday Racism: A Book for All Americans* (Sourcebooks, Inc.).

Berry, Brewton. 1969. *Almost White* (Collier-Macmillan Books).

Binzen, Peter. 1970. *Whitetown, USA: A Firsthand Study of How the "Silent Majority" Lives, Learns, Works and Thinks* (Vintage).

Bonilla-Silva, Eduardo. 2001. *White Supremacy and Racism in the Post-Civil Rights Era* (Lynn Rienner Publishers).

Brodkin, Karen. 1999. *How Did Jews Become White Folks and What That Says About Race in America* (Rutgers University Press).

Doane, Ashley and Eduardo Bonilla-Silva. 2003. *White Out: The Continuing Significance of Racism* (Routledge).

Fanon, Franz. 1967. *Black Skin, White Masks* (New York: Grove Press).

Fine, Michelle, Lois Weis, Linda Powell Pruitt, and April Burns. 2004. *Off White: Readings on Power, Privilege, and Resistance* (Routledge).

Gallagher, Charles. *Rethinking the Color Line: Readings in Race and Ethnicity*, 5th ed. (McGraw-Hill).

Guglielmo, Jennifer and Salvatore Salerno. 2003. *Are Italians White?: How Race Is Made in America* (Routledge).

Ignatiev, Noel. 2008. *How the Irish Became White* (Routledge).

Jensen, Robert. 2005. *The Heart of Whiteness: Confronting Race, Racism and White Privilege* (City Lights Publishers).

Jordan, Winthrop. 1968. *White Over Black*: *American Attitudes Toward the Negro, 1550–1812* (The University of North Carolina Press).

Lipsitz, George. 2006. *The Possessive Investment in Whiteness: How White People Profit from Identity Politics* (Temple University Press).

Lipsitz, George. 2011. *How Racism Takes Place* (Temple University Press).

Roediger, David R. 2005. *Working Toward Whiteness: How America's Immigrants Became White* (Basic Books).

Rosenkranz, Mark. 2009. *White Male Privilege: A Study of Racism in America 50 Years After the Voting Rights Act*, 3rd ed. (Law Dog Books).

Rothenberg, Paula. 2011. *White Privilege: Essential Readings on the Other Side of Racism* (Worth Publishers).

Stanley Crouch, Stanley. 2004. *The Artificial White Man: Essays on Authenticity* (Basic Books).

Sullivan, Shannon. 2006. *Revealing Whiteness: The Unconscious Habits of Racial Privilege* (Indiana University Press).

Williams, Lind, Faye. 2003. *The Constraint of Race: Legacies of White Skin Privilege in America* (The Pennsylvania State University Press).

Wise, Tim. 2005. *White Like Me: Reflections on Race from a Privileged Son* (Soft Skull Press).

Internet References . . .

Color Lines

http://colorlines.com/

Public Broadcasting System

www.pbs.org/

The Occidental Observer

www.theoccidentalobserver.net

Selected, Edited, and with Issue Framing Material by:
Wind Goodfriend, *Buena Vista University*

ISSUE

Do Minorities and Whites Engage in Self-Segregation?

YES: Beverly D. Tatum, from "Identity Development in Adolescence," Basic Books (1997)

NO: Debra Humphreys, from *Campus Diversity and Student Self-Segregation: Separating Myths from Facts,* Diversity Web Association of American Colleges and Universities (1999)

Learning Outcomes

After reading this issue, you will be able to:

- Present an informed understanding of racial identity development of American youth.
- Develop an appreciation of self-segregation as a mode of intergroup relations.
- Understand how this issue illuminates the continuing legacy of Jim Crow living within American society.
- Explain and apply concepts such as social distance, separatism, desegregation, assimilation, multiculturalism, and diversity to the discussion of this issue.
- Identify and examine factors that contribute to self-segregation within institutional settings.

ISSUE SUMMARY

YES: Beverly D. Tatum, an African American clinical psychologist and president of Spelman College, examines identity development among adolescents, especially black youths, and the behavioral outcomes of this phenomenon. She argues that black adolescents' tendency to view themselves in racial terms is due to the totality of personal and environmental responses that they receive from the larger society.

NO: Debra Humphreys is the director of Programs, Office of Education and Diversity Initiatives, at the Association of American Colleges and Universities in Washington, DC. She notes that today's university students are matriculating on very diverse campuses that are "leading to significant educational and social benefits for all college students. In such an environment, students have many opportunities to interact and associate with students of different backgrounds than themselves." She cites research that tends to show that rather than self-segregating, students are interacting across racial and ethnic lines in significant numbers.

In confronting this issue, students are challenged to develop a more comprehensive understanding of the scope and impact of legal segregation that existed in the United States prior to the civil rights movement. Many Americans, especially youth, have a tendency to associate racial segregation solely with the American South. They fail to recognize that segregation of the races was a national phenomenon. Segregation was not a social aberration; rather it was mandated by the *Plessy v. Ferguson* 1896 decision and the separate but equal doctrine that applied throughout the nation. In the wake of the Plessy decision, Jim Crow laws were passed in many states. The substantially desegregated society, which Americans experience today, is very different than the conditions that prevailed during the segregation era. It is the civil rights movement and the resulting legislation upon which today's race relations exist.

Blacks who experienced Jim Crow were forced to adjust their expectations and behavior to accommodate segregation. They became conditioned to a Jim Crow lifestyle and responded accordingly. Blacks learned not to seek services or employment within a plethora of institutions, including barbershops, bars, golf courses, restaurants, and many other public accommodations that were racially segregated. Private clubs and associations were clearly off limits to blacks. They wanted to avoid the humiliation that rejection due to skin color generated. Meritocracy did not apply to blacks in pursuit of upward mobility. In examining this issue, students should consider whether the response of blacks to such conditions was due to self-segregation or a pragmatic response to the real world.

American colleges and universities are major institutional domains in which the isolation of African American students and other ethnic groups is a reality that has generated interest, concern, and controversy. African American students tend to be the primary focus of such concerns on our campuses, though they are not the only group involved in what many Americans, both scholars and others, characterize as "self-segregation." The clustering and grouping together of whites can also be seen as self-segregation. The focal concern of this social issue is often stated within the question: "Why are all the black kids sitting together in the cafeteria?" However, the larger and perhaps more relevant question is why do all racial groups tend to congregate together?

Beverly Tatum notes that the quest for personal identity is a fundamental aspect of human experience. As black youth proceed in their development from childhood through adolescence, the question of identity evolves and grows, according to Tatum and other psychologists.

This identity development of black youth is influenced by an evolving racial consciousness within their perceptions of self. According to Tatum, these racially focused self-perceptions and identities that black youth develop in response to their experiences within an environment intensify due to messages and treatments they receive in interacting with whites. The challenges facing black youth in their attempts to engage the dominant white world range from having to confront and effectively deal with prejudice and discrimination to resisting stereotypes and affirming other more positive definitions of themselves. In response to these challenges, Tatum examines significant coping strategies that are developed by these youth including self-segregation.

Tatum maintains that black youth develop strategies to affirm and protect themselves from the deleterious effects of their involvement within a society with embedded stereotypes concerning blacks. So, Tatum answers the question, "Why are all the black kids sitting together in the cafeteria?" She does so by exploring the responses of black youth to the stresses of race in American society, and their need to seek meaning, sensitivity, understanding, and support from their black peers.

Debra Humphreys, in the NO selection, offers an interesting challenge to Tatum. Humphreys views self-segregation as an advantage that contributes to the overall adjustment of minorities in a new environment. At the same time, she points out that racial minorities increase their social interaction with whites. She reviews studies of self-segregation (homogeneous groups) and additional levels of friendship. Citing studies by Richard Light of Harvard, a 1991 study of student life at Berkeley, and a 1997 study at the University of Michigan, Humphreys points out that all racial and ethnic groups want to meet and become friends with more students from different ethnic and cultural backgrounds than their own. Hence, she sees an increase of multiculturalism and diversity on the college campuses, overtaking the tendency toward self-segregation.

Understanding voluntary segregation, in contrast to exclusion, challenges one to comprehend the complexities of identity. Given the goal of equality, what are the functions of self-segregation? On one hand, as Tatum points out, it offers a means to cope with rejection. Humphreys agrees and goes further to point out that self-segregation among minority college students does not impede intergroup contact. How might self-segregation impact upon social cohesion? What can be understood from John Matlock's article in *Diversity Digest* (Summer 1997), "Student Expectations and Experiences," which found that white students had the most segregated friendship patterns on campus of all students?

The United States has a legacy of conflict-ridden race and ethnic relations rooted in such institutions as slavery, segregation, and related policies and practices of discrimination. Despite this legacy, minority students are more likely to interact with students of different backgrounds than are whites. Humphreys writes, "the reality is that students of color have much more intergroup contact than do white students but their pattern of interaction needs to be understood in light of their psychological development."

Many of the nation's campuses have not achieved multicultural sensitivity. We still have hate crimes and other manifestations of race and ethnic conflict. Confederate flags and other incendiary symbols of American racist tradition are still able to penetrate communities of higher learning. Given such realities, the black "table in the cafeteria" is expected to persist within the educational institutions of the United States. Essentially, as stated above, Tatum describes black students congregating around these tables as engaging in positive identity formation. Their peers provide them with the reaffirmation and support that they need to affirm that their blackness is a positive quality. The immersion of these youth within the circle of their peers around the black table can facilitate their development of positive senses of self-esteem and self-worth to serve as effective antidotes to the negativity that they often encounter in dealing with the dominant society. Thus, Tatum argues that self-segregation is a social adaptation by blacks and other youth in order to function effectively on campus.

Both Tatum and Humphreys offer the reader insight into the complex problem of race and American identity. Students may want to consider the following questions for further reflection: Is self-segregation truly voluntary? To what extent is self-segregation on campuses a threat to a common American identity?

YES ↩

Beverly D. Tatum

Identity Development in Adolescence

Walk into any racially mixed high school cafeteria at lunch time and you will instantly notice that in the sea of adolescent faces, there is an identifiable group of Black students sitting together. Conversely, it could be pointed out that there are many groups of White students sitting together as well, though people rarely comment about that. The question on the tip of everyone's tongue is "Why are the Black kids sitting together?" Principals want to know, teachers want to know, White students want to know, the Black students who aren't sitting at the table want to know.

How does it happen that so many Black teenagers end up at the same cafeteria table? They don't start out there. If you walk into racially mixed elementary schools, you will often see young children of diverse racial backgrounds playing with one another, sitting at the snack table together, crossing racial boundaries with an ease uncommon in adolescence. Moving from elementary school to middle school (often at sixth or seventh grade) means interacting with new children from different neighborhoods than before, and a certain degree of clustering by race might therefore be expected, presuming that children who are familiar with one another would form groups. But even in schools where the same children stay together from kindergarten through eighth grade, racial grouping begins by the sixth or seventh grade. What happens?

One thing that happens is puberty. As children enter adolescence, they begin to explore the question of identity, asking "Who am I? Who can I be?" in ways they have not done before. For Black youth, asking "Who am I?" includes thinking about "Who am I ethnically and/or racially? What does it mean to be Black?"

As I write this, I can hear the voice of a White woman who asked me, "Well, all adolescents struggle with questions of identity. They all become more self-conscious about their appearance and more concerned about what their peers think. So what is so different for Black kids?" Of course, she is right that all adolescents look at themselves in new ways, but not all adolescents think about themselves in racial terms.

The search for personal identity that intensifies in adolescence can involve several dimensions of an adolescent's life: vocational plans, religious beliefs, values and preferences, political affiliations and beliefs, gender roles, and ethnic identities. The process of exploration may vary across these identity domains. James Marcia described four identity "statuses" to characterize the variation in the identity search process: (1) *diffuse,* a state in which there has been little exploration or active consideration of a particular domain, and no psychological commitment; (2) *foreclosed,* a state in which a commitment has been made to particular roles or belief systems, often those selected by parents, without actively considering alternatives; (3) *moratorium,* a state of active exploration of roles and beliefs in which no commitment has yet been made; and (4) *achieved,* a state of strong personal commitment to a particular dimension of identity following a period of high exploration.

An individual is not likely to explore all identity domains at once, therefore it is not unusual for an adolescent to be actively exploring one dimension while another remains relatively unexamined. Given the impact of dominant and subordinate status, it is not surprising that researchers have found that adolescents of color are more likely to be actively engaged in an exploration of their racial or ethnic identity than are White adolescents.

Why do Black youths, in particular, think about themselves in terms of race? Because that is how the rest of the world thinks of them. Our self-perceptions are shaped by the messages that we receive from those around us, and when young Black men and women enter adolescence, the racial content of those messages intensifies. A case in point: If you were to ask my ten-year-old son, David, to describe himself, he would tell you many things: that he is smart, that he likes to play computer games, that he has an older brother. Near the top of his list, he would likely mention that he is tall for his age. He would probably not mention that he is Black, though he certainly knows that he is. Why would he mention his height and not his racial group membership? When David meets new adults, one of the first questions they ask is "How old are you?" When David states his age, the inevitable reply is "Gee, you're tall for your age!" It happens so frequently that I once overheard David say to someone, "Don't say it, I know. I'm tall for my age." Height is salient for David because it is salient for others.

When David meets new adults, they don't say, "Gee, you're Black for your age!" If you are saying to yourself, of course they don't, think again. Imagine David at fifteen, six-foot-two, wearing the adolescent attire of the day, passing adults he doesn't know on the sidewalk. Do the women hold their purses a little tighter, maybe even cross the street to avoid him? Does he hear the sound of the automatic door locks on cars as he passes by? Is he being followed around by the security guards at the local mall? As he stops in town with his new bicycle, does a police officer hassle him, asking where he got it, implying that it might be stolen? Do strangers assume he plays basketball? Each of these experiences conveys a racial message. At ten, race is not yet salient for David, because it is not yet salient for society. But it will be.

Understanding Racial Identity Development

Psychologist William Cross, author of *Shades of Black: Diversity in African American Identity*, has offered a theory of racial identity development that I have found to be a very useful framework for understanding what is happening not only with David, but with those Black students in the cafeteria. According to Cross's model, referred to as the psychology of nigrescence, or the psychology of becoming Black, the five stages of racial identity development are *pre-encounter, encounter, immersion/emersion, internalization,* and *internalization-commitment.* For the moment, we will consider the first two stages as those are the most relevant for adolescents.

In the first stage, the Black child absorbs many of the beliefs and values of the dominant White culture, including the idea that it is better to be White. The stereotypes, omissions, and distortions that reinforce notions of White superiority are breathed in by Black children as well as White. Simply as a function of being socialized in a Euro-centric culture, some Black children may begin to value the role models, lifestyles, and images of beauty represented by the dominant group more highly than those of their own cultural group. On the other hand, if Black parents are what I call race-conscious—that is, actively seeking to encourage positive racial identity by providing their children with positive cultural images and messages about what it means to be Black—the impact of the dominant society's messages is reduced. In either case, in the pre-encounter stage, the personal and social significance of one's racial group membership has not yet been realized, and racial identity is not yet under examination. At age ten, David and other children like him would seem to be in the pre-encounter

stage. When the environmental cues change and the world begins to reflect his Blackness back to him more clearly, he will probably enter the encounter stage.

Transition to the encounter stage is typically precipitated by an event or series of events that force the young person to acknowledge the personal impact of racism. As the result of a new and heightened awareness of the significance of race, the individual begins to grapple with what it means to be a member of a group targeted by racism. Though Cross describes this process as one that unfolds in late adolescence and early adulthood, research suggests that an examination of one's racial or ethnic identity may begin as early as junior high school.

In a study of Black and White eighth graders from an integrated urban junior high school, Jean Phinney and Steve Tarver found clear evidence for the beginning of the search process in this dimension of identity. Among the forty-eight participants, more than a third had thought about the effects of ethnicity on their future, had discussed the issues with family and friends, and were attempting to learn more about their group. While White students in this integrated school were also beginning to think about ethnic identity, there was evidence to suggest a more active search among Black students, especially Black females. Phinney and Tarver's research is consistent with my own study of Black youth in predominantly White communities, where the environmental cues that trigger an examination of racial identity often become evident in middle school or junior high school.

Some of the environmental cues are institutionalized. Though many elementary schools have self-contained classrooms where children of varying performance levels learn together, many middle and secondary schools use "ability grouping," or tracking. Though school administrators often defend their tracking practices as fair and objective, there usually is a recognizable racial pattern to how children are assigned, which often represents the system of advantage operating in the schools. In racially mixed schools, Black children are much more likely to be in the lower track than in the honors track. Such apparent sorting along racial lines sends a message about what it means to be Black. One young honors student I interviewed described the irony of this resegregation in what was an otherwise integrated environment, and hinted at the identity issues it raised for him.

> It was really a very paradoxical existence, here I am in a school that's 35 percent Black, you know, and I'm the only Black in my classes. . . . That always struck me as odd. I guess I felt that I was different from the other Blacks because of that.

In addition to the changes taking place within school, there are changes in the social dynamics outside school. For many parents, puberty raises anxiety about interracial dating. In racially mixed communities, you begin to see what I call the birthday party effect. Young children's birthday parties in multiracial communities are often a reflection of the community's diversity. The parties of elementary school children may be segregated by gender but not by race. At puberty, when the parties become sleepovers or boy-girl events, they become less and less racially diverse.

Black girls, especially in predominantly White communities, may gradually become aware that something has changed. When their White friends start to date, they do not. The issues of emerging sexuality and the societal messages about who is sexually desirable leave young Black women in a very devalued position. One young woman from a Philadelphia suburb described herself as "pursuing White guys throughout high school" to no avail. Since there were no Black boys in her class, she had little choice. She would feel "really pissed off" that those same White boys would date her White friends. For her, "that prom thing was like out of the question."

Though Black girls living in the context of a larger Black community may have more social choices, they too have to contend with devaluing messages about who they are and who they will become, especially if they are poor or working-class. As social scientists Bonnie Ross Leadbeater and Niobe Way point out,

> The school drop-out, the teenage welfare mother, the drug addict, and the victim of domestic violence or of AIDS are among the most prevalent public images of poor and working-class urban adolescent girls. . . . Yet, despite the risks inherent in economic disadvantage, the majority of poor urban adolescent girls do not fit the stereotypes that are made about them.

Resisting the stereotypes and affirming other definitions of themselves is part of the task facing young Black women in both White and Black communities.

As was illustrated in the example of David, Black boys also face a devalued status in the wider world. The all too familiar media image of a young Black man with his hands cuffed behind his back, arrested for a violent crime, has primed many to view young Black men with suspicion and fear. In the context of predominantly White schools, however, Black boys may enjoy a degree of social success, particularly if they are athletically talented. The culture has embraced the Black athlete, and the young man who can fulfill that role is often pursued by Black girls and White girls alike. But even these young men will

encounter experiences that may trigger an examination of their racial identity.

Sometimes the experience is quite dramatic. *The Autobiography of Malcolm X* is a classic tale of racial identity development, and I assign it to my psychology of racism students for just that reason. As a junior high school student, Malcolm was a star. Despite the fact that he was separated from his family and living in a foster home, he was an A student and was elected president of his class. One day he had a conversation with his English teacher, whom he liked and respected, about his future career goals. Malcolm said he wanted to be a lawyer. His teacher responded, "That's no realistic goal for a nigger," and advised him to consider carpentry instead. The message was clear: You are a Black male, your racial group membership matters, plan accordingly. Malcolm's emotional response was typical—anger, confusion, and alienation. He withdrew from his White classmates, stopped participating in class, and eventually left his predominately White Michigan home to live with his sister in Roxbury, a Black community in Boston.

No teacher would say such a thing now, you may be thinking, but don't be so sure. It is certainly less likely that a teacher would use the word *nigger,* but consider these contemporary examples shared by high school students. A young ninth-grade student was sitting in his homeroom. A substitute teacher was in charge of the class. Because the majority of students from this school go on to college, she used the free time to ask the students about their college plans. As a substitute she had very limited information about their academic performance, but she offered some suggestions. When she turned to this young man, one of few Black males in the class, she suggested that he consider a community college. She had recommended four-year colleges to the other students. Like Malcolm, this student got the message.

In another example, a young Black woman attending a desegregated school to which she was bussed was encouraged by a teacher to attend the upcoming school dance. Most of the Black students did not live in the neighborhood and seldom attended the extracurricular activities. The young woman indicated that she wasn't planning to come. The well-intentioned teacher was persistent. Finally the teacher said, "Oh come on, I know you people love to dance." This young woman got the message, too.

Coping with Encounters: Developing an Oppositional Identity

What do these encounters have to do with the cafeteria? Do experiences with racism inevitably result in so-called self-segregation? While certainly a desire to protect oneself from further offense is understandable, it is not the only factor at work. Imagine the young eighth-grade girl who experienced the teacher's use of "you people" and the dancing stereotype as a racial affront. Upset and struggling with adolescent embarrassment, she bumps into a White friend who can see that something is wrong. She explains. Her White friend responds, in an effort to make her feel better perhaps, and says, "Oh, Mr. Smith is such a nice guy, I'm sure he didn't mean it like that. Don't be so sensitive." Perhaps the White friend is right, and Mr. Smith didn't mean it, but imagine your own response when you are upset, perhaps with a spouse or partner. He or she asks what's wrong and you explain why you are offended. Your partner brushes off your complaint, attributing it to your being oversensitive. What happens to your emotional thermostat? It escalates. When feelings, rational or irrational, are invalidated, most people disengage. They not only choose to discontinue the conversation but are more likely to turn to someone who will understand their perspective.

In much the same way, the eighth-grade girl's White friend doesn't get it. She doesn't see the significance of this racial message, but the girls at the "Black table" do. When she tells her story there, one of them is likely to say, "You know what, Mr. Smith said the same thing to me yesterday!" Not only are Black adolescents encountering racism and reflecting on their identity, but their White peers, even when they are not the perpetrators (and sometimes they are), are unprepared to respond in supportive ways. The Black students turn to each other for the much needed support they are not likely to find anywhere else.

In adolescence, as race becomes personally salient for Black youth, finding the answer to questions such as, "What does it mean to be a young Black person? How should I act? What should I do?" is particularly important. And although Black fathers, mothers, aunts, and uncles may hold the answers by offering themselves as role models, they hold little appeal for most adolescents. The last thing many fourteen-year-olds want to do is to grow up to be like their parents. It is the peer group, the kids in the cafeteria, who hold the answers to these questions. They know how to be Black. They have absorbed the stereotypical images of Black youth in the popular culture and are reflecting those images in their self-presentation.

Based on their fieldwork in U.S. high schools, Signithia Fordham and John Ogbu identified a common psychological pattern found among African American high school students is this stage of identity development. They observed that the anger and resentment that adolescents feel in response to their growing awareness of the systematic exclusion of Black people from full participation in U.S. society leads to the development of an oppositional

social identity. This oppositional stance both protects one's identity from the psychological assault of racism and keeps the dominant group at a distance. Fordham and Ogbu write:

> Subordinate minorities regard certain forms of behavior and certain activities or events, symbols, and meanings as *not appropriate* for them because those behaviors, events, symbols, and meanings are characteristic of white Americans. At the same time they emphasize other forms of behavior as more appropriate for them because these are *not* a part of white Americans' way of life. To behave in the manner defined as falling within a white cultural frame of reference is to "act white" and is negatively sanctioned.

Certain styles of speech, dress, and music, for example, may be embraced as "authentically Black" and become highly valued, while attitudes and behaviors associated with Whites are viewed with disdain. The peer groups's evaluation of what is Black and what is not can have a powerful impact on adolescent behavior.

Reflecting on her high school years, one Black woman from a White neighborhood described both the pain of being rejected by her Black classmates and her attempts to conform to her peer's definition of Blackness:

> "Oh you sound White, you think you're White," they said. And the idea of sounding White was just so absurd to me. . . . So ninth grade was sort of traumatic in that I started listening to rap music, which I really just don't like. [I said] I'm gonna be Black, and it was just that stupid. But it's more than just how one acts, you know. [The other Black women there] were not into me for the longest time. My first year there was hell.

Sometimes the emergence of an oppositional identity can be quite dramatic, as the young person tries on a new persona almost overnight. At the end of one school year, race may not have appeared to be significant, but often some encounter takes place over the summer and the young person returns to school much more aware of his or her Blackness and ready to make sure that the rest of the world is aware of it, too. There is a certain "in your face" quality that these adolescents can take on, which their teachers often experience as threatening. When a group of Black teens are sitting together in the cafeteria, collectively embodying an oppositional stance, school administrators want to know not only why they are sitting together, but what can be done to prevent it.

We need to understand that in racially mixed settings, racial grouping is a developmental process in response to an environmental stressor, racism. Joining with one's peers for support in the face of stress is a positive coping strategy. What is problematic is that the young people are operating with a very limited definition of what it means to be Black, based largely on cultural stereotypes.

Oppositional Identity Development and Academic Achievement

Unfortunately for Black teenagers, those cultural stereotypes do not usually include academic achievement. Academic success is more often associated with being White. During the encounter phase of racial identity development, when the search for identity leads toward cultural stereotypes and away from anything that might be associated with Whiteness, academic performance often declines. Doing well in school becomes identified as trying to be White. Being smart becomes the opposite of being cool.

While this frame of reference is not universally found among adolescents of African descent, it is commonly observed in Black peer groups. Among the Black college students I have interviewed, many described some conflict or alienation from other African American teens because of their academic success in high school. For example, a twenty-year-old female from a Washington, D.C., suburb explained:

> It was weird, even in high school a lot of the Black students were, like, "Well, you're not really Black." Whether it was because I became president of the sixth-grade class or whatever it was, it started pretty much back then. Junior high, it got worse. I was then labeled certain things, whether it was "the oreo" or I wasn't really Black.

Others described avoiding situations that would set them apart from their Black peers. For example, one young woman declined to participate in a gifted program in her school because she knew it would separate her from the other Black students in the school.

In a study of thirty-three eleventh-graders in a Washington, D.C., school, Fordham and Ogbu found that although some of the students had once been academically successful, few of them remained so. These students also knew that to be identified as a "brainiac" would result in peer rejection. The few students who had maintained strong academic records found ways to play down their academic success enough to maintain some level of acceptance among their Black peers.

Academically successful Black students also need a strategy to find acceptance among their White classmates. Fordham describes one such strategy as *racelessness,* wherein individuals assimilate into the dominant group by de-emphasizing characteristics that might identify them as members of the subordinate group. Jon, a young man I interviewed, offered a classic example of this strategy as he described his approach to dealing with his discomfort at being the only Black person in his advanced classes. He said, "At no point did I ever think I was White or did I ever want to be White. . . . I guess it was one of those things where I tried to de-emphasize the fact that I was Black." This strategy led him to avoid activities that were associated with Blackness. He recalled, "I didn't want to do anything that was traditionally Black, like I never played basketball. I ran cross-country. . . . I went for distance running instead of sprints." He felt he had to show his White classmates that there were "exceptions to all these stereotypes." However, this strategy was of limited usefulness. When he traveled outside his home community with his White teammates, he sometimes encountered overt racism. "I quickly realized that I'm Black, and that's the thing that they're going to see first, no matter how much I try to de-emphasize my Blackness."

A Black student can play down Black identity in order to succeed in school and mainstream institutions without rejecting his Black identity and culture. Instead of becoming raceless, an achieving Black student can become an *emissary,* someone who sees his or her own achievements as advancing the cause of the racial group. For example, social scientists Richard Zweigenhaft and G. William Domhoff describe how a successful Black student, in response to the accusation of acting White, connected his achievement to that of other Black men by saying, "Martin Luther King must not have been Black, then, since he had a doctoral degree, and Malcolm X must not have been Black since he educated himself while in prison." In addition, he demonstrated his loyalty to the Black community by taking an openly political stance against the racial discrimination he observed in his school.

It is clear that an oppositional identity can interfere with academic achievement, and it may be tempting for educators to blame the adolescents themselves for their academic decline. However, the questions that educators and other concerned adults must ask are, How did academic achievement become defined as exclusively White behavior? What is it about the curriculum and the wider culture that reinforce the notion that academic excellence is an exclusively White domain? What curricular interventions might we use to encourage the development of an empowered emissary identity?

An oppositional identity that disdains academic achievement has not always been a characteristic of Black adolescent peer groups. It seems to be a post-desegregation phenomenon. Historically, the oppositional identity found among African Americans in the segregated South included a positive attitude toward education. While Black people may have publicly deferred to Whites, they actively encouraged their children to pursue education as a ticket to greater freedom. While Black parents still see education as the key to upward mobility, in today's desegregated schools the models of success—the teachers, administrators, and curricular heroes—are almost always White.

Black Southern schools, though stigmatized by legally sanctioned segregation, were often staffed by African American educators, themselves visible models of academic achievement. These Black educators may have presented a curriculum that included references to the intellectual legacy of other African Americans. As well, in the context of a segregated school, it was given that the high achieving students would all be Black. Academic achievement did not have to mean separation from one's Black peers.

The Search for Alternative Images

This historical example reminds us that an oppositional identity discouraging academic achievement is not inevitable even in a racist society. If young people are exposed to images of African American academic achievement in their early years, they won't have to define school achievement as something for Whites only. They will know that there is a long history of Black intellectual achievement.

This point was made quite eloquently by Jon, the young man I quoted earlier. Though he made the choice to excel in school, he labored under the false assumption that he was "inventing the wheel." It wasn't until he reached college and had the opportunity to take African American studies courses that he learned about other African Americans besides Martin Luther King, Malcolm X, and Frederick Douglass—the same three men he had heard about year after year, from kindergarten to high school graduation. As he reflected on his identity struggle in high school, he said:

> It's like I went through three phases. . . . My first phase was being cool, doing whatever was particularly cool for Black people at the time, and that was like in junior high. Then in high school, you know, I thought being Black was basically all stereotypes, so I tried to avoid all of those things. Now in college, you know, I realize that being Black means a variety of things.

Learning his history in college was of great psychological importance to Jon, providing him with role models he had been missing in high school. He was particularly inspired by learning of the intellectual legacy of Black men at his own college:

> When you look at those guys who were here in the Twenties, they couldn't live on campus. They couldn't eat on campus. They couldn't get their hair cut in town. And yet they were all Phi Beta Kappa. . . . That's what being Black really is, you know, knowing who you are, your history, your accomplishments. . . . When I was in junior high, I had White role models. And then when I got into high school, you know, I wasn't sure but I just didn't think having White role models was a good thing. So I got rid of those. And I basically just, you know, only had my parents for role models. I kind of grew up thinking that we were on the cutting edge. We were doing something radically different than everybody else. And not realizing that there are all kinds of Black people doing the very things that I thought we were the only ones doing. . . . You've got to do the very best you can so that you can continue the great traditions that have already been established.

This young man was not alone in his frustration over having learned little about his own cultural history in grade school. Time and again in the research interviews I conducted, Black students lamented the absence of courses in African American history or literature at the high school level and indicated how significant this new learning was to them in college, how excited and affirmed they felt by this newfound knowledge. Sadly, many Black students never get to college, alienated from the process of education long before high school graduation. They may never get access to the information that might have helped them expand their definition of what it means to be Black and, in the process, might have helped them stay in school. Young people are developmentally ready for this information in adolescence. We ought to provide it.

Not at the Table

As we have seen, Jon felt he had to distance himself from his Black peers in order to be successful in high school. He was one of the kids *not* sitting at the Black table. Continued encounters with racism and access to new culturally relevant information empowered him to give up his racelessness and become an emissary. In college, not only did he sit at the Black table, but he emerged as a campus leader, confident in the support of his Black peers. His example illustrates that one's presence at the Black table is often an expression of one's identity development, which evolves over time.

Some Black students may not be developmentally ready for the Black table in junior or senior high school. They may not yet have had their own encounters with racism, and race may not be very salient for them. Just as we don't all reach puberty and begin developing sexual interest at the same time, racial identity development unfolds in idiosyncratic ways. Though my research suggests that adolescence is a common time, one's own life experiences are also important determinants of the timing. The young person whose racial identity development is out of synch with his or her peers often feels in an awkward position. Adolescents are notoriously egocentric and assume that their experience is the same as everyone else's. Just as girls who have become interested in boys become disdainful of their friends still interested in dolls, the Black teens who are at the table can be quite judgmental toward those who are not. "If I think it is a sign of authentic Blackness to sit at this table, then you should too."

The young Black men and women who still hang around with the White classmates they may have known since early childhood will often be snubbed by their Black peers. This dynamic is particularly apparent in regional schools where children from a variety of neighborhoods are brought together. When Black children from predominantly White neighborhoods go to school with Black children from predominantly Black neighborhoods, the former group is often viewed as trying to be White by the latter group. We all speak the language of the streets we live on. Black children living in White neighborhoods often sound White to their Black peers from across town, and may be teased because of it. This can be a very painful experience, particularly when the young person is not fully accepted as part of the White peer group either.

One young Black woman from a predominantly White community described exactly this situation in an interview. In a school with a lot of racial tension, Terri felt that "the worst thing that happened" was the rejection she experienced from the other Black children who were being bussed to her school. Though she wanted to be friends with them, they teased her, calling her an "oreo cookie" and sometimes beating her up. The only close Black friend Terri had was a biracial girl from her neighborhood.

Racial tensions also affected her relationships with White students. One White friend's parents commented, "I can't believe you're Black. You don't seem like all the Black children. You're nice." Though other parents made similar comments, Terri reported that her White friends didn't start making them until junior high school, when

Terri's Blackness became something to be explained. One friend introduced Terri to another White girl by saying, "She's not really Black, she just went to Florida and got a really dark tan." A White sixth-grade "boyfriend" became embarrassed when his friends discovered he had a crush on a Black girl. He stopped telling Terri how pretty she was, and instead called her "nigger" and said, "Your lips are too big. I don't want to see you. I won't be your friend anymore."

Despite supportive parents who expressed concern about her situation, Terri said she was a "very depressed child." Her father would have conversations with her "about being Black and beautiful" and about "the union of people of color that had always existed that I needed to find. And the pride." However, her parents did not have a network of Black friends to help support her.

It was the intervention of a Black junior high school teacher that Terri feels helped her the most. Mrs. Campbell "really exposed me to the good Black community because I was so down on it" by getting Terri involved in singing gospel music and introducing her to other Black students who would accept her. "That's when I started having other Black friends. And I thank her a lot for that."

The significant role that Mrs. Campbell played in helping Terri open up illustrates the constructive potential that informed adults can have in the identity development process. She recognized Terri's need for a same-race peer group and helped her find one. Talking to groups of Black students about the variety of living situations Black people come from, and the unique situation facing Black adolescents in White communities, helps to expand the definition of what it means to be Black and increases intragroup acceptance at a time when that is quite important.

For children in Terri's situation, it is also helpful for Black parents to provide ongoing opportunities for their children to connect with other Black peers even if that means traveling outside the community they live in. Race-conscious parents often do this by attending a Black church or maintaining ties to Black social organizations such as Jack and Jill. Parents who make this effort often find that their children become bicultural, able to move comfortably between Black and White communities, and able to sit at the Black table when they are ready.

Implied in this discussion is the assumption that connecting with one's Black peers in the process of identity development is important and should be encouraged. For young Black people living in predominantly Black communities, such connections occur spontaneously with neighbors and classmates and usually do not require special encouragement. However, for young people in predominantly White communities they may only occur with active parental intervention. One might wonder if this social connection is really necessary. If a young person has found a niche among a circle of White friends, is it really necessary to establish a Black peer group as a reference point? Eventually it is.

As one's awareness of the daily challenges of living in a racist society increase, it is immensely helpful to be able to share one's experiences with others who have lived it. Even when White friends are willing and able to listen and bear witness to one's struggles, they cannot really share the experience. One young woman came to this realization in her senior year of high school:

> [The isolation] never really bothered me until about senior year when I was the only one in the class. . . . That little burden, that constant burden of you always having to strive to do your best and show that you can do just as much as everybody else. Your White friends can't understand that, and it's really hard to communicate to them. Only someone else of the same racial, same ethnic background would understand something like that.

When one is faced with what Chester Pierce calls the "mundane extreme environmental stress" of racism, in adolescence or in adulthood, the ability to see oneself as part of a larger group from which one can draw support is an important coping strategy. Individuals who do not have such a strategy available to them because they do not experience a shared identity with at least some subset of their racial group are at risk for considerable social isolation.

Of course, who we perceive as sharing our identity may be influenced by other dimensions of identity such as gender, social class, geographical location, skin color, or ethnicity. For example, research indicates that first-generation Black immigrants from the Caribbean tend to emphasize their national origins and ethnic identities, distancing themselves from U.S. Blacks, due in part to their belief that West Indians are viewed more positively by Whites than those American Blacks whose family roots include the experience of U.S. slavery. To relinquish one's ethnic identity as West Indian and take on an African American identity may be understood as downward social mobility. However, second-generation West Indians without an identifiable accent may lose the relative ethnic privilege their parents experienced and seek racial solidarity with Black American peers in the face of encounters with racism. Whether it is the experience of being followed in stores because they are suspected of shoplifting, seeing people respond to them with fear on the street, or feeling overlooked in school,

Black youth can benefit from seeking support from those who have had similar experiences.

An Alternative to the Cafeteria Table

The developmental need to explore the meaning of one's identity with others who are engaged in a similar process manifests itself informally in school corridors and cafeterias across the country. Some educational institutions have sought to meet this need programmatically. Several colleagues and I recently evaluated one such effort, initiated at a Massachusetts middle school participating in a voluntary desegregation program known as the Metropolitan Council for Educational Opportunity (METCO) program. Historically, the small number of African American students who are bussed from Boston to this suburban school have achieved disappointing levels of academic success. In an effort to improve academic achievement, the school introduced a program, known as Student Efficacy Training (SET) that allowed Boston students to meet each day as a group with two staff members. Instead of being in physical education or home economics or study hall, they were meeting, talking about homework difficulties, social issues, and encounters with racism. The meeting was mandatory and at first the students were resentful of missing some of their classes. But the impact was dramatic. Said one young woman,

> In the beginning of the year, I didn't want to do SET at all. It took away my study and it was only METCO students doing it. In the beginning all we did was argue over certain problems or it was more like a rap session and I didn't think it was helping anyone. But then when we looked at records. . . . I know that last year out of all the students, sixth through eighth grade, there was, like, six who were actually good students. Everyone else, it was just pathetic, I mean, like, they were getting like Ds and Fs. . . . The eighth grade is doing much better this year. I mean, they went from Ds and Fs to Bs and Cs and occasional As. . . . And those seventh-graders are doing really good, they have a lot of honor roll students in seventh grade, both guys and girls. Yeah, it's been good. It's really good.

Her report is borne out by an examination of school records. The opportunity to come together in the company of supportive adults allowed these young Black students to talk about the issues that hindered their performance—racial encounters, feelings of isolation, test anxiety, homework dilemmas—in the psychological safety of their own group. In the process, the peer culture changed to one that supported academic performance rather than undermined it, as revealed in these two students' comments:

> Well, a lot of the Boston students, the boys and the girls, used to fight all the time. And now, they stopped yelling at each other so much and calling each other stupid.

> It's like we've all become like one big family, we share things more with each other. We tease each other like brother and sister. We look out for each other with homework and stuff. We always stay on top of each other 'cause we know it's hard with African American students to go to a predominantly White school and try to succeed with everybody else.

The faculty, too, were very enthusiastic about the outcomes of the intervention, as seen in the comments of these two classroom teachers:

> This program has probably produced the most dramatic result of any single change that I've seen at this school. It has produced immediate results that affected behavior and academics and participation in school life.

> My students are more engaged. They aren't battling out a lot of the issues of their anger about being in a White community, coming in from Boston, where do I fit, I don't belong here. I feel that those issues that often came out in class aren't coming out in class anymore. I think they are being discussed in the SET room, the kids feel more confidence. The kids' grades are higher, the homework response is greater, they're not afraid to participate in class, and I don't see them isolating themselves within class. They are willing to sit with other students happily. . . . I think it's made a very positive impact on their place in the school and on their individual self-esteem. I see them enjoying themselves and able to enjoy all of us as individuals. I can't say enough, it's been the best

thing that's happened to the METCO program as far as I'm concerned.

Although this intervention is not a miracle cure for every school, it does highlight what can happen when we think about the developmental needs of Black adolescents coming to terms with their own sense of identity. It might seem counterintuitive that a school involved in a voluntary desegregation program could improve both academic performance and social relationships among students by *separating* the Black students for one period every day. But if we understand the unique challenges facing adolescents of color and the legitimate need they have to feel supported in their identity development, it makes perfect sense.

Though they may not use the language of racial identity development theory to describe it, most Black parents want their children to achieve an internalized sense of personal security, to be able to acknowledge the reality of racism and to respond effectively to it. Our educational institutions should do what they can to encourage this development rather than impede it. When I talk to educators about the need to provide adolescents with identity-affirming experiences and information about their own cultural groups, they sometimes flounder because this information has not been part of their own education. Their understanding of adolescent development has been limited to the White middle-class norms included in most textbooks, their knowledge of Black history limited to Martin Luther King, Jr., and Rosa Parks. They sometimes say with frustration that parents should provide this kind of education for their children. Unfortunately Black parents often attended the same schools the teachers did and have the same informational gaps. We need to acknowledge that an important part of interrupting the cycle of oppression is constant re-education, and sharing what we learn with the next generation.

BEVERLY D. TATUM is a clinical psychologist and current president of Spelman College. She is the author of *Why Are All the Black Kids Sitting Together in the Cafeteria? And Other Conversations About Race* (Basic Books, 1997).

Debra Humphreys  **NO**

Campus Diversity and Student Self-Segregation: Separating Myths from Facts

When students went off to college this Fall, they entered more diverse campuses than ever before. For many students, in fact, their college community is the most diverse they have ever encountered. Most students entering college today come from high schools that are predominantly or exclusively one racial or ethnic group. Given this reality, how are students interacting with one another educationally and socially in college? How socially segregated are college campuses? Is campus diversity leading to educational benefits for today's college students or are students too separated into enclaves on campus to benefit from campus diversity?

> A survey of the most recent research suggests that, indeed, campus diversity is leading to significant educational and social benefits for all college students. It also suggests that, contrary to popular reports, student self-segregation is not, in fact, a dominant feature of campus life today. This paper summarizes new research on campus diversity and on the actual extent of student self-segregation and interaction across racial/ethnic lines on college campuses today.

This new research is little known outside of the academic community and critics have ignored it as they describe campus life today to reflect their own political agendas. Critics of both affirmative action and campus diversity programs are skeptical about the educational benefits of campus diversity; they allege that racial and ethnic self-segregation among students is widespread and that it undermines the educational promise of a genuinely multicultural college community. In addition, some critics suggest that campus diversity programs themselves, including African American and Ethnic Studies programs, racial/ethnic student groups, theme houses and dorms, encourage separation rather than community and undermine intergroup contact and the learning that can result from it.

The latest educational research suggests a very different picture of campus life.

While the phenomenon does not appear to be widespread, given the degree of continuing segregation in America's schools and communities, it isn't surprising that college students today do sometimes choose to live, socialize, or study together with other students from similar backgrounds. Contrary to many commentators' claims, however, research suggests that this clustering isn't widespread; it doesn't prevent students from interacting across racial/ethnic lines; and it may be an essential ingredient in many students' persistence and success in college.

Is Student Self-Segregation Prevalent on Today's Diverse College Campuses?

While there are situations in which college students may cluster in racial/ethnic groups, research suggests that there is a high degree of intergroup contact on college campuses and that self-segregation by race/ethnicity is not a dominant feature on diverse college campuses today.

In a recent study, Anthony Lising Antonio, assistant professor of education at Stanford University, examined the extent to which students perceive racial balkanization at the University of California, Los Angeles (UCLA) and whether their perceptions reflect the reality of actual close friendship patterns.[1]

Compared to many American colleges and universities, UCLA is a very diverse campus. When this study was conducted (between 1994 and 1997), the undergraduate student body was approximately 40% white, 35% Asian American, 16% Latino, 6% African American, and just over 1% Native American.

Antonio found that students at UCLA do, indeed, view their campus as racially balkanized.

More than 90% of students in his surveys agreed that students predominantly cluster by race and ethnicity on campus. A small majority (52%) said that students rarely socialize across racial lines.

Antonio, however, didn't stop at just measuring perceptions. He also calculated the actual racial/ethnic diversity or homogeneity of close friendship groups on campus. Antonio categorized the racial diversity of each student's friendship groups as one of the following: 1) Homogenous—the largest racial/ethnic group makes up 100% of the friendship group; 2) Predominantly one race/ethnicity—the largest racial/ethnic group makes up 75–99% of the friendship group; 3) Majority one race/ethnicity—the largest racial/ethnic group makes up 51–74% of the friendship group; and 4) No majority—the largest racial/ethnic group makes up 50% or less of the friendship group.

Just 17% of UCLA students, or about one in six, reported having friendship groups that were racially and ethnically homogenous.

Homogenous groups and those groups with predominantly one race/ethnicity together account for about one-quarter of the sample.

The most common friendship group on campus (46%), however, was racially and ethnically mixed with no racial or ethnic group constituting a majority.

At the level of student friendship groups, then, racial and ethnic balkanization is not a dominant, overall campus characteristic at UCLA. Several other earlier studies also suggest a high degree of student interaction across racial and ethnic lines at campuses across the country, especially among students of color.

A 1991 study that examined patterns of intergroup contact at 390 institutions across the country confirmed that self-segregation is not a general pattern among students of color. The authors of this study examined the frequency with which students dined, roomed, socialized, or dated someone from a racial/ethnic group different from their own.[2]

Chicano, Asian American, and African American students reported widespread and frequent interaction across race/ethnicity in these informal situations. White students were least likely to report engaging in any of these activities across race/ethnicity.

Sixty-nine percent of Asian Americans and 78% of Mexican American students frequently dined with someone of a different ethnic or racial background compared with 55% of African American students and 21% of white students.

Nearly 42% of Asian American students reported interracial or interethnic dating compared with 24% of Mexican Americans, 13% of African Americans, and 4% of white students.

What Characterizes Student Interactions within and across Racial/Ethnic Lines on Campus? Why Do Some Students Cluster by Race/Ethnicity on College Campuses?

Understanding student interactions across racial/ethnic lines requires an appreciation of the influence of the widespread residential segregation that characterizes American society. It also requires an appreciation of how white American higher education still is, despite its increasing diversity. Most students of color who do not attend historically black colleges or universities attend overwhelmingly white institutions.

A 1991 study of student life at Berkeley, an unusually diverse college campus, describes the experience of campus life as a complex phenomenon that encompasses both some student-initiated racial/ethnic clustering and substantial amounts of interracial interactions.[3]

This study also found, however, that 70% of all undergraduates agreed with the statement, I'd like to meet more students from ethnic and cultural backgrounds that are different from my own.

A forthcoming book by Richard Light of Harvard University also suggests that students from a wide array of racial/ethnic groups desire intergroup contact and see the educational and social benefits of such interactions.

The widespread segregation by race that still characterizes much of the rest of American life is, however, having an impact on how students interact with one another on college campuses.

A 1997 study at the University of Michigan found that students' friendship patterns closely reflected the make-ups of their high schools and home neighborhoods. This study confirmed that a majority of all students, but a very high percentage of white students, came from highly segregated high schools and neighborhoods.

The Michigan study also found that white students had the most segregated friendship patterns on campus of all ethnic groups.[4]

The reality is that students of color have much more intergroup contact than do white students, but their patterns of interaction need to be understood in light of their psychological development. Research by psychologist Beverly Daniel Tatum, Dean of the College at Mt. Holyoke College, suggests that there are complex psychological reasons why college students may choose to cluster in racial/ethnic groups. She argues that racial grouping is a developmental process in response to an environmental stressor, racism. Joining with one's peers for support in the face of stress is a positive coping strategy. There is a developmental need on the part of many college students to explore the meaning of one's identity with others who are engaged in a similar process.[5]

What Difference Does Racial/Ethnic Clustering Make When It Does Occur?

Recent research, including Tatum's and that of others, suggests that racial/ethnic clustering can be an important component contributing to the psychological health and educational success of many students. Research also suggests that this clustering need not prevent students from achieving the educational benefits of intergroup contact within college classrooms and on college campuses.

The 1991 study of 390 institutions cited above found that ethnic-specific activities were not impeding intergroup contact for the students who participated in them. Programs like racial/ethnic theme houses and study groups seem to help students of color persist and succeed in college and seem to increase their involvement overall with other areas of college life in which they interact frequently across racial/ethnic lines.

Other studies confirm these findings:

- A 1994 study of Latino students suggests that students belonging to Latino organizations increased their adjustment and attachment to their colleges and universities.[6]
- Two other studies, one in 1994 and another in 1996, also found positive benefits of participation in racial and ethnic groups and that these groups also fostered rather than impeded intergroup contact.[7]
- Another 1989 study found that a targeted student support program was positively related to African American students' persistence in college and their degree status.[8]

Given the Relatively High Level of Intergroup Contact and the Existence of Some Racial/Ethnic Clustering, What Is the Impact of Campus Diversity on Today's College Students?

Research suggests a variety of positive educational outcomes that result from being educated in a diverse

environment. It also suggests a positive impact for those students with high degrees of intergroup contact.

Patricia Gurin, professor of psychology at the University of Michigan, recently compiled a report summarizing three parallel empirical analyses of university students. Her report suggests that,

> A racially and ethnically diverse university student body has far-ranging and significant benefits for all students, non-minorities and minorities alike. Students learn better in such an environment and are better prepared to become active participants in our pluralistic, democratic society once they leave school. In fact, patterns of racial segregation and separation historically rooted in our national life can be broken by diversity experiences in higher education.

Gurin's research demonstrates that the diverse environment provided by many colleges today contributes to students' intellectual and social development. She suggests that racial diversity in a college or university student body provides the very features that research has determined are central to producing the conscious mode of thought educators demand from their students.

Gurin also found that these positive effects of campus diversity extend beyond graduation.

Diversity experiences during college had impressive effects on the extent to which graduates in the national study were living racially and ethnically integrated lives in the post-college world. Students with the most diversity experiences during college had the most cross-racial interactions five years after leaving college.[9]

The study by Antonio mentioned above also confirms that campus diversity is having a positive impact on today's college students.

Antonio examined the impact of the diverse friendship groups he found to be common at UCLA. Controlling for important background information such as gender, socio-economic status, and the racial diversity of pre-college friendship groups, Antonio found that friendship group diversity contributed to greater interracial interaction outside the friendship group and stronger commitments to racial understanding.

Another important arena of college life, of course, is the classroom. On diverse campuses, many students are now being educated in highly diverse classrooms in which they are studying a much wider array of subjects that include content about previously neglected groups. These classes are also having a significant positive educational impact on both majority and minority students as well.[10]

Conclusions: Is There Cause for Alarm, Hope, or Celebration?

There is little cause for alarm, some cause for celebration and much hope for what lies ahead. The reality is that while there is still a long way to go before American higher education will truly reflect the full diversity of American society, college campuses are becoming much more diverse and their diverse campus environments are having a significant positive effect on this generation of students.

College campuses are not dominated by widespread racial/ethnic segregation and the racial/ethnic clustering that does occur isn't impeding intergroup contact. In fact, the existence of racial/ethnic groups and activities, along with other comprehensive campus diversity initiatives, is contributing to the success of today's college students and preparing them to help build a healthier multicultural America for the future.

Notes

1. Antonio, Anthony Lising, "Racial Diversity and Friendship Groups in College: What the Research Tells Us," *Diversity Digest,* Summer, 1999, (Washington, DC: Association of American Colleges and Universities, 1999): 6–7.
2. Hurtado, S., Dey, E., and Treviño, J., "Exclusion or Self-Segregation? Interaction Across Racial/Ethnic Groups on College Campuses," paper presented at American Educational Research Association Conference, New Orleans, LA, 1994.
3. Duster, Troy, "The Diversity Project: Final Report," Institute for the Study of Social Change. University of California, Berkeley, 1991.
4. Matlock, John, "Student Expectations and Experiences: The Michigan Study," *Diversity Digest,* Summer, 1997, (Washington, DC: Association of American Colleges and Universities, 1997): 11.
5. Tatum, Beverly Daniel. *Why Are All the Black Kids Sitting Together in the Cafeteria?* (New York: Basic Books, 1997): 62;71.
6. Hurtado, S., and D.F. Carter, "Latino Students' Sense of Belonging in the College Community: Rethinking the Concept of Integration on Campus," paper presented at the annual meeting of the American Educational Research Association, New Orleans, LA, 1994.
7. Gilliard, M. D., "Racial Climate and Institutional Support Factors Affecting Success in Predominantly White Institutions: An Examination of African American and White Student Experiences," unpublished Ph.D. dissertation, University of Michigan, 1996; Hurtado, S., Dey, E., and Treviño, J., "Exclusion or Self-Segregation? Interaction Across Racial/Ethnic Groups on College Campuses," paper presented at American Educational Research Association Conference, New Orleans, LA, 1994.
8. Trippi, J., and H.E. Cheatham, "Effects of Special Counseling Programs for Black Freshman on a Predominantly White Campus," *Journal of College Student Development* 30, (1989): 35–40.
9. Gurin, Patricia, "New Research on the Benefits of Diversity in College and Beyond: An Empirical Analysis," *Diversity Digest,* Spring, 1999, (Washington, DC: Association of American Colleges and Universities, 1999): 5/15.
10. For information on the impact of diversity courses, see "Diversity and The College Curriculum," http://www.inform.umd.edu/EdRes/Topic/Diversity/Response/Web/Leadersguide/CT/curriculum_briefing.html.

DEBRA HUMPHREYS is a former director of programs, Office of Education and Diversity, Equity and Global Initiatives, at the Association of American Colleges and Universities in Washington, DC. Currently, she is vice president for communications and public affairs at AACU. She has written columns in *The Chronicle of Higher Education* and *USA Today.*

EXPLORING THE ISSUE

Do Minorities and Whites Engage in Self-Segregation?

Critical Thinking and Reflection

1. How do adolescents develop a sense of racial identity? How is the understanding of racial identity developed among adolescents important for understanding this issue?
2. Why do young people choose self-segregation as their way of dealing with interracial environments?
3. What is the link between Jim Crow society and self-segregation?
4. How do these concepts inform the discussion of this issue?
5. What social and psychological factors lead to self-segregation of adolescents? How may self-segregation extend to areas of life beyond high school and college?

Is There Common Ground?

The separation of blacks from whites within American society is the prevailing context within which race relations develop throughout history. The long-standing tradition of segregated schools, neighborhoods, and even churches in the United States is being challenged by the growing multiculturalism and the diversity ideal. However, some levels of segregation persist, especially in the area of housing. It is important to note that any tendency toward self-segregation is an outcome of the traditional Jim Crow that dominated the country for many years. Neither Tatum nor Humphreys challenges the reality of self-segregation within institutional settings today. Both Tatum and Humphreys recognize that self-segregation is part of the collegiate experience, as it is in other areas of life. For many students, the university is the first truly integrated experience of their lives. At the same time, Humphreys points out that college campuses are not dominated by widespread self-segregation and, when it occurs, the self-segregation does not impede intergroup contact. Additionally, Tatum and Humphreys both view self-segregation as a means for all students—whites and minorities—to adjust to a new experience. Campus diversity is having a positive impact on today's college students.

Additional Resources

Anderson, Elijah. 1978. *A Place on the Corner* (University of Chicago Press).

Anderson, Elijah. 1999. *Code of the Street: Decency, Violence, and the Moral Life of the Inner City* (W. W. Norton & Co.).

Anderson, Elijah. 2012. *The Cosmopolitan Canopy: Race and Civility in Everyday Life* (W. W. Norton & Co.).

Antonio, Anthony Lising. 1999. "Racial Diversity and Friendship Groups in College: What the Research Tells Us," *Diversity Digest* (Summer, 6–7).

Bow, Leslie. 2010. *Partly Colored: Asian Americans and Racial Anomaly in the Segregated South* (New York University Press).

Chan, Priscilla. 2004. "Drawing the Boundaries," in Arar Han and John Hsu, eds. *Asian American X: An Intersection of 21st Century Asian American Voices* (University of Michigan Press).

Conley, Dalton. 2000. *Honky* (Vintage).

Cose, Ellis. 1993. *The Rage of a Privileged Class* (HarperCollins, 1993).

DuBois, W. E. B. 1951. *The Souls of Black Folk* (Fawcett World Library).

Duster, Troy. 1991. "The Diversity Project: Final Report" (Institute for the Study of Social Change, University of California, Berkeley, CA).

Hurtado, Sylvia. 1994. *Exclusion of Self-Segregation?: Interaction Across Racial/Ethnic Groups Across College Campuses* (S. Hurtado, distributor).

Massey, Douglas and Nancy Denton. 1993. *American Apartheid: Segregation and the Making of the Underclass* (Harvard University Press).

Matlock, John. 1997. "Student Expectations and Experiences: The Michigan Study," *Diversity Digest* (Summer, 11).

Nathan, Rebekah. 2005. *My Freshman Year: What a Professor Learned by Becoming a Student* (Penguin Books).

Norman, Brian. 2010. *Neo-Segregation Narratives: Jim Crow in Post-Civil Rights Literature* (University of Georgia Press).

Royster, Deidre A. 2003. *Race and the Invisible Hand: How White Networks Exclude Black Men from Blue Collar Jobs* (University of California).

Thurman, Howard. 1986. *The Search for Common Ground* (Friends United Press).

Thurman, Howard. 1989. *The Luminous Darkness: A Personal Interpretation of the Anatomy of Segregation and the Ground of Hope* (Friends United Press).

West, Cornel. 1993. *Race Matters* (New York: Vintage Books).

Wilson, William Julius. 1980. *The Declining Significance of Race* (University of Chicago).

Internet References . . .

Diversity Web

http://www.diversityweb.org/

Selected, Edited, and with Issue Framing Material by:
Wind Goodfriend, *Buena Vista University*

ISSUE

Does Intergroup Contact Work to Reduce Prejudice?

YES: **Muzafer Sherif**, from "Experiments in Group Conflict," *Scientific American* (1956)

NO: **Jennifer C. Cornell**, from "Prejudice Reduction Through Intergroup Contact in Northern Ireland: A Social-Psychological Critique," *Journal of Conflict Studies* (1994)

Learning Outcomes

After reading this issue, you will be able to:

- Explain the basic idea of the "contact hypothesis" and how it predicts reduction in prejudice between two groups.
- Summarize the purpose, procedures, and results of the famous Sherif experiments using boys at a summer camp to test hypotheses about intergroup conflict.
- Discuss how the contact hypothesis has been applied in attempts to decrease conflict in Northern Ireland, and identify at least one problem with how it has been implemented there.
- Apply the contact hypothesis and the idea of "superordinate" (common) goals to at least one modern conflict you see in the world around you, and how this theory might be used to decrease that conflict, if the circumstances were right.

ISSUE SUMMARY

YES: In a classic and famous article, social psychologist Muzafer Sherif describes studies he completed in which young boys learned prejudice in a summer camp setting. While simple intergroup contact failed to decrease this prejudice, working together toward common goals did work. Sherif discusses how this particular type of intergroup contact is therefore successful for producing harmony and cooperation between groups.

NO: Jennifer Cornell argues that in Northern Ireland attempts at peaceful intergroup contact have been tried for several decades. Even though the contact is structured, collaborative, and long-term, it has not worked to reduce prejudice and anger between Catholics and Protestants in that province.

Many sports movies have been made over the years with the same basic premise: Each player comes to the team initially wary, with dislike for at least some of the other players due to one form of prejudice or another. The beginning of the movie highlights the players' conflicts and shows how they appear to dislike each other more and more. However, as time passes and the players must form a true "team" mentality, individual prejudices erode. Eventually, by the end of the movie, the teammates have found unlikely friends, overcome their prejudice, and (most likely) come out of the season as champions.

The basic premise of this scenario highlights several ideas from within social psychology, but perhaps the most salient idea is one called the "contact hypothesis." One of the central tenets of the contact hypothesis is that intergroup prejudice is caused because people from different groups do not spend time with each other. In other words, we tend to form stereotypes about people from different groups because we simply don't know them very well. This leads to "outgroup homogeneity," or the assumption that everyone from the other group is the same as everyone else in that group—"they're all the same." In contrast, because we spend much more time with people in our own group, we can see the wide variety and diversity of individuals, so we see "ingroup heterogeneity." Outgroup homogeneity leads to stereotypes and prejudice, because all we know about this different group is what we hear or see from media messages.

Thus, the contact hypothesis suggests that stereotypes and prejudice toward outgroups would be decreased if we simply spent more time with people from that group, and got to know them as individuals. This would serve two functions: (1) we would have to acknowledge that different members of that group are also different from each other in various ways, and that they are not all the same, and (2) we would become friends with some of those individuals, thus leading to positive, liking attitudes and behaviors instead of negative, prejudiced behaviors.

The contact hypothesis has been the subject of scores of studies over the years, but perhaps the most famous study, considered a classic now, is the series of boys' summer camps conducted by Muzafer Sherif and his colleagues. An article summarizing some of these camps serves as the "yes" side of this debate. Sherif gathered young boys of similar backgrounds to summer camps, without their knowledge that they were really being studied by psychologists. He wanted them to all be similar to each other at the beginning so that they wouldn't have pre-formed prejudices upon arrival. This ensured that he could experimentally manipulate their ingroups, outgroups, and prejudices toward each other, which he did very successfully. He divided the boys into two groups and created a series of competitions that led the boys to dislike each other very much.

The next step, of course, was to attempt to experimentally erase this newly formed prejudice. Sherif's first test of the contact hypothesis was simple, unrestricted contact. Sherif states in the article, "We first undertook to test the theory that pleasant social contacts between members of conflicting groups will reduce friction between them." This first attempt failed, and in fact may have made the prejudice between groups worse. However, Sherif then tried another test, which was a particular *type* of contact. He writes, "Just as competition generates friction, working in a common endeavor should promote harmony. . . . Where harmony between groups is established, the most decisive factor is the existence of 'superordinate' goals which have a compelling appeal for both but which neither could achieve without the other." This form of contact worked to bring the two groups of boys together.

However, some people doubt whether contact between groups can really achieve such lofty goals. In the "no" side of this debate, Jennifer Cornell presents a thorough explanation of how positive intergroup contact has been attempted between Catholics and Protestants in Northern Ireland. Historically, these two groups have held extremely zealous and passionate dislike for each other, consistently erupting in violence over many years. She describes how the Department of Education Northern Ireland (DENI) tried to have young people from both groups interact, thus attempting to apply the contact hypothesis to this very volatile situation. She then describes how this attempt failed.

After you read each side of the debate, consider other real-life intergroup conflicts, and whether it would be possible for the prejudice held on both sides to be reduced due to the "right" kind of contact. Is it possible—or are all those sports movies a modern fairy tale, fooling us with their "happily ever after" endings?

YES ↵

Muzafer Sherif

Experiments in Group Conflict

Conflict between groups—whether between boys' gangs, social classes, "races" or nations—has no simple cause, nor is mankind yet in sight of a cure. It is often rooted deep in personal, social, economic, religious and historical forces. Nevertheless, it is possible to identify certain general factors which have a crucial influence on the attitude of any group toward others. Social scientists have long sought to bring these factors to light by studying what might be called the "natural history" of groups and group relations. Intergroup conflict and harmony is not a subject that lends itself easily to laboratory experiments. But in recent years there has been a beginning of attempts to investigate the problem under controlled yet lifelike conditions, and I shall report here the results of a program of experimental studies of groups which 1 started in 1948. Among the persons working with me were Marvin B. Sussman. Robert Huntington, O. J. Harvey, B. Jack White, William R. Hood and Carolyn W. Sherif. The experiments were conducted in 1949, 1953 and 1954; this article gives a composite of the findings.

We wanted to conduct our study with groups of the informal type, where group organization and attitudes would evolve naturally and spontaneously, without formal direction or external pressures. For this purpose we conceived that an isolated summer camp would make a good experimental setting, and that decision led us to choose as subjects boys about eleven or twelve years old, who would find camping natural and fascinating. Since our aim was to study the development of group relations among these boys under carefully controlled conditions, with as little interference as possible from personal neuroses, background influences or prior experiences, we selected normal boys of homogeneous background who did not know one another before they came to the camp.

They were picked by a long and thorough procedure. We interviewed each boy's family, teachers and school officials, studied his school and medical records, obtained his scores on personality tests and observed him in his classes and at play with his schoolmates. With all this information we were able to assure ourselves that the boys chosen were of like kind and background: all were healthy, socially well-adjusted, somewhat above average in intelligence and from stable, white, Protestant, middle-class homes.

None of the boys was aware that he was part of an experiment on group relations. The investigators appeared as a regular camp staff—camp directors, counselors and so on. The boys met one another for the first time in buses that took them to the camp, and so far as they knew it was a normal summer of camping. To keep the situation as life-like as possible, we conducted all our experiments within the framework of regular camp activities and games. We set up projects which were so interesting and attractive that the boys plunged into them enthusiastically without suspecting that they might be test situations. Unobtrusively we made records of their behavior, even using "candid" cameras and microphones when feasible.

We began by observing how the boys became a coherent group. The first of our camps was conducted in the hills of northern Connecticut in the summer of 1949. When the boys arrived, they were all housed at first in one large bunkhouse. As was to be expected, they quickly formed particular friendships and chose buddies. We had deliberately put all the boys together in this expectation, because we wanted to see what would happen later after the boys were separated into different groups. Our object was to reduce the factor of personal attraction in the formation of groups. In a few days we divided the boys into two groups and put them in different cabins. Before doing so, we asked each boy informally who his best friends were, and then took pains to place the "best friends" in different groups as far as possible. (The pain of separation was assuaged by allowing each group to go at once on a hike and campout.)

As everyone knows, a group of strangers brought together in some common activity soon acquires an informal and spontaneous kind of organization. It comes to look upon some members as leaders, divides up duties, adopts unwritten norms of behavior, develops an *esprit de corps*. Our boys followed this pattern as they shared a series of experiences. In each group the boys pooled their efforts, organized duties and divided up tasks in work and play. Different individuals assumed different responsibilities. One boy excelled in cooking. Another led in athletics. Others, though not outstanding in any one skill, could be counted on to pitch in and do their level best in anything the group attempted. One or two seemed to disrupt activities, to start teasing at the wrong moment or offer useless suggestions. A few boys consistently had good suggestions and showed ability to coordinate the efforts of others in carrying them through. Within a few days one person had proved himself more resourceful and skillful than the rest. Thus, rather quickly, a leader and lieutenants emerged. Some boys sifted toward the bottom of the heap, while others jockeyed for higher positions.

We watched these developments closely and rated the boys' relative positions in the group, not only on the basis of our own observations but also by informal sounding of the boys' opinions as to who got things started, who got things done, who could be counted on to support group activities.

As the group became an organization, the boys coined nicknames. The big, blond, hardy leader of one group was dubbed "Baby Face" by his admiring followers. A boy with a rather long head became "Lemon Head." Each group developed its own jargon, special jokes, secrets and special ways of performing tasks. One group, after killing a snake near a place where it had gone to swim, named the place "Moccasin Creek" and thereafter preferred this swimming hole to any other, though there were better ones nearby.

Wayward members who failed to do things "right" or who did not contribute their bit to the common effort found themselves receiving the "silent treatment," ridicule or even threats. Each group selected symbols and a name, and they had these put on their caps and T-shirts. The 1954 camp was conducted in Oklahoma, near a famous hideaway of Jesse James called Robber's Cave. The two groups of boys at this camp named themselves the Rattlers and the Eagles.

Our conclusions on every phase of the study were based on a variety of observations, rather than on any single method. For example, we devised a game to test the boys' evaluations of one another. Before an important baseball game, we set up a target board for the boys to throw at, on the pretense of making practice for the game more interesting. There were no marks on the front of the board for the boys to judge objectively how close the ball came to a bull's-eye, but, unknown to them, the board was wired to flashing lights behind so that an observer could see exactly where the ball hit. We found that the boys consistently overestimated the performances by the most highly regarded members of

their group and underestimated the scores of those of low social standing.

The attitudes of group members were even more dramatically illustrated during a cook-out in the woods. The staff supplied the boys with unprepared food and let them cook it themselves. One boy promptly started to build a fire, asking for help in getting wood. Another attacked the raw hamburger to make patties. Others prepared a place to put buns, relishes and the like. Two mixed soft drinks from flavoring and sugar. One boy who stood around without helping was told by others to "get to it." Shortly the fire was blazing and the cook had hamburgers sizzling. Two boys distributed them as rapidly as they became edible. Soon it was time for the watermelon. A low-ranking member of the group took a knife and started toward the melon. Some of the boys protested. The most highly regarded boy in the group took over the knife, saying, "You guys who yell the loudest get yours last."

When the two groups in the camp had developed group organization and spirit, we proceeded to the experimental studies of intergroup relations. The groups had had no previous encounters; indeed, in the 1954 camp at Robber's Cave the two groups came in separate buses and were kept apart while each acquired a group feeling.

Our working hypothesis was that when two groups have conflicting aims—i.e., when one can achieve its ends only at the expense of the other—their members will become hostile to each other even though the groups are composed of normal well-adjusted individuals. There is a corollary to this assumption which we shall consider later. To produce friction between the groups of boys we arranged a tournament of games: baseball, touch football, a tug-of-war, a treasure hunt and so on. The tournament started in a spirit of good sportsmanship. But as it progressed good feeling soon evaporated. The members of each group began to call their rivals "stinkers," "sneaks" and "cheaters." They refused to have anything more to do with individuals in the opposing group. The boys in the 1949 camp turned against buddies whom they had chosen as "best friends" when they first arrived at the camp. A large proportion of the boys in each group gave negative ratings to all the boys in the other. The rival groups made threatening posters and planned raids, collecting secret hoards of green apples for ammunition. In the Robber's Cave camp the Eagles, after a defeat in a tournament game, burned a banner left behind by the Rattlers; the next morning the Rattlers seized the Eagles' flag when they arrived on the athletic field. From that time on name-calling scuffles and raids were the rule of the day.

Within each group, of course, solidarity increased. There were changes: one group deposed its leader because

Friendship choices of campers for others in their own cabin are shown for Red Devils (*white*) and Bulldogs. (*gray*). At first, a low percentage of friendships were in the cabin group (*left*). After five days, most friendship choices were within the group (*right*).

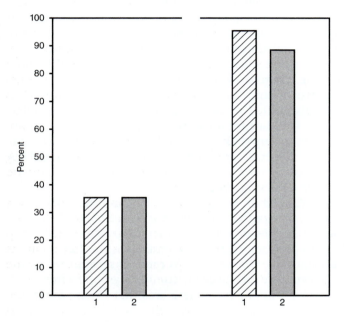

During conflict between the two groups in the Robber's Cave experiment, there were few friendships between cabins (*left*). After cooperation toward common goals had restored good feelings, the number of friendships between groups rose significantly (*right*).

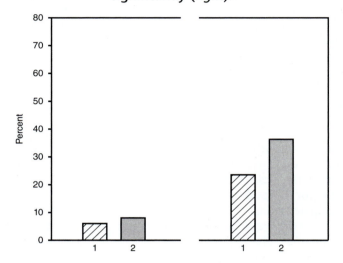

he could not "take it" in the contests with the adversary; another group overnight made something of a hero of a big boy who had previously been regarded as a bully. But morale and cooperativeness within the group became stronger. It is noteworthy that this heightening of cooperativeness and generally democratic behavior did not carry over to the group's relations with other groups.

We now turned to the other side of the problem: How can two groups in conflict be brought into harmony? We first undertook to test the theory that pleasant social contacts between members of conflicting groups will reduce friction between them. In the 1954 camp we brought the hostile Rattlers and Eagles together for social events: going to the movies, eating in the same dining room and so on, But far from reducing conflict, these situations only served as opportunities for the rival groups to berate and attack each other. In the dining-hall line they shoved each other aside, and the group that lost the contest for the head of the line shouted "Ladies first!" at the winner. They threw paper, food and vile names at each other at the tables. An Eagle bumped by a Rattler was admonished by his fellow Eagles to brush "the dirt" off his clothes.

We then returned to the corollary of our assumption about the creation of conflict. Just as competition

generates friction, working in a common endeavor should promote harmony. It seemed to us, considering group relations in the everyday world, that where harmony between groups is established, the most decisive factor is the existence of "superordinate" goals which have a compelling appeal for both but which neither could achieve without the other. To test this hypothesis experimentally, we created a series of urgent, and natural, situations which challenged our boys.

One was a breakdown in the water supply. Water came to our camp in pipes from a tank about a mile away. We arranged to interrupt it and then called the boys together to inform them of the crisis. Both groups promptly volunteered to search the water line for the trouble. They worked together harmoniously, and before the end of the afternoon they had located and corrected the difficulty.

A similar opportunity offered itself when the boys requested a movie. We told them that the camp could not afford to rent one. The two groups then got together, figured out how much each group would have to contribute, chose the film by a vote and enjoyed the showing together.

One day the two groups went on an outing at a lake some distance away. A large truck was to go to town for food. But when everyone was hungry and ready to eat, it developed that the truck would not start (we had taken care of that). The boys got a rope—the same rope they

Negative ratings of each group by the other were common during the period of conflict (*left*) but decreased when harmony was restored (*right*). The graphs show percentage who thought *all* (rather than *some* or *none*) of the other group were cheaters, sneaks, and so forth.

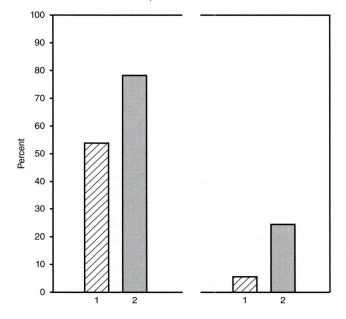

own initiative they invited their former rivals to be their guests for malted milks.

Our interviews with the boys confirmed this change. From choosing their "best friends" almost exclusively in their own group, many of them shifted to listing boys in the other group as best friends. They were glad to have a second chance to rate boys in the other group, some of them remarking that they had changed their minds since the first rating made after the tournament. Indeed they had. The new ratings were largely favorable.

Efforts to reduce friction and prejudice between groups in our society have usually followed rather different methods. Much attention has been given to bringing members of hostile groups together socially, to communicating accurate and favorable information about one group to the other, and to bringing the leaders of groups together to enlist their influence. But as everyone knows, such measures sometimes reduce intergroup tensions and sometimes do not. Social contacts, as our experiments demonstrated, may only serve as occasions for intensifying conflict. Favorable information about a disliked group may be ignored or reinterpreted to fit stereotyped notions about the group. Leaders cannot act without regard for the prevailing temper in their own groups.

What our limited experiments have shown is that the possibilities for achieving harmony are greatly enhanced when groups are brought together to work toward common ends. Then favorable information about a disliked group is seen in a new light, and leaders are in a position to take bolder steps toward cooperation. In short, hostility gives way when groups pull together to achieve overriding goals which are real and compelling to all concerned.

had used in their acrimonious tug-of-war—and all pulled together to start the truck.

These joint efforts did not immediately dispel hostility. At first the groups returned to the old bickering and name-calling as soon as the job in hand was finished. But gradually the series of cooperative acts reduced friction and conflict. The members of the two groups began to feel more friendly to each other. For example, a Rattler whom the Eagles disliked for his sharp tongue and skill in defeating them became a "good egg." The boys stopped shoving in the meal line. They no longer called each other names, and sat together at the table. New friendships developed between individuals in the two groups.

In the end the groups were actively seeking opportunities to mingle, to entertain and "treat" each other. They decided to hold a joint campfire. They took turns presenting skits and songs. Members of both groups requested that they go home together on the same bus, rather than on the separate buses in which they had come. On the way the bus stopped for refreshments. One group still had five dollars which they had won as a prize in a contest. They decided to spend this sum on refreshments. On their

Reference

Sherif, Muzafer, and Sherif, Carolyn W. *Groups in harmony and tension*. Harper & Brothers, 1953.

Muzafer Sherif is credited as being one of the founders of social psychology through his work on group processes, inner group conflict, and social norms. He was born in Turkey, but obtained a master's at Harvard University and a PhD at Columbia University. He passed away in 1988 as a distinguished name in the field of social psychology, a decorated educator, and the author of over 60 articles and 24 books.

Jennifer C. Cornell

 **NO**

Prejudice Reduction Through Intergroup Contact in Northern Ireland: A Social-Psychological Critique

Introduction

The Equal Status Contact (ESC) hypothesis, of which the Integration Through Play (ITP) model is a variant, has its roots in the post-World War II era, and was originally developed with the aim of improving race relations in the United States. The theory is based upon three assumptions. First is that the fundamental problem of intergroup conflict is individual prejudice. Second is that prejudice is an educational as well as a psychological problem. Finally, is the view that prejudicial attitudes may be altered by re-education; this accomplished, behavioral changes will necessarily follow.

The simplistic view that prejudice stems from ignorance and that ignorance can be cured by contact was elevated to "a cultural truism and a plan for action" in the early 1950s, and has been at the heart of the study of intergroup relations, particularly in the US, ever since. In 1962, Berkowitz proposed the ESC hypothesis as the only successful means of reducing hostilities across racial divides. Subsequently, cross-community contact schemes were widely deployed throughout the period of the civil rights movement in America. Like many aspects of that period, which made their way across the Atlantic, the concept of contact as a means of improving relations between divided communities received considerable support from those working for reconciliation between Catholics and Protestants in Northern Ireland at that time, and is still the prevailing philosophy behind many cross-community endeavors in the province today.

The ESC Model as a Form of Education

The implementation of the ESC hypothesis in Northern Ireland has taken many forms, all of which may be said to be educational in nature, whether or not they take place in the classroom. Nevertheless, it is in a formal educational setting, where equality of contact is most pronounced, that the hypothesis should, in theory, be best put to the test. In such a setting equality exists not only in terms of age and environment, but also in program of study, criteria for individual assessment, rules of conduct, and even (in some cases) code of dress. Because attendance is compulsory, contact between students is regular, consistent, and long-term: most children spend more than forty hours a week engaged in school-related activities, nine months out of every year, for more than a decade.

Education for Mutual Understanding (EMU) has been developed to introduce a cross-community theme into the design of school curricula at all levels throughout the province; it also forms the basis of the European Studies Project jointly sponsored by the Education Departments of Northern Ireland, England, Wales, the Republic of Ireland and Belgium. EMU principles may be implemented either as a specific project involving teachers and pupils from more than one school and from both communities, or as a general approach to teaching, which informs the presentation of all areas of study. In either form its aim is to bridge divisions and dispel prejudice, and to promote improved community relations by teaching students self-respect as well as respect for the cultural traditions, backgrounds and beliefs of others.

The call for a program of formal education for peace to challenge Northern Ireland's segregated school system has also been answered by the integrated school movement. Thirteen such schools have come into existence, since the first, Lagan College, opened in 1981, twelve at the primary level and Hazlewood College; a further two opened in September 1992. This pattern of steady incremental growth is repeated in the enrollment figures, and reflects an increasing interest in integrated education on the part of parents from both sides of the community.

There is, however, a considerable gap between the amount of support for the idea of integrated education and its actual extent. Development of an extensive system of

From Jennifer C. Cornell (1994), "Prejudice Reduction Through Intergroup Contact in Northern Ireland: A Social-Psychological Critique." *Journal of Conflict Studies*, vol. 14, 30–46.

integrated schools is further impeded by opposition from some church and community leaders on both sides of the divide. By contrast, extracurricular cross-community contact is rarely met with such official resistance, and therefore more children are still likely to experience contact in this context rather than in the classroom. For this reason, and because EMU is only just beginning to take effect in schools, this essay will focus on programs of nonformal, rather than formal, education for peace.

The Point of Contact: Interpersonal Versus Intergroup

The only real criterion for assessing programs of intergroup contact is the extent to which they achieve their goals. Some aim simply to provide participants with a respite from the stress and deprivation that have characterized life for many people in the province since the onset of the Troubles. Others, however, clearly hope to exert a positive influence on community relations in the long term, beyond the confines of the contact situation they provide.

In a publication released in 1983, the Department of Education Northern Ireland (DENI) described cross-community holiday schemes as "a practical means of facilitating the coming together of children and young people in circumstances that will contribute to increased understanding between the two traditions." In other words, DENI's goal was not simply to encourage *interpersonal* contact—contact between individuals leading to a personal and unique relationship of a more or less intimate nature, the course and dimensions of which are determined by the characteristics of the individuals involved. Rather, DENI aimed to promote real and lasting *intergroup* contact, which occurs "whenever individuals belonging to one group interact, collectively or individually, with another group or its members in terms of their *group* identifications."

Since 1983, the guidelines issued to applicants for government funding have become more stringent. Programs must now be "coherent, ongoing and systematic" and should "result in cross-community contact which is purposeful and require *(sic)* a genuinely collaborative effort to achieve its aims;" moreover, a preference is stated for projects whose participants have previously been in contact. Each of these conditions makes the possibility of effective exchange between participants all the more likely, and indeed, some such programs do appear to make a real contribution to improving intergroup relations.

Nevertheless, many projects still follow the model established in the wake of the much-cited Doob and Foltz workshop. Those that do are based upon the assumption that "short-term intergroup *(sic)* contact in an isolated

setting . . . does have a positive effect," and that "good 'human relationships'"—which are believed to develop naturally and inevitably between individuals in contact as the "common humanity" they share becomes evident to them all —"will promote [widespread] community harmony in Northern Ireland."

This view that relatively short-term contact between small groups of individuals is an effective means of improving community relations generally is still espoused by the Department of Education. Although the premises upon which such a view is based have been challenged by contemporary analyses of intergroup contact, many of those working for peace in the province, particularly at the community level, have adopted programs in which this view remains enshrined. The most prevalent of these, and the focus of this essay, is the Integration Through Play model.

The Integration Through Play Model

The theory behind the ITP variant of the contact hypothesis is as follows. First, individuals from different groups engaged in joint recreational activity will come to know and respect each other as individuals because such activity stimulates conversation and "creates opportunities for mutual recognition," which inevitably reveal fundamental similarities between participants. Second, strong interpersonal relationships will develop as a result. Third, these interpersonal relationships will challenge preconceptions held by members of one group about those of the other and thus make stereotypical thinking and other forms of prejudice impossible. Finally, prejudice reduction at the individual level resulting from this kind of contact will produce a reduction in prejudice at the community level (i.e., the group level).

In practice, TP initiatives offered by local community centers are limited by their very design. First, most are short-term, intensive immersion programs, or else involve a schedule of limited, irregular contact. Second, recreational programs, which assume that "mutual recognition" will take place spontaneously as participants converse, rarely provide more structured opportunities for exchange. (The same holds for those programs of joint cultural inquiry and/or community action currently favored by DENI.) Third, groups are often together only for the duration of the activity; by arriving at the venue separately and then departing the same way, the contact experience is further isolated from the participants' everyday lives. Finally, few staff members have acquired formal training in prejudice reduction or community conflict skills and therefore are uncomfortable in the role of facilitator; many opportunities for constructive exchange are lost as a result.

ITP projects also suffer from the same obstacles faced by all community-based youth schemes, no matter what their purpose or design. Such projects are inevitably low-budget and often rely on financial contributions from participants to defray their costs. As a consequence, cross-community contact schemes must be "sold," and are usually advertised to their potential participants as "holidays." Because the term connotes entertainment rather than education, this label obscures the function and value of the experience as an opportunity for intergroup contact and exchange. . . .

In theory, the success of ITP schemes depends upon the growth of strong interpersonal relationships between participants, links that can be weakened or even destroyed by inconsistencies in the composition of the groups involved. Such inconsistencies, however, are inevitable, and ironically become more pronounced the more extensive and long term the program. The financial strain posed by the cost of frequent holidays can be prohibitive, particularly for parents with several children, making programs of regular contact difficult to sustain. Older children often have other obligations, either to their families or their schoolwork, which can prevent them from regular participation in any extracurricular activity. Often, too, high unemployment and the need to seek work elsewhere will force a family to move. This can be disastrous for some schemes: siblings and cousins often join a club together, and the participation of any one child in its activities is frequently dependent on that of the others. All these factors make programs of regular, extended contact difficult to sustain in their original form. . . .

All these factors have contributed to the failure of ITP projects to produce real improvements in relations between estranged communities, wherever they've been employed. Yet, while such obstacles admittedly are difficult to surmount, there is another reason for this failure, which can be easily rectified, and that is the failure of the model to take certain fundamental principles of group dynamics into account.

Why the ITP Model Fails

In pursuit of their goals, projects modeled on ITP theory tend to focus on the similarities between groups in contact; they may even avoid divisive issues altogether. In so doing the organizers of these schemes are guilty of ignoring the nature of prejudice, and of stereotyping in particular. They also appear to disregard the extent to which the pressure to conform influences behavior, both during and following contact. Research into the psychology of social interaction has stressed the distinction between interpersonal and intergroup contact on the grounds that each involves

its own mode of behavior and thought; yet the success of the ITP model depends upon the participants' ability to switch easily between the two. ITP theorists appear to imagine that individual prejudice is confirmed or dispelled in much the same manner as a scientific hypothesis—on the basis of empirical evidence, objectively observed. In practice, however, individuals employ both conscious and unconscious strategies to protect themselves from the need to reassess their assumptions, and thus from emotional and psychological harm.

In brief, ITP projects share three basic characteristics, each of which is premised upon assumptions largely invalidated by the field of social-psychology. First is a focus on similarities to the exclusion of differences. Second is an effort to dispel stereotypes as a means of reducing prejudice between groups. Finally, there is a tendency to mobilize normative rather than informational influences in their attempts to combat conformity.

The Denial of Differences

According to Enloe, a society is ethnically divided if each of its communities distinguishes itself from the others by virtue of a bond of shared culture. That culture may be defined in terms of language, religion, ideology, tradition, values, beliefs or some combination thereof. But whatever its form, it has the power to convey upon each member of that group a sense of collective identity that exists alongside but apart from his or her identity as an individual. By this definition Northern Ireland is clearly a divided society. Moreover, Fields and others have noted a marked contrast between the political influences, objectives, and philosophy of republican paramilitaries and those of loyalists, particularly as expressed in their publications and in the wall murals that appear in the areas they each control. Fraser has commented that the form and nature of prejudice within the two communities differ, while McLachlan goes so far as to suggest that beyond those differences that arise from divergent historical experience, there are those that "derive from psychological differences due in great measure to conflicting elements in Roman Catholicism and Protestantism." Why, then, is the existence of cultural difference between the two communities in the province largely ignored or obscured if not denied by ITP scheme organizers? . . .

Hewstone and Brown suggest that contact schemes would be better engaged in working to establish a sense of *mutual intergroup differentiation* than attempting to deprive individuals of the collective identities they value so much. Each group should be seen as it wishes to be seen, and differences should be highlighted as desired. At the same time, those who adopt this approach must be careful to discourage ethnocentrism, avoid the implication that one group is better than the other, and prevent the development of out-group discrimination whereby in-groups appropriate the most valued dimensions of identity for themselves. Such a strategy is clearly difficult and potentially risky, and it may be for these reasons that it has only rarely featured in contact programs of any form. Whatever its challenges, however, it is a strategy that must be part of ITP schemes in the future if they are to have a lasting effect.

The Destruction of Stereotypes

The ability to categorize is an essential human cognitive process. The segmentation and organization of the social world into categories or groups serves to reduce the complexity of incoming information, facilitate rapid identification of stimuli, and to guide behavior. To paraphrase Heider, categorization allows us to understand, predict and control our environment, to describe the unknown in familiar terms. As such, it is an adaptive strategy for survival that pervades the structure of both human language and society. Stereotyping, one form of the categorization process, likewise serves explicit psychological and social functions. Although stereotyping has traditionally been dismissed either as "an inferior cognitive process in the form of an overgeneralization or oversimplification, or as a process that was morally wrong because it categorized people who had no desire to be categorized," such definitions have since been proven false. Stereotyping is not the psychological aberration suggested by early contact theorists; on the contrary, stereotypes are employed by all human beings, all of whom are prone to biased thinking. . . .

It is important to remember that these behaviors are the natural result of inherent perceptual and cognitive limitations, and do not indicate a conscious desire to misperceive. Often, as Taylor and Moghaddam suggest, misperception is simply a result of unfamiliarity: the less familiar we are with a group, the more likely we are to have a uniform stereotype of that group. (It is, of course, this form of misperception that ESC schemes seek to correct.) Moreover, when societies are under stress, misperception may arise as an adaptation (i.e., as a means of denying one's own responsibility for events or actions), or from fear (in the form of psychosis due to stress), or from hostility (as an expression of anger, a desire for revenge, or as part of a search for scapegoats). All these responses are interrelated, yet ITP programs address themselves only to the last of the three. They attempt to reduce hostility without examining the reasons why hostility exists; they seek to alter opinions without challenging the opinion-making process. At

best the ITP model prescribes a cure for a local manifestation of a larger disease. At worst, it provides an inadequate dosage of an ineffectual drug.

Conformity: Normative versus Informational Pressures

Like many contact schemes, ITP programs often claim to be successful if children from different communities are observed playing harmoniously together within the context of the contact situation. It is then concluded that the experience has been positive, and that the contact hypothesis approach in general "works."

Such a conclusion may be premature. The pressure to conform, to behave in such a way as to facilitate cohesion within and between groups, may be placed upon one individual by another or by a group. Such pressures can be classified as follows. First are *informational influences*, which are exerted when new information, knowledge, or arguments are presented to the individual that succeed in altering his or her views or behavior. This type of influence tends to be long-lasting and resilient in the face of efforts to challenge it. Second are *normative influences*, which are experienced by an individual who seeks acceptance by the group. This type of influence tends to be fragile, temporary and dependent upon the continued existence of the group. The normative forces that influence the dynamics of groups in contact are likely to produce a superficial cohesion, which cannot withstand the greater pressures exerted by pre-existing informational influences after re-entry. Given that the need to be accepted by one's peers is especially great among children, this phenomenon is perhaps the primary reason why ITP schemes so frequently fail to achieve their long-term goals. . . .

Belonging to a group can provide identity, security and a source of self-verification, as long as the general perception of that group is positive. The views and behaviors to which we conform as children are often learned from others—e.g., our parents, relations, peers, and community leaders. These fall under the heading of "informational influences" and it is often acutely uncomfortable for us to hear them challenged. When we are asked to critically examine—let alone to reject—the views and opinions of those we most respect and to whom we are usually bound by much closer ties than those that link children to their educators, formal or otherwise, we necessarily cast doubt upon the basis of our own identity. Few adults are able to subject themselves to such an unpleasant and potentially threatening self-analysis; it is not surprising that children should be unwilling to do so. . . .

Conclusion

It is now more than twenty-five years since the onset of the Troubles and it is difficult to be anything but pessimistic about the likelihood of reconciliation between the two communities. As one generation after another matures with no experience of a society at peace, the chances of empowering people to confront their habituation to violence and to take charge of their future grow ever more slim. Seligman has described the phenomenon of "learned helplessness" whereby a sense of one's own inability to change the nature or structure of one's society results in one's abandoning all efforts to do so; this process has already begun in Northern Ireland.

Proponents of the contact hypothesis in the province believe strongly that "positive contact"—whatever its form—"under 'micro' conditions is better than no contact at all." Indeed. Lemish argues that "the primary accomplishment of the Contact Approach in plural societies is that . . . meetings [between groups in conflict] take place," even if such encounters produce only superficial modifications in the outcome of the larger conflict. For despite the evidence that contact in and of itself has little or no direct impact on personal or group ideologies, the social isolation that would result in its absence would only serve to widen the divide between estranged communities. The use of violence then becomes justified in defense of what are perceived to be opposing values, and opportunities for reconciliation are reduced as each community's interpretation of events increasingly diverge.

With this in mind, Fisher has proposed that the following assertions be incorporated into Pettigrew's original outline of the contact hypothesis. First is that institutional discrimination is at the core of the problem of intergroup conflict rather than individual prejudice, which, while important, is not fundamental. Second is that prejudice is based on a variety of cognitive processes involving misperception and stereotyping and is embedded in the culture of society. The final point is that education is a woefully insufficient remedy in contrast to institutional change requiring new intergroup behavior to reshape intergroup attitudes. Though it is of course true that intergroup conflict may arise in the absence of institutional bias, to acknowledge its possible role in the perpetuation of a conflict can only improve the odds of a successful resolution. Without tackling the problem of individual prejudice, attempts to implement institutional change will be met with suspicion and fear; in the face of such resistance they will proceed only impartially, if they do not founder altogether. At the same time, impatience with (and accusations regarding) the slow pace of change on the one hand, and resentment against its scope on the other, will continue to flourish in the absence of concerted efforts toward prejudice reduction at the grassroots level.

Intergroup contact works, when and if it does, because it changes the nature of the intergroup relationship, and not because it encourages or permits interpersonal friendships between members of different groups; such relationships are a result, not a cause, of positive changes generally. Whether or not contact serves to strengthen "the *readiness* for intergroup relations" depends as much on the general socio-political climate as the dynamics that develop each time contact takes place. While it is encouraging, then, that the concept of integrated education appears to have full official support at last, and that increasingly children participating in holiday schemes will have been involved in joint-work arising from Education for Mutual Understanding activities in their classrooms, nevertheless without real political progress toward a climate conducive to social change such efforts will be of little use. Indeed, should the commitment and creativity of all those working for peace in the province be wasted because of the intransigence of their representatives—both paramilitary and political, on both sides of the border and on both sides of the Irish Sea—it will only deepen their frustration and lead to despair.

Jennifer Cornell is an assistant professor of English in the College of Liberal Arts at Oregon State University.

EXPLORING THE ISSUE

Does Intergroup Contact Work to Reduce Prejudice?

Critical Thinking and Reflection

1. One of the learning outcomes for this controversy was: "Apply the contact hypothesis and the idea of 'super-ordinate' (common) goals to at least one modern conflict you see in the world around you, and how this theory might be used to decrease that conflict, if the circumstances were right." Try to do this, and explain how you think contact or common goals could help.

2. Think of a time when you disliked someone or disliked a particular group, but you changed your mind after spending time with them. Then, think of a time when you disliked someone or disliked a group, and spending time with them made your negative opinion even stronger. What was the difference in the two experiences? Can you identify variables that explain the two different outcomes?

3. Think about a nearby elementary or high school, or even your own college. Identify two groups at that school who don't seem to get along, and design a procedure for how they might get along better if they had a common goal to work toward. Do you think this procedure could actually help? Why or why not?

Is There Common Ground?

On the surface, it may seem that both authors agree that the contact hypothesis does *not* work. Sherif concluded that simple contact only made prejudice between the two camps of boys even worse. Cornell came to the same decision and stated that "contact in and of itself has little or no direct impact on personal or group ideologies." Are both of the articles thus really on the "no" side, that contact is useless?

In fact, both authors actually agree that contact *can* work, if it is done correctly, with all of the proper circumstances. Sherif notes that contact between groups will reduce prejudice *if* the groups are working together toward a common goal. Cornell hesitatingly agrees when she writes, "Intergroup contact works, when and if it does, because it changes the nature of the intergroup relationship." While Cornell is clearly more doubtful about contact, she acknowledges that it might work, given the right kind of contact. This is the conclusion that most social psychologists have come to as well; contact works, under the right circumstances.

Additional Resources

Alderfer, C. P. (1991). Changing race relations in organizations: A critique of the contact hypothesis. *Canadian Journal of Administrative Sciences, 8,* 80–88. doi: 10.1111/j.1936-4490.1991.tb00547.x

Brener, L., von Hippel, W., & Kippax, S. (2007). Prejudice among health care workers toward injecting drug users with hepatitis C: Does greater contact lead to less prejudice? *International Journal of Drug Policy, 18,* 381–387.

Pettigrew, T. F., & Tropp, L. R. (2000). Does intergroup contact reduce prejudice? Recent meta-analytic findings. In S. Oskamp (Ed.), *Reducing prejudice and discrimination* (pp. 93–114). Mahwah, NJ: Lawrence Erlbaum Associates.

Wilson, T. C. (1996). Prejudice reduction or self-selection? A test of the contact hypothesis. *Sociological Spectrum, 16,* 43–60. doi: 10.1080/02732173.1996.9982119

Internet References . . .

Muzafer Sherif

http://www.muskingum.edu/~psych/psycweb/history
/sherif.htm

Simply Psychology: Robber's Cave

http://www.simplypsychology.org/robbers-cave.html

**The Inquisitive Mind: Intergroup Contact
Theory**

http://www.in-mind.org/article/intergroup-contact
-theory-past-present-and-future

**Understanding Prejudice: The Contact
Hypothesis**

http://www.understandingprejudice.org/apa/english
/page24.htm